I WILL RUN WILD

OSPREY
PUBLISHING

I WILL
RUN WILD

THE PACIFIC WAR
FROM PEARL HARBOR TO MIDWAY

THOMAS McKELVEY
CLEAVER

OSPREY PUBLISHING
Bloomsbury Publishing Plc
Kemp House, Chawley Park, Cumnor Hill, Oxford OX2 9PH, UK
1385 Broadway, 5th Floor, New York, NY 10018, USA
E-mail: info@ospreypublishing.com
www.ospreypublishing.com

OSPREY is a tradeMark of Osprey Publishing Ltd

First published in Great Britain in 2020

A catalog record for this book is available from the British Library.

ISBN: HB 9781472841339; PB 9781472841346; eBook 9781472841322;
ePDF 9781472841308; XML 9781472841315

20 21 22 23 24   10 9 8 7 6 5 4 3 2 1

Maps by www.bounford.com
Index by Zoe Ross
Originated by PDQ Digital Media Solutions, Bungay, UK
Printed and bound in Great Britain by CPI (Group) UK Ltd, Croydon CR0 4YY

Cover image: US Douglas SBD-3 Dauntless dive bombers patrolling coral reefs off Midway Island,
prior to the naval engagement, searching for Japanese troops.
(Frank Scherschel/The LIFE Picture Collection via Getty Images/Getty Images)

Osprey Publishing supports the Woodland Trust, the UK's leading woodland conservation charity.

To find out more about our authors and books visit www.ospreypublishing.com.
Here you will find extracts, author interviews, details of forthcoming events and the
option to sign up for our newsletter.

CONTENTS

LIST OF MAPS

LIST OF ILLUSTRATIONS

FOREWORD

This is a terrific book, fast-moving and loaded with facts. I have read a number of books about World War II in the Pacific. Most go from Pearl Harbor to Coral Sea to Midway and on to Guadalcanal. *I Will Run Wild* brings you to all the places in between and then covers the big ones we heard about. I really had little knowledge about the air battles in the South Pacific near Australia other than Coral Sea and Midway. The author has really done his homework! He covers in great detail the thinking and actions of the great young heroes as well as the key players, with great background detail as to how the two navies viewed each other for the twenty years before the war, as well as the development of the weapons used by both sides. Of particular note is the political detail provided – I really knew nothing about the history of Thailand and I suspect many others will find this highly interesting. As a former combat aviator myself, I was impressed with how little flight time many of the young aviators had when they went into battle, and how they met the challenges they faced regardless. No punches are pulled in this book. Both sides made mistakes and at times showed poor judgement. The author treats General MacArthur with candor. Java, Dutch Borneo, Darwin and many places you might never have heard of are integrated into this fast-paced historical work. There are many lessons in this book, but the most important is how people rose to challenges they would never have believed they would face until the events were upon them, and how they gave it everything they had. This is a story for our times. It is a great read for young and old.

RADM H. Denny Wisely USN (Ret.)
Former commander, USS *John F. Kennedy*
Author of *Green Ink: Memoirs of a Fighter Pilot*

INTRODUCTION

When I was in junior high school, I discovered that my home room teacher, Mr. Dennis Main, was a veteran of the early part of the Pacific War, having been a radioman in the 19th Bomb Group during the fighting in the Philippines and during the first year of the war in the South Pacific. He saw I was sincerely interested, and consented to answer my many questions, thus becoming the first World War II veteran I ever interviewed. I remember that Mr. Main was bitter about the way the war he had fought was viewed in America. I've always remembered him telling me, "Everyone thinks it was just a time of losing, but the truth is it was the foundation of victory." From that, I found myself always interested in that period of the war that so many think of as the dark days of defeat. This book is the result of that long-ago interest on the part of a budding historian.

When he received orders in November 1941 to execute the planned attack on Pearl Harbor, Imperial Navy Combined Fleet commander Admiral Isoroku Yamamoto informed his superiors, "I will run wild for six months. After that, I can promise nothing." He missed his prediction by three days: the Japanese did indeed "run wild," from December 7, 1941, when aircraft from six carriers sank or severely damaged the battle fleet of the United States Pacific Fleet, to June 4, 1942, when aircraft from two American carriers sank four of the six Pearl Harbor attackers in six deadly minutes at the Battle of Midway. The loss cut the heart out of Japanese naval aviation.

The first six months of the Pacific War were indeed a period of almost unrelieved catastrophe upon catastrophe for the United States and its allies, as the wages of hubris and underestimation of the enemy were paid.

Most Americans who read about this period focus only on the initial attack, the "revenge" of the Doolittle Raid four months later, followed by the battles of the Coral Sea the next month and Midway the month following. As General George S. Patton Jr. once observed, "Americans love a winner and will not tolerate losing."

Many wartime myths were created during these months: Captain Colin P. Kelly, the bomber pilot who sank a battleship; Marines fighting a "Pacific Alamo" at Wake Island; "the battling bastards of Bataan;" the doctors and nurses in Malinta Tunnel on "the rock" at Corregidor who refused evacuation; General MacArthur's miraculous escape aboard PT-boats. When General Wainwright messaged President Franklin Roosevelt that he must surrender his forces to the Japanese enemy, the President replied, "You and your devoted followers have become the living symbol of our war aims and the guarantee of victory."

Indeed they had, but not quite in the way wartime propaganda portrayed those events. To this day, the *Encyclopedia Britannica* states that Colin P. Kelly sank a battleship and doesn't even cite the correct date for the event. Kelly was indeed a hero who sacrificed his own life to save his crew; he just didn't do what the wartime mythology said he did. The Marines at Wake did indeed fight outnumbered against an overwhelming enemy; they never said "Send us more Japs" – that was "padding" in a message in which the commander informed his superiors that they were outnumbered, running out of supplies and ammunition, and would have to surrender in a matter of days if they did not receive reinforcements, reinforcements that were ordered to turn back at the last minute; the officers commanding the force made their admiral leave the room with their vehement refusal of orders, admonishing them he would not "hear talk of mutiny." "The battling bastards of Bataan" would have been better served had their commander, Douglas MacArthur, not deluded himself in the six months before the war that he could "stop the enemy at the beaches" and made certain that the supplies they would need to make a stand on Bataan were there for their use. The doctors and nurses at Corregidor really did refuse evacuation.

That the stories were not accurate does nothing to diminish actual bravery in the face of overwhelming odds. Indeed, there are many stories throughout the period of Americans, members of the Commonwealth, and the Dutch, who made their stands regardless of the opposition. Most of these accounts are almost unknown today. It's my hope that gathering and telling the stories that I have will lead the reader to look for further information.

I was very fortunate in 1999 to meet Lieutenant Colonel Lamar Gillet, when he came to speak at the Planes of Fame Air Museum in Chino, California. From that meeting, I was able to conduct several interviews with him, which provided a unique and previously unknown personal perspective on the fall of the Philippines, and his later survival of the Bataan Death March, and three years as a prisoner of the Emperor in Japan. I first told Lamar's amazing story in *Flight Journal*, a magazine for which I was a contributing editor, in 2002. It is also a privilege to finally set the historical record straight as to who exactly was the only P-35 flyer to shoot down a Zero, an accomplishment that has long been credited to the wrong pilot due to a mix-up at the time as to who did what, with the incorrect story being told by those who escaped to Australia while Lamar endured his years of captivity.

I was privileged during the last ten years of his life to know and be friends with the remarkable Richard Halsey Best, Jr., the naval aviator whose actions at Pearl Harbor and Midway bookend this account. Educated and erudite, a man of true integrity, Dick Best to me epitomizes the best of America. Hearing the accounts of his experiences led me to look further into the history of this period. His oath made at Pearl Harbor to "make the bastards pay" was made good over the Japanese fleet six months later, ending Admiral Yamamoto's wild run. He is a hero whose actions are not well known today; I hope this book changes that.

It would have been impossible to write a book like this had I not been privileged to know Erik Shilling for 25 years. His friendship opened the door for me to get to know several other of the Tigers, including R.T. Smith and Charles Older (a truly "forbidding presence" never known to suffer fools), and ground crewman Chuck Baisden. Among other things, Erik taught me to barrel roll my Bonanza, telling me, "One of these days, you'll be on final approach behind an airliner and the tip vortices will spin you upside-down. It's good to know how to do this." I never had cause to use that knowledge, but it was good to know it. Erik was a tiger to the end, dying at age 84 the night before he was to commence chemotherapy for cancer. He'll always be missed.

The searing experience of the first six months of the Pacific War set the stage for all that came after. Men at all levels whose skill and ability had not previously been fully recognized came to the fore and their accomplishments allowed them to become the leaders who would bring about victory. It is a stirring story worth knowing.

As I look at the completed manuscript of this book, I realize there was a reason why I was compelled to write this. This is a story of Americans – and their allies – in the worst of circumstances, standing and doing the right thing, regardless of the consequences and despite the ominous possibility of defeat. The American republic stands today because of their sacrifice. Reading the daily news, this is a parable for all Americans living here today.

And I'd like to think that if Mr. Main was here today, he'd appreciate that the student who learned his story finally told it.

Thomas McKelvey Cleaver

CHAPTER ONE

"I KNEW MY PLANS HAD CHANGED"

The flight deck of USS *Enterprise* (CV-6) echoed with the command over the loudspeaker from the bridge: "Pilots! Man your planes!" Thirty-one-year-old Lieutenant Richard H. "Dick" Best, Jr., operations officer of Bombing 6, watched from near the ship's island as the crews of the 12 Douglas SBD-3 Dauntlesses of Scouting 6 and five SBD-2s of Bombing 6 climbed aboard their airplanes and wished he was one of the Bombing 6 crews who would be the first of the squadron to arrive home at NAS Ford Island, since he was eager to go on leave with his wife and four-year-old daughter who were waiting for him in Honolulu. He glanced up and saw Vice Admiral William F. Halsey, Jr. – universally known in the Navy as "Bull," though no one ever used that to his face – watching the preparations for takeoff from the admiral's bridge as commander of Carrier Division Two. Best could see the four heavy cruisers of Cruiser Division 5 led by Rear Admiral Raymond A. Spruance aboard his flagship USS *Northampton* (CA-26) and six destroyers that constituted Task Force 16 as gray shapes on the horizon.

Commander Howard L. "Brigham" Young climbed aboard the blue-gray over light-gray Dauntless marked "Commander Enterprise Group" on its flank, designating it as the group commander's airplane that would lead the five Bombing 6 SBD-2s. The admiral's assistant operations officer, Lieutenant Commander Bromfield Nichol, eased himself into the gunner's rear seat in Young's airplane; seven years before, then-Lieutenant Nichol had been then-Captain Halsey's flight instructor at Pensacola when Halsey had been awarded his Wings of

Gold on May 15, 1935 at age 52, the oldest man to ever qualify as a naval aviator. Nichol's briefcase carried Halsey's report to Pacific Fleet Commander Admiral Husband E. Kimmel regarding the Wake Island operation.

Eighteen R-1830 radial engines coughed to life and soon their throbbing rumble filled the air. For the first time since November 28 when Task Force 16 had departed Pearl Harbor, the sky was clear and the rising sun could be clearly seen. The heavy seas encountered during the return from Wake Island, where the task force had delivered 12 F4F-3 Wildcats of the Marines' VMF-212 to provide air defense for the US-held island 1,993 miles from Japan, had prevented the destroyers from refueling and forced the carrier to reduce speed so that the "small boys" could keep station. *Enterprise* had been scheduled to drop anchor in Pearl Harbor the previous afternoon, December 6. Instead, here she was on Sunday, December 7, 1941, launching a full-scale 90-degree search perimeter from 225 miles south of the Hawaiian Islands to ensure the safety of the ships as they returned to the major American naval base in the Pacific.

Relations between the United States and Japan had steadily deteriorated since the previous July, when President Roosevelt had embargoed oil exports to Japan following the Japanese occupation of the French colony of Indochina. On August 17, 1941, Roosevelt warned Japan that the United States was prepared to take action if "neighboring countries" were attacked. On Monday, November 24, 1941, the Gallup poll found 52 percent of Americans expected war with Japan; 27 percent did not; and 21 percent had no opinion.

When *Enterprise* departed Pearl Harbor at the end of November, Admiral Halsey issued Battle Order No. 1, placing the fleet on a wartime footing in expectation of a possible encounter with Japanese forces. Training ammunition was stored below and replaced with "service ammo," while the pilots of Air Group 6 were cleared to attack any ship or aircraft spotted because there were no "friendlies" ahead of Task Force 16. The admiral had concluded, "If anything gets in my way, we'll shoot first and argue afterwards. When put to the test, all hands keep cool, keep your heads, and FIGHT."

Lieutenant Best was in complete agreement with his commander. A graduate in the Class of 1932 from Annapolis, Best entered flight training in 1934, following two years' sea duty. His outstanding record at Pensacola saw him given orders to join "The Flying Chiefs" of Fighting 2 aboard the USS *Lexington* (CV-2) as a flight leader, where he served under record-breaking naval aviation pioneer Lieutenant Commander Apollo Soucek. Following his tour with the Chiefs, he returned to Pensacola for two years as an instructor in Squadron 5, the advanced training unit. By the summer of 1940 when his tour was up, "It was clear to me that the only question regarding the war was when we would become involved." Best put in a request to transfer from fighters to a torpedo squadron. "I wanted to be sure I was part of the striking force, which fighters were not at that time." Lacking the seniority to be assigned to a flight leader position since the torpedo squadrons were the "battleships" of naval aviation at the time, he took assignment to Bombing 6 aboard *Enterprise*, joining the squadron on May 31, 1940 as flight officer (operations officer), while they were still equipped with the Northrop BT-1 dive bomber that became the progenitor of the SBD Dauntless after Douglas Aircraft acquired Northrop later that year.

For those in the Navy and Marine Corps out on the pointed end of the spear, the intentions of the Japanese had become plain over the four years since dive bombers of the Imperial Japanese Naval Air Force based aboard the carrier *Kaga* sank the gunboat USS *Panay* on December 12, 1937, as she was tied up to the dock at Nanking on the Yangtze River, killing three sailors and wounding 43 sailors and five civilians; the Japanese "apology" always rang hollow.

Several months later, then-18-year-old USMC Private James F. Eaton, Jr. arrived fresh from boot camp at Parris Island for duty with the Marine Legation guards in Tientsin, China, just before the Imperial Japanese Army captured the city. The 150 Marines, armed with .30-caliber 1903 Springfield rifles and two water-cooled .30-caliber light machine guns, were under orders not to provoke an incident, but also not to let the Japanese "walk all over us," as Eaton later remembered. Within weeks, the Japanese began testing the Marines. The ex-German Legation quarters the US diplomatic mission had moved to after the fall of Beijing had no water on the premises. There was, however, a fire engine in the barn: an ancient 1914 La France tractor and an even older pumper that had originally been drawn by horses. Both had solid rubber wheels that were nearly as tall as the 6-foot Eaton. When the Japanese erected roadblocks around the Legation to force American recognition of their control of the city, by happenstance they set up roadblocks between the Legation and the nearest fire hydrant.

After a day's standoff, the Marines announced they were holding a fire drill. Because of his size, Eaton was chosen to drive, since he could control the huge steering wheel of the massive fire truck. "We went roaring out the gate laying hose behind us, and the skipper told me to keep my foot on the gas. We went through the Japs like a bowling ball through ten pins." In answer to the Japanese protest, the Marine commander coolly stated he was only concerned with saving the city; if the Legation caught fire and it could not be controlled, the Japanese-occupied city would be at risk of burning down. Flummoxed, the Japanese could only accept the explanation and never made any other provocations. In June 1941, Eaton, by then promoted to lance corporal, was one of the last of the "China Marines" to get out of the country before the war. On this Sunday, he was celebrating promotion to corporal as a member of the newly formed 1st Marine Division at newly built Camp Lejeune, North Carolina.

Still, even with the events of the previous four years, in the face of the news over the previous five months, despite the fact a majority of their fellow citizens expected a war, most of the men aboard Task Force 16 could not bring themselves to believe that a war with Japan could truly be imminent. Yeoman 2/c Bill Norberg, who worked in the captain's office aboard *Enterprise*, later remembered, "We in the captain's office never mentioned impending war. We looked on the Japanese as squint-eyed midgets due to lack of knowledge. Battle order Number One was to us somewhat comparable to The Second Coming – it'll happen someday, but certainly not this week or month."

At 0615 hours that Sunday morning, *Enterprise* turned into the wind and commenced launching the 18 Dauntlesses. No American knew that at the same time, some 500 miles north of *Enterprise*'s position, six Japanese aircraft carriers that had departed Hokkaido two days before *Enterprise* departed Pearl Harbor were launching 183 fighters, dive bombers and torpedo bombers: nine Nakajima B5N2 bombers armed with 800-kilogram (1,760-pound) armor-piercing bombs; 40 B5N2 bombers carrying Type 91 aerial torpedoes; 51 Aichi D3A1 dive bombers with 249-kilogram (550-pound) general-purpose bombs; and 43 Mitsubishi A6M2 Type 0 fighters. One B5N2, three D3A1s, and two A6M2s failed to launch.

The 18 search planes set off in nine formations of two, each assigned a segment of the search area. By 0730 hours, they had reached the end of their patrols, and the pilots turned for Pearl Harbor. Since they were operating under radio silence, several of the backseaters took the opportunity to practice radio homing, tuning their sets to Honolulu radio stations KGMB and KGU.

After the takeoff, Dick Best returned to his office near the Bombing 6 ready-room, to complete his paperwork. The compartment had a speaker that relayed the radio messages from the airborne aircraft. Shortly after 0800 hours, his paperwork was forgotten when he heard Bombing 6's Ensign Manuel Gonzalez's high-pitched shout over the radio, "Don't shoot! This is an American plane! Do not shoot!"

Gonzalez and his wingman, Ensign Fred Weber, had been assigned the northernmost search area. Just as they finished their search, they were suddenly surrounded by six strange aircraft with fixed landing gear – what would later become known as "Val" dive bombers. Before Gonzalez's rear seater, Aviation Radioman 3/c Leonard Kozalek, could deploy his machine gun, the Dauntless caught fire when it was hit by bullets fired by the strange airplanes. As the Dauntless headed toward the ocean below, carrying the first two *Enterprise* fliers to die in the Pacific War, Weber dived away and escaped his pursuers by flying 25 feet above the waves.

For the 36 *Enterprise* fliers, their entry into World War II was "come as you are." Air group commander Young and his wingman, Ensign Perry Teaff, were passing over Barber's Point when they spotted aircraft in the sky above the Marine air station at Ewa. Young commented that it was early for the Army to be flying on a Sunday. An instant later, he saw antiaircraft explosions in the sky over the base. At the same time, Teaff spotted a low-wing single-engine aircraft closing on the formation. A moment later, he saw bullet strikes in the tail of Young's airplane. As the attacker adjusted his aim, Teaff saw the red circles of the Japanese rising sun on its wings.

The enemy pilot overshot the two Dauntlesses and turned to make a second attack. Teaff's radioman unlimbered his single .30-caliber machine gun, but the unknown fighter took aim at Young. "Follow me!" the group commander ordered, and Teaff followed his leader as the two dive bombers dove for the hills below. They managed to land successfully at Ford Island through a barrage of fire from the defenders.

Lieutenant Clarence E. Dickinson had been looking forward to landing at Ford Island, where his gunner, Aviation Radioman 3/c William C. Miller, would finish his enlistment in the Navy. Dickinson and his wingman, Ensign R. McCarthy, were approaching Barber's Point from the south at an altitude of 1,500 feet when he spotted flak bursts over the base. Beyond, he saw the explosions aboard the battleships moored to Ford Island at Battleship Row. Climbing for a better look, the two Navy fliers came across two enemy fighter pilots who immediately attacked. Dickinson dived away, followed by McCarthy, and ran into four more enemy fighters. They quickly shot down McCarthy and set his Dauntless afire. McCarthy was able to bale out, landing in a tree and breaking a leg in so doing, while his gunner, Aviation Radioman 3/c Mitchell Cohn, died in the crash.

Dickinson, pursued by three of the enemy, kept turning to see his wounded gunner Bill Miller fire at the fighters as they flashed past. In a few minutes, Miller ran out of ammo and was wounded a second time. As one of the enemy planes crossed his nose, Dickinson cut loose with his two .50-caliber machine guns. The enemy fighter caught fire at the same moment his controls went slack under the fire of another on his tail. His left wing caught fire and the Dauntless spun in.

Dickinson was at 1,000 feet when he managed to overcome the G-forces and get out of the cockpit. He saw Miller slumped over his gun as he threw himself off the wing. A moment later he pulled the ripcord, and landed in a cane field in time to see his airplane hit the ground and explode. Twenty-two-year-old Bill Miller died on the day that was supposed to be his last in the Navy.

The *Enterprise* fliers weren't the only American pilots struggling to get into action. At the Army's Wheeler Field, second lieutenants Ken Taylor and George Welch of the 47th Pursuit Squadron were surprised in their barracks by the sound of aircraft overhead and bomb explosions on the airfield. Both young pilots had spent the night before dancing in the officers' club. After the club had closed, the two had become involved in an all-night poker game in the barracks. The game had only just wrapped up and the two were in their room, still in their tuxedo pants and shirts, trying to decide whether to go to sleep or take a morning swim.

Stepping out of the barracks, they saw burning buildings and more explosions. Strange enemy fighters dived low and strafed the P-40s that were lined up wingtip to wingtip to protect them from attempted sabotage. Fortunately, a week earlier the 47th Squadron had been sent on gunnery practice and relocated to Haleiwa Field, 11 miles from Wheeler. Without orders, Taylor called Haleiwa and commanded the ground crew to prepare their Curtiss P-40 Tomahawks for takeoff.

Welch jumped into Taylor's new Buick and started it up. He stopped in front of the barracks long enough for Taylor to jump in and stepped on the gas. It took them less than ten minutes to drive the 11 miles to Haleiwa; Welch later recalled reaching 100 miles an hour along the way.

They found their airplanes fueled but not fully armed. Cranking up, they managed to get airborne and attracted the attention of some Zeros immediately. Evading the enemy fighters, they came on a formation of bombers. When Welch closed to open fire, he discovered the .50-caliber weapons in the airplane's nose were disconnected, but he was able to fire the four .30-caliber wing guns. In quick succession, two of the enemy airplanes caught fire and fell away. Taylor's guns all worked and he made quick work of one bomber and damaged another before they were both forced to break off with the arrival of Zeros on the scene.

By now both were low on ammunition. As the enemy aircraft of the first wave flew off, they landed at Wheeler, where they thought they could get serviced faster. The ground crews went to work quickly. A senior officer ordered them to stay on the ground, but when the second wave of attackers appeared overhead, they climbed back in their fighters and took off into the swarming enemy.

Even though his plane had been damaged on the first sortie, Welch managed to find another formation of enemy bombers and the two attacked. Welch was still limited to his wing guns, but managed to shoot down two while Taylor shot down a third and took a fourth under fire before a rear gunner managed to hit him. A bullet pierced his canopy and hit his arm while shrapnel hit his leg. Welch had opened fire on a fifth bomber when Taylor radioed he'd been hit. Both planes were now too badly damaged, not to mention Taylor's wounds; Welch broke off his attack to cover Taylor, and they returned to Wheeler.

Back aboard *Enterprise*, Admiral Halsey had just poured himself a second cup of coffee when his aide dashed into the cabin. "Admiral, there's an air raid on Pearl!" Halsey's first thought was that the Army, which had been scheduled to conduct a readiness exercise the week before, was taking things too far. He leapt to his feet, telling his aide to radio Kimmel that the Army was "shooting down my own boys!" A second aide entered with a message direct from Admiral Kimmel: "AIR RAID PEARL HARBOR X THIS IS NO DRILL."

Officer of the Deck Lieutenant John Dorsett ordered general quarters. Nineteen-year-old Seaman Jim Barnill, one of *Enterprise*'s four buglers, sounded the staccato notes of "Boots and Saddles." Twenty-eight-year-old First Class Bosun's Mate, Max Lee, played his pipe over the 1MC then called "General Quarters! General Quarters! All hands man your battle stations!" Lee's enlistment was almost up. After the war, he remembered that he then turned to OOD Dorsett and said, "We're at war and I'll never get out of the Navy alive."

Dick Best remembered coming onto the flight deck shortly after general quarters had been called and looking up at the island. "The first thing I saw was the biggest American flag I had ever seen, flying from the masthead and whipping in the wind. It was the most emotional sight of the war for me."

Enterprise's fighter commander, Lieutenant Commander Clarence Wade McClusky, rushed to the flag bridge to urge that the 18 F4F-3As of Fighting 6 be launched to help protect Pearl Harbor. Halsey demurred; with an enemy force of unknown size somewhere in the vicinity, the 18 fighters were needed to defend *Enterprise*. At 1645 hours, the admiral ordered a search-and-strike mission for the 18 TBD Devastators of Torpedo-6, with an escort of six Wildcats. In the event the planes found nothing, inasmuch as the Mobile Fleet had turned to the northwest after recovering its second Pearl Harbor strike. The torpedo bombers managed to recover without first dropping their torpedoes, but the effort took time and the six fighters were ordered to fly on in to Ford Island. It was a fatal order.

The six Wildcats arrived over Pearl Harbor at night, with their lights out and having maintained radio silence. As Ford Island came into sight, they switched on their running lights. On the ground, shell-shocked trigger-happy gunners saw the lights and immediately opened fire.

Two of the Wildcats went down immediately, while the survivors doused their lights, raised their landing gear, and increased power to get away from the storm of fire. The Wildcats were extremely low on fuel, and two pilots elected to bale out rather than attempt a go-around and try to land in the confused situation below. The last pair managed to land on Ford Island, where Ensign Gale Herman found the gunners still firing at him as he taxied in from the runway. When he finally climbed out, Herman found 18 bullet holes in his airplane. He was lucky. The pilot of the first Wildcat to go down was killed in his plane, while two others died of their wounds the next day. The other two survivors spent a harrowing night in the cane fields after baling out, attempting to convince the defenders they were on the same side.

The Japanese strike had accomplished its goal. The battleships that still formed the backbone of the battle fleet in contemporary strategy were sunk or damaged, while both Ford Island Naval Air Station and Wheeler Field had been hard hit. Losses totaled 188 aircraft destroyed and 159 damaged, for a total Japanese loss of 29. George Welch and Ken Taylor became the first American pilots of the war to be awarded the Distinguished Service Cross. Welch was nominated for the Medal of Honor, but it was denied when his superior officers claimed he had taken off without proper authorization and against orders. Taylor received the Purple Heart.

Five thousand three hundred miles west of *Enterprise*, Army Air Forces Second Lieutenant Lamar Gillet and the other members of the 17th Pursuit Squadron at Clark Army Airfield in the Philippines faced even longer odds of survival than the men at Pearl Harbor. While the Japanese came and left Pearl Harbor, everyone in the Philippines knew that when they came, they'd come to stay, since the islands were at the end of a long trans-Pacific supply line that the Navy had determined six months earlier they could not defend in the event of war. Indeed, Rainbow Five, the US military's war plan, recognized that the only action to be taken if Japan went to war in Asia was to organize a withdrawal from the Philippines. These facts were unknown to the young pilots at Clark Field.

Gillet had reported to the squadron in July, 1941, a freshly commissioned second lieutenant right out of Army flight school. The Air Force in the Philippines was so under-equipped that the 17th Pursuit Squadron had only given up their Boeing P-26C fighters, the Air Corps' first metal monoplane fighter, some six months earlier when they were replaced by 48 Seversky P-35As the Army had sequestered from an order made by the Swedish Air Force. These were replaced by 50 new Curtiss P-40Es that arrived in early October, 1941. However, Gillet was so junior that he was unable to get more than a basic checkout in the new fighter and continued to fly the P-35A whenever he could to build time.

Gillet recalled the outbreak of war in the Philippines:

We weren't surprised that the Japanese attacked us, other than it happened the day it happened. We were expecting something. The week before, Japanese aircraft had been spotted over the Philippines on several occasions, but they were too high for us to catch them before they turned away. The report of the attack at Pearl Harbor arrived in the Philippines around 0300 on Monday, December 8. Everyone was roused. We expected the Japanese attack to come at dawn, and all the fighters took off on patrol as soon as the sun rose.

While the American pilots circled Manila Harbor, 500 miles to the north, thick sea fog lay heavily over the Japanese airfields on southern Formosa as their frustrated crews fumed at the delay. Takeoff had originally been scheduled for 0400 hours, to put the strike over Manila at dawn, as the Americans expected, but the fog had rolled in from the Formosa Sea around 0300 hours. When they were informed of the Pearl Harbor attack, they were certain the Americans would send their vulnerable bombers to airfields further south out of range and be ready and able to repel them by the time the fog lifted.

The original plan of attack had been developed over the summer of 1941, and called for the A6M2 Type 0 fighters of the Tainan Air Corps to be loaded aboard three smaller Japanese carriers – *Ryūjō* , *Zuiho*, and *Chitose* – which would carry the fighters within 200 miles of the American bases around Manila on Luzon Island. Saburo Sakai, who would become a leading ace of the Imperial Japanese Naval Air Force following the outbreak of war, recalled that while the three carriers were theoretically capable of carrying 90 fighters, "in reality it was closer to 50, and even this number would be restricted in the event of bad weather at sea." Over the preceding months, Sakai and his fellow pilots had learned to extend the range of their aircraft. Sakai recalled, "The Zero was designed to remain in the air a maximum of six or seven hours. We stretched this figure to 10–12 hours, and did so on mass formation flights. I personally established the record low consumption of 17 gallons per hour; on the average, our pilots reduced their consumption from 35 gallons per hour to only 18."

Throughout the Philippines campaign, the Americans would be convinced there was a Japanese carrier fleet lurking offshore; the truth that the Zero could fly 500 miles, engage in air combat with high fuel consumption, and return 500 miles to its base was considered impossible since no single-engine fighter operated by the Allies was capable of such performance. Yet that was exactly how the Japanese fought the Philippines campaign.

Finally, at 1000 hours, the fog lifted over Formosa. By 1045 hours, 53 twin-engine G4M1 Type 1 Land Attack bombers of the 1st Kōkūtai and Kanoya Kōkūtai and 45 A6M2 escorts were climbing to their cruising altitude of 10,000 feet, headed for Manila. While 24 A6Ms remained with the bombers, 21 – including Sakai's – climbed to 19,000 feet and flew on to arrive first and deal with the expected enemy aerial opposition.

"At 1335 hours, we turned in from the China Sea and headed toward Clark Field," Sakai recalled. "The sight which met us was unbelievable." Sakai and his fellow pilots marveled at the sight of the American fighters and bombers, lined up wingtip-to-wingtip at Clark and Nichols fields, because Colonel Charles A. Willoughby, MacArthur's intelligence chief, had decreed the threat of sabotage was greater than the possibility of air attack.

In one of those strange twists of war that gives advantage to one side that the other cannot overcome, the Japanese attack could not have been timed better. As Lieutenant Gillet remembered, "Our fighters had first taken off at dawn, then when they didn't come we launched patrols every two hours. It just happened that by mid-day, all of our planes were on the ground being refueled, which took longer than expected since the ground crews weren't prepared for such constant activity."
Sakai and his fellow pilots circled Clark Field and maintained their altitude. "We could not believe they didn't have fighters in the air waiting for us. Finally, I spotted five Americans below us at 15,000 feet. We dropped our fuel tanks and armed our weapons, but they refused to fight us and we were under orders to wait for the arrival of the bombers."
At 1345 hours, the 27 G4M1s of the first wave arrived over Clark. Sakai recalled: "The attack was perfect. Long strings of bombs fell from the

bays and their accuracy was phenomenal – the most accurate bombing I ever witnessed by our own planes throughout the war."

Gillet remembered the attack:

Planes were blowing up and there was smoke and fire everywhere. Our antiaircraft defenses were pathetic. The gunners were all National Guardsmen from New Mexico who had arrived that summer, and had not had much opportunity to train with their weapons. What was worse was the discovery that the guns didn't have the range to hit the bombers as they cruised overhead at 10,000 feet.

Their bomb runs completed, the G4M1s turned back for Formosa. Sakai and the other fighter pilots escorted them out to sea, then turned back for Clark Field. "With my two wingmen tied to me as if by invisible lines, I pushed the stick forward and dove at a steep angle for the ground. I selected two undamaged B-17s on the runway for our targets. The three of us poured a fusillade of bullets into the big bombers and they caught fire."

Sakai recalled events after he pulled off his run:

Five American P-40s jumped us. I spiraled sharply to the left, then yanked back on the stick for a sudden climb, which threw their attack off. Four of the Americans arced up to the right and disappeared in the smoke, but the fifth turned left, out of the smoke. I turned and approached from below. He half-rolled and began a loop. At 200 meters, I had his belly in my sight and I closed the distance to 50 yards as he tried to get away. A short burst of my cannon walked into the cockpit, blowing the canopy off. The fighter seemed to stagger in the air, then fell off and dived into the ground.

Moments later, the A6Ms turned north to return to Formosa. Gillet and the other survivors on the ground looked around at the fires and smoke on the field. "When the Japanese left, nearly all of our air force in the Philippines was smoking ruins."

Back in the United States, the month of December 1941 was, comparatively, the warmest month of the year, with average temperatures ranging from a high of nine degrees above normal in North Dakota to seven degrees above normal along most of the east coast. In Greenville,

North Carolina, the day was sunny and about 60 degrees at two o'clock in the afternoon. Newly commissioned Ensign John D. Bridgers was on leave, awaiting orders to a fleet squadron, having recently become a naval aviator after he joined the Navy in February 1941. A 1940 graduate of East Carolina Teachers' College with a double major in mathematics and science, Bridgers' ambition had been to go on to medical school; however, with his family still dealing with the effects of the Great Depression, he knew he had to go to work before following his dream.

He recalled in his memoirs that "A beginning teacher in North Carolina received a monthly salary of $96.50. From this, one was expected to house, clothe, and feed oneself as well as suffer pension withholdings and pay taxes." Though he had never been particularly interested in airplanes or aviation, he read of the expansion of the Navy's Aviation Cadet Program.

> I learned I could make $105.00 per month in the Navy as an aviation cadet with board, lodging, and clothing furnished. In a year, if successful in flight training, I would be commissioned as an ensign in the US Naval Reserve with a $250.00 per month salary, again with lodging provided and an allowance for food, and with a half-month's bonus for flight pay. Further, for foregoing four formative years one typically spent on temporary employment, the reserve aviator would receive a $1,000.00 per year bonus at discharge: $4,000. To a son of the Depression, these seemed princely sums, and the flight bonus would provide a nest egg if I needed more college before medical school.

He joined the Navy in February 1941, and had returned home only three days earlier, after pinning on his Wings of Gold following graduation from flight school at Pensacola on December 3, 1941, with an assignment as a dive bomber pilot.

That afternoon, Bridgers and his father listened to the broadcast of the New York Giants football game on the NBC Blue Network. At 2:30 pm, the broadcast was interrupted with the news no one who heard it would ever forget: Pearl Harbor had been attacked. "I knew my plans had changed."

John Bridgers wasn't the only North Carolinian affected by the news on the radio. At Craig Army Air Field, outside Birmingham, Alabama,

22-year-old Aviation Cadet George E. Preddy, Jr., born and raised in Greensboro, North Carolina, had spent the previous day putting in extra hours in a North American AT-6 trainer, in expectation of his graduation and commissioning as an Air Forces second lieutenant the coming Thursday, December 12. When Preddy heard the news, he knew his dream of being a fighter pilot would be realized. Unlike John Bridgers, Preddy had been in love with airplanes and flying ever since his neighbor in Greensboro Hal Foster took him along in his 1933 Aeronca C-3 on a 30-minute flight over the 50 miles from Greensboro to Danville on November 13, 1938. Afterwards, Preddy had written, "I see now how great the airplane is. That trip was the most wonderful experience I ever had. I *must* become an aviator!"

Within a few months, Preddy was taking lessons from his friend Bill Teague, who ran the local A&P grocery store in Greensboro and owned a 1931 Waco GXE Model 10 biplane he kept on a dirt airstrip at Vandalia, 6 miles south of Greensboro, where he gave flight instruction. Preddy soloed in a bit over six hours and shortly thereafter Teague suggested they each invest $75 to purchase a second Waco, an early 1921 Model 4, based on the World War I Curtiss Jenny and powered by a 90 hp OX-5 engine. They then barnstormed all over North Carolina during the summer of 1939. By the summer of 1940, Preddy had accumulated 80 hours in the Waco and – more importantly – completed the necessary two years of college to qualify for admission to the Navy's AvCad program. He was rejected due to the fact he was only 5 feet 4 inches tall and didn't weigh enough. The Navy rejected him twice again that year, after which he joined the Coast Artillery while awaiting a response from the Army to his application to enter the Army Aviation Cadet program; he just missed being sent to Puerto Rico before he was called up and sent to basic training in April 1941. His previous flight experience allowed him to excel in his training, which put him on track for achieving his dream with assignment to "pursuit aviation" – fighters.

On the west coast, the news of the Pearl Harbor attack arrived at 11:30 am. Aviation Cadet Victor Tatelman was preparing to go to lunch at the Fresno Army Air Field where he was about to graduate from basic training, having joined the Aviation Cadet program the week after Labor Day in September, following completion of two years' study of engineering at the University of Indiana. Tatelman was another young man enamored of airplanes and flying. He had learned to fly at age 16 in 1936 in a neighbor's Alexander Eagle Rock, a biplane produced by the Alexander Aviation Co. in Colorado Springs, Colorado. Tatelman had accumulated 50 hours by the time he went off to college, and added another 50 hours through the Civilian Pilot Training (CPT) program by the time he was accepted as an aviation cadet. He recalled that a thrill went down his back when a friend passed the news: "I had no idea what that news was going to mean to me, but being young and stupid, it seemed exciting to contemplate."

Seventy-five miles north of Fresno at Stockton Army Airfield, Aviation Cadet John D. Landers already knew he would receive an assignment to fighters when he graduated the next Thursday. Born in Oklahoma and raised in west Texas, Landers had completed two years at the Arkansas State Teachers' College when he decided to apply for flight training. He had entered basic training in April 1941, at almost the same time as George Preddy, and demonstrated superior ability in the AT-6 during advanced training at Stockton.

Newly promoted Marine Captain Marion E. Carl was busy in the hangars at North Island Naval Air Station in San Diego, supervising final checks of the Brewster F2A-3 fighters that equipped Marine fighter squadron VMF-221 before they were loaded for transportation to Hawaii aboard the carrier *Saratoga* that had docked at the air station the previous Wednesday. The young captain had been interested in aviation since a barnstormer landed in a field on his family farm in Hubbard, Oregon, when he was 12. Carl learned to fly while attending Oregon State College and soloed after only two-and-a-half hours of dual instruction. Graduating in 1938, he accepted a commission in the Army Reserve, then entered Navy flight training in December 1939. On graduation, he took a commission in the Marines, where he was assigned to VMF-1 in the summer of 1940. A year later, he arrived back at Pensacola, where he joined the instruction staff in Squadron 5. Promoted to captain in November 1941 with 1,300 flying hours, he was assigned as a division leader in newly formed VMF-221, where those flying hours and instruction experience would be useful to bring the fresh-caught second lieutenants just graduated from Pensacola up to speed. He later remembered that when the word of the attack was passed, "we worked all that night and the next day to prepare the planes to go aboard *Saratoga*."

Dick Best lifted his SBD-2 off of *Enterprise* at noon that fateful Sunday, leading a search for the enemy fleet. "We were lucky we didn't find the Japs," he recalled later. "We only had 18 fighters, 18 dive bombers and 18 torpedo bombers aboard, and if we'd have run across them they'd have made a quick hash of us." Incorrect intelligence and bad guesses led Best and the others to search southwest of Hawaii, where all they found were other American ships.

On Monday, December 8, the crew listened to President Roosevelt's address to Congress over the loudspeakers. The speech concluded:

> With confidence in our armed forces, with the unbounding determination of our people, we will gain the inevitable triumph – so help us God.
>
> I ask that the Congress declare that since the unprovoked and dastardly attack by Japan on Sunday, December 7th, 1941, a state of war has existed between the United States and the Japanese empire.

That evening, *Enterprise* and her escorts, all low on fuel, crept into Pearl Harbor. Crewmen stared in awe at the battleship *Nevada*, beached near the entrance to the harbor, and at the still-smoking ruins of the other ships. After dropping anchor, the crew set to work in the dark, their shadows cast by the still-burning *Arizona*, as they hauled aboard provisions brought out to the ship by lighters.

Dick Best and the other Air Group 6 flyers had already landed at Ford Island in the last light of day. "I climbed out of my plane, and looked around at the damage, and thought of the good friends I knew who were already dead, and I swore I'd make the bastards pay for this."

At 0600 hours the next morning, *Enterprise* cleared the harbor channel and returned to the vast Pacific.

CHAPTER TWO

THE RISING SUN

The Pacific War was an event long expected and planned for by both of the major antagonists. While the United States Navy first took notice of Japan as a potential competitor and opponent following the smashing Japanese victory over the Russian fleet at the Battle of Tsushima Strait in 1905, their Japanese counterparts did not begin to look similarly at the United States until 1907, when discrimination against Japanese immigrants reached a peak with the "Yellow Peril" campaign on the US west coast that broke out that year.

Japanese naval officers had become aware of the writings of Captain Alfred Thayer Mahan with the 1890 publication of *The Influence of Sea Power Upon History*, as had sailors in the Royal Navy and the German Imperial Navy. The book was translated into Japanese before it was translated into any other language and Mahan's works were required reading for Imperial Navy officers, both during their training and during their careers. Saneyuki Akiyama, "the father of Japanese naval strategy," had served as an observer aboard Admiral Sampson's flagship during the Spanish-American War and had earlier personally met and spoken with Mahan. In terms of acceptance of basic strategy for a naval war, both navies were a mirror image of the other.

For the Japanese, Mahan's emphasis on a climactic battle that would give to the victor "command of the seas" confirmed their experiences in the 1894–95 war with China, where Admiral Ito had destroyed the Chinese fleet at the 1894 Battle of the Yangtze, and the annihilation of the Russian fleet by Admiral Togo at Tsushima in 1905 that led to Japanese victory in the Russo-Japanese War. Thus the Japanese "battleship admirals" controlled the Imperial Navy throughout the years of planning and the actual Pacific War; there was no "Pearl Harbor" to challenge their ascendancy.

The Imperial Navy's basic plan for the Pacific War saw initial seizure of the Philippines and Guam, the American possessions in the western Pacific. This would force the American fleet to sortie westward to recover these possessions. Interestingly, the US Navy's various "Orange Plans" – the plans for the conduct of the Pacific War – also began with these events. Both sides foresaw a decisive fleet action that would happen somewhere north of the Marianas, south of the Japanese Home Islands.

Following the end of World War I, in which Japan gained control of the former Imperial German Pacific possessions in the Marshalls and Carolines and Marianas, Japanese strategy changed to a two-stage fight: an "attrition stage" in which forces operating from these island bases attacked and harried the American fleet as it moved west, and a "decisive battle" stage in which the American fleet would arrive at the final battle in a depleted condition similar to that of the Imperial Russian Navy at Tsushima, where the fresh Japanese main force, operating close to its bases, would be victorious despite the enemy fleet outnumbering it.

While the Imperial Army's war plan was always focused on the Asian mainland and saw Imperial and later Soviet Russia as the main adversary, with the main battle front of a future war in the Russian Far East, the leaders of the Navy looked to what was called the "South Seas," or "Southern Region" – French Indochina, the Dutch East Indies, British Malaya – where success would provide Japan with essential resources. The Army agreed that such an advance was desirable, but the generals argued that the Soviet Union must first be defeated. The admirals claimed the southern advance should have priority and the Army should avoid provocations with the USSR.

In 1936, the Japanese cabinet adopted a document titled "Fundamental Principles of National Policy." Under its terms, Japan would secure a firm diplomatic and military position in East Asia and an extension of national influence to the South Seas. The South Seas advance would be accomplished "gradually and by peaceful means," while on the Asian mainland "extreme caution would be exercised to avoid trouble with the Soviet Union." The Army would expand by ten divisions and additional aviation squadrons so it could resist the forces the Soviet Union would be able to deploy in the Far East, while the

Navy would expand with the addition of two battleships, seven aircraft carriers, and 20 destroyers to secure command of the western Pacific against the US Navy. Whether such geographic expansion was peaceful or not, expansion in China, confrontation with the Soviet Union, and penetration of the South Seas would inevitably result in conflict with the USSR, Great Britain or the United States.

Throughout the period after World War I, a dominant feature of the competition between the Imperial Navy and the US Navy was the Washington Naval Treaty of 1922. The treaty, also known as the Five-Power Treaty, the Four-Power Treaty, and the Nine-Power Treaty, was signed in 1922 by the major nations that had won World War I, and was intended to prevent another arms race like that between Britain and Germany before the war by limiting naval construction. The signatories – the United Kingdom, the United States, France, Italy, and Japan – agreed to limit construction of battleships, battlecruisers, and aircraft carriers; significantly, the treaty did not limit other categories of warships, including cruisers, destroyers, and submarines.

The trigger that ultimately led to the treaty was the announcement by the Wilson Administration of the expansion plan for the US Navy between 1916 and 1919 with the construction of an enormous fleet of 50 modern battleships. While this plan was ultimately aborted by the Senate, the British – who had a policy of maintaining the Royal Navy as the equal of the next two naval powers – saw the program as a threat in the aftermath of a war that had seen the nation lose its pre-eminent world position. Still, the 1921 British Naval Estimates planned construction of four battleships and four battlecruisers, with four additional battleships to follow in 1922. The Japanese government responded with parliamentary approval to construct warships that would see the Imperial Navy achieve its goal of a fleet with eight modern battleships and eight battlecruisers; work was immediately started on four new battleships and four new battlecruisers, all larger and more powerful than preceding ships of those classes. France and Italy, which were both nearly prostrate in the aftermath of the war, were unable to match such expansion.

President Wilson's 1919 naval expansion plan was disapproved by the Republican-controlled Congress following the end of the war. During the 1920 presidential election campaign, the successful Republicans returned to the prewar policy of non-interventionism and exhibited little enthusiasm for expansion. In late 1921, the Harding Administration learned Britain was planning to call a conference to deal with the strategic situation in the Pacific and East Asia. Not wishing to have the British take the lead in dealing with issues of importance to the US in the Philippines, and to satisfy domestic calls for an international disarmament conference, Secretary of State Charles Evans Hughes issued a call in November 1921 for a naval conference to scrap over 1,900,000 tons of naval construction, to be held in Washington.

During the first plenary session in Washington on November 21, 1921, Secretary Hughes opened with the statement "The way to disarm is to disarm," which received an enthusiastic reception when reported in the press and likely abbreviated the conference. He then presented the US proposal, which called for a ten-year pause or "holiday" in construction of battleships and battlecruisers, including immediate suspension of all current capital ship construction. He included a proposal to scrap existing or planned capital ships to provide a 5:5:3:1.75:1.75 tonnage ratio for Britain, the United States, Japan, France and Italy, respectively, and further tonnage limits of secondary vessels (i.e., cruisers and destroyers), though there was no limit on the numbers which could be built.

While the British government was willing to accept these limits, they were controversial in British public opinion when first reported. The Royal Navy leadership was outraged that accepting such limits would mean it was no longer possible for Britain to deploy adequate fleets simultaneously in the North Sea, the Mediterranean, and the Far East. However, the fact that there was little likelihood of military competition or risk of war with the United States meant that the traditional policy of maintaining a fleet the equal of two potential antagonists was not considered; the fact that Britain was implementing major budget decreases due to the postwar recession led to acceptance of the American proposal.

The proposal divided the Japanese delegation. Imperial Navy doctrine required maintenance of a fleet that was 70 percent the size of the US Navy, which was considered the minimum necessary to defeat the US fleet in any war; this made a 5:3 ratio, or 60 percent, unacceptable. Navy Minister Admiral Tomosaburō Katō, leader of the delegation, preferred accepting the ratio since the relative industrial strength of the two counties would mean Japan would lose such an arms race with the

United States, pointing out that at the time Japan had only 55 percent of US capital ships and 18 percent of American GDP. He also pointed out that the lack of limits on the numbers of cruisers and destroyers would mean that the Imperial Navy could continue development of these two types, which were most useful in the Navy's South Seas strategy.

Admiral Tomosaburō Katō's view was strongly opposed by Admiral Kanji Katō, president of the Naval Staff College, who represented the influential "big navy" opinion that, in the event of war, the United States could build more warships indefinitely due to its industrial power, thus requiring Japan to prepare thoroughly in anticipation of the inevitable conflict. In the end, Tomosaburō Katō convinced the Navy's high command to accept the ratio, even with the limitation on the sizes of cruisers and destroyers added to the treaty; however, the treaty would be a cause of controversy within the Imperial Navy until its abrogation 14 years later.

Importantly, Article XIX prohibited construction of any new fortifications or naval bases in the Pacific by Britain, Japan, and the United States, though existing fortifications in Singapore, the Philippines, and Hawaii were allowed to remain. This was significant for Japan, since additional fortified British or American bases would be a serious obstacle in any future war. The article essentially guaranteed Japanese dominance in the western Pacific and was pivotal to Japanese acceptance of the capital ship limits.

Domestically, both within the Army and Navy and newly active ultranationalist civilian political groups, the 5:5:3 ratio was seen as another snub by the West. Given that during the term of the treaty the United States and Britain did not build out their navies to the treaty limits, the result was the Imperial Navy could muster a greater concentration of force in the western Pacific than either potential opponent. Over the period of the treaty, the terms provoked controversy in the Imperial Navy between the "Treaty Faction" and the "Fleet Faction," with the latter allied with the ultranationalists in the Japanese Army and other parts of the Imperial government. This led to political instability and assassinations of political and military leaders seen as insufficiently "pro-Japan" in the late 1920s and early 1930s when the Japanese military began the expansion that led first to war in Manchuria, then China and eventually to the Pacific War. The perception of inequality was responsible for the failed relationship between the United States and Japanese governments during this period. The 1930 extension of the Washington Treaty was only approved by Japan due to the economic uncertainties created by the worldwide economic depression. The internal rivalries finally resulted in Japan's renunciation of the Second London Naval Treaty in 1936 and the subsequent overthrow of the "Treaty Faction" in the Imperial Navy's leadership by the "Fleet Faction."

While Admiral Isoroku Yamamoto had personally opposed the 1930 treaty, after its adoption he argued that Japan should remain in the treaty. His opinion was based on his direct experience of traveling through the United States in the 1920s, which led him to understand that in the event of war the United States could outproduce Japan by far more than the 5:3 ratio due to the huge US industrial production advantage. His position was that "Anyone who has seen the auto factories in Detroit and the oilfields in Texas knows that Japan lacks the power for a naval race with America... The ratio works very well for Japan – it is a treaty to restrict the other parties."

Nevertheless, the government gave formal notice on December 14, 1934 that Japan intended to terminate the treaty. Its provisions remained in force formally until December 31, 1936. In the end, Admiral Yamamoto would be proven right following passage of the Two Ocean Navy Act of 1940 by the US Congress, which created the navy that eventually won the war both sides had foreseen for 30 years.

While the senior leadership of the Imperial Navy continued to plan for the "decisive battle," one Japanese admiral saw the future more accurately. Vice Admiral Shigeyoshi Inoue, a brilliant, iconoclastic, and eccentric officer in a navy where all those qualities worked against acceptance of his views, was head of the Navy Ministry's Naval Affairs Bureau. Throughout the final treaty years, he urged his fellow admirals to cease thinking of the decisive battle and instead prepare for protracted air and amphibious warfare across the Pacific, and to use the fleet's submarines as commerce raiders rather than limiting them to directly working with the main fleet. Most importantly, he urged development of a significant antisubmarine capability with large numbers of escort vessels to defend Japan's crucial merchant marine from American submarines. His reward was to be sidelined after his perceived "failures" in the initial six months of the Pacific War – particularly the failure to take New Guinea and to defeat the US Navy at the Battle of the Coral Sea, for which he was held responsible as the senior commander – until

1944 when he was finally appointed Navy vice minister with the power to initiate his plans, years too late.

An essential point in understanding how the Japanese military would fight the Pacific War relates to the political control of the armed forces. Unlike the American military, which is firmly under the control of the civilian political authority, the ministers of the Army and Navy in the Imperial government were the heads of the respective force. These officers were given direct contact with the emperor, which allowed them to operate independently of the civilian political leaders. Any time either service wanted to bring the operation of the civilian government to a halt, they had only to withdraw their minister and refuse to participate in the government.

With the Army looking north and west, and the Navy looking east and south, Japanese interwar policy was necessarily schizophrenic. While the Imperial General Headquarters was created in 1937 ostensibly to establish unity of command, with the Army and Navy general staffs participating in meetings held at the Imperial Palace twice a week, operational control of the forces in the field remained separate. At the outbreak of the Pacific War, the Army and Navy were still separate and equal, each jealously guarding its prerogatives against the other. If the Army and Navy could not agree on a proposed operation, it would be either postponed or abandoned. There was never an overall commander with authority over both services who could enforce cooperation, as was established in American theater commands. This division of military authority and its independence from civil political control would hobble Japan in creating an effective strategy to fight the Pacific War, and ultimately prolong it far past the ability of Japan to fight effectively.

Since they saw themselves operating from a position of material weakness, prewar Japanese planners and strategists counted on what they saw as the superior toughness, morale, and fighting spirit of the soldiers and sailors, the "Japanese spirit" that brought victory in the wars with China and Russia. This meant the development of new and superior weapons and incessant training in the use of those weapons to bring that spirit to the forefront.

During the 1930s, the Imperial Navy became the world leader in the development of the torpedo and torpedo-carriers. Design of a torpedo to be used by surface warships began in 1931 and in 1933 the first Type 93 torpedo was produced. At the same time, the Type 95 submarine torpedo was developed. Both were 24 inches in diameter, completely oxygen-fueled, with a range of 24 miles at 39 knots or 12 miles at 49 knots, with a 1,000-pound high explosive warhead. Oxygen fuel provided five times the energy of conventional compressed air and greatly extended range. These torpedoes were extensively subjected to live-fire tests under operational conditions, and mass production of the torpedo was instituted in 1935. Every Japanese combat ship from heavy cruisers to destroyers was equipped to use it, since the terms of the Washington Treaty allowed unlimited armament development of these classes of warship.

Additionally, the Imperial Navy operated on a training schedule that was jokingly known to crews as "all weekdays," and emphasis was directed toward developing a fleet-wide capability for successful night fighting using torpedoes as the primary attack weapon. Ships were damaged and a few were lost in this training during pre-radar days, which was considered acceptable by senior fleet commanders as the cost of being fully prepared for combat. During the surface battles in the South Pacific of 1942–43, Japanese destroyers and cruisers routinely launched torpedoes at unsuspecting Allied warships that did not expect torpedo attacks from ships further away than 5 miles while 12 miles away, which ran to their targets at a stunning 49 knots while the ships that launched them closed to gun range.

In comparison, development of the American Mark XIV submarine and aerial torpedo and concurrent Mark XV surface ship torpedo, which was the main American weapon during the war, also began in 1931. This torpedo was 21 inches in diameter with a maximum range of 15,000 yards at 27 knots or 6,000 yards at 45 knots, with a significantly smaller 825-pound warhead and powered by compressed air. Significantly, the smaller warhead was meant to explode under the target's keel, using a Mark VI magnetic exploder developed from a German World War I design for magnetically exploded mines. While the magnetic exploder was extensively tested using torpedoes with instrumented heads, amazingly no live-fire test was ever done, since the authorities were loath to sacrifice a $10,000 torpedo or supply a target ship even if it was one due for scrapping.

The Naval Torpedo Station at Newport had been designated the sole designer, developer, builder, and tester of torpedoes in the United States by congressional order in 1923. During the development of the

Mark XIV, no independent or competing group was allowed to verify the test results. Only destroyers and submarines were to be armed with torpedoes, and there was little training of any sort in their use and no training at all in night fighting due to the fear of ship damage or loss in training accidents. Other manufacturers were not brought into the Mark XIV program until after Pearl Harbor. By the time of the Japanese attack, the government factories at Newport and Alexandria, Virginia were producing a total of 23 torpedoes per day, and only 2,000 additional torpedoes were produced in all of 1942. Even with additional manufacturers, there would be a torpedo shortage in the Navy throughout the war. Worst of all, however, was the fact that without live-fire exercises, it was not known that the Mark VI exploder was faulty, that it was not strong enough and could be deformed when the torpedo hit a target, leading to a dud. The majority of American torpedoes fired in the first 24 months of the war were duds, and the problem was not solved until 1943 when Admiral Charles Lockwood, commander of the Pacific Fleet submarines, finally forced a live-fire test to be held that conclusively demonstrated the problem.

In addition to developing a torpedo for surface ship and submarine use, the Imperial Navy also developed the Type 91 aerial torpedo, which achieved service production status in 1934. The weapon was 17¾ inches in diameter and 18 feet long, weighing 1,841 pounds with a 450-pound warhead, and was powered by compressed air. It had a range of 2,200 yards and a speed of 42 knots. Most importantly, from the outset the torpedo was designed so that it could be dropped successfully by an aircraft flying at a speed of 180 knots at an altitude of 70 feet. By the outbreak of the Pacific War, further development allowed it to be dropped in a power-glide torpedo-bombing run at a maximum speed of 200 knots and an altitude of 500 feet.

In 1935, the Nakajima Aircraft Company began design of the B5N1, which first flew in 1937 and was quickly ordered into production as the Type 97 Carrier Attack Bomber. A total of 1,150 B5N1 and B5N2s were produced. Its maximum speed was 206 mph with a range of 1,230 miles. Like the contemporary American TBD-1, it was the first Imperial Japanese Naval Air Force carrier type to feature all-metal monoplane construction with fully retractable landing gear, a fully enclosed cockpit, and power-folding wings. The B5N1 first saw combat in China in 1938, primarily in its secondary role as a level bomber; the aircraft was further developed into the B5N2 by the outbreak of the Pacific War. Known to Americans as the "Kate," in the initial carrier battles of 1942, the performance of the B5N2 with the Type 91 torpedo making high-speed higher-altitude attacks astounded its US Navy opponents, who expected a torpedo attack similar to that which their torpedo bomber could perform. At Coral Sea, the attacking Japanese bombers outran the defending US fighters, with fatal results for the carrier *Lexington*.

US Navy torpedo bombers were armed with the Mark XIII aerial torpedo. Developed from a 1925 design, the torpedo had been subject to changing requirements that resulted in on-and-off development. Early versions were prone to running on the surface or not running at all, even when dropped from low altitude at slow speeds. The torpedo was unusually squat for its type, with a diameter of 22½ inches and length of 13 feet 5 inches. It had a top speed of 33½ knots – 12.8 knots slower than the Mark XIV – and a range of 6,300 yards. The version in service at the outset of the Pacific War and during the first two years had to be launched at a speed of 100 mph at an altitude of exactly 100 feet with the aircraft flying straight and level with no G-force, which was suicidal for the attacking airplane. If the bomber flew lower, the torpedo would "porpoise" when it went into the water; if dropped from higher altitude, the torpedo would explode when it hit the water and any G-force experienced at the time of drop would harm the guidance system.

The US Navy's Douglas TBD-1 torpedo bomber was ordered in 1934; it first flew in 1935 and entered service in 1937. For the Navy, the airplane was "revolutionary" – the first all-metal low-wing monoplane with fully enclosed cockpit and power-folding wings. At the time, it was called the most advanced carrier-based airplane in the world, since the Navy knew nothing of the B5N that entered service at almost the same time. Only 129 were built, with prewar attrition reducing that number to 100 at the outbreak of war. The airplane had a top speed of 206 mph and a cruising speed of 128 mph, with a range of only 435 miles. After the Battle of Midway, the remaining TBDs aboard the carriers were quickly replaced by the Grumman TBF-1 Avenger, a vastly superior aircraft, though it was still armed for shipping attack with the same poorly performing torpedo.

By far the most important American technical development in the 1930s was the creation of the scout-bomber. Fleet exercises had clearly demonstrated that the side which first disabled or sank the opposing aircraft carrier would win the battle. The scout-bomber was developed to allow discovery of the enemy carrier, with the opportunity to place one or two bombs in the flight deck after radioing the location, effectively knocking the enemy carrier out of the fight from the beginning. Dive-bombing, which provided the best chance for accuracy, was the tactic to be used. Design work at the Northrop Corporation in El Segundo, California, on what would become the BT-1 began in 1935, with a young engineer named Ed Heineman working under the supervision of Jack K. Northrop, who at the time was responsible for some of the most advanced aircraft construction techniques in the US. The BT-1 used all of Northrop's advanced technology to create an all-metal low-wing airplane with an enclosed cockpit. Unfortunately, the 750-horsepower Wright engine only allowed a 500-pound bomb load. Douglas Aircraft acquired the Northrop Corporation in 1937, which became the El Segundo Division of Douglas. Northrop's active projects continued, and the BT-2 was developed with more aerodynamic landing gear and a more powerful engine. In response to a BuAer request for a more modern dive bomber, Heineman's design team created the XSBD-1 (Scout Bomber, Douglas) in the spring of 1939. It was powered by a 1,000-horsepower Wright R-1820 Cyclone engine and could carry a 1,600-pound semi-armor-piercing bomb. The SBD-1 went into production in the summer of 1940. The aircraft was short-ranged and the 57 produced were passed on to the Marine Corps while 87 SBD-2s with increased fuel capacity arrived in the Navy in the spring of 1941. That fall, the SBD-3, which had self-sealing fuel tanks and increased fuel capacity, entered production; 584 would eventually see service. At the outbreak of war, the US Navy's scouting (VS) and bombing (VB) squadrons were all equipped with the SBD-2 and SBD-3, now known as the Dauntless. Few airplanes would live up to their name as well as the SBD, which would turn in a truly dauntless performance during the crucial first year of the Pacific War, where it would become the Navy's premier ship-killer.

The cutting edge of Japanese aerial success in the first year of the Pacific War was the astounding Mitsubishi A6M2 Type 0 Carrier Fighter, *rei-shiki-kanjō-sentōki*, or A6M Rei-sen. The A6M was called the "Reisen" ("zero fighter") by its pilots, "00" being the last digits of the imperial year 2600 (1940) when it entered service with the Imperial

Japanese Naval Air Force. It became known as the "Zero" or "Zeke" to its opponents. At the time it entered service in 1940, it was the most advanced carrier-based fighter in the world, and the first carrier-based fighter to have superior performance to its land-based opponents. In the hands of pilots who were the products of the most demanding aviation training program in the world, the Zero attained nearly legendary status both in its home country and in the minds of those who flew against it as it established a 12:1 victory-loss ratio during 1942.

Development of what became the A6M began when the IJN issued "Planning Requirements for the ProtoType 12-shi Carrier-based Fighter" to Nakajima and Mitsubishi on October 5, 1937. At the time, the Mitsubishi A5M1, the first all-metal low-wing carrier fighter in the world, was just entering service with the IJNAF. Both companies commenced initial design work in anticipation of more definitive requirements. At the end of October, the updated requirements were issued; the new fighter should be capable of a speed of 600 km/h (370 mph) and climb to 3,000 meters (9,800 feet) in 3.5 minutes. Flight endurance should be two hours at normal power, with six to eight hours at economical cruising speed. Armament was set at two 20mm cannon and two 7.7mm (.303in.) machine guns. The aircraft was to be equipped with radio and an RDF for long-range navigation. Maneuverability should at least equal that of the A5M, with a wingspan less than 12 meters (39 feet) for carrier use. The aircraft was to be powered by an available engine, which was a significant design limitation.

In January 1938, Nakajima's design team concluded the requirements exceeded the capability of the industry to achieve and withdrew from the competition. At Mitsubishi, chief designer Jiro Horikoshi, who had created the A5M, concluded the requirements could be met if the aircraft was as light as possible. Accordingly, he utilized every possible weight-saving measure in the design. The airframe was built from a new top-secret aluminum alloy, "extra super duralumin" (ESD), that had been developed by Sumitomo Metal Industries in 1936 and was lighter, stronger, and more ductile than other aluminum alloys though it was prone to corrosion, which made it brittle. This was countered by the application of an anticorrosion coating after fabrication. The design did not include armor for the pilot, engine or other vital points and it did not include self-sealing fuel tanks.

The result was the most maneuverable, longest-ranged single-engine fighter of World War II. In return for this astounding performance, the design tradeoff in weight and the construction material used meant it was likely to catch fire and explode when hit by enemy fire.

The wide-track landing gear made it easy to land on either a carrier or a land base. The airfoil gave high lift at low speeds; combined with low weight, the stalling speed was below 60 knots, which was the basis of the phenomenal maneuverability that allowed it to out-turn any contemporary opponent. The large ailerons, which provided the amazing maneuverability at lower speeds, required servo tabs due to increased heaviness of control forces at speeds over 250 mph, with the ailerons losing most of their effectiveness at speeds over 350 mph. When this fault was discovered during testing of a captured A6M2 in 1942, Allied fighter pilots were instructed to keep their speed up in combat with the Zero, which negated its maneuverability.

During the war, there were several claims that the aircraft was either a copy or highly influenced by some contemporary Western designs. However, a thorough analysis of the Zero in later years revealed that it was an incredibly original design, unlike any other at the time.

The A6M first entered service in July 1940. On September 13, Lieutenant Saburo Shindo led 13 A6M2s that attacked 27 Soviet-built I-152s and I-16s of the Chinese Nationalist Air Force, shooting down all 27 without loss. The event passed without notice in the West and the Zero was unknown when the war broke out. This was despite the fact the Chinese had captured an early example and examined it, and a report of this examination and of combat experience was forwarded by Major Claire A. Chennault to the Pentagon at least eight months before the attack on Pearl Harbor. American myopia about Japanese achievements and capabilities was nearly impenetrable before the war, and was then quickly replaced by a belief in superhuman superiority that was equally misplaced.

On December 7, 1941, the IJNAF possessed 521 Zeros, 328 in first-line units such as Saburo Sakai's Tainan Air Corps and the six carriers of the Mobile Fleet. The A6M2 Model 21 had a range of more than 1,600 miles that could be extended by skilled fliers such as those in the Tainan Air Corps who managed to convince MacArthur's command that there were at least two carriers operating in the Philippines when there were actually none, due to their ability to fly to the Philippines from bases on Formosa. The Zero's fearsome reputation came from inexperienced Allied fighter pilots who attempted to engage it in traditional air combat maneuvering at which it excelled. The fighter ranged over the Central Pacific, the Philippines, and the Netherlands East Indies, sweeping nearly all before it.

While the Imperial Navy had developed aircraft that were the equals if not the superiors of their Western opponents, this was not the case with the Imperial Japanese Army Air Force. At the outbreak of the Pacific War, most JAAF (Japanese Army Air Force) fighter units were equipped with the Nakajima Ki-27 *Kyūnana-shiki sentōki*, or Type 97 Fighter. The fighter had been developed in a 1935 Imperial Japanese Army competition between Nakajima, Mitsubishi, and Kawasaki to design a low-wing monoplane to replace the Kawasaki Ki-10 (Army Type 95 Fighter) biplane, which was also to have a better performance than the experimental Mitsubishi Ki-18 that was the prototype for what became the A5M1. The Ki-27 made its first flight on October 15, 1936. Though it displayed a lower top speed and worse climb performance than its competitors, the Kawasaki Ki-28 and the Mitsubishi Ki-33 (a modification of the A5M1), the Army chose the design for the outstanding turning ability provided by its remarkably low wing loading. Conservative Army pilots were still wedded to the high-G close-in maneuvering of biplane fighters. Like the A5M, it was armed with two 7.62mm (.30-caliber) machine guns. While the A5M had been relegated to second-line status by the outbreak of war, the Ki-27 was the primary JAAF fighter during the battles in the Philippines, Malaya, and the Indies. While it was more maneuverable than its Allied opponents, its light armament and slow speed put it at a disadvantage as opponents learned not to fight it on its own terms.

The closest JAAF equivalent to the Zero was the Nakajima Ki-43 *Hayabusa* (Peregrine Falcon) Army Type 1 Fighter (for its adoption in the year 2601). Eventually known by the Allied reporting name "Oscar," the Ki-43 was frequently mistaken throughout the war for the Zero by Allied pilots due to its resemblance to the Mitsubishi fighter; both had a generally similar low-wing layout with similar round cowlings and bubble-type canopies. The initial Ki-43-I that entered combat in limited numbers just at the outset of the war was armed with just two 7.62mm machine guns, though this was later increased to two 13mm (.50-caliber) weapons in subsequent series development.

At the outbreak of war, the JAAF could only field two sentais equipped with the Ki-43. Due to its light construction without armor or self-sealing fuel tanks, Allied pilots often reported that the Ki-43 was a difficult target, but that only a few hits were needed to set it afire or break it apart. Like the Zero and the IJNAF, the Ki-43 remained the primary JAAF fighter throughout the Pacific War and was credited with shooting down more Allied aircraft than any other Japanese fighter. Nearly all JAAF aces achieved the majority of their victories while flying the *Hayabusa*.

While the US Navy had engaged throughout the 1930s in fleet exercises that demonstrated the rules of carrier warfare, the Japanese had concentrated on the nuts and bolts of creating a well-trained fighting force able to put to use the most advanced weapons they could create. The result was a desperate struggle for the first 18 months of the Pacific War in which the United States, despite its greater strength, faced defeat at several points.

Throughout the interwar years, the Japanese doctrine of strategic defense remained a fixture in Japanese fleet exercises. American naval intelligence had broken the prewar Japanese naval codes, so that as early as 1927, it had been possible to monitor the Imperial Navy's annual grand maneuvers and know that the Japanese strategic posture was largely defensive. However, there was virtually no intelligence penetration within Japan, so that the change in strategic outlook of the late 1930s was unknown. The official American intelligence estimate as late as 1941 was that the Imperial Navy would largely remain in home waters to await the American move west. American naval war planning, epitomized in WPAC-46 under Admiral Kimmel promulgated in the summer of 1941, counted on this inaction, calling for an advance across the Central Pacific once hostilities began.

With the defeat of France and the Netherlands in 1940, their colonies in Indochina and the East Indies were unprotected and vulnerable. Britain's fight for survival in Europe meant that the entire British Empire in Asia – Malaya, Burma, and India itself – was vulnerable to attack. Under Army pressure, Japanese premier Admiral Matsumoto Yonai resigned his position, to be replaced by Prince Funimaro Konoye, an aristocrat of considerable intelligence and experience who was nevertheless weak, irresolute, and unable to stand up to pressure from the Army for action to take advantage of the new situation. The new foreign minister, the ultranationalist Yosuke Matsuoka, was described by a fellow cabinet member as "crazy."

In September 1940, the Vichy French authorities in Indochina allowed Japan to establish air bases around Hanoi that enabled more wide ranging air attacks against southwestern China and positioned Japanese bombers to threaten the rest of Southeast Asia. At the same time, negotiations proceeded for an alliance with Germany and a non-aggression pact with the Soviet Union. Japan joined Germany and Italy in the Tripartite Pact in November 1940. The Imperial Army had discovered that the Red Army was a more dangerous opponent than expected during the 90-day "Nomonhan Incident" in the fall of 1939, and was thus eager to secure that front; the Japan–USSR Non-Aggression Pact was signed on April 13, 1941. Japan had chosen the South Seas for expansion.

This was not a unanimous decision. The Navy opposed a war that would involve both the United States and Great Britain, with the Imperial Navy hopelessly outnumbered by the two largest naval powers, not to mention that the Navy and the entire Japanese civil economy was dependent on imports from the United States. Vice Navy Minister Admiral Yamamoto and clear-eyed Admiral Shigeyoshi Inoue led the Navy's resistance to the Army's desires. At the time the Tripartite Pact was signed, the two men were targeted by right-wing extremists, with the situation becoming so threatening that tanks and machine guns manned by Special Naval Landing Force troops were set up to guard the Navy Ministry, while Yamamoto was the target of several serious assassination plots that resulted in his changing his residence from night to night.

Japanese planning was assisted by the fact that in November 1940, just after the signing of the Tripartite Pact, the German raider *Atlantis* captured and boarded the British SS *Automedon*, where they found top secret documents including a copy of the British War Cabinet minutes of August 1940 that included a summary of British Far Eastern strategy and admitted the indefensibility of Malaya and Hong Kong. Crucially, the papers indicated Britain would not go to war over the fate of French Indochina. The Germans gave the documents to the Japanese, which allowed them to assess correctly the weakness of Britain in the Far East.

With this information in hand, the Navy came around and accepted the argument in favor of South Seas expansion. Junior officers were pro-German, and the leaders came to accept Foreign Minister Matsuoka's argument that the alliance with Germany and Italy would deter the United States and Britain from acting in response to Japanese expansion. Admiral Yamamoto left Tokyo for the safer assignment of commander of the Combined Fleet.

In late May 1940, President Roosevelt had given orders that the Pacific Fleet would remain in Pearl Harbor, following the end of Fleet Problem XXI, turning the Hawaiian base from an advanced deployment base to the main American base in the Pacific. The President had hoped this change would act as a deterrent to Japan. However, the move put the Pacific Fleet's radio communications within range of the Japanese radio intelligence listening station of the First Detachment of the Sixth Communications Unit on Kwajalein in the Marshalls. This allowed the Japanese, who had over the years developed a similar radio intelligence capability to the US Navy, to gather much more intelligence.

The Japanese Telephone and Telegraph Ministry was able to monitor commercial telegrams and radio telephone calls made by Pacific Fleet sailors to the mainland. Additionally, sailing schedules, supply-train arrivals, unit manning, and ship locations were available through open communications in Hawaiian media. At the end of 1940, this Japanese capability was revealed when the US Army Signal Corps began testing a new speech-scrambler system designed by AT&T for radio telephone calls between Honolulu and San Francisco. The device was already being used for communication between Washington and American embassies in Europe. During testing, an operator in Tokyo broke in to ask if there was a problem with the channel, since he could not understand the voice transmission between the two US terminals. This knowledge that the Japanese were monitoring calls between Honolulu and the United States was the reason why General George Marshall would direct that the final warning of impending Japanese attack be sent to Hawaii by commercial telegraph rather than by telephone.

With the Navy having come around to agreeing with the Army regarding future strategy, Admiral Yamamoto proposed the idea of a surprise attack on Pearl Harbor in January 1941. The proposal overturned 20 years of naval strategic thinking and the Navy General Staff initially opposed his idea. However, in July 1941, Vichy France agreed to complete Japanese occupation of Indochina. Surprisingly, President Roosevelt responded to this action immediately by embargoing the sale of American oil and aviation gasoline to Japan. The Navy was now faced with the fact that, in the aftermath of the US embargo, it had fuel supplies for only 18 months of wartime operations, while the country as a whole had barely enough resources to support two years of war. The chief of the naval staff, Admiral Osami Nagano, stated "there is no choice left but to fight and break the iron chains strangling Japan."

Following imposition of the US embargo, the General Staff finally agreed that Admiral Yamamoto should develop a plan that would allow Japan to prevent the immediate move forward across the Central Pacific by the US Pacific Fleet after the outbreak of war. Initial planning, training, and war games conducted in September 1941 demonstrated technical and operational shortcomings that had to be fixed if the plan was to be successful. Significantly, Yamamoto had imposed radio silence on the September war games, which meant that US naval intelligence did not detect the change in thinking and continued to believe the fleet would stay in home waters. All the admiral had to do to ensure surprise was to convince the Americans they should continue to think that way.

Timing of the outbreak of war was constrained by weather. The monsoon dominated all thinking. December and January were the two months during which the weather would be favorable to the attackers in invasions of the Philippines and Malaya; after that the northeastern monsoon would make conditions progressively more difficult until they became impossible in late spring. On November 5, 1941, an imperial conference concluded that if no diplomatic agreement could be reached with the United States by the beginning of December, Japan would go to war. With the majority of the Imperial Army tied down in China, and the main striking force of the Navy involved in the Pearl Harbor operation, Japanese military planners foresaw that speed would be essential in catching the enemy off guard and then defeating him in detail. While Allied forces in the southern region appeared formidable on paper, they were dispersed throughout the area rather than concentrated; additionally, they suffered from a lack of command unity since there were three national armed forces facing the unified Japanese. Furthermore, much of the enemy's current equipment on-hand was obsolescent. The Japanese plan allowed 50 days for the conquest of the Philippines, 100 days for Malaya, and 150 for the Indies.

The carrier striking force, Kido Butai, departed Hokkaido on November 26, 1941, headed across the northern Pacific for the surprise strike on Pearl Harbor. The key to success lay in Japanese radio denial-and-deception actions. In March and June 1941, when the carriers had been dispatched south to support the Japanese move in French Indochina, it had been discovered that the British radio monitoring station in Hong Kong had identified and tracked the ships. While it was unknown that US naval radio intelligence had been equally as successful, it was assumed such was possible. A counterplan was created.

In mid-November 1941, the Imperial Navy held a week-long communications drill with a series of scheduled radio contacts between certain ships and stations. This drill began as Kido Butai moved to its initial rendezvous in the Inland Sea. At that point, Japanese radio operators left the ships and continued these communications, so as to appear to US radio monitors in Hawaii and the Philippines as the same exercise. Kido Butai, in the meantime, instituted strict radio silence from their departure for the Kuriles on November 17. The monitored transmissions reinforced the American expectation that the carriers were in home waters. On the crucial day of November 17, American ambassador Joseph C. Grew cabled from Tokyo that internal security in Japan was now so tight that the embassy was no longer able to monitor activity and provide any sort of early warning of warlike moves.

The false transmissions were picked up by the monitoring station on Corregidor in the Philippines. Using direction-finding gear, analysts plotted lines of bearing on the call signs; the lines crossed the naval bases of Sasebo, Kure, and Yokosuka. American naval intelligence analysts in Washington, Hawaii, and the Philippines stated their conclusion that the carriers were still in home waters, preparing for the expected emergence of the Pacific Fleet from Pearl Harbor.

Unfortunately, at this point, the Navy cryptanalysts had not broken JN-25, so they did not know that a daily radio broadcast from Tokyo, to which Kido Butai did not respond, contained updated information from the Japanese spy in Honolulu regarding Pacific Fleet ship movements and information that Navy aerial reconnaissance was not being flown into the stormy northern Pacific. The Japanese operational security had beaten American intelligence.

In the end, the Japanese mistake was to attack the United States at all. Isolationist sentiment still dominated domestic American politics. Had Japan attacked the British and Dutch possessions and ignored those of the US, President Roosevelt would likely not have had the ability to win congressional political support for the military defense of distant European colonies in Asia. Had Roosevelt not been able to lead a crusade to avenge Pearl Harbor on December 8 with a virtually unanimous congressional declaration of war against Japan, Hitler would not have adhered to his promises in the Tripartite Pact and declared war on the United States on December 10. Without the German declaration of war, the United States Congress would likely never have declared war unilaterally against Germany. Though it would take two dangerous years for the full military force of the United States to be felt, Churchill was entirely right when he recorded that on the night of December 7, 1941, he "slept the sleep of the saved."

CHAPTER THREE

PREPARATION IN THE PHILIPPINES

Throughout the prewar years, US Navy planners recognized that, in any war with Japan, the Philippines were doomed, since the Japanese could overwhelm the defenders long before the main American force in the Pacific could arrive on the scene. It was estimated that within the first month of war, the Japanese could land 300,000 men on Luzon, which would easily defeat the 11,000 American troops and 6,000 members of the Philippine constabulary. This knowledge on the part of American Army and Navy leaders was kept from the Congress and the American people throughout the interwar years.

By the time the Navy's Orange Plan was adopted in 1924, the American forces in the Philippines were charged with holding Manila Bay against the enemy until the fleet arrived. When it was proposed in 1940 that US forces in the Philippines be increased to 40,000 by 1942, General Douglas MacArthur dissented, stating it would take a minimum of 400,000 troops to hold the Philippines against a Japanese assault.

During the 1920s and '30s, the Naval War College held "war games" applying the various versions of War Plan Orange 127 times. Admiral Nimitz later stated that "the courses were so thorough that nothing that happened in the Pacific War was strange or unexpected." By 1937, the Army and the Navy were at loggerheads regarding a future war with Japan. General Stanley B. Embick, chief of the Army War Plans Division, called War Plan Orange "an act of madness" and advocated that the United States withdraw in the Pacific to the "natural strategic peacetime frontier in the Pacific," along the Alaska–Hawaii–Panama line, which would create an almost-invulnerable defensive position. The Navy, which considered that the Pacific War would be a naval war and not a land war, demurred. The Joint Board directed General Embick and the Navy's chief planner, Rear Admiral James O. Richardson, to develop a compromise Orange Plan.

The result, which was adopted by the Joint Board in February 1938, avoided the important differences between the Army's defensive outlook and the Navy's offensive position. While US forces would position themselves initially in line with the Army concept, they would prepare to take the offensive against the Japanese-held Central Pacific mandates and then proceed to the Philippines. This was implicitly a multiyear task, but the forces in the Philippines were still directed to hold out in Manila while it played out.

In 1939, in the face of international political and military changes and the prospect of a world war breaking out, the Orange Plan was put aside in favor of the Rainbow Plans, which foresaw the United States fighting on multiple fronts with multiple allies against multiple enemies. The primary result of this was the adoption in 1941 of the "Germany First" position advocated by the Army, while the Pacific War would be a secondary fight with the United States taking a defensive position until forces could be brought to bear following the defeat of Germany in Europe. While the Navy officially went along with the decision, none of the senior naval leadership agreed with it. The Pacific War would still be the Navy's fight against Japan.

General Douglas MacArthur had retired as Army chief of staff in 1937 and taken the position of military advisor to the Commonwealth Government of the Philippines. He was also made commander of the Philippine Army with the rank of field marshal. During three frustrating years leading the under-manned and ill-equipped Philippine Army, he had chafed at the reality that in any foreseeable conflict he was to oversee the loss of the islands and the surrender of the Army to Japan. Raised since birth to see himself as a "man of destiny," such a role was inconceivable.

The general was recalled to active duty in the US Army in July 1941, with the possibility of war with the Empire of Japan looming in the foreseeable future. He was named commander of United States Army Forces in the Far East (USAFFE), which united the Philippine Army and US Army in the Philippines under one command, with MacArthur now the most senior general in the Army. The mobilization provided American pay to Filipino soldiers; their army was viewed with contempt by American officers in the islands, many of whom subscribed to the view that Filipino soldiers knew two things: "One, when an officer appeared, to yell attention in a loud voice and jump up and salute, and the other to demand three meals a day."

MacArthur had a history throughout his career of confusing his personal desires with reality. Once returned to active service, he pointed out that he would soon have an additional ten divisions in the Philippine Army, as these units were activated starting in September 1941; in addition to the American troops under his command, this would provide a force of 200,000 men. MacArthur assured his superiors in Washington that with such a force he could defend all of the Philippines, rather than cling to defending Manila Bay. His words fell on responsive ears, since most Americans in the government and the military who were aware of War Plan Orange chafed at the thought of sacrificing the Philippines so easily. MacArthur was telling Secretary of War Henry Stimson and Army Chief of Staff General George C. Marshall what they secretly wanted to hear.

That such a plan was impossible never entered MacArthur's mind. The ten divisions were impressive only in numbers. The units were being called up one regiment at a time and most of the troops received no training whatsoever before September 1941. MacArthur was assured by his staff, led by Chief of Staff Major General Richard K. Sutherland and intelligence chief Colonel Charles A. Willoughby – both of whom owed their careers to MacArthur and were viewed with disdain by the Army senior command in Washington – that his forecast the Japanese would not attack before April 1942 at the earliest allowed sufficient time to train this force. MacArthur announced his strategy was to meet the invaders on the beaches and throw them back into the sea.

In August 1941, MacArthur was told by Colonel Leonard T. Gerow, chief of the War Plans Division in Washington, that American war production was now moving into high gear, making it possible to supply the Philippines with modern military equipment. By the end of September, the army in the Philippines was scheduled to be the first to re-equip with the new Garand M-1 rifle and the new M2A1 105mm howitzer to replace the World War I-vintage French 75mm field howitzers.

American naval power in Asia was composed of the Asiatic Fleet based at Manila and commanded by Admiral Thomas C. Hart. The fleet included the heavy cruiser USS *Houston* (CA-30) and the light cruiser USS *Marblehead* (CL-12), supported by four World War I-era "four-piper" destroyers. The fleet's primary striking force was 23 submarines, of which 17 were among the latest fleet submarine classes. Submarine Squadron (SubRon) 2 was composed of six *Salmon*-class fleet submarines and six World War I-vintage "S"-class submarines, while SubRon 5 had 11 *Porpoise*- and *Sargo*-class fleet submarines. Six new PT (Patrol-Torpedo) boats of Motor Torpedo Boat Squadron 3, commanded by Lieutenant John D. Bulkeley, arrived in September 1941. Patrol Wing 10, with two squadrons of Consolidated PBY-4 "Catalina" flying boats, was available for reconnaissance and patrol missions.

Reinforcing the Air Corps units in the Philippines held high priority. In November 1940, the 17th Pursuit Squadron arrived to join the 20th and 21st pursuit squadrons of the 24th Pursuit Group. Formerly a squadron in the elite 1st Pursuit Group and the lineal descendant in the Army Air Corps of the famed American-manned Lafayette Escadrille of World War I, the pilots of the 17th Squadron were amazed at the equipment that waited for them at Clark Field. Back at Selfridge Field outside Detroit, they had been flying the Seversky P-35 and Curtiss P-36, the first "modern" fighters adopted by the USAAC with all-metal construction, low wings, retractable landing gear, and enclosed cockpits. The pilots of the 24th Pursuit Group in the Philippines were still flying ancient Boeing P-26 "Peashooters" that were thoroughly obsolete in 1940 by any standard.

The P-26s remained the front-line fighter defense of the Philippines through the rest of 1940. At the end of the year, they received new equipment that had come into the Air Corps' inventory following the June 18, 1940 government embargo on the export of military equipment to any nation other than Great Britain. The action resulted in the seizure that September of 60 Seversky EP-106 fighters developed from the P-35 that had been ordered by Sweden; 48 of these, now designated P-35A, with their flight instruments still metric and their flight manuals written in Swedish, arrived at Clark Field in February 1941 to replace the ancient Boeings. Powered by a 1,050 horsepower Pratt & Whitney Wasp, the P-35A had a top speed of 310 mph and was armed with two .30-caliber machine guns in the nose and a .50-caliber weapon in each wing.

Lacking spare parts, the planes were soon in poor shape. That summer, 20 Curtiss P-40B fighters, hand-me-downs from stateside units re-equipping with the new P-40E, arrived. While the 17th Pursuit Squadron flew the P-35s, the 20th Pursuit Squadron considered themselves fortunate to receive the P-40Bs. Unfortunately, the pilots of both squadrons were unable to ever engage in any gunnery training with their new mounts due to a shortage of .50-caliber ammunition.

Newly commissioned Second Lieutenant Lamar Gillet arrived at Clark in May 1941, assigned to the 17th Squadron. "They were operating P-35As and still had a few P-26s. As a very junior pilot, I got to fly what was available, which meant I got to put in quite a bit of time in the P-26. Of all the planes I flew in the Air Force over 25 years, it was my favorite."

While most of the 17th's pilots cursed the P-35As, Gillet was happy to fly them whenever the schedule allowed. "I became quite proficient in that airplane, which – as it turned out – was fortunate." As war clouds gathered, the P-35As lost their shiny prewar aluminum look under a coat of quickly applied olive drab paint. "There wasn't enough paint in the Philippines to paint them right. There was no primer, so the paint was applied directly over the bare metal. The first time you flew one through a rainstorm, and there were a lot of rainstorms in the Philippines, most of the paint came off. After only a few flights the airplanes looked like they had already been through a war."

When the first new Curtiss P-40E Kittyhawks arrived in September 1941, the 17th Squadron happily handed down their Severskys to the newly arrived 34th Pursuit Squadron at the end of October. The 3rd and 21st pursuit squadrons were equipped with the last P-40Es to arrive in the Philippines during November and early December; the pilots of the 3rd Squadron found their oxygen masks didn't work, which meant they could not fly above 13–15,000 feet. With the exception of the 17th Squadron, most of the pilots in the other squadrons were newly commissioned graduates of flight school with only a few hundred flying hours. The new fighters were subject to several teething problems, most prominently an unfortunate tendency for engine fires. The armorers received an AAF Technical Order to disable the hydraulic gun-charging system, which meant that the guns could only be manually charged on the ground prior to takeoff and it was impossible to re-charge the guns in-flight should they jam.

Again, due to the shortage of ammunition, none of the new fighters ever had their guns fired before the outbreak of hostilities.

Due to his lack of seniority, Gillet only received a basic transition flight in the P-40E while the more senior pilots flew them as often as possible to become familiar with their new mounts. "Unfortunately, we didn't get that much opportunity to fly, since the monsoon is at its height in the Philippines in October and November. The senior pilots in my squadron had perhaps ten hours in the P-40 and the others a lot less." The 17th kept several P-35As on strength, so Gillet continued to build time and experience in them.

General Henry H. "Hap" Arnold, commander of the newly renamed US Army Air Forces, planned to base 300 B-17s in the Philippines, which were expected to take offensive action against Japanese-held territory in eastern China, Formosa, and even perhaps Japan itself. The 30th and 93rd bomb squadrons of the 19th Bombardment Group were selected for initial service in the Philippines. The group's other two squadrons would not make it to the Philippines before the war broke out.

The 19th Group's deployment was delayed while their B-17Cs were brought up to B-17D standards; thus nine B-17Ds of the 14th Provisional Squadron, composed of crews from the 5th and 11th bomb groups, led by Major Emmet C. "Rosie" O'Donnell, Jr., departed from Hawaii bound for the Philippines on September 5, 1941. Among the pilots was Captain Colin P. Kelly, Jr., who had been assigned from the 11th Bomb Group. Their route staged from Hawaii to Midway to Wake to Port Moresby in New Guinea, to Australia. The leg from Wake to Port Moresby was flown at night at high altitude as they transited near the Japanese-held island of Ponape in the eastern Carolines, part of the Japanese-controlled Central Pacific island chains. Pilot First Lieutenant Henry C. Godman remembered that "At Wake, our machine guns were loaded, test-fired and readied to ward off an attack as we flew near the Mandate Islands."

Among the pilots in O'Donnell's provisional squadron was First Lieutenant Frank Kurtz. In 1927, enamored of the exploits of Charles A. Lindbergh like many other youths of his generation, Kurtz managed to convince a pilot at his local airfield in Hollywood, California, to teach him to fly at age 16. While a student at the University of Southern California in 1933, he qualified for the US Olympic Team, winning a bronze medal in diving from the 10-meter platform; he qualified as fifth in the event at the 1936 Berlin Olympics. Following graduation, Kurtz bought an airplane and over the next two years established six speed records for light planes; in 1935 he set the national junior transcontinental speed record for a flight from Los Angeles to Mexico City to Washington, DC and back to Los Angeles, after which he joined the Air Corps.

At Port Moresby, native tribesmen refueled the planes by hand, a process that took four hours per plane. They then flew on to Darwin, Australia, before heading north for Clark. Three hundred miles south of their destination, they ran into a typhoon. First Lieutenant Edward C. Teats, flying B-17D 40-3078, recalled, "We let down to within 100 feet of the water and bored right through with rain drops as big as goose eggs slamming the windows." Lieutenant Godman remembered, "At times we could see maybe two or three miles ahead and as an island would loom up, we would veer to the left or right – talk about frightening! We were flying under the typhoon!" After a 7,000-mile trans-Pacific trip, the longest overseas flight yet attempted by the Army Air Force, the only casualty happened when the last plane to land at Clark taxied off the runway and accidentally tore off its tail section when it hooked a derelict airplane by the runway. Every crewman was awarded the Distinguished Flying Cross for accomplishing the feat.

On October 16, nine B-17Cs of 30th Bombardment Squadron departed from Hamilton Field north of San Francisco, bound for Hawaii. They were followed on October 20 by 19th Bomb Group commander Lieutenant Colonel Eugene L. Eubank leading 17 shiny silver bombers. At Hickam Field, Hawaii, the bombers were armed with 100 rounds per gun and given orders that "In the event of contact in the air with planes of a possibly belligerent nation, do not hesitate to bring them under immediate and accurate fire."

The 26 B-17s made the trans-Pacific flight in two 13-plane formations. The first departed Hawaii on October 24, followed by the second on October 27. En route to Port Moresby, the first formation ran into bad weather and three bombers were forced to land at Rabaul to refuel while the others continued on, arriving in New Guinea on October 31; the second group arrived the next day with the airplanes nearly out of gas. Both groups arrived at Darwin on November 2 and left for the Philippines that night, arriving at Clark on November 3.

Once the 19th was at Clark, O'Donnell's 14th Provisional Squadron became the group's 14th Bombardment Squadron. The 35 B-17s constituted the largest American heavy bomber unit outside the United States. Clark Field was the only base in the Philippines that could handle them. The main runway was hard-packed sod, 6,700 feet long. The land surrounding the runway was too soft to take the weight of the B-17s, so the bombers were forced to park alongside the runway. By the end of November, only two protective revetments had been completed.

Morale was high. Second Lieutenant Edgar D. Whitcomb remembered:

> The feeling of American superiority had a strong hold on each of us. Since childhood, we had been taught that American machines, American planes, American equipment and American men were superior in quality to all others on the face of the earth. Why then, should any of us doubt that we would be able to crush the Japanese in a very short time if they were foolish enough to attack us?

Lieutenant Godman recalled, "The feeling of war was in our veins and we wanted some action."

An October 1941 report by the War Plans Division stated that "American air and ground units now available or scheduled for dispatch to the Philippines in the near future have changed the entire picture in the Asiatic area." Major General Lewis H. Brereton arrived in Manila on November 5 to take command of the newly constituted Far East Air Force (FEAF).

On December 6, Colonel Harold George, commander of FEAF Fighter Command, spoke to his pilots about the gathering threat from Japan and his expectation that war would break out in a matter of days. He ended by saying, "You're not a suicide squadron yet, but you are damned close to it."

CHAPTER FOUR

"ALL HANDS HAVE BEHAVED SPLENDIDLY"

The booming surf was so loud that Navy Commander Winfield Scott Cunningham, one of the original naval aviators who had first flown from USS *Langley* back in 1922, couldn't hear the four engines of the Pan American Martin "China Clipper" flying boat as they coughed to life at the mid-lagoon buoy where the big flying boat had awaited better weather over the Pacific since flying in from Manila on the previous Thursday. The plane cast off and taxied for takeoff, headed for Honolulu with four passengers. It lifted off and was soon silhouetted against the rising sun through the cloud decks and the approaching squall line.

Cunningham couldn't hear the shouts from Captain Wilson, the officer in charge of the US Army radio unit, until the man was a mere 10 feet away. "Commander! Sir! War!"

All thoughts of the difficulties he had been consumed with since assuming command ten days earlier on November 28 left Cunningham's mind as he incredulously read the words on the paper Wilson handed to him: "AIR RAID PEARL HARBOR X THIS IS NO DRILL." The booming waves suddenly sounded to him like the sound of naval gunfire. Enemy naval gunfire. He ordered Captain Wilson to contact the Clipper and tell it to return.

On Wake Island, 2,298 miles west of Honolulu and only 1,991 miles southeast of Tokyo, it was Monday, December 8, 1941. Cunningham would later remember that it was around 0730 hours when he read the message. The American force on Wake was pitifully small to face the oncoming enemy: ten officers and 58 naval personnel; six officers and 173 men of the 1st Marine Defense Battalion who had arrived on the island the previous August 19, now fleshed out by nine more officers and 200 men who had arrived on November 5, commanded by Major James P.S. Devereaux, who had arrived on October 15; and a detachment of 12 F4F-3 Wildcat fighters from VMF-211 commanded by Major Paul A. Putnam, which had landed on the half-finished air strip four days earlier, having been transported by the carrier USS *Enterprise*. The fighters were supported by 47 Marine ground support personnel from Marine Air Group 21 (MAG-21) who had been dropped off by the seaplane tender USS *Wright* (AV-1) on November 28, along with Commander Cunningham.

Cunningham was also responsible for the safety of 1,221 civilian employees of the Morrison-Knudsen Civil Engineering Company who had been on the island since February 1941 constructing the airfield and gun emplacements. There were an additional 45 Guamanian Chamorros, employed by Pan American Airways at the company's hotel on Wake, one of the stops on Pan Am's trans-Pacific service.

Wishbone-shaped Wake Atoll contains three islands: Wake, the largest, Wilkes, and Peale. Comprising only 2,600 acres in total, the islands were not the bare sandy coral found on most Pacific atolls, but were rather covered by large boulders, stubby trees, and thick underbrush; no part of the three islands was further than 1,100 yards from the sea. Wake is one of the most isolated places in the world, 592 miles northwest of the nearest inhabited island, Utirik Atoll in the Marshall Islands. Spanish explorer Álvaro de Mendaña first discovered the atoll in 1586, naming it "San Francisco." The name "Wake" was given it by the British master of a whaling ship who happened upon it in 1796. A few Americans became aware of the island during a survey voyage commanded by Commodore Charles Wilkes, who left his name on the second-largest island in 1840. The atoll was formally claimed by the United States in 1898 by a ship of the United States Expeditionary Force on its way to Manila following Commodore Dewey's victory over the Spanish fleet.

After a further 36 years of neglect, Wake was officially placed under the jurisdiction of the Navy Department in 1934. It gained a measure of renown the following year when Pan American World Airways chose it as a stop for the China Clipper service between San Francisco and Shanghai and built a hotel for overnight stays by passengers bound for the Philippines and China. In 1938, the Hepburn Board recommended the atoll be developed as a Navy seaplane base for long-range reconnaissance into the Japanese-held Marshall Islands of the Central Pacific; work on the base did not begin until February 1941. With an air base on Wake to provide air defense, a seaplane base for the proposed reconnaissance patrols was to be established on Peale.

The Navy was well aware of Wake's exposed position should war break out with Japan. On April 18, 1941, Pacific Fleet commander Admiral Husband E. Kimmel had written a prophetic letter to Chief of Naval Operations Admiral Harold R. Stark:

> To deny Wake to the enemy, without occupying it ourselves, would be difficult; to recapture it if the Japanese should seize it in the early period of hostilities would require operations of some magnitude. Since the Japanese Fourth Fleet (based in the mandated islands) includes transports and troops with equipment especially suited for landing operations, it appears not unlikely that one of the initial operations of the Japanese may be executed against Wake.
>
> If Wake be defended, then for the Japanese to reduce it would require extended operations of their naval force in an area where we might be able to get at them; thus affording us opportunity to get at naval forces with naval forces. We should try, by every possible means, to get the Japanese to expose naval units. In order to do this, we must provide objectives that require such exposure.

The official Marine Corps 1941 Table of Organization called for 43 officers and 939 enlisted men to man the island defenses formed around six 5-inch/.51-caliber artillery pieces for coastal defense, with an additional 12 3-inch/.50-caliber antiaircraft guns with one working fire control director among them, of which only six could be operated at one time, which had been removed from the battleship USS *Texas* (BB-35). The defenders were also armed with 18 Browning .50-caliber water-cooled heavy machine guns, and 30 .30-caliber water- and air-cooled light machine guns, none of which had a full set of maintenance tools or spare parts to fight off invaders. The Marines were personally armed with 1903 Springfield rifles with 100 rounds per man.

The VMF-211 Wildcats operated from the single paved runway, 5,000 feet long, but less than 100 feet wide, so narrow that aircraft could not take off while recently landed aircraft turned around and taxied back on the runway. There was a parking area adjacent to the runway, but the protected revetments the civilian workers had started the week before were not yet completed. The squadron, which had been VMF-2 when its pilots flew their Grumman F3F-2 biplanes for the cameras during the filming of the popular aviation movie *Dive Bomber* the previous spring, had become VMF-211 (Marine Air Group 21, 1st Squadron) on July 1, 1941. At the end of September, they traded their biplanes for new F4F-3 Wildcat monoplanes; most of the pilots had less than 20 hours' flight experience in their new mount by the time they landed aboard *Enterprise* for transport to Wake. None of the 47 recently arrived ground support personnel were experienced airframe or engine mechanics; the two senior gunnery sergeants were both ordnancemen. The island's air-ground radio set consistently malfunctioned.

VMF-211 detachment commander Major Paul A. Putnam had joined the Marines in 1925 after attending Iowa State University for one year and was commissioned as a second lieutenant on March 4, 1926. After a tour of duty in Nicaragua as an aerial observer fighting Sandinista insurgents, he was sent to flight training at Pensacola where he graduated in 1928 and served two more tours in Nicaragua as a pilot. Promoted to major in the summer of 1941, he had joined VMF-211 as executive officer in October and been assigned command of the 12-plane detachment the squadron sent on to Wake.

Putnam's acting executive officer of the detachment was the senior division leader, 36-year-old Captain Henry T. Elrod, a Georgian who had enlisted in the Marines in 1927 after three years of study at Georgia University and Yale. Promoted to corporal in 1930, he was assigned to Marine Observation Squadron 8 (VO-8M), a unit of the West Coast Expeditionary Force based at NAS San Diego, in March 1930. That July, he entered officer training at the Marine Barracks in Washington, DC, where he was commissioned as a second lieutenant on February 10, 1931. In April 1933, he was ordered to flight training at Pensacola and received his Wings of Gold in February 1935 when he was also promoted to first lieutenant. Promoted to captain in September 1937, Elrod, known to his fellow Marine aviators as "Hammerin' Henry," had joined VMF-2 in September 1940.

Since the arrival of the Wildcats, Commander Cunningham had ordered that a four-plane patrol be flown at dawn and just before sunset in hopes of spotting any incoming Japanese attackers and providing warning to the island in time to launch the other defending fighters. By the time Cunningham arrived back at the island headquarters in his pickup truck, Major Devereaux had ordered the bugler play "Call to Arms" and the Marines had manned their coastal defense artillery and the two batteries of antiaircraft guns that were operational.

Major Putnam and his three pilots soon landed from the morning patrol. With news of the Pearl Harbor attack, an additional patrol was immediately sent out with Captain Elrod leading second lieutenants Carl R. Davidson and John E. Kinney, and Tech Sergeant William Hamilton. Climbing to 12,000 feet through an overcast at around 5,000 feet, they split into sections, with Elrod and Davidson heading southeast while Kinney and Hamilton headed southwest. Any Japanese attack would most likely come from the Marshall Islands some 600 miles to the south, the nearest Japanese-controlled territory to Wake.

At about the time the Wildcats took off, the 34 Mitsubishi G3M Type 96 Land-Based Attack Aircraft of the 24th Air Flotilla's Chitose Kōkūtai, known to the IJNAF as the "Rikko" and soon to be known to Allied fliers as the "Nell," descended from their 10,000-foot cruising altitude to 1,500 feet so they could approach their target from beneath the overcast through the end of a rain squall. The bombers had taken off from their base on Roi Island of the Kwajalein Atoll in the central Marshalls shortly after dawn for the 720-mile flight, led by Lieutenant Commander Hideo Matsuda. By the time Elrod's two Wildcats reached the limit of their search and turned back toward Wake, the Japanese bombers had flown beneath them, out of sight below the cloud deck in the squall-filled sky.

At approximately 1158 hours, Major Putnam spotted dots in the sky to the south, which quickly resolved themselves as what he recognized to be Japanese bombers. There was no time to get the other Wildcats into the air. They were grouped closely together in the paved parking area and Putnam wished that the Japanese had delayed their attack two hours, when the sandbagged revetments were supposed to be ready to shelter his fighters. Now, the eight fighters were sitting ducks.

Only Battery D of the antiaircraft guns had a full set of fire-control equipment. Battery E had a director but no height-finder, and had to rely on telephone calls from Battery D to obtain information about target altitude. The six guns were the island's sole air defense, since there were not enough trained men to crew the other six guns. Marines and civilian workers ran for the recently dug slit trenches while the bombers wheeled around to head into the wind as they approached their bombing point. First Lieutenant Lewis, commanding Battery E, made an estimate of the enemy's height and opened fire when the 100-pound fragmentation bombs began to fall from the bombers. Battery D opened up, and the gunners manning the .50-caliber heavy machine guns raised their barrels as high as possible and opened fire.

The bombers couldn't miss from only 1,500 feet. In a matter of minutes, seven of the Wildcats were blown apart and set afire while bomb splinters savaged the eighth. The two 12,500-gallon aviation fuel tanks were set afire, with black smoke rising over the island. The planes came around again, lower this time; their gunners strafed the island repeatedly. When they left ten minutes after first being spotted, flames from the gas tanks were flooding the parking area, setting other gasoline drums on fire. The oxygen tanks exploded when the flames reached them, and what tools and spares they had were smashed to pieces. The malfunctioning radio was wrecked almost beyond repair. Camp One, where the Marines had their tents, was wiped out, along with much of the fresh food supplies.

In a matter of minutes, Wake's aerial defenders had lost two-thirds of their strength and most of the fuel the surviving planes would need to fly and fight. In the sky above, the four Wildcats were north of the atoll, unaware of the battle beneath the clouds until Lieutenant Kinney and his wingman Sergeant Hamilton swung southeast and Kinney spotted the black smoke from the burning fuel supply rising through the clouds. He increased speed and flew toward Wake. Suddenly, the enemy bombers emerged into clear air from beneath the clouds and Kinney spotted the two formations. Kinney, with Hamilton on his wing, pushed his throttle full forward and dived after the enemy planes, but lost them in the clouds. Short on fuel now, the two Wildcats turned back to Wake.

Captain Elrod and Lieutenant Davidson knew even less about the fight than Kinney and Hamilton did as they dropped beneath the cloud deck, where they spotted the fires and black smoke rising from the island. On landing, Elrod struck his propeller on runway debris. His Wildcat was now plane number nine either destroyed or damaged beyond repair, since there was no propeller on the other eight that could be used as a replacement. Wake was now down to three aircraft for defense, and it was obvious the enemy would return.

Staff from the civilian hospital joined the surviving Navy corpsmen and began treating the wounded. VMF-211 had 23 either dead or dying, including VMF-211 pilots second lieutenants Graves and Holden, who were killed, and Lieutenant Conderman, who was so badly injured he died later that night. Eleven other squadron personnel were badly wounded, including Lieutenant Webb. Major Putnam, Captain Tharin, and Staff Sergeant Arthur were also wounded, but could still fly. Ten Pan Am employees were dead and the Clipper that had landed just before the arrival of the Japanese was holed but still flyable. Twenty-five civilian workers were dead and several others wounded. All of the wounded military personnel and civilians were taken to the civilian hospital in Camp Two for further treatment by Navy doctor Lieutenant Gustave Kahn with his available corpsmen and civilian doctor Lawton Shank and his hospital employees.

Two hours later, the Clipper departed after several attempts to start its engines with its five passengers, along with the 26 surviving white Pan Am employees, but leaving behind the Chamorro hotel staff as it headed to Midway and then Honolulu. Commander Cunningham noted in his log that he felt "it was an unfortunate moment to draw the color line."

The first day of the Pacific War found Task Force 12, centered around the carrier USS *Lexington* (CV-2) and her accompanying three heavy cruisers and five destroyers, under the command of Rear Admiral John H. Newton, 500 miles southeast of Midway Island and about 1,200 miles east of Wake. The ships had departed Pearl Harbor two days before, tasked with delivery of 18 Marine Vought SB2U-3 Vindicator dive bombers of VMSB-241 to provide the garrison at Midway with an air component. Two hours after receiving news of the attack, the ferry mission was canceled; Task Force 12 was ordered to rendezvous with a force commanded by Vice Admiral Wilson Brown 100 miles west of Niihau Island and conduct an aerial search for the Japanese fleet with the combined force now designated Task Force 11.

Lexington's flight deck was crowded with Air Group Two's 65 planes and the 18 Marine dive bombers. In order to increase flight operations, Captain Frederick C. Sherman used the ship's unique ability to reverse the phase of the electric propulsion motors to steam at full speed astern, which allowed the launch of a new Combat Air Patrol (CAP); resuming forward motion, the carrier could then recover the current CAP. Sherman's unorthodox operation meant that *Lexington* could maintain a continuous CAP, launching and recovering aircraft without the lengthy delay caused by moving aircraft fore and aft to allow flight operations.

Lexington's task force spent the next five days sailing between Johnston Island and Hawaii, as they reacted to several false alerts. Bad weather on December 11 and 12 prevented the carrier refueling her escorting destroyers and Task Force 12 was forced to return to Pearl Harbor on December 13.

While *Lexington* and her escorts unsuccessfully sought to find the enemy in mid-Pacific, the defenders of Wake faced a continuing assault. VMF-211 had lost all the aviation mechanics and the engineering officer, First Lieutenant Graves Kinney and Sergeant Hamilton were put in charge of keeping the three remaining Wildcats flying, with Putnam offering Kinney "a medal as big as a pie" if he could accomplish the task. They set about salvaging everything they could strip from the wreckage. In addition to the dawn and dusk patrols, a mid-day patrol was set to meet the Japanese bombers if they took off from their Marshalls base at dawn. Defensive works were created at a fever pitch. The three Wildcats were now protected by sandbagged revetments, and more trenches were dug around the island. Construction equipment was driven onto the airstrip when it was not in use to prevent a possible Japanese air landing.

Kinney and Hamilton, joined by Aviation Machinist's Mate 1/c James F. Hesson, managed to replace the most heavily damaged blade on Elrod's Wildcat, and by dawn on December 9 they reported that four Wildcats were now available. The three men would eventually work wonders of improvisation in keeping airplanes in shape to fight throughout the battle for Wake, which epitomized the flair for improvisation that was a major feature of the battles during the opening months of the war. Major Putnam wrote of the trio:

These three, with the assistance of volunteers among the civilian workmen, did a truly remarkable and almost magical job. With almost no tools and a complete lack of normal equipment, they performed all types of repair and replacement work. They changed engines and

propellers from one airplane to another, and even completely built
new engines and propellers salvaged from wrecks. They replaced
minor parts and assemblies, and repaired damage to fuselages and
wings and landing gear; all this in spite of the fact they were working
with new types with which they had no previous experience and
were without instruction manuals of any kind. In the opinion of the
squadron commander, their performance was the outstanding event
of the whole campaign.

General quarters was sounded at 0500 hours on December 9. Forty-
five minutes later the four Wildcats took off for the dawn patrol, flying
80 miles to the south and returning at 0730 hours to report they had
seen nothing of the enemy. The rest of the morning was devoted to
work on improving the defenses.

Major Putnam led two of the Wildcats off at 1100 hours, followed
by Second Lieutenant David Kliewer and Sergeant Hamilton. The four
defending fighters were at 14,000 feet when 26 G3Ms of the Chitose
Kōkūtai, again led by Lieutenant Commander Matsuda, were spotted
to the south, approaching at 13,000 feet in the clear air. Kliewer and
Hamilton managed to dive on the formation's tail-end stragglers and set
one aflame. As the bombers closed on Wake, the six guns of Batteries
D and E opened fire and the Wildcats pulled away. While the bombers
wheeled over the island, 12 of the 25 were holed by defending fire, but
all managed to successfully return to their base.

The damage inflicted was heavy. Camp Two, where the contractors
lived on Wake, was hit; the civilian hospital and the Pan American hotel
were set afire and burned out. Navy doctor Kahn, civilian doctor Shank,
and the civilian hospital staff managed to pull many of those wounded
the previous day out of the burning hospital, but four Marines and
55 civilians were killed. The rangefinder for Battery A's 5-inch coastal
defense artillery was damaged, as well as one of Battery E's four 3-inch
AA guns, while the Navy radio station was damaged.

To Major Devereaux, it was obvious the Japanese were working to
a planned schedule of destruction, taking out the air defenses in the
first raid and the support facilities in the second. He ordered the three
surviving guns of Battery E be moved several hundred yards from their
current position, since they had obviously been spotted by the attackers.
Commander Cunningham ordered that the ammunition in the two

underground storage bunkers be moved so that the bunkers could be converted for use as hospitals.

While the defenders at Wake endured the second day of attacks, USS *Saratoga* (CV-3) departed NAS North Island and cleared Point Loma. Flying the flag of Rear Admiral Aubrey Fitch as flagship of Carrier Division 1 and Task Force 15, the accompanying fleet included the heavy cruisers *Astoria* (CA-34), *Minneapolis* (CA-36), and *San Francisco* (CA-38), nine destroyers, the seaplane tender-transport USS *Tangier* (AV-8), and the fleet oiler USS *Neches* (AO-5). Once clear of land, *Saratoga* turned into the wind and brought Air Group 3 aboard. First to catch a wire on the freshly renovated carrier was Lieutenant Commander John S. "Jimmy" Thach, commanding Fighting 3's 18 F4F-3s and the Navy's leading exponent of aerial gunnery; he was soon followed by senior division leader Lieutenant Edward H. "Butch" O'Hare, who had graduated from Pensacola in May 1940 and started in the squadron as Thach's wingman. As executive officer at that time, Thach was responsible for the squadron's gunnery training; he later declared O'Hare was the best gunnery student he had ever encountered in his ten years as a naval aviator. During the fleet gunnery competition that November, eight of 16 Fighting 3 pilots had qualified for the coveted "Gunnery E," and Ensign O'Hare won the fleet trophy for best gunnery.

Once the 36 SBD-3 Dauntless dive bombers of Scouting and Bombing 3, and the 18 TBD Devastator torpedo bombers of Torpedo 3 had been brought aboard, the LSO landed Marine Major Verne McCaul and his 18 Brewster F2A-3 fighters of VMF-221. Senior division leader Captain Marion Carl was fourth to catch a wire. The Marines were the reason for haste: *Saratoga* was headed for Wake Island, where VMF-221 would reinforce the embattled VMF-211. The fleet took a heading of 270 degrees and headed for Hawaii at flank speed; they would arrive at Pearl Harbor on December 12.

On December 10, the Japanese bombers arrived earlier than expected at 1045 hours and focused their attack on outlying Wilkes Island and Battery E on Wake. Fortunately, the morning patrol was airborne when the 26 G3Ms arrived over Peacock Point. Captain Elrod was leading the defending Wildcats. He dove through the enemy formation from rear to front, taking aircraft under fire as he put his sights on them. By the time he completed his pass, two of the bombers were headed for the ocean below, their wings wrapped in fire.

Following the previous day's raid, the AA guns of the unmanned Battery F on Peale had been relocated in case the Japanese had photographed their positions. Wooden replicas had been erected in their place, which the Japanese attacked. A lucky strike on the civilian cache of 125 tons of dynamite set off a chain reaction that destroyed the 3-inch and 5-inch ready ammunition for the guns on Wilkes, crippling the defense on that side of the atoll.

Seizure of Wake Atoll was the responsibility of Admiral Shigeyoshi Inoue's Fourth Fleet based at Kwajalein. By December 10, the Japanese estimated there were no more than five defending fighters and a maximum of 600 defenders and perhaps that many civilian workers left on the island. It was time to act.

Rear Admiral Kajioka commanded the Japanese invasion force from his flagship, the light cruiser *Yūbari*. The fleet was composed of the light cruisers *Yūbari*, *Tenryū*, and *Tatsuta*; destroyers *Yayoi*, *Mutsuki*, *Kisaragi*, *Hayate*, *Oite*, and *Asanagi*; two older *Momi*-class destroyers converted to patrol boats – Patrol Boat 32 and Patrol Boat 33 – each carrying 225 Special Naval Landing Force troops, and two medium transports carrying heavy equipment. The fleet arrived off Wake before dawn on December 11.

The invaders closed to within 5,000 yards of the atoll. At 0500 hours, the three light cruisers opened fire, hitting the diesel fuel tanks on Wake. With shells exploding around them, the four Wildcats sped down the runway and lifted into the air. Kinney, Hamilton, and Hesson had somehow devised bomb racks and each fighter carried two 100-pound high-explosive bombs.

Yūbari had fired only one broadside when Battery A on Wake replied with four salvoes. The cruiser turned away and opened the range. Battery A's third and fourth salvoes finally found their target and two 5-inch shells hit the cruiser at a range of 6,000 yards as she attempted to move out of range. *Yūbari* belched smoke and steam and slowed as she disappeared over the horizon.

Tenryū, *Tatsuta*, three destroyers, and the two destroyer-transports closed on Wilkes as *Yūbari* fought Battery A. Battery L's three guns took on the ships. At 0650 hours, the battery's third salvo caught the leading destroyer *Hayate* amidships. Moments after being struck, she exploded and broke in two – the first Imperial Navy ship sunk by US forces in the Pacific War. When they saw the destroyer blow up, the Battery L gunners spontaneously cheered. Hard-bitten Gunnery Sergeant Henry Bedell restored them to reality in a voice that carried over the sounds of battle: "Knock it off you bastards and get back on the guns! What d'you think this is? A ball game?"

Destroyer *Oite*, following *Hayate*, turned away and made smoke to hide herself from the sharpshooting artillerymen ashore, but took a hit before the smoke hid her. Battery L then fired on and hit one of the destroyer-transports, which turned away and made smoke. Nine thousand yards from Wilkes, the cruiser *Tatsuta* took a hit from Battery L that forced her to withdraw.

On Peale, Battery B engaged three destroyers. Fire from the ships knocked out the communication system and disabled one of the two guns, but the Marines continued to engage with the remaining gun and scored hits on *Yayoi*, which turned away, followed by her sisters.

After 45 minutes, the Japanese were in retreat. At that moment, Major Putnam and captains Elrod, Freuler, and Tharin dove into action, strafing the ships relentlessly and bombing them. One of Freuler's bombs hit the transport *Kongo Maru* on her stern, while destroyer-transport Patrol Boat 33 was also hit. With their ammunition expended and the enemy in retreat, the Wildcats landed. Two were quickly refueled and rearmed. Engineering miracle worker Kinney took off in one and caught the destroyer *Kisaragi* 20 miles offshore. His bombing run was perfect and the destroyer blew up in an explosion that could be seen and heard ashore at 0815 hours. The Marine casualties were Freuler's Wildcat, which took hits in the engine with damage to the oil cooler and one cylinder, and Elrod's Wildcat, which took a hit from shipboard AA that severed his fuel line. His plane was wrecked when he crashed short of the runway. The defenders were now reduced to two Wildcats.

The Japanese had lost two destroyers sunk, and suffered severe damage to seven other ships including the cruisers *Yūbari* and *Tatsuta*, with 407 Japanese sailors and troops killed or wounded. Admiral Kajioka credited the fighter attack with turning back the invasion attempt.

Word of the successful defense of Wake electrified the American media, which had for the previous four days been consumed by dark news. The *Washington Post* compared the stand made by the Marine defenders to the Alamo. Topping the news and sending a wave of pride through the country was the news that the defenders had radioed, "Send more Japs!" In fact, the words were padding to the real message that Cunningham sent, listing critical equipment – gunsights, spare parts, and fire-control radar – and reporting that half his equipment had been destroyed and morale among the civilians was low.

Saratoga's task force arrived in Pearl Harbor the evening of December 13. Over the next two days, the seaplane tender *Tangier* took aboard the officers and men of the 4th Marine Defense Battalion along with 9,000 5-inch rounds, 12,000 3-inch rounds, and 3,000,000 .50-caliber rounds, as well as ammunition for mortars and other small arms. Two radar sets and their operators also came aboard.

Lexington's task force had arrived back in Pearl from their unsuccessful search for the Mobile Fleet a few hours before *Saratoga's* arrival. After an overnight stay, *Lexington* and her escorts, under command of Admiral Wilson Brown, as Task Force 11 departed Pearl on December 14. Their mission was to mount a diversionary raid on the Japanese base at Jaluit in the Marshalls to provide cover to the Wake Island relief mission.

Vice Admiral Frank Jack Fletcher came aboard *Saratoga* and relieved Admiral Fitch as Commander Task Force 14. *Saratoga's* task force departed Pearl Harbor headed for Wake on December 15. Within a day, the fleet was battling heavy seas in a midwinter Pacific storm, their speed reduced in order that the old oiler *Neches* could keep up and provide fuel for the escorting destroyers.

At Wake, the Japanese had sent bombers four hours after the invasion force had been forced to withdraw. Lieutenants Davidson and Kinney were airborne in the two surviving Wildcats when the 30 enemy bombers were sighted. Davidson shot down two while Kinney downed a third; the AA batteries on Wake shot down a fourth in flames and sent three heading south trailing smoke. The surviving bombers continued on nevertheless and sent more bombs crashing into the defenses.

The next day, two Kawanishi H6K Type 97 four-engine flying boats that had taken off from Majuro lagoon at midnight arrived over Wake at dawn after an 840-mile flight. Captain Tharin, flying a solo morning patrol, downed one of the flying boats, while the other dropped bombs on the runway without effect. During the course of the morning, Kinney and his men managed to patch together another Wildcat from parts taken from the other wrecks. There were now three defenders.

Everyone on the island was amazed on December 13 when the enemy failed to put in an appearance. However, one of the three Wildcats suffered a flat tire on takeoff and went off the runway, reducing the defense again to two. The next morning, the flying boats returned, though they turned away when the two defending Wildcats intercepted them. At 1100 hours, 30 G3Ms from Roi appeared in the distance. Their bombs killed two VMF-211 Marines and wounded a third, while also getting a direct hit on one of the Wildcats. Kinney, Hamilton, and Hesson rebuilt the engine from that Wildcat over the next two days to return the force to two fighters. The next day, December 17, they finished work on two more. On December 19, 27 bombers from Roi arrived at 1050 hours. When they departed 20 minutes later, they left only four of the 3-inch AA guns operational. Two Wildcats had gotten airborne in time to remain safe and the bombers had missed the two newly returned from the graveyard. On December 20, a PBY Catalina from Pearl landed in the lagoon at 1530 hours, bringing word of the relief convoy that expected to arrive in 72 hours. It took off at 0700 hours the next morning headed back to Hawaii with reports from the senior commanders on the island and letters written by the men to their families and loved ones. Ninety minutes after the PBY departed, 29 Japanese D3A dive bombers, escorted by 18 A6M2 Zero fighters, bombed and strafed all three islands, destroying the two newly repaired Wildcats. Three hours after these attackers departed, 33 G3Ms from Roi bombed the island, destroying all but one 3-inch AA gun of Battery D. Major Devereaux had Battery D's fire control equipment moved to Battery B.

The radioed report of the attack by carrier-based bombers confirmed the information Navy communications intelligence had received that the carriers *Sōryū* and *Hiryū* had been detached from the Mobile Fleet as it returned to Japan, to support a second landing attempt at Wake. Vice Admiral William S. Pye, acting commander of the Pacific Fleet, canceled the planned attack on Jaluit and ordered Task Force 11 to turn northwest and cover Task Force 14 as it neared Wake. There was concern that a carrier battle could break out at any time. The next day, both US task forces experienced difficulty refueling their destroyers in the heavy seas, slowing their progress even more; *Saratoga* was forced to refuel her escorts that had been unable to hook up with *Neches*. Task Force 14 still planned to arrive at Wake on December 23.

The morning of December 22 found Captain Freuler and Lieutenant Davidson on patrol. They spotted a large formation coming from the north, which turned out to be 33 B5N Type 97 level bombers, escorted by six Zeros, from *Sōryū* and *Hiryū*. Freuler dived through the formation and managed to shoot down one B5N, then turned and hit a second bomber in a fight so close that flying fragments from the exploding enemy damaged his controls. He saw Davidson engage the escorting fighters. As he headed down toward Wake, another Zero closed on his tail. He saw Davidson for the last time, chasing a Zero with a second on his tail. A second Zero closed on Freuler and opened fire. Shot through the shoulder, he managed to crash land on the runway. Davidson was never seen again. Petty Officer 3rd Class Isao Tahara was credited with shooting down both Wildcats. The bomb aimer of the second B5N Freuler shot down was Petty Officer 1st Class Noburo Kanai, who had been credited with dropping the bomb that penetrated the magazine of USS *Arizona* (BB-39) at Pearl Harbor, causing the massive explosion that sank the battleship.

Wake was now without air defense. The surviving 20 members of VMF-211 were issued rifles and ammunition. They were now "mud Marines."

At Pearl Harbor, the report from Wake of the raid by carrier-based aircraft confirmed for Admiral Pye that Japanese carriers were now in the vicinity. A carrier battle was imminent. He could not risk two-thirds of his carrier force and a majority of the Pacific Fleet's remaining surface capital ships in such a fight.

At 0800 hours on December 22, when *Saratoga* was 427 miles from Wake, Admiral Pye ordered admirals Fletcher and Wilson to turn their task forces around and return to Pearl Harbor. Admiral Fletcher's staff officers called for him to ignore the orders and he went below so that he would not officially hear such "mutinous talk." Pilots in their ready rooms aboard *Saratoga* broke down in tears on hearing the order and the Marine fliers begged to be launched to fly in to Wake. Aboard *Tangier*, senior Marine officers intervened to prevent the Marines aboard from taking over the ship and sailing it to Wake in spite of orders. Admiral Halsey, who was aboard *Enterprise*, providing cover from the northeast with Task Force 8, later wrote he could not understand why the plan to send *Tangier* into Wake with the reinforcements was not carried out. No one knew that at the time the order was received, four Japanese heavy cruisers, including *Tone* and *Chikuma*, were patrolling east of Wake without air cover, or that the Japanese fleet that had arrived at dusk was disposed around the atoll with no security measures against surface attack. The outcome could have been different.

On Wake, the night of December 22–23 was stormy, with rain squalls and high seas. The Marines were alerted to the presence of the enemy at 0200 hours on December 23 when the cruisers *Tenryū* and *Tatsuta*, which had missed the atoll in the stormy darkness, opened fire without effect. At 0245 hours, Patrol Boats 32 and 33 were run through the reef and put aground on Wake Island, carrying 1,000 men of the Maizuru 2nd Special Naval Landing Force, which had been sent from their base at Saipan to finish the operation at Wake. Marines manning machine guns opened up when flares fired from Peale illuminated the approaching ships. Lieutenant Robert Hanna turned the last 3-inch gun of Battery D on the two ships, hitting Patrol Boat 33 14 times and breaking its back while killing seven and wounding 25 Japanese. He then took Patrol Boat 32 under fire with his target illuminated by the explosion of Patrol Boat 33, but the SNLF troops were already ashore. The gun was defended by the survivors of VMF-211, led by Major Putnam and Captain Elrod. Lieutenant Uchida led his detachment to surround the American position just as dawn broke, when shots rang out. There was 20 minutes of hard fighting to take the position, during which 62 Japanese were killed as well as 14 of the 20 defending fliers. "Hammerin' Henry" Elrod was killed by a SNLF trooper hiding beneath a pile of casualties as he rose to throw a grenade at the advancing enemy.

Dive bombers from the carriers and gunfire from the cruisers offshore provided support to the invaders, who took 125 casualties before Commander Cunningham, seeing the American situation was hopeless, ordered Devereaux to surrender at 0700 hours. Fighting continued throughout the morning on Wilkes and Peale, where the gunners of Battery L made a final stand. It took until 1330 hours for Major Devereaux to reach Wilkes and find 25 Marines still alive. They had killed all four Japanese officers and their 90 troops who had landed on Wilkes that morning.

The Marines lost 49 killed, two missing, and 49 wounded during the 16-day siege of Wake Island. Three Navy personnel and at least 70 US civilians were killed, including the ten Chamorro employees left behind by Pan American, with 12 civilians wounded. Four hundred and thirty-three Americans became prisoners of war with the surrender. Japanese losses were 140 SNLF troops and four sailors aboard ships. Three Japanese destroyers were sunk by artillery and aerial bombing along with both invasion vessels. Twenty-eight Japanese aircraft were either shot down or damaged.

The next day, Christmas Eve of 1941, *Saratoga* was 180 miles south of Midway Island. Marion Carl and the other pilots of VMF-221 were launched to fly to the atoll and provide air defense for the next American Pacific possession in the line of fire after Wake.

In January 1942, the surviving American military personnel as well as most of the civilians were loaded aboard the *Nitta Maru* and transported to prison camps in China. On the night of October 7, 1943, following the raid by aircraft from the new carriers *Lexington* and *Yorktown*, the 98 American civilians still on Wake were lined up on the beach and killed by machine gun fire.

Captain Henry T. Elrod was posthumously promoted to major on November 8, 1946, when his widow was presented his Medal of Honor by President Truman. He was the first Marine in World War II to be so honored.

Major Putnam's report to the commander of Marine Air Group 21, which was taken to Hawaii in the PBY the morning of December 21, ended: "All hands have behaved splendidly and held up in a manner of which the Marine Corps may well tell."

OPENING RIOT

CHAPTER FIVE

OPENING BLOW IN THE PHILIPPINES

On November 28, 1941, General Brereton was informed that negotiations with Japan had broken down. He placed all FEAF units on a war footing. Blackouts were ordered on all airfields and a 24-hour alert was established for half the squadrons. B-17 pilot Lieutenant Whitcomb recalled:

> We were ordered to wear our .45s, carry a bulky gas mask, and wear a steel helmet. Flight training now included reconnaissance missions towards Formosa. Every day, at least two planes flew pie-shaped search missions in the vicinity of the Japanese-held island. They were under War Department orders to "avoid any overt act."

At first, they flew two-thirds of the distance from northern Luzon and southern Formosa, with the northern boundary soon changed to the International Boundary of Formosa. First Lieutenant Frank Kurtz in "Old 99" was over a cloud deck when he looked down through an opening. "My God! We were over a big Japanese base. A big hunk of something that was forbidden. I didn't want to become the first international incident, so I got out of there quick."

Several days later, Major Gibbs flew across southern Formosa at 2,000 feet and reported "landing fields literally stacked with Japanese bombers." General MacArthur's intelligence chief, Colonel Charles A. Willoughby, discounted the report. First Lieutenant Earl R. Tash of the 19th Group, who also got close enough to see what was on Formosa, later recalled, "General MacArthur was of the opinion that these Japanese preparations were not for a strike against us but against Malaya." Colonel Eubank began painting the shiny B-17s with a coat of olive drab paint; without primer, the paint wore off quickly when the planes flew in rainstorms.

On December 2, a Japanese C5N1 reconnaissance airplane, later known as "Babs," overflew Clark Field and returned to Formosa with photos of 32 B-17s on the airfield. On December 4, General Brereton decided to move some of his bombers to Mindanao, where they would be out of range of the Japanese, despite Chief of Staff General Sutherland's dislike of the idea. Brereton wrote that "The overcrowding at Clark Field invited attack." On December 5, Major O'Donnell led his eight B-17s of the 14th Squadron to Del Monte Field, followed by eight bombers of the 93rd Squadron. Lieutenant Teats was unimpressed by the new airfield, recalling:

> In reality, it was just a big cow pasture backed up against some mountains. There were no shops, no hangars, no adequate servicing facilities, and the upper end of the runway slanted down like a ski run. Contrary to our expectations, the Del Monte Pineapple company had a country club nearby with golf, tennis and a swimming pool. But we still had to live in our tents. The one and only spray gun on Mindanao was operated day and night to give the planes a coat of olive drab paint.

The night of December 7, 1941, General Brereton was informed that "in the opinion of the War and Navy departments hostilities may break out at any time." He immediately ordered his airfields to go on "full combat alert" at first light on December 8.

The Asiatic Fleet headquarters in downtown Manila intercepted the message from Pearl Harbor announcing the Japanese attack at 0230 hours local time on Monday, December 8. When Brereton heard the news, he later recalled, "It came as a surprise to no one." At 0340 hours, General Sutherland heard the commercial radio broadcast announcing the attack; he awakened MacArthur and informed the general of the news. Shocked that the enemy would dare to behave differently than he had declared they would, the commander of the Philippines retired to his private quarters in the penthouse atop the

Army and Navy Club in downtown Manila, where he would remain incommunicado for the next crucial week.

As word spread, commanders immediately began making plans to counter the expected Japanese invasion. Many men didn't believe the news, thinking it only a rumor, until well-known Manila radio announcer Don Bell announced, "Japanese aircraft have attacked Pearl Harbor. There is no report of the damage at this time."

FEAF commander Brereton arrived at MacArthur's Manila headquarters at 0500 hours, demanding permission to launch a B-17 raid against Japanese bases on Formosa. General Sutherland refused him permission to see MacArthur on the grounds the general was busy. Brereton returned to his own headquarters at Nielsen Field and ordered his commanders to prepare the mission; he also ordered the bombers to take off and remain in a holding pattern over southern Luzon so they would not be caught on the ground by the Japanese air strike he expected momentarily. Having heard nothing from Sutherland by 0700 hours, he again returned to MacArthur's headquarters, where Sutherland told him to stand by for orders and said there could be no attack before a photo-reconnaissance mission was flown to Formosa. At 0940 hours, Sutherland called and authorized the reconnaissance mission. Thirty minutes later he again called Brereton and informed him MacArthur had authorized the bombing mission. In fact, this was Sutherland covering for his commander, who was in no state to issue any orders.

Finally, at around 1030 hours, while Saburo Sakai and his fellow pilots of the Tainan Air Group were finally free of fog on their Formosa airfields and able to take off, the B-17s, which had been sent off to avoid the dawn attack that had not materialized, were ordered to land at Clark and refuel. With Sutherland's permission to fly the mission, Brereton teletyped orders to the 19th Bomb Group at Clark, and at 1130 hours the ground crews began to fuel and arm the B-17s in preparation for takeoff at 1400 hours to bomb Formosa at night. The 20th Pursuit Squadron's P-40Bs that had covered the landing of the B-17s then landed to refuel, while the 17th Pursuit Squadron took off from Nichols and landed at Clark to provide defense while the 20th Squadron refueled. The pilots were served lunch before they went on alert in their cockpits shortly after 1100 hours.

At 1127 hours, the radar station at Iba Field detected a formation inbound from the north, 130 miles distant. Two minutes later, the radar spotted a second formation to the west of the first force, and the officer in charge alerted FEAF headquarters and called the command post at Clark Field where he informed the 17th Squadron's commander, Major Orrin L. Grover, of the incoming raids. FEAF ordered the 3rd Pursuit Squadron at Iba Field to take off at 1145 hours and intercept the western force, which appeared headed for Manila. The P-40s became separated after they became airborne due to dust problems on the field during takeoff and never found the enemy.

Two flights of the 21st Squadron at Nichols also took off at 1145 hours, led by First Lieutenant William E. "Ed" Dyess. After starting for Clark, they were diverted to Manila Bay to provide support to the 3rd Squadron. A third flight of the 21st took off five minutes after and headed toward Clark, where the 17th Squadron took off at 1215 hours with orders to patrol over the Bataan Peninsula and Manila Bay. The 20th Squadron completed refueling and was ready for takeoff, but had not received orders to do so. At 1230 hours, when a line chief spotted the incoming Japanese formation, section commander First Lieutenant Joseph H. Moore ordered a scramble.

Lieutenant Frank Kurtz recalled the briefing for the Formosa mission.

The operations tent was crowded with about 40 pilots and navigators waiting for the briefing to begin. As we waited, I snapped on my radio and we all listened to Manila. Don Bell announced Clark Field had been bombed and he could see big plumes of smoke rising from the burning bombers. We all smiled at this. We didn't know that he, from Manila, could see around the little hill over in the direction of Iba Field, and that those plumes of smoke were burning P-40s.

Out on the field, a private spotted an approaching formation. "Oh gee," he said, "look at the pretty Navy formation." First Lieutenant Lee Coats looked up. "Navy hell! Here they come!"

The 27 G3M2 bombers of the 23rd Kōkūtai arrived over Clark Field at 1240 hours. Even though they had been tracked by US radar, and with three defending fighter squadrons airborne, the Japanese had achieved complete tactical surprise. The B-17s were still on the ground, while the P-40Bs of the 20th Squadron were just starting to taxi toward the runway; only four would make it off the ground, as the G3Ms were followed minutes later by the 26 G4M1s of the 21st Kōkūtai. The 53 bombers dropped 636 60-kilogram (130-pound) bombs on Clark Field as they flew above the range of the defending antiaircraft guns. When the bombers turned away, 34 Zero fighters strafed the undamaged planes on the ground.

Sergeant Lloyd Kimmerle of the 19th Group remembered, "As the apex of the first V approached the field, the bombs began falling, and as the V widened out the area of the bombing widened out. As the last of the first group of bombers left the far end of the field, the first of the second group started." Hiding in a slit trench behind the operations tent, Lieutenant Kurtz remembered, "We could think of nothing except this earthquaking roar and grinding and the whistling of a mighty storm moving down the field. At its mildest, the hard dirt quivered like a steel-tired truck thundering over cobblestones, and at its worst bucked and pitched like a bronco."

At 1247 hours, 53 G4Ms dropped 486 60-kilogram (130-pound) bombs and 26 250-kilogram (550-pound) bombs on Iba Field, followed by strafing Zero fighters. All but four of the 3rd Pursuit Squadron's P-40Es were caught in their landing pattern short of fuel and were destroyed by the Japanese or crashed from lack of fuel, while strafing Zeros turned nearly all the P-40Bs of the 20th Squadron and the P-40Es of the 3rd that were on the field into smoking junk. The destruction inflicted at Iba was so complete the Zeros flew over to Clark Field, where they were able expend their remaining ammunition on what was left there.

Second Lieutenant Randall D. Keator was one of three 20th Squadron pilots who managed to get into the air ahead of the attacking enemy. Thirty miles west of Clark, he came across a Zero that made a head-on pass at him. He opened fire and the enemy fighter exploded, to become the first American victory of the Philippines campaign. The 17th and 21st squadrons had been circling over Manila Bay when they were called in to oppose the enemy over Clark. Several managed to engage the enemy fighters, where they quickly learned that tales of Japanese aerial inferiority were untrue. Nine victories were credited to five pilots, but over half the airborne P-40s were shot down, while nearly all the others sustained hits; the Japanese reported a loss of two.

In the course of the Japanese attacks, FEAF had lost half its effective combat force on the war's first day. Lieutenant Whitcomb remembered that "when I was finally able to stand up, I wiped the sand out of my eyes. There, across the field, we could see our beautiful silver Flying Fortresses burning and exploding right before our eyes." During the hour-long Japanese attack, 12 of the 17 B-17s on the ground at Clark were destroyed and four were damaged, while two that were flying patrols were unharmed. In the aftermath of the attack, Lieutenant Whitcomb recalled he could not walk 30 feet in any direction without finding a bomb crater. Nearly all the buildings had been hit and set afire, while a gasoline dump behind the hangars caught fire from a direct hit, shooting a dense cloud of black smoke skyward.

Two B-17s that had just been painted were in a hangar that caught fire. First Lieutenant Fred T. Crimmins, Jr. ran into the hangar to see if he could save one. There was a ten-minute lull in the attack, during which he was able to get two engines started. Just as he began to taxi out of the hangar, the Japanese fighters returned and strafed the field. He swung the Fortress' tail to face the enemy, just as bullets began to ricochet off the armor behind his seat and a 20mm cannon shell exploded in the instrument panel. He was hit in his hand as he tried to shut down the engines, then was hit in the shoulder. He squirmed out of his seat to get out of the plane and was creased by a bullet through his scalp. Flying shell fragments and pieces of the bomber ripped his head, neck, and arms. Finally able to drop out of the nose hatch, Crimmins ran across the tarmac to a gun pit, where he assumed command as they fired on the attackers. His action resulted in the award of the Distinguished Service Cross.

First Lieutenant Ray Cox and Second Lieutenant Austin Stitt followed Crimmins into the hangar and managed to get the other B-17 started. The bomber was strafed as it moved out of the hangar and caught fire. The two pilots barely managed to bale out through the nose hatch before the plane was engulfed in flames, along with the one Crimmins had rescued. Tech Sergeant Anthony Holub jumped into another of the B-17s and manned the twin .50-caliber mount in the radio compartment. After running out of ammunition, he ran across to another bomber, grabbed as many ammo cans as he could, ran back to the first bomber, and opened fire on the attackers again.

Lieutenant Tash had flown up from Del Monte, arriving just as the attack began. He began circling to see if he might be able to land. After the bombing, he attempted a landing but the strafing Zeros sent him climbing back to altitude for a return to Del Monte. South of the field, he was jumped by three Zeros. Gunner Staff Sergeant Michael Bibbin, manning the right waist gun, was hit in both shoulders. Raking the big bomber from tail to nose, the enemy fighters damaged the superchargers, severed the aileron cables, and put holes in the propellers. As they continued their attack, Private Arthur Norgaard fired at them from the radio compartment and hit the third Zero, which caught fire and crashed into the jungle below to make Norgaard the first American gunner to shoot down an enemy plane from an American airplane in the war. Despite the damage, Tash tried to get back to Del Monte, but the bomber was nearly uncontrollable. Finally he turned around to return to Clark. He arrived around 1700 hours, with his tanks nearly empty, and managed to land despite having no aileron control.

As the Zeros departed, men began to climb out of the slit trenches. Sergeant Kimmerle remembered:

> The field was covered with a pall of smoke and there was an unearthly mixture of sounds; the moans of the dying, the crackling flames, the boom and flash of exploding gas tanks, the cries of the wounded and the shouts of the work crews braving the shrapnel to aid the wounded and fight the fires. It all reminded me of a horrible nightmare.

Twenty-year-old Corporal Dennis Main, a gunner in the 19th Bomb Group, who had joined the Air Corps after graduating from high school in 1940, remembered the attack as the most terrifying event he experienced during the war. "I was bombed several other times during my year in the Pacific, but the first such event is the one that stays with you forever."

Frank Kurtz found "Old 99" at the end of the field. "Everything about 'Old 99' was still there, only melted and bent and ruined." He found his eight crewmen where they fell when they ran from the burning plane and were killed in the explosion. "There they were, lying so very still, my eight boys in a senseless, irregular line. Some of the bodies were entirely naked, having lost their clothing in the blast." Total casualties at Clark Field were 100 dead and some 250 wounded. The badly wounded Lieutenant Crimmins was taken to the Fort Stotsenberg Hospital, where he remembered, "Kids were dying all night, crying out and calling for the nurses. Men who had gone to sleep would wake up shouting." Some of the dead at Clark were not recovered and buried for more than a week.

Second Lieutenant John H. Posten of the 17th Squadron landed back at Clark that evening and later wrote in his diary, "That night everything was confusion. The hangars were still burning and every once in a while ammunition would go off. Automobiles, trucks and airplanes were wrecked and burning all over the place. We all went into the hills to sleep."

Shortly before dawn on December 9, a flight of four P-40s took off from Clark to provide cover for the inbound Flying Fortresses returning from Mindanao. The first Warhawk to take off hit a bomb crater and lost control, slamming into Colonel Eubank's B-17D, one of three bombers on the field still relatively undamaged. The B-17's tanks were ruptured and the two planes caught fire, with bullets cooking off from the heat and keeping fire fighters at a distance. The other three fighters crashed on takeoff due to poor visibility from the dust. The crashes reduced the number of operational P-40s to 54, from a total of 100 available 24 hours earlier.

The Del Monte B-17s and the two Clark survivors spent the day of December 9 in fruitless searches for the Japanese carriers everyone was convinced must be off the Luzon coast. Finally, at 1700 hours, the Del Monte B-17s began to land at Clark.

Bad weather throughout the day prevented further American losses, since the Japanese were unable to mount any attack successfully. Saburo Sakai remembered:

> We were forced to turn back from a mission to Luzon by the weather. Torrential rains broke up our formation on its return flight. The rain was incredible; it lashed at the planes in the worst downpour I have ever encountered. Swirling masses of clouds drove us to the ocean's surface. I had no choice but to fly at this low altitude, my two wingmen hugging my tail, desperate to not lose sight of my plane. For hours we fought our way northward, our fuel gauges dropping lower and lower. Finally, after what seemed like countless hours, the southern tip of Formosa came into view.

On Luzon, the 14th Squadron was diverted from Clark to a new airfield at San Marcellino that was only 4,000 feet long. Nevertheless, the B-17s were able to operate successfully from the field. Lieutenant Teats wrote, "We found out a lot about those big Fortresses that we hadn't known. We discovered we could take off from any field we could land in. We took off and landed no matter what the wind directions was. We threw the book away." By December 10, the 19th was ready for action, with seven B-17s at Clark, eight at San Marcellino and four at Del Monte. General Brereton decided to abandon Clark as a base and use it only as a forward staging field.

On December 10, the Japanese Fourteenth Army, commanded by Lieutenant General Masaharu Homma, commenced the invasion of the Philippines. The 48th Yuitsu Tsuchihashi Division, which was specially trained in amphibious operations, invaded northern Luzon, landing at Vigan, Aparri, and Gonzaga.

Despite his lack of familiarity with the P-40, Lieutenant Gillet was surprised and happy to find himself on the list of pilots who would fly that day. The P-40s were assigned to escort the 16 P-35As from the 34th Squadron that had survived the morning attack at Del Carmen and were assigned to strafe the newly landed Japanese forces in northern Luzon.

The P-40s were in line for takeoff when First Lieutenant Joe Kreuzel jumped on the wing of Gillet's airplane and told him to go see the squadron commander, First Lieutenant Boyd D. "Buzz" Wagner. "He told me he'd hold the plane for me, so I got out. I went to Wagner's airplane but he was just ready to take off. When I got back to my plane, Kreuzel was taxying away. He'd stolen it!"

Gillet's loss of his airplane was fortunate. The ex-cavalrymen of the New Mexico National Guard manning the antiaircraft guns defending the field promptly shot down three P-40s and damaged the one Kreuzel had stolen badly enough to force his return. "Those guys couldn't tell a P-35 from a P-40 from a Zero. If it flew, they shot at it! I think they shot down as many of our airplanes as the Japs did." Eight of the P-35As in the attack force suffered failures of their worn engines, forcing them to return to Del Carmen. By the time the defenders arrived over the invasion beaches, there were eight P-35As and only 12 P-40Es. Five B-17s of the 93rd Squadron, each armed with 20 100-pound bombs, participated in the attack on the invading troops. The Fortresses attacked from 12,000 feet as the 34th Squadron commander, First Lieutenant Sam Marrett, led his P-35As to attack the ships in the gulf. Marrett made several runs on the minesweeper W-10 until the ship blew up

MAP 1: ADVANCE JAPANESE LANDINGS IN THE FAR EAST, DECEMBER 8–20, 1941.

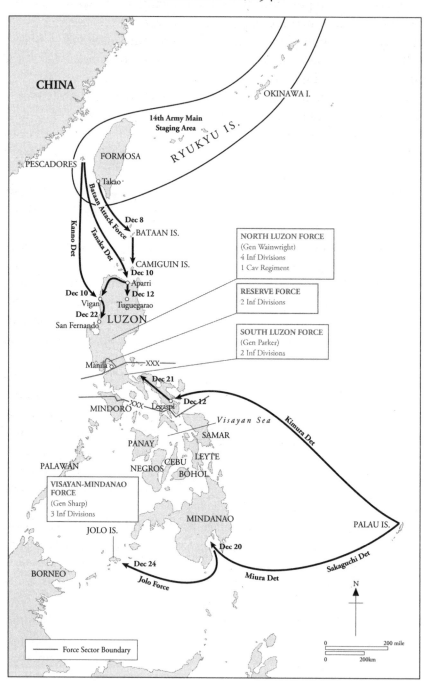

in an explosion so powerful that Marrett's wing was torn off as he flew over his target, to become the first USAAF fighter pilot aerial combat casualty in the Philippines. The 93rd's Lieutenant Vandevanter recalled that "there was heavy antiaircraft fire, but it was mostly behind us." The bombers hit two ships, claiming one sunk.

In the midst of this battle, Buzz Wagner claimed his first victories that would make him the first ace of the USAAF of the war a week later. Eleven of the P-40s sent on the mission were lost to enemy fighters and antiaircraft fire. By that evening, there were only 22 P-40Es and eight P-35As left flyable.

While the pilots of the 17th and 34th squadrons prepared to fly their futile mission against the Japanese invaders in Lingayen Gulf on December 10, Saburo Sakai and 26 other Zero pilots of the Tainan Air Group departed Taiwan at 1000 hours, headed for Luzon. As the Japanese headed south, Captain Colin P. Kelly, Jr., a 1937 West Point graduate who had arrived in the Philippines with the 14th Provisional Squadron, lifted his Boeing B-17C, 40-2045, off the main strip of Clark Field, having flown over earlier from San Marcellino to bomb up. He and his crew were also assigned to attack the invaders in Lingayen Gulf along with other single B-17s from the 14th Squadron.

Sakai and the others arrived over Clark Airfield at around 1300 hours. "We circled the burned-out American base for 30 minutes, but were unable to find an American plane on the ground or in the air." The Zeros turned north to provide air cover for the invasion. They maintained their patrol over the invasion force for 20–25 minutes, circling at 18,000 feet. "Suddenly I noticed three large water rings near the ships. They were unmistakable. There was a bomber somewhere above us attacking them."

The attacker was Colin Kelly. Bombardier Corporal Meyer Levin closed the bomb bay doors, having dropped the three 600-pound bombs they were carrying. He reported to Kelly that they had hit their target, which he identified as the Japanese battleship *Haruna*. The target was actually the light cruiser *Natori*, which was undamaged. Kelly turned to the south to return to Clark. Sakai searched for the intruding bomber.

After a few minutes searching for the enemy, squirming around in my cockpit, I saw a lone B-17 about 6,000 feet above us, speeding southward. We continued looking for the others we were sure were part of the attacking force. Unbelievable as it seemed, the B-17 had made a lone attack despite our presence. The pilot certainly did not lack for courage.

Sakai signaled the others to follow and began climbing after the enemy bomber. "The B-17 was surprisingly fast, and only with full throttle did we manage to get within range. Approximately 50 miles north of Clark field, we caught up." The thin air at 22,000 feet reduced the Zero's performance.

We swung out in a long file and made individual attacks on the bomber, one after the other. Amazingly, after all ten had fired on it, we were flabbergasted as it appeared not a single bullet or shell had touched the plane! This was our first experience with the B-17 and the airplane's huge size caused us to misjudge our firing distance. In addition, the bomber's extraordinary speed, for which we made no allowance, threw our sights off. All through the attack, the B-17 crew fired at us from their gun positions. Fortunately, their accuracy was no better than our own.

We were now over Clark Field and it seemed certain the bomber had called for help. We had to destroy it quickly before we became caught in a trap of our own making. I decided to approach close from the stern. Fortunately, this was an early model B-17 without a tail gun position, or I might not have survived. Two others joined me and we raced in for the kill. I opened fire and pieces of metal flew off the right wing, then a thin white film sprayed back. I exhausted my ammunition at the same time the white film became flames as the bomber burned from inside the fuselage. I turned aside and the others attacked.

Kelly's radio operator, Private Robert E. Altman, described the Japanese attack:

The first heavy burst from the fighters went right through the middle of our ship and burst the instrument panel. The top of Sergeant Delahanty's head was sliced off. They also set us on fire in the middle of the ship. We had all those gasoline lines and oxygen lines in there. We were on fire like an acetylene torch.

Sakai recalled the end of the fight. "The damage had been done and the B-17 nosed down, still with the wings level. I dropped below and saw three men parachute from the now-flaming plane. It disappeared into an overcast. Since no Japanese pilot saw the B-17 actually crash, no credit was given at the time."

What Sakai failed to see was that Captain Kelly held the burning bomber under control while the rest of his crew baled out. Bombardier Levin and navigator Joe M. Bean managed to get out of the nose hatch after a struggle, while Altman and waist gunner Staff Sergeant James Halkyard went out the open bomb bay. Moments after the last man was clear, the B-17 blew up, killing Kelly while blasting co-pilot Second Lieutenant Donald D. Robins clear of the plane; he was able to deploy his parachute successfully. A second explosion tore the Fortress apart and three burning sections struck the ground 6 miles north of Clark Field. Kelly's body was found a few yards from the nose section, while Sergeant Delahanty's body was in the tail section. The five parachuting crewmen were strafed in their parachutes by the other group of Zeros that had joined in Sakai's attack, with Halkyard later reporting that each counted over 100 holes in his parachute canopy after they landed; only Bean was wounded, being grazed in his ankle.

Kelly became the first hero of a nation desperate for heroes. Early reports mistakenly identified the heavy cruiser *Ashigara*, which was present, as the battleship *Haruna*, which was nowhere near the Philippines. Kelly was feted as "the man who sank a battleship," when in fact bombardier Levin hit nothing. This is unsurprising, given that throughout the war, very few bombs dropped on ships in motion from high altitude struck their target and no capital ship on either side was sunk by high-altitude level bombing attacks other than the battleship *Arizona* at Pearl Harbor. The light cruiser *Natori*, the ship that was actually attacked, was lightly damaged by shrapnel from one near-miss bomb. In the popular mind of the time, Kelly was awarded the Medal of Honor for diving his plane into the Japanese battleship after his crew baled out, when in fact the Air Force decorated him with a posthumous Silver Star for his willingness to stay with his airplane and allow his crew to escape. As of the 2006 edition, the *Encyclopedia Britannica* continues to state that Kelly bombed and sank either *Haruna*, *Natori* or *Ashigara*, and that the date of the bombing was December 9, 1941, and not December 10.

The Army Air Forces were not the only units to attack the Japanese invaders. The lumbering PBY Catalinas of Patrol Wing 10 were also involved. In fact, the invading force had originally been spotted just after dawn by a PBY-4 flown by VP-101's Lieutenant Clarence Keller, who had spotted some ships 250 miles off the west coast of Luzon, which the crew mistakenly initially identified as the British warships HMS *Prince of Wales* and *Repulse*, which were at the time in Singapore, readying for what would be their final combat engagement. Keller swung away, searching for Japanese ships, but when he flew back over the "British" ships, his identification was quickly revised when he came under antiaircraft fire from the ships below.

Keller's 0800 sighting report resulted in PatWing 10 commander Captain Frank Wagner ordering five bombed-up Catalinas at their advanced seabase at Laguna de Bay to attack the ships Keller had found. Around noon, the five PBYs found the fleet and dropped 20 500-pound bombs, just missing the stern of the heavy cruiser *Ashigara*. The Catalina crews reported seeing the cruiser slow and circle as the other ships moved away. All five flying boats returned to base safely. Wagner then ordered four VP-101 Catalinas at the Sangley Point seaplane base in Manila Bay to load with torpedoes and bombs for a second strike against the fleet.

Before this mission could be organized and get off, 27 G3M "Nells" of the 1st Kōkūtai, led by Lieutenant Commander Tateo Ozaki and escorted by 12 Zeros of the Tainan Kōkūtai, arrived over Cavite at 24,000 feet, well above the maximum altitude range of 18,000 feet for the antiaircraft guns manned by the Marine defenders, at around 1245 hours, while the other bomber units went after Clark and Nichols. Ozaki made a circuit over Cavite before taking up a heading into the wind for his bomb run. There were a number of ships tied up to the docks at Cavite, including the British destroyers HMS *Thanet* and *Scout*, which had arrived that morning after escaping from Hong Kong. The submarines *Seadragon* and *Sealion* were moored side by side at Machina Wharf, along with the submarine rescue vessel *Pigeon*, a converted minesweeper, and the minesweepers *Bittern* and *Quail*. Two old "four-piper" destroyers, *Pillsbury* and *Peary*, were moored to either side of Central Wharf, undergoing repairs after colliding back in October. The four armed PBYs had just been launched from the ramp at Sangley Point and were readying for takeoff. Several other smaller vessels were also in the harbor.

As the Japanese bombers entered their bomb run, the four PBYs gunned their engines and attempted to get airborne and escape the attack. Ensign McConnell staggered into the air where the PBY was riddled by strafing Zeros, but he managed to stay airborne and make it to Laguna de Bay, where he made a forced landing. Lieutenant Harmon T. Utter, pilot of the second heavily loaded Catalina to get airborne, found his plane surrounded by enemy fighters. Utter held the flying boat low and made wide sweeping turns to throw off the enemy's aim, while Chief Boatswain Earl D. Payne, Utter's bow gunner, fought it out with the enemy using his single .30-caliber machine gun. One attacking Zero overshot and flew in front of the Catalina at close range, and Payne filled it with bullets. The Zero smoked, caught fire, and crashed into Manila Bay to become the first US Navy air-to-air victory of the Pacific War. Utter managed to make a hard landing; fortunately, the other enemy fighters had scattered to strafe the Navy yard. The Catalina was patched up overnight to be ready for operations the next morning. Utter was awarded the Distinguished Flying Cross for the action, the citation concluding: "Despite the fact that the plane was heavily laden with a torpedo and bombs, his skillful landing of his injured plane in a heavy sea without further injury to it or its personnel, made it possible to have the plane in service again on the following day." Chief Payne was awarded the Silver Star for his victory.

Three Grumman J2F-2 "Ducks" and an OS2U-1 "Kingfisher" managed to get off the water and evade the Zeros.

The Nells passed overhead on their first run without dropping their bombs. Ozaki then came around on a second run, carefully lining up the navy base below. The first building hit was the power plant. Lieutenant J.A. Steward was inside and he shut down the key machinery, which avoided an explosion even though the base lost power. He was later awarded the Navy Cross for his cool-headed action. The rest of the base was mostly closely spaced wooden buildings, which caught fire as they were hit, with the fires quickly spreading. *Quail* and *Pigeon*, which were moored together, managed to pull away from the dock, still tied together, and move into the harbor as their crews fired their single 3-inch guns at the high-flying enemy to no effect. The two ships then cut the lines that held them together and moved back toward the Navy yard to aid in the rescue of those who survived the bombing of the other ships.

The destroyer *Peary* was near-missed, then struck in the bridge, which caught fire. *Pillsbury* caught fire from burning pieces of *Peary* that flew across the wharf and hit her. The minesweeper *Whippoorwill*, which had been on patrol in the bay, moved in to fight *Peary*'s fires and attempt to pull the burning destroyer away from the dock before her fires spread to the torpedo stowage building. Unfortunately, the torpedo storage did catch fire, and suddenly the torpedoes stowed within began exploding. With torpedoes exploding and falling bombs making a rain of further explosions, "*Whip's*" commander made a final effort to pull *Peary* free and succeeded. The senior officer aboard *Pillsbury*, Lieutenant R.W. Germany, ordered her to get underway despite her repaired engines having not been tested. *Pillsbury* moved into the bay. *Peary* would survive, though she suffered 23 dead and 19 wounded of a ship's company of 130.

Seadragon and *Sealion* were also hit by the bombs, with *Sealion* hit by two bombs, one on the conning tower and one aft that penetrated to the engine room where it exploded. As *Sealion*'s crew abandoned ship, open paint cans on *Seadragon*'s deck caught fire. *Seadragon* couldn't move because *Bittern* was tied up to her and had also caught fire. At that moment, the submarine rescue vessel *Pigeon* returned, and managed to pass a line to *Seadragon*, by which she was able to pull the submarine away from the dock and save her. Just as the submarine pulled free of the dock, a large fuel tank on the wharf exploded, sending burning fuel right where *Seadragon* had been moored. *Sealion* lay by the wharf, half sunk, the first US submarine lost in the Pacific War.

The bombers made four runs over Cavite, attacking in nine-plane groups. The G4M "Bettys" of the Takao Kōkūtai, which had been unable to attack Del Carmen Airfield, joined the Nells, adding even more bombs to the attack. The bombers departed by 1500 hours, with Cavite Navy Base aflame from end to end. For those ashore, the situation was dire. Power for fire-fighting pumps was dead. The city of Cavite outside the base was also on fire and could spare no resources to help. Firefighting efforts went on throughout the afternoon and evening, but were unable to get control. By 2100 hours it looked like the fires would get to the Ammunition Depot. At that point Admiral Rockwell, the base commander, ordered complete evacuation. Across the bay in Manila, Admiral Hart needed no one to tell him Cavite was gone, though amazingly the Ammunition Depot did not explode.

There was no effective air defense left in Luzon. Reluctantly, the admiral ordered his surviving ships of the Asiatic Fleet to abandon Manila. Shortly after giving the order, Hart learned of the fates of *Prince of Wales* and *Repulse* earlier that day. The Japanese attack on Cavite was the most thorough and devastating attack on a US naval installation since the British burned the Washington Navy yard in 1814. Carl Mydans of *Life* magazine and Mel Jacoby of *Time* had witnessed the attack. Mydans, who had reported from the Russo-Finnish War, remarked he had never seen such an accurate bombing attack. There was no effective air defense left in Luzon, and with the losses of *Repulse* and *Prince of Wales* and the destruction of Cavite, there was now no effective Allied naval force in Asia to oppose the Japanese Navy.

By dusk on December 10, the opportunity for any effective defense of the Philippines was gone. All but three of the B-17s on Luzon had been ordered to return to Del Monte. Flying through a weather front, two of the three planes were forced down at emergency strips while low on gas, and the third ditched in the Sulu Sea with the crew surviving. The 19th Bomb Group now had only 17 B-17s left. There was no organized aerial opposition to the Japanese hitting targets of their choice at their will. The American attacks that day had spread disarray among the invaders, but by the night of December 12, following a second landing that day, the Japanese were firmly in control of Lingayen Gulf. The only question now was how long it would take them to conquer all of Luzon and the rest of the Philippines.

CHAPTER SIX

A FIGHTING RETREAT

Following the successful Japanese landings in northern Luzon Island at Lingayen Gulf, no one knew where the next blow would land. The fate of American forces on Luzon was quickly sealed. Over the next two weeks, American forces in the Philippines reeled from unrelenting Japanese attacks.

The pilots of the American fighter squadrons on Luzon were quickly reduced to making hit and run raids of as many as two pairs of P-40s per mission, and most were flown by only two or even one aircraft. On December 12, Boyd "Buzz" Wagner flew a solo reconnaissance mission to Aparri, where it was believed the Japanese were now basing aircraft. Intercepted by two Zeros at low altitude, Wagner claimed them as victories on his return to Nichols, raising his score to four. On December 17, Wagner led lieutenants Allison W. Strauss and Russell M. Church, Jr. to attack a Japanese airstrip near Vigan in northern Luzon. Church was hit by defending fire on his run and stayed with his burning P-40 to complete his pass before the plane crashed and exploded, while Wagner and Strauss continued the attack. A Zero took off and attempted to attack Wagner; he chopped his throttle and the enemy fighter overshot him. Once in position Wagner shot it down, to be credited as the first USAAF ace of World War II.

While Wagner claimed all five of his victories were "Zeros," later research indicates these were actually Nakajima Ki-27 fighters of the Japanese Army Air Force's 5th Air Group commanded by Lieutenant General Hideyoshi Obata, which had been transferred from Manchuria to Formosa, then flown to Luzon following the Lingayen invasion. This would square Wagner's account of his victories with the fact that the Tainan Air Group and the Kaiohsung Wing, which operated the only Zeros in the region, never relocated from Taiwan to the Philippines. Being unfamiliar with Japanese types at the beginning of the war, most American pilots in 1942 claimed to be fighting Zeros even when the nearest IJNAF unit equipped with the now-mythological fighter were hundreds if not thousands of miles distant. While the Ki-27 was among the most maneuverable fighters, it did not have the performance of the Zero and JAAF pilots were not trained to the same level as their Imperial Navy counterparts.

On December 14, the 19th Group's First Lieutenant Hewitt T. Wheless was assigned to lead a flight of three B-17s from Del Monte to bomb a new invasion at Legaspi on southern Luzon. Wheless had difficulty starting his plane and the other two proceeded without him. He managed to get off and ended up alone over the invasion fleet some 15 minutes after the others had unsuccessfully attacked. "By this time, the other planes had pretty well stirred up the Japanese there," Wheless recalled. He had just begun his bomb run at 9,500 feet, when the Flying Fortress was swarmed by 18 defending Zeros.

Radio operator Private 1/c W.G. Killin was manning the guns in the belly bathtub position when the first burst of fire from the Zeros tore off the top of his head, killing him instantaneously. Assistant radio operator Corporal W.W. Williams, who manned the radio compartment guns, was hit by an explosive bullet that ripped his leg open from hip to knee. Right waist gunner Sergeant Russell Brown was hit in his right wrist, while left waist gunner Sergeant John Gootee had his right hand almost shot off. As the enemy continued their attacks, Brown fired the waist guns with one hand while Gootee ignored his pain after fashioning a tourniquet and swung the guns for Brown with his good hand. Together, they managed to shoot down three enemy fighters.

Wheless later described the fight:

Sometime during the fight, my number four gas tank was hit by an explosive bullet, knocking a hole in it about six inches in diameter and allowing the fuel to leak out. The intercom was shot out in the cockpit and the oxygen system was entirely shot out. Out of 11 control cables, only four remained, which made it very difficult to maneuver the ship and almost impossible to turn.

The enemy followed the B-17 for 75 miles over 30 minutes before giving up. Wheless fought to stay airborne as darkness fell. "With the controls shot out, I could only fly straight ahead." Realizing he couldn't make it over the mountains of Mindanao to get to Del Monte, Wheless landed on a small field near Cagayan, on the northern side of the island. He came in low and hit some palm trees. "The plane, on hitting the ground, rolled some 200 yards then the brakes locked, causing it to stand straight up on its nose. It settled back on the ground and all were able to get out unhurt." B-17D 40-3096 was a total loss.

Sergeant Benjamin Kimmerlee reported, "The inside was covered with blood, the propellers had bullet holes in them, the tail was almost completely shot away and one could hardly put his hand on the wing or fuselage without touching a bullet hole." A mechanic gave up counting the bullet holes when he reached 1,200! Wheless later stated, "Don't let anyone tell you the B-17 can't take it." He would be awarded the Distinguished Service Cross and mentioned by name in President Roosevelt's Fireside Chat on April 28, 1942. Over a 28-year Air Force career, Wheless would rise to lieutenant general and serve as deputy commander of the Strategic Air Command before retiring in 1968 as assistant vice chief of staff of the Air Force.

After attempting more unsuccessful missions against the invaders from Mindanao, the surviving B-17s at Del Monte Field were flown to Darwin, Australia, between December 17 and 20. Lieutenant Teats recalled, "The primary fact in the whole situation was just this: we had to go someplace where we could get decent maintenance on the planes and where the crews could get some rest." The bombers had to fly up to Clark three at a time to be fitted with bomb-bay gas tanks for the 1,700-mile flight, arriving at dusk and departing for Australia before dawn with as many men as could be carried crammed inside. Teats recalled, "We ignored the rated maximum load; there wasn't such a thing. The only criterion was how much we could carry and still get to Australia." Eventually, 145 men escaped aboard the 12 B-17Ds and two B-17Cs that made it to Batchelor Field south of Darwin. On December 18, a Japanese reconnaissance plane found Del Monte and the Japanese attacked on December 19. Six B-17s were still there, and two were destroyed. The next day, the Japanese landed on Mindanao. On December 22, nine Fortresses flew from Darwin and bombed the invaders at Davao. The Japanese later admitted that the dock area had been set afire, that a 10,000-ton troop ship had been sunk, and a heavy cruiser damaged badly enough it had to return to Japan for repair. Refueling at Del Monte in a driving rainstorm, five of the bombers managed to bomb the main Japanese landing at Lingayen Gulf at 0300 hours on December 23, but were only able to inflict light damage. They were forced to divert to the Dutch island of Ambon to get fuel to return to Australia on December 25.

The main Japanese landing in Lingayen Gulf occurred on December 22. Buzz Wagner led the 17th Squadron's last six P-40Es, along with the last six P-40Bs of the 20th Squadron, in a strafing attack. The two formations became separated in the pre-dawn darkness and Wagner, with his wingman, Second Lieutenant William J. "Bill" Hennon, proceeded alone. They dropped their fragmentation bombs among the landing barges on the beach, then circled around to make a strafing run. Before they could, they were jumped by a formation of Ki-27 fighters. Wagner's P-40 was hit several times and the windshield was shattered, spraying his face and eyes with glass while he was hit in the shoulder by another bullet. He managed to make it back to Clark, covered by Second Lieutenant George E. Kiser, but his days as a fighter pilot in the Philippines were over. The next day, he was evacuated to Australia for treatment.

The two Philippine Army divisions guarding northern Luzon were decimated in the days following the landings, with the weather proving a greater hindrance to the Japanese than the poorly trained, ill-equipped Filipino troops. MacArthur was forced to realize that his cherished plan of defending all of Luzon was impossible as the defenders fell back in the face of the enemy's advance from Lingayen Gulf. Field commanders were notified on December 24 that the old War Plan Orange was in effect, and Manila was declared an open city; the evacuation of the city was complete by December 31. MacArthur was taken by ship across Manila Bay to Corregidor, where he, his wife and son, and the rest of the staff took up residence in Malinta Tunnel.

On the morning of December 24, Lieutenant Gillet was sent to pick up a newly repaired P-40E at Clark Field and return it to Nichols Field, where the 17th Squadron was still operating. A sudden Japanese air raid saw the airplane destroyed before he could touch it. At the same time, Captain Moore, the commander of the 20th Pursuit Squadron, learned of a possible Japanese landing at Lamon Bay on the west coast of Luzon. If the report were true, American forces around Manila would be threatened with encirclement. Moore asked for volunteers to fly a reconnaissance mission. "The guys in the 20th weren't too anxious to go up against the Zero, and there weren't too many volunteers." Gillet was among the few who raised their hands.

With squadron executive officer First Lieutenant Anderson assigned as leader, Gillet and two other pilots he didn't know manned the four surviving P-35As that were wheeled from under the trees. "They were not in the best of shape, and only mine and one other started up right away. Lieutenant Anderson signaled us to go ahead and take off."

Once airborne, Gillet noticed that the other P-35A was flying wing to him.

He thought I was Lieutenant Anderson, but I knew he had to be senior to me because I was about the most junior second lieutenant in the Philippines. I slid back to fly wing on him, but he slid back again. Finally I just took the lead and headed out toward the coast. I knew if I took off from Clark Field and headed west to the ocean, then turned south and followed the shoreline, I would come across Lamon Bay at some point. But I wasn't sure how far south it was.

In Lamon Bay, the sky was overcast with the threat of rain as Japanese troops of the 16th Susuma Morioka Division climbed into the waiting invasion barges. North of the invasion fleet, the bad weather forced the two P-35As lower and lower as they headed down the coast. Gillet recalled, "I was at about 900 feet when we came over the hills and there was the Japanese fleet in the bay. I started counting the transports. I had gotten up to about 50 when two destroyers spotted us and opened fire."

As Gillet tried to count the fleet below, he didn't know that in the clouds above, Petty Officer 3/c Toshio Kikuchi of the Tainan Air Group was part of the Zero air cover for the invasion fleet. Equally befuddled by the weather, Kikuchi saw the ships open fire and dived to investigate.

I was trying to evade the anti-aircraft fire, when all of a sudden a Zero popped out of the overcast practically right beside me. I don't think he ever saw me, because he immediately turned away. I just turned immediately to my right and was directly on his tail. I opened fire, and realized the tracers from my wing guns were converging ahead of him. I couldn't throttle back to open the distance, but then he just dove and headed for the ocean as I realized my two .30-caliber nose guns were tearing up the rear fuselage in back of the cockpit. They tell you not to get target fixation, but I just stuck right behind him, firing all the way till he impacted the ocean, on fire all over. Looking back, I think I probably killed him with the first burst, but I was too green to know that.

Gillet became separated from the other P-35A when he turned to go after the Zero.

I pulled out and I was right over an invasion barge with a tank in it and the Japs were jumping over the sides into the water. Just past it, there were other ships and I fired at them. I turned, strafed another ship, then came back on that barge with the tank and shot at it and it rolled over and sank. Just at that moment, I ran out of ammo, because I'd wasted so much shooting at that Zero. I pulled up, saw four Zeros headed toward me, and climbed up into the overcast.

Once in the clouds, Gillet set course for Clark. "I wasn't instrument-rated, but I stayed in the clouds because I didn't want the Japs to see where I was going. They had Nichols Field and Clark Field pretty well covered, and they knew where we'd be going and chase us there and shoot us down when we tried to land." After a few minutes, Gillet felt safe to drop out of the clouds. "I looked out through the rain and saw another airplane in the distance with a radial engine. I couldn't tell if it was a Zero or maybe my wingman."

Gillet then spotted Clark Field and turned to enter the landing pattern.

Just as I dropped my gear, I felt the impact of bullets in the airplane. I thought to myself that the airplane I'd seen was a Zero and now he'd gotten me. I retracted the gear, dived across the field and down into one of the canyons beyond. I looked around and didn't see anyone, so I turned back to Clark and got a green flare and landed.

As Gillet taxied in to where the other airplanes were hidden, a sergeant ran out and told him the field was under attack.

I shut down, got out and watched the Japanese bombers come overhead. Our antiaircraft defense was pathetic. I later figured out it was our gunners who were the ones that shot me up when I tried to land the first try. There were 24 .50-caliber holes in my airplane from just behind the cockpit to the tail. I was lucky they were as bad with their shooting as they were with airplane identification.

After the Japanese departed, Gillet caught a ride across the field to the 20th Squadron's headquarters, where he found the unknown pilot who had flown with him. "We were talking, and he told me how Lieutenant Anderson had shot down a Zero over the invasion fleet. He described the whole thing and I told him, 'That wasn't Lieutenant Anderson, that was me. Anderson never took off.'" Second Lieutenant Lamar Gillet had just become the only P-35 pilot to ever shoot down an enemy airplane. The mistake was finally rectified by the Air Force in 1986 when retired Lieutenant Colonel Gillet was awarded the Bronze Star for his feat in shooting down a Zero on Christmas Eve, 1941. However, as recently as 2003, a book on the P-35 put out by Squadron Publishing assigned credit for the victory to Anderson.

Christmas Day saw the 19th Bomb Group fly its final Philippine mission when the three B-17s still at Del Monte made their escape to Australia, each bombing Davao as they departed. Lieutenants Shaetzel and Mueller were followed by defending fighters and climbed to 28,000 feet where they believed the Fortresses were safe from the enemy. The Japanese fighters were at their maximum altitude, but they continued their attacks. Mueller's airplane was seemingly ignored while the Zeros concentrated on Shaetzel. By the time the enemy departed, Shaetzel's airplane was badly damaged, though both managed to make it to Australia, where his B-17 was written off and Mueller's was only used afterwards as a transport. The 19th now had 11 Flying Fortresses left after 18 days of war, but only two of the 24 lost had been shot down.

Had the Japanese pressed harder, they might have destroyed the defending army south of Lingayen Gulf, but General Homma had orders to take Manila and Japanese planners had expected the defenders to fight the big battle on Luzon to defend the city; there were no plans to counter a retreat by the Americans into Bataan. From his headquarters on Corregidor, MacArthur ordered the army to retreat into the Bataan Peninsula. The Japanese had no plans to counter a retreat by the Americans into Bataan.

On December 30, General Homma finally realized the full extent of MacArthur's change in strategy and the 48th Division was ordered to press forward in order to cut off the American retreat into Bataan. Between January 2 and January 4, 1942, the Philippine Army's 11th and 21st divisions, the 26th Cavalry of the Philippine Scouts and the Provisional Tank Group were able to keep the road from San Fernando to Dinalupihan at the neck of the peninsula open so the retreating units of the South Luzon Force could enter the peninsula before making good their own retreat. The 194th Tank Battalion suffered the loss of half its M-2 tanks, but that unit and a supporting battery of M-3 antitank halftracks armed with the M1897A4 75mm cannon of the Provisional Field Artillery Brigade were able to repeatedly stop the Japanese thrusts as they became the last units to enter Bataan.

Unfortunately, following MacArthur's change of strategy before the war, the necessary supplies of food and ammunition that should have been waiting on the peninsula for the American last stand had not been positioned; there was not enough time to move sufficient supplies into the peninsula before the evacuation of Manila. Within a week of the retreat the defenders were forced to go on half-rations. Lacking fresh fruits and vegetables as well as medical supplies, scurvy, beriberi, and dysentery soon broke out, followed by malaria.

The day War Plan Orange was reactivated, the five remaining flyable P-35As were ordered to fly to Bataan and land at Lubao Airfield. Two were lost when nervous Army gunners mistook the P-35As for Zeros and shot the planes down as they circled to land. Gillet remembered, "I was headed to the field when suddenly I was fired on. There was oil all over my windshield and when I glanced at my instruments, the oil pressure was zero. I slid open the cockpit and rolled inverted to bale out, and then saw the field right below me, so I rolled upright and brought her in dead stick." The ground crews examined the airplane and informed Gillet it would take ten days to change the engine and make repairs. "I was ordered to become an infantryman."

Lieutenant Posten was one of seven pilots from the 17th and 21st squadrons who managed to land P-40s at Bataan Field. Captain Ed Dyess, commander of the 21st, was placed in overall command. After escaping Japanese imprisonment in 1943, he recalled their last stand on Bataan: "At the time, we had five planes from the 21st and two from the 17th, and two old civilian airplanes. We used these for bombing, strafing, recon work, dropping ammunition, and ferrying in medical supplies from the south." Dyess named his P-40 "Kibosh," and fitted it with a camera in the baggage compartment; he flew aerial reconnaissance missions, as well as one-man bombing raids.

Over the week following the American retreat, Japanese actions concentrated on reconnaissance and necessary preparations to attack the Main Battle Line from Abucay to Mount Natib to Mauban. Believing that the jungle-covered Mount Natib was impassable, the American defenders had not located any defensive positions on the steep slopes. In accordance with previous plans, the experienced 48th Division that had been responsible for the Japanese success was replaced by the less-capable 65th Brigade that had been intended as a garrison force. On January 5, 1942, the JAAF 5th Air Group was also pulled off operations to accompany the 48th Division to the Netherlands East Indies. The American forces commenced an unsuccessful counterattack on January 16, but the Japanese counterattack forced the Philippine Division to withdraw to the Reserve Battle Line on January 26.

On January 23, a battalion of the Japanese 16th Division attempted to make amphibious landings behind the lines. Lieutenant Gillet and the other airmen-turned-infantrymen, along with US Navy sailors, were able to turn back this attack successfully in desperate fighting in the dense jungle, with high casualties on both sides in what became known as the Battle of the Points. Additional Japanese landings to reinforce the survivors on January 26 and February 2 were disrupted by air attacks from the last few American fighters based on Bataan. The Japanese were trapped and annihilated on February 13 in the Battle of the Pockets. Lamar Gillet recalled, "They came in barges at night, and we managed to stop them on three occasions."

Following the final battle that stopped the Japanese, Gillet managed to get back to Lubao Airfield, where he learned that his airplane and the other remaining flyable P-35A had been ordered to fly out to Del Monte Airfield, on Mindanao in the southern Philippines. "The P-35A had a wet wing, so it had the longest range of any of our fighters. It also had a large baggage compartment right behind the cockpit. Each of those planes left for Mindanao with two other pilots crammed in there."

Gillet rejoined the Air Corps infantrymen he'd been with, who were commanded by a Lieutenant Sloan.

One day a few weeks later, I complained to a colonel about the World War I ammunition we were being given to use. There were a lot of duds and a lot of misfires. He got terribly angry with me, asked who my commanding officer was, and when I told him he told me to have Sloan go over to Corregidor to explain himself to the colonel in charge of ordnance.

When Gillet informed Sloan, he was told to go to Corregidor and explain things himself. "I ended up on Corregidor for three days, until I could see that colonel. When I told him why I was there he told me to return to my unit and he would take care of that colonel." On his return, Gillet discovered Sloan and two other officers he was friends with had been killed by artillery fire called in from Corregidor during another attempted landing.

General Homma was forced to request reinforcement to overcome the American resistance. Japanese forces were stretched thin with the simultaneous assaults on Malaya and Singapore, and it was not until the British bastion had fallen that additional troops could be sent to the Philippines. Reduced to a single brigade on the front line, the Japanese dug in and commenced siege operations. The Army was not equipped for jungle warfare, and the troops suffered many of the same diseases as their American opponents.

Lamar Gillet recalled that during this time the cavalrymen of the 26th Cavalry were forced to kill and eat their horses, and that he and his fellow involuntary infantrymen hunted water buffalo to supplement their dwindling rations.

Most of the meat was tougher than shoe leather, but when you're down to living on 1,200 calories a day, which is not supposed to be enough to support an active human being and you have to fight on that, you take what's offered. If you boiled it long enough, it became almost soft enough to eat. The guys who had scurvy were in bad shape because their teeth were falling out, which made it even more difficult to eat.

Men hoped and believed that reinforcement was coming. It was, but it was now too late to reinforce those on the front line in the Philippines.

CHAPTER SEVEN

THE FORGOTTEN CAMPAIGN

The Netherlands East Indies, which contained among many other important natural resources the largest source of sweet crude oil in Asia that was the basis of the fuel oil for the Imperial Navy and the aviation gasoline that was crucial to the IJNAF and JAAF, became the focus of the Japanese southern seas strategy as plans were developed to put the strategy into action. For Japan, the Indies would be the "crown jewel" in their new empire. By the fall of 1940, with the defeat and surrender of the Netherlands to Hitler's armies and the isolation of Britain in its stand against potential invasion, both the British colony of Malaya and the Dutch-controlled East Indies seemed ripe for conquest with little difficulty.

Like the Americans in the Philippines and the Dutch in the East Indies, life before the war in Singapore was good, at least for some. An RAF (Royal Air Force) pilot who flew from Seletar and lived in Singapore with his wife wrote:

> Few of us in Singapore knew anything of the reality of war. War will never reach us, we had always thought, and like ostriches with our heads in the sands of splendid isolation we enjoyed our lives. At night the clubs and restaurants were crowded with tuxedo-clad men and bare shouldered women drifting together round the dance floors. At Seletar Airdrome, life was especially good. It was reputed to be the most comfortable of RAF stations in the Far East; it had its own golf course, a yacht club, a swimming pool and private taxis available for all ranks at about £1 for all day hire. The Singapore civilians accepted us with studied tolerance and most of the town's amenities were open to us.

Like most of the rest of Britain's eastern empire, white Europeans lived the good colonial life. However, the British class system was still present; places such as the Raffles Hotel were out of bounds to other ranks, as they were in Rangoon or New Delhi.

While the colonials may have believed that "it can't happen here," both the British government and the Dutch government-in-exile in London were aware of the likelihood of a Japanese invasion. For the Dutch, there was little possibility of further reinforcement in the Indies, though the colonial government there had worked to modernize the colony's defenses. The Royal Netherlands East Indies Army Air Force (Militaire Luchtvaart van het Koninklijk Nederlands-Indisch Leger, ML-KNIL), the air arm of the Royal Netherlands East Indies Army and a separate organization from the Royal Netherlands Air Force, had been expanded beginning two years before the outbreak of the war in 1939 through the purchase of American aircraft: 144 Brewster Model B-339C and 339D export versions of the US Navy's Brewster F2A-2 fighter had been ordered, though only 71 had been delivered by the fall of 1941; these were lighter than the RAF's B-339Es, since the armament was reduced from .50-caliber machine guns to .30-caliber weapons, while the engine was the same 1,200 horsepower Wright Cyclone used in the F2A-2. Additionally, 24 Curtiss Hawk 75A-7s, the export version of the Air Corps' P-36 fighter, had been delivered in 1940; they had flown so many hours by the outbreak of the Pacific War that their engines were in need of overhaul. A further 24 Curtiss-Wright CW-21s, a lightweight interceptor developed specifically for export, arrived in Java in February 1941. The CW-21's lightweight construction gave rise to structural problems on operations, and nearly half had been grounded by cracks in their undercarriage that had not yet been repaired when the war broke out.

A force of bombers had been created, beginning in 1938 with the initial purchase of an eventual 121 Martin Model 139WH and Model 166 bombers, export versions of the Martin B-10, the Air Corps' first all-metal twin-engine monoplane bomber, which had entered service in 1932.

By the fall of 1941, the ML-KNIL was composed of five groups, with three or four squadrons assigned to each group.

The two fighter groups were based on Java, the central island of the archipelago. The IVe JachtVliegtuiggroep (4th Air Group – Fighter) was based at Maospati Airfield outside Madioen, where the 1e JachtVliegAfdeling (1st Fighter Squadron, 4th Fighter Group) operated 12 H-75A-7s alongside the 2e Afdeling's 16 CW-21s and the 12 B-339Ds of 3e Afdeling. The Ve JachtVliegtuiggroep (5th Air Group – Fighter) was based at Semplak Airfield outside Buitenzorg; the B-339Ds of the 1e Afdeling operated two flights at Samarinda II Airfield and three flights at Singkawang Airfield in Dutch Borneo, while the 2e Afdeling and 3e Afdeling operated their B-339Ds from Semplak Airfield, with 3e Afdeling basing a detachment of four B-339Ds at Ambon Airfield on a rotating basis following the outbreak of hostilities.

The three bomber groups were also based on Java. Ie Vliegtuiggroep (1st Air Group) operated nine Martin 139s each of the 1e Afdeling and 2e Afdeling from Andir Airfield, outside Bandoeng, Java, with detachments deployed to Tarakan and Samarinda airfields in Dutch Borneo. IIe Vliegtuiggroep (2nd Air Group) was based at Singosari Airfield, near Malang, Java, where the 1e Afdeling was equipped with 12 Model 139s. IIIe Vliegtuiggroep operated from Tjililitan Airfield outside the capital of Batavia, with 1e, 2e, and 3e Afdeling each assigned nine Model 139s. They were joined on December 15 by the newly mobilized reserve 7e Afdeling Horizontale Bommenwerpers (7th Horizontal Bombing Squadron) with nine more Model 139s of various sub-types.

Two independent army cooperation squadrons were also based on Java, with Verkenningsafdeling 1 (1st Cooperation Squadron) operating 12 two-seat CW-22s at Tjikembar airfield and Verkenningsafdeling 2 (2nd Cooperation Squadron) at Djokjakarta. These were under the control of ML-KNIL headquarters and assigned to provide battlefield aerial reconnaissance.

In addition to the ML-KNIL units, the Marine Luchtvaartdienst (MLD), the Royal Netherlands East Indies Naval Air Force, operated 24 Dornier Do-24K trimotor flying boats and six Catalina flying boats throughout the colony for maritime patrol. The Do-24s were assigned in *groepen vliegtuigen* (aircraft groups) of three each to Pontianak, West Borneo; Sorong, Netherlands Papua; Surabaya, Java; Sambas, West Borneo; Ternate, Moluccas; Morokrembangan, Java; Tarakan, Dutch Borneo; and Paeloe Samboe, Sumatra. The six Catalinas operated in units of three each from Tanjong Priok on Java, and Halong on Ambon.

Dutch naval units in the region were organized into three sea forces (*zeemacht Nederlands-Indië*). Submarine and mine warfare forces were controlled by the Netherlands Indies Navy (Nederlands Indie Marine), while cruisers and destroyers were under the control of the Netherlands Indies Squadron (Nederlands Indië Eskader), led by Admiral Karel Doorman. A customs and patrol force similar to the American Coast Guard, the Militarized Government Navy (Gemilitairiseede Gouvernementsmarine) provided coastal control.

The Netherlands Indies Squadron was divided into two task forces. Task Force One, based in Java and directly commanded by Admiral Doorman with his flag in the light cruiser *De Ruyter*, included the light cruiser *Tromp* and destroyers *Van Ghent*, *Kortenaer*, *Piet Hein*, *Witte de With*, and *Banckert*. Task Force Two, based in Sumatra, included the light cruiser *Java* and destroyers *Evertsen* and *Van Nes*. Fifteen submarines in four squadrons were based at Surabaya.

The British in Malaya and Singapore were also hard-stretched to provide a defense. British military strategy in the Far East had been undermined in the decades after the end of World War I by a lack of attention on the part of both the Royal Navy and Army, and a lack of funding by Parliament. Major General William Dobbie, the General Officer Commanding (GOC) Malaya, wrote in 1937 that during the monsoon season which lasted from October to March, an enemy could land on the east coast of Malaya and Siam at Songkhla and Pattani in Siam, and Kota Bharu in Malaya. His predictions would turn out to be correct, but his recommendation that additional forces be sent to the colony were ignored. The British plan of defense involved stationing a strong fleet at Singapore to defend both Malaya and the sea lanes through the Straits of Malacca that led to Australia.

Dobbie's recommendation was updated in 1940 by Lieutenant General Lionel Bond, who stated that stationing a fleet at Singapore would not deter a Japanese invasion and that a successful defense of Singapore required that the Malayan peninsula be defended. He estimated that an air force of 300–500 aircraft would be required for a successful defense. By then, the army and the RAF were in no position to achieve either goal.

It was obvious to the British and Dutch that the defense of Southeast Asia required action by all three major powers with possessions in the region, operating as allies with a coordinated strategy and command. Unfortunately, despite some low-level discussions of this with Americans from the Asiatic Fleet in the Philippines, no plans for such cooperation could be made because there was no American commitment to enter a war that might break out if the Japanese only attacked the British and Dutch possessions. Given that US war plans for the Pacific foresaw a quick loss of the Philippines to the Japanese, there was little that could be done in the way of planning any defense before a war actually broke out. Additionally, Churchill and Roosevelt had agreed during their conferences in 1941 that if a war broke out in Asia, it would take second priority to finishing the war against Germany in Europe. So far as Washington and London were concerned, the only policy in Southeast Asia would be to contain a Japanese advance to the extent that was possible.

To defend Singapore, the RAF decided that the fighter units would be equipped with the Brewster B-339E export version of the US Navy's Brewster F2A-2 fighter which the RAF had named Buffalo Mk I. One hundred and seventy Model 339Es had been ordered by the British Purchasing Commission in early 1940, even though the Air Ministry had determined in October 1939 that the fighter was unsuitable for the RAF. Since British prewar air intelligence regarding the equipment of the Japanese air forces was as faulty as that of the United States, with Japanese aircraft considered not up to Western standards, it was decided that the Buffalo fighters would not have any difficulty dealing with "second rate" opposition. This despite the fact the 1,100 horsepower Wright R-1820-G105 Cyclone engine, which offered 100 horsepower less than the engine that powered the F2A-2, had fuel starvation problems above 18,000 feet since the Buffalo did not use the same fuel line pressurization system as the F2A-2; also the single-stage supercharger reduced performance at higher altitudes.

Once the airplanes were flown at Singapore, it was discovered that the tropical climate caused the engine to overheat, spraying oil over the windscreen. With pilot armor and an armored windscreen, gross weight rose 1,000 pounds more than the F2A-2 to 6,500 pounds; the increased weight coupled with the less-powerful engine made the airplane underpowered. Maximum speed dropped to 330 mph, while rate of climb was reduced to 2,600 feet per minute. The extra weight increased the wing loading and landing speed, while reducing maneuverability. The second batch of Buffalos produced for the British order were forced to use reconditioned engines that had been used in DC-3s.

One hundred and sixty-seven Buffalos began arriving in Singapore in the spring of 1941 to provide the air defense of Singapore, Malaya, and Burma, and were assigned to each of the five Commonwealth squadrons. By the outbreak of war, the main fighter base was at Kallang Airfield on Singapore, where 453 Squadron RAAF (Royal Australian Air Force) had 18 Buffalos and 243 Squadron RAF had 15, while 488 Squadron RNZAF (Royal New Zealand Air Force) – the least-trained unit and not yet fully operational – had 17; 21 Squadron RAAF was equipped with 18 Buffalos, based at Sungei Patani in northwest Malaya, while RAF 67 Squadron's 16 fighters were moved in the fall of 1941 to Mingaladon Airdrome outside Rangoon, Burma.

A shortage of pilots meant that additional squadrons could not be formed, so many of the Buffalos went into storage. Most of the Commonwealth pilots were new and inexperienced, which led to the loss of 20 Buffalos in training accidents during the fall of 1941. Among the pilots at Singapore was RNZAF Flight Sergeant Geoff Fisken. A sheep farmer's son from Gisborne, the 25-year-old had first learned to fly at age 16, taking lessons in a D.H.60 Gypsy Moth. He had finally joined the RNZAF in the summer of 1940, and had arrived in Singapore in February 1941 after completing flight training.

Fisken was first assigned to 205 Squadron, which at the time was still flying the ancient Shorts Singapore I biplane flying boats. Shortly after his arrival, the Singapores were transferred to 5 Squadron RNZAF, which resulted in his being sent on a fighter conversion course, followed by assignment to 67 Squadron, an RAF unit that was filled primarily with New Zealanders. When 67 Squadron was posted to Rangoon in October, Fisken was transferred to 243 Squadron and remained at Singapore.

Unlike most of the pilots, Fisken did not dislike the Buffalo. In describing his experience with the airplane, he later recalled having accrued a total of 150 flying hours by the time he first met the Buffalo in early 1941. Compared to the other inexperienced pilots, he was considered "high time." Due to having a few hours of time in the Oxford, which had a retractable landing gear, he was assigned as a test pilot for the newly assembled Buffalos and also delivered them to their respective squadrons. The Buffalo was his first "real fighter." He thought it was quite easy to fly and landed as easily as it flew, and enjoyed doing aerobatics in it. However, he quickly found that it was underpowered, with poor turn, and "climbed like a brick," taking 15–20 minutes to stagger up to 15,000 feet. His opinion overall was that it was not a suitable aircraft with which to fight the Japanese, but if it had been given an additional 300 horsepower, the outcome would have been different. By the time the squadrons had received their full organization of pilots, Fisken had over 300 hours flying the Buffalo in his logbook. In conclusion, he recalled that he had heard the Americans thought Buffalos were awful, an opinion with which most of the others he flew with agreed; however, Fisken found he enjoyed flying it even in combat. It is likely his 300 hours in the airplane when most others had far less than 50 when the Japanese attacked colored his opinion. That experience would allow him to survive battle with the enemy where many others did not.

The offensive force based at Singapore consisted of 27, 34, 60, and 62 squadrons (RAF), equipped with Bristol Blenheim I and IV light bombers; 1 and 8 squadrons (RAAF), operating Lockheed Hudson maritime reconnaissance bombers; and 36 and 100 squadrons (RAF) flying the ancient and obsolete Vickers Vildebeest biplane torpedo bomber, though 36 Squadron also had some equally obsolete Fairey Albacore carrier biplanes. 205 Squadron RAF had recently transferred their Shorts Singapore biplane flying boats to the RNZAF, but only two Catalina II flying boats of 18 planned for had arrived for long-range maritime patrol duties.

All of the units faced numerous operational problems, including a lack of adequate spare parts and ground support maintenance personnel as well as no clear and coherent command structure. There was no radar for early warning of air raids, which meant the airfields on Singapore and the Malayan mainland were difficult to defend against air attack. The Australians received the full force of the "Singapore Mentality," being ostracized by the RAF and other British servicemen. In Singapore, clubs, bars, and hotels refused entry to anyone under the rank of lieutenant, while they got a cold reception from most civilians; this reinforced the anti-British sentiment most Australians held, and the pilots responded by ignoring their British allies whenever possible and calling them all "bloody Pommies." On top of all that, there was a Japanese spy in the Army air liaison staff.

On top of all that, there was a Japanese spy in the Army air liaison staff: Patrick Stanley Vaughan Heenan, a captain in the British Indian Army. After the outbreak of war, others in the staff found it remarkable that the Japanese seemed to know the correct recognition codes, despite the fact that they were changed every 24 hours. Heenan was caught red-handed with a radio during an air raid on December 12 and arrested. He was court-martialled for treason in January 1942. By February 13, as the Japanese closed in, Heenan began taunting his guards that he would be free while they became prisoners. British military police cut cards to determine who would execute him and he was taken to the docks where he was shot in the back of the head by a sergeant, who then dumped the body in the harbor.

The attitude of Singapore at the moment the war began was caught by an Australian soldier whose unit arrived in the colony shortly before the outbreak of hostilities: "I still have very vivid memories of my first mental reactions on our arrival in Singapore. The first sight that met our eyes on the first evening was officers in mess dress and women in evening dress. It was not only incongruous, it was wrong. Either we were crazy or they were crazy."

An RAAF pilot recalled that RAF Seletar was like a holiday camp with excellent accommodations and plentiful good food, with cheap alcohol and tobacco available. Officers lived a life of relative luxury compared to conditions in the UK, with most of the married ones accompanied by their wives. In a service where British class-consciousness was pervasive, even the "other ranks" did very nicely, with the result that there was a softness and never-never land atmosphere. Prior to the outbreak of hostilities, there were even many Japanese employed as servants and manual workers, some of whom may have been spies.

The Royal Navy's contribution to the defense of Singapore was Force Z, comprising the battleship HMS *Prince of Wales* and the battlecruiser HMS *Repulse*, commanded by Vice-Admiral Sir Tom Phillips with his flag in *Prince of Wales*, which arrived in Singapore on December 2. The task force had originally included the aircraft carrier HMS *Indomitable*, which was detached after it ran aground off Jamaica on October 27 and was unable to rendezvous with the rest of the force in Ceylon.

While the British and the Dutch prepared as best they could for what was seen as an inevitable Japanese attack, the Imperial Navy did not devote any real attention to the seizure of the Dutch colony until a map exercise was held in the spring of 1940, the only time before the outbreak of war that such planning was conducted. The results were disconcerting, since the primary lesson was that any action by Japan to gain control of the Dutch Indies would inevitably result in a protracted war with the United States, which the Japanese had only a slight chance of winning. While the results were reported to the Navy minister and Imperial Navy's chief of staff, the Navy's leadership did not share this information with Japanese political leaders or with the Imperial Army.

By the summer of 1941, the Imperial Army and Imperial Navy strategists saw four alternative strategies for the southern move. The first entailed seizure of the Dutch East Indies, followed by Malaya and the Philippines; the second foresaw a step-by-step advance to the Philippines, then to Borneo, Java, Sumatra, and Malaya; the third involved taking Malaya first, followed by the Philippines, in an attempt to delay hostilities with the United States; the fourth plan involved seizing the Philippines and Malaya simultaneously, followed by seizure of the Dutch East Indies. While the last was the most difficult, bringing on a tricky problem of timing and coordination that entailed a dangerous dispersion of force, it was, however, the only plan on which both the Army and the Navy agreed, which led to its adoption.

This was typical of Japanese decision-making, which would be a major influence on the outcome of the Pacific War. Throughout the war, a compromise that allowed the two competitive services to offer the appearance of unanimity was more likely to be adopted regardless of its realistic chance of success. After the war, an Imperial Army planner lamented, "When agreement was fairly unanimous, it was easier to join the group than to cause trouble... Hence as a general rule no one said anything even when assailed by doubts." The Army also had what turned out to be misplaced confidence in the ability of the Imperial Navy to hold back the United States Navy. The Navy's leadership said nothing to the Army leadership regarding their own doubts as to their ability in this task.

The Imperial Navy had used the probability of war with the United States in the Pacific as the primary argument in support of its relative power position within the military bureaucracy throughout the interwar years. Faced with the reality of what they had proclaimed for so long, the admirals could not now retreat from their public position that they would be victorious in the grand confrontation.

The first Japanese move in the southern campaign following the occupation of French Indochina in the summer of 1941 was against Thailand, which was seen as a crucial base for operations against Malaya, Burma, and the Netherlands East Indies.

Over the years since the Siamese Revolution of 1932, Thailand had become increasingly fascist under the rule of Major General Plaek Phibunsongkhram. Known throughout the country in the years following the revolution as Phibun, the general began as foreign minister of the revolutionary government. Following his appointment by the king as prime minister in December 1938, the previous military-civilian cooperation broke down. An admirer of Benito Mussolini, Phibun arrested 40 political opponents, both monarchists and democrats, in early 1939. Following rigged trials, 18 were executed; these were the first political executions in Siam in more than 100 years. Prince Damrong and Phraya Songsuradej were exiled with many others, while Phibun launched a campaign against the Chinese business class that was hated by native Thai. As with Hitler in Germany with the Jews, taxes on Chinese businesses were increased to confiscatory levels and Chinese schools and newspapers were closed.

Phibun and Luang Wichitwathakan, the government's ideological spokesman, followed these moves with a campaign that created a domestic cult of the leader. The ex-monarch, King Prajadhipok, an outspoken critic of the Phibun regime, was banned and sent into exile in Switzerland. The government passed laws which gave the authorities almost unlimited arrest powers and complete press censorship.

On June 23, 1939, the country's name was changed from Siam to Prathet Tha, "Land of the Free." A campaign of pan-Thai nationalism was organized against the Malay and Chinese ethnic minorities to integrate the Shan, Lao, Burmese, Vietnamese, and Thai ethnic communities into a "Great Kingdom of Thailand." "Modernization" required all Thais to salute the flag, sing the national anthem, and speak the national language. Performance of traditional Thai music, dance, and theater was abolished. Phibun's photo was ordered to be displayed at the end of every motion picture as if it were the king's portrait; the audience was ordered to stand and bow. Phibun adopted the title of "Than Phu Nam," Thai for "the leader."

Phibun's regime also revived old territorial claims against French Indochina, demanding restoration of former Thai territory in Cambodia and Laos. Confronted with American opposition and British hesitancy regarding these claims, Phibun turned to Japan for support. In the aftermath of the surrender of France to Nazi Germany in 1940, the Franco–Thai War erupted that October. Sporadic battles along Thailand's eastern frontier ended with an invasion of Laos and Cambodia in January 1941 that saw the Thai armed forces occupy the disputed territories. Japan intervened diplomatically and used its influence with the Vichy government, and in March 1941 France agreed to cede 54,000 square kilometers of Laos west of the Mekong and the majority of the Cambodian province of Battambang to Thailand, which renamed the territory its original name, Phra Tabong Province.

In fact, the Japanese forced Thailand to accept only a quarter of this territory, and to pay six million piasters to the French, since the Japanese wished to maintain their relationship with Vichy. Phibun's government proclaimed themselves the victors over a hated European colonial power, which increased Phibun's domestic reputation and popular support and allowed him to change his policy and begin courting the British and Americans in hope of blocking what he now saw was an imminent Japanese invasion. His first step was to declare Thailand neutral in any future regional war, a move that came too late.

At 2300 hours on December 7, the Thai government was presented with a Japanese ultimatum with a two-hour response deadline to allow the Japanese military to enter Thailand. With no response from the Thai government by the deadline of 0100 hours on December 8, the Imperial Army invaded Thailand at dawn from their bases in French Indochina. After several hours of fighting, the Thai government acceded to the Japanese demands, and aircraft of the Japanese Army Air Force began landing on Thai airfields to provide bases for the planned attacks on Burma and Malaya. Phibun assured the country in a radio message that the Japanese action was agreed to by the Thai government. On December 21, Phibun announced a "mutual assistance pact" with Japan. On December 30, the pact was revised to provide Japan full access to Thai railways, roads, airfields, naval bases, warehouses, communications systems, and barracks. Phibun's government declared war on Britain and the United States on January 25, 1942. However, Seni Pramoj, the Thai ambassador to the United States, refused to present the declaration of war. As a result, the United States did not declare war on Thailand. Seni, a publicly anti-Japanese conservative aristocrat, began organizing the Free Thai Movement, using the Thai assets frozen by the United States. Thai students in the country worked with the Office of Strategic Services (OSS) during the war.

MAP 2: JAPANESE 25TH ARMY OPERATIONS IN MALAYA, DECEMBER 1941–JANUARY 1942.

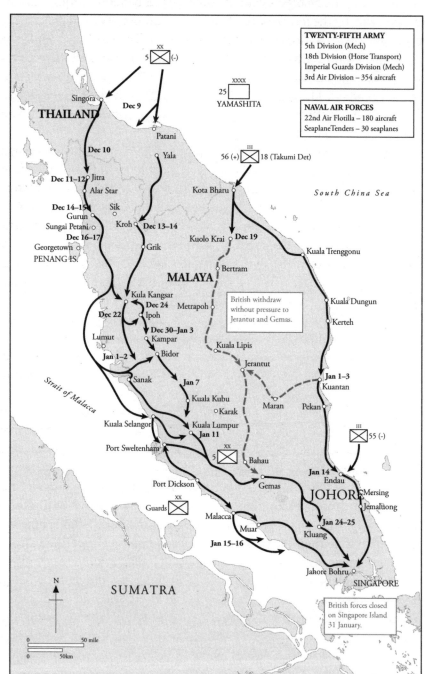

Following the Malayan campaign, Thailand benefited from Phibun's cooperation by the return of the four northernmost Malay states. During the war, Japan stationed 150,000 troops in Thailand and built the infamous Death Railway using Allied prisoners of war, and the country was treated as an "ally" by the Japanese the same way the Germans treated Finland, Hungary, and Romania as allies in the European war. For all Phibun's efforts, both the Allies and the Japanese called Thailand "The Italy of Asia." It was not meant as a compliment.

The Japanese air forces available for the Malayan and Indies campaign totaled 464 aircraft, compared with the 160 operational British aircraft in Malaya, Singapore and Burma, the 180 airplanes available to the Dutch, and 18 P-40s of the American Volunteer Group's "Hell's Angels" squadron.

The Imperial Navy was represented by the 22nd Kōkū Sentai (Air Flotilla), comprising the Genzan, Mihoro, and Kanoya Kōkūtai (air groups) equipped with 33 Mitsubishi G3M2 Type 96 Land-based Attack Aircraft (Nell) and 25 A5M4 Type 96 fighters (Claude), under the command of Vice Admiral Sadaichi Matsunaga and based at three airfields near Saigon in southern French Indochina. The 21st Kōkū Sentai's 1st Kōkūtai and Kanoya Kōkūtai were equipped with the new Mitsubishi G4M1 Type 1 Land-based Attack Bomber (Betty), while the Toko Kōkūtai's four-engined Kawanishi H6K1 Type 97 Large Flying Boat (Mavis) provided maritime search capability.

The Japanese Army Air Force provided 354 aircraft for the coming attack. The JAAF 3rd Hikō Shudan (Air Corps) was composed of the 3rd Hikodan (Air Division) with the 59th Hikō Sentai that flew Nakajima Ki-27 Type 97 fighters (Nate); the 27th Hikō Sentai operating the Mitsubishi Ki-51 Type 99 Assault Plane, (Sonia); and the 75th and 90th Hikō Sentai equipped with the Mitsubishi Ki-30 Type 97 Light Bomber (Ann). The 7th Hikodan's 64th Hikō Sentai was the first to take the new Nakajima Ki-43 *Hayabusa* (Peregrine Falcon) Type 1 Fighter (Oscar), that had only entered service in September. The 47th Independent Chutai was equipped with the first 14 Ki-44 *Shoki* (Demon) fighters (Tojo). The 12th, 68th, and 98th Hikō Sentai flew the Mitsubishi Ki-21 Type 97 Heavy Bomber (Sally). The independent 1st and 11th Hikō Sentai were also equipped with Ki-27 fighters. Reconnaissance units were equipped with the Mitsubishi Ki-15-I, Type 97 Command Reconnaissance Plane (Babs) and the new Mitsubishi Ki-46 Type 100 Command Reconnaissance Aircraft

(Dinah), which could outrun any Allied fighter. All these aircraft were based on airfields in Thailand near the Malayan border.

Over the course of the month following the outbreak of the Pacific War, the need for a joint Allied command became painfully obvious. During the three-week "Arcadia" conference attended by President Roosevelt and Prime Minister Churchill in Washington to develop the Allied master strategy for the war, ABDACOM – which stood for the United States (America), Great Britain (Britain), the Netherlands East Indies (Dutch), and Australia – was created on December 29, 1941. Its mission was to coordinate the joint defense of the "Malay Barrier."

British General Sir Archibald Wavell, Commander in Chief of British Forces in India, was appointed commander of ABDACOM, with American General George H. Brett appointed deputy commander. RAF Air Marshal Sir Richard Peirse was appointed commander of air forces (ABDAAIR) with US General Lewis H. Brereton as his deputy. US Asiatic Fleet commander Admiral Thomas C. Hart was appointed commander of the combined ABDA navies (ABDAFLOAT); Hart was succeeded in command by Dutch Admiral Conrad Helfrich on February 12, 1942.

When American Army chief of staff General George C. Marshall proposed that the top commander be British, General Sir Alan Brooke, chief of the Imperial General Staff, saw it as an American "set up" to be able to blame the British for what was seen as an obviously inevitable defeat. While General Wavell had the responsibility of command, he did not have authority, since the top subordinate commanders from the four component nations could override his orders if they believed such orders ran counter to their nation's national interest. Wavell was generally considered to have a brilliant mind and was admired by his staff, but he lacked charisma.

By the time General Wavell arrived in Singapore on January 7, 1942, the situations in the Philippines and Malaya were too late to save, while the Indies would soon come under attack. Ten days later, on January 18, Wavell moved his headquarters to Lembang near Bandoeng on Java, where he was joined by Air Marshal Peirse and the ABDA AIR staff. Throughout the campaign, the joint Allied command would be playing catch-up as they reacted to the continuing series of Japanese offensives.

CHAPTER EIGHT

THE MALAY BARRIER

On December 6, 1941, a 205 Squadron Catalina sighted a Japanese troop convoy through the clouds, headed south in the Gulf of Siam toward the Malayan coast.

Shortly after dawn on December 8, the airfields at Alor Star, Sungai Petani, and Butterworth on the Malay peninsula were struck by Mitsubishi Ki-21 bombers of the 7th Hikodan. Without an effective early-warning system, over 60 RAF aircraft were destroyed on the ground. Losses included 23 Blenheims and 12 Buffalos. The pilots who did manage to get off the ground in their Buffalos quickly discovered that the "intelligence" they had received regarding the inferiority of Japanese aircraft and pilots was the opposite of reality. The fact that the Nakajima Ki-27 and the newer Ki-43 *Hayabusa* fighters were each armed with only two 7.62mm machine guns was the saving grace for the Commonwealth pilots, since their Buffalos were not so easily shot down, though both Japanese fighters could fly circles around their opponents and eventually overwhelmed them with sheer numbers, while many of the JAAF pilots were veterans of fighting in China and the Nomonhan Incident and were thus skilled in air combat.

The 64th Sentai, the first JAAF unit equipped with the *Hayabusa*, was led by Major Takeo Kato, who became the most celebrated and distinguished ace of the JAAF during the war. Joining the Imperial Army in 1925, Kato had transferred to the JAAF in 1927. He was a captain commanding the 1st Chutai, which was equipped with the Nakajima Ki-10 Type 95 biplane fighter, when the war in China began in July 1937. On March 25, 1938, he shot down four Polikarpov I-16

Type 5 fighters in one combat. Three weeks later, now flying the brand-new Ki-27, he shot down three Polikarpov I-15 fighters on April 10. When he returned to Japan at the end of April, he was the leading ace of the war with nine victories. Commanding the 64th Sentai at the outset of the Malayan campaign, Major Kato disallowed individual victory credits for the sake of teamwork and led his pilots personally as they claimed an eventual 260 victories over Malaya and Burma by the end of April 1942 to become the leading JAAF fighter unit of the campaign. The Sentai would be joined a few weeks into the campaign by the 59th Sentai, the second unit to equip with the *Hayabusa*.

When the Japanese 25th Infantry Division landed at Kota Bharu, four Lockheed Hudson bombers flown by pilots of the RAAF's 1 Squadron attacked the invasion fleet. The transport *Awazisan Maru* was sunk while the transports *Ayatosan Maru* and *Sakura Maru* were damaged in the attack. Two of the Hudsons were shot down at 0118 hours local time, an hour before the planes of Kido Butai arrived over Pearl Harbor.

Following Japanese air raids on Singapore during the day of December 8, the Royal Navy's Force Z departed the harbor, with orders to attack the Japanese invasion fleet at Kota Bharu. HMS *Prince of Wales* and *Repulse* were escorted by the destroyers HMS *Electra*, *Express*, *Tenedos*, and HMAS *Vampire*. Shortly after dawn on December 9, the fleet was spotted by the Japanese submarine I-65. Shortly thereafter, *Prince of Wales*' radar failed, depriving the fleet of any early warning of an air attack.

While Force Z steamed through the Gulf of Siam during the day of December 9 searching for the enemy, invading troops seized Kota Bharu, supported by fighters based at Singora and Patani airfields in Thailand. Eight Blenheim I bombers from 62 Squadron took off from Butterworth Airdrome to attack Singora, but quickly ran into the fighter escorts of an unreported incoming Japanese raid which shot down all but one of the RAF bombers. The surviving Blenheim, flown by 28-year-old Squadron Leader Arthur Scarf who was leading the mission, managed to evade the enemy fighters and fly on to Singora, where he successfully bombed the airfield. Returning to Butterworth, Japanese fighters caught up with Scarf's Blenheim and shot it up thoroughly, severely wounding him and shattering his left arm. Despite drifting in and out of consciousness, he managed to keep the airplane in the sky until the Japanese turned back and then successfully crash-landed the shot-up bomber at Alor Star Airdrome. His navigator-bombardier Sergeant Paddy Calder and gunner Sergeant Cyril Rich were uninjured, but Scarf died of his wounds two hours later in the hospital. His pregnant wife, a nurse based at Alor Star, had just been evacuated south that morning. In 1946, when the facts of the mission became known, Scarf was awarded the Victoria Cross, making him the first British soldier of the Pacific War to receive the highest award for valor.

During the daylight hours of December 9, the H6K flying boats of the Toko Kōkūtai searched for Force Z, finally spotting the ships at the end of the day, though the searchers were unable to maintain contact in the darkness. Shortly after midnight on December 10, Admiral Philips received a message that the Japanese were landing at Kuantan and he was ordered to investigate. The submarine I-58 spotted Force Z at 0220 hours and fired five torpedoes that missed after reporting their position. At dawn, the Toko Kōkūtai launched 11 H6K "Mavis" flying boats to search for the British ships. Force Z arrived off Kuantan at 0800 hours, to find the reported landings were a diversion, and was spotted by a Mavis 30 minutes later.

Shortly after 0900 hours, 86 bombers from the 22nd Kōkū Sentai in Saigon took off to attack the British ships. A G3M2 "Nell" of the Genzan Kōkūtai spotted Force Z at 1015 hours; the pilot was ordered to maintain contact and broadcast a directional signal the rest could follow. At 1100 hours, eight G3M2s of the Genzan Kōkūtai were spotted visually as they entered their bomb runs over the fleet. Each carried six 250-kilogram (551-pound) bombs and attacked *Repulse*; the first two bombs straddled the battlecruiser, while the third passed through the hangar roof and exploded on the 1-inch armor plating of the main deck. *Repulse*'s antiaircraft fire damaged five bombers, two so badly that they immediately turned back to Saigon.

Thirty minutes later, 17 torpedo-carrying "Nells" of the Mihoro Kōkūtai were spotted as they divided into two groups for a "hammer and anvil" attack. *Repulse*'s commander, Captain Bill Tennant, managed by skillful handling to avoid nine Type 93 torpedoes aimed at the ship as well as bombs dropped by six other Nells of the Genzan Kōkūtai.

The eight other torpedo-armed Nells attacked *Prince of Wales*, which was struck by one torpedo on the port side next to "Y" Turret. The blast wrecked the outer port propeller shaft and destroyed bulkheads along the shaft all the way to B Engine Room; power to the electric dynamos was lost, which stopped the pumps and caused uncontrollable rapid flooding that put the entire electrical system in the after part of the ship out of action. With much of the interior plunged into total darkness, attempts by the damage repair parties to counter the flooding were slowed and the battleship soon took on a heavy list.

Flight Sergeant Fisken and the other pilots of 243 Squadron at Ipoh Airdrome were sent off to provide air cover when news of the attack was received at Singapore. As the Buffalos winged north, *Repulse* was able to avoid nine more torpedoes in a third attack by the Mihoro Kōkūtai. But minutes later, 17 torpedo-carrying G4M1 "Betty" bombers of the 21st Kōkū Sentai's 1st Kōkūtai and Kanoya Kōkūtai arrived and made a third "hammer and anvil" attack. *Repulse* was hit by five torpedoes in rapid succession that gutted her. *Repulse*'s gunners shot down two attackers from the 1st Kōkūtai and heavily damaged eight more, but the damage inflicted by the torpedoes was fatal. *Repulse* listed severely to port at 1228 hours and quickly capsized, taking 508 officers and men down with her. Minutes later, Fisken and another pilot arrived overhead. He later described that he saw the bow sticking out of the sea, surrounded by an oil slick and many bodies as the destroyers HMS *Electra* and HMAS *Vampire* rescued the survivors. The squadron remained overhead watching the final struggle of Force Z until they were relieved by the Australians of 453 Squadron.

Prince of Wales had also been attacked by six G4M1s from the Kanoya Kōkūtai, which hit her with three torpedoes that caused further damage and flooding. Six G4M1s armed with 500-kilogram (1,100-pound) armor-piercing bombs also attacked. One bomb hit the catapult deck and penetrated to the main deck, where it hit near the makeshift aid station and killed many of the wounded. Several other bombs were near misses that popped rivets and split hull plates along the seams, increasing flooding. With the approval of Admiral Phillips, Captain Leach gave the order to abandon ship at 1315 hours, and five minutes later the battleship that had first fought the *Bismarck* and later carried Prime Minister Churchill to his first meeting with President Roosevelt capsized and sank. The admiral and captain were among the 327 lost with the ship. The 20-year question of whether or not aircraft could sink battleships capable of maneuvering and defending themselves had finally been resolved in favor of the aviators.

That evening, after returning from their unsuccessful mission to defend Force Z, 243 Squadron was transferred from Ipoh to Kuala Lumpur. The Japanese invasion was well underway by December 11, with bombing raids on the airfields of Alor Star, Sungei Patani and Butterworth, and the city of Penang. The single fighter unit up north, 21 "City of Melbourne" Squadron, suffered heavy losses due to strafing and was badly mauled. Squadron leader Flight Lieutenant Tim Vigors led 453 Squadron to Ipoh on December 12 as reinforcement for 21 Squadron, which was pulled back from Sungei Patani to Ipoh.

The next day, Vigors led five 453 Buffalos on to Butterworth. They had just landed to refuel when the field was attacked by Ki-27s. Vigors and his wingman managed to get airborne, but both were quickly shot down. While the other three were taking off, they were attacked and Flight Sergeant Ronald Oelrich was shot down in flames, while another made a forced landing in a rice paddy and Wing Commander L.J. Neale crashed, surviving with injuries in what became known as "the Butterworth Massacre."

Back at Ipoh on December 15, 12 453 Squadron Buffalos intercepted a force of JAAF Nakajima Ki-48 *shiki-souhatu-keibaku* Army Type 99 twin-engined light bombers (Lily) and Mitsubishi Ki-51 Type 99 Sonias. Flight Lieutenant R.D. Vanderfield scored the first confirmed aerial victories for a Buffalo pilot by shooting down two Ki-48s, while flight sergeants Neville Read and V.A. Collyer claimed a Ki-51 each. The squadron's first day of combat cost one pilot killed, two pilots wounded, and five Buffalos written off.

Butterworth was raided again on December 17, and three Buffalos intercepted an attack on Ipoh. Eight more Buffalos were scrambled; while they were engaged with the first force, a second formation of Japanese bombers raided the airfield, destroying buildings and aircraft. The raids on Ipoh continued on December 18. On December 19, six Buffaloes of 453 Squadron and one 21 Squadron survivor were flown back to Singapore, leaving nine working aircraft and five pilots at Ipoh. Another Japanese raid that evening left two aircraft. After six days at Ipoh, 453 and 21 squadrons withdrew to Kuala Lumpur in southern Malaya, where they re-equipped with new aircraft.

Before the war, Sunga Bresi airfield at Kuala Lumpur had been home to a flying club whose clubhouse became 453's headquarters. On December 20, the day Butterworth was occupied by the enemy, the

Buffalos flew defensive patrols. The next day, a formation of bombers appeared over the airfield. Flight sergeants Leys and Peterson attacked the formation. Leys was shot down but baled out, while Peterson claimed two Ki-48s.

On December 22, 18 of the 64th Sentai's Ki-43 *Hayabusas*, led by Major Kato, appeared in force just after the standing patrol landed to refuel. Six Buffalos managed to get airborne, but were shot down or crash-landed. Flight Sergeant Read rammed a Ki-43; both pilots were killed in the crash. That afternoon, four Ki-43s strafed the airfield, shooting down and killing Pilot Officer Drury when he tried to take off. By the end of the day, 453 had lost three pilots killed and four injured, with three Buffalos shot down and four seriously damaged. The next day, the four serviceable Buffalos were flown back to Sembawang Airfield on Singapore, and on December 25 the survivors of 21 and 453 squadrons were combined into a new 21/453 Squadron under command of Squadron Leader Harper. The Japanese had established air superiority over Malaya in less than a week.

The pilots had quickly discovered their fighter was underpowered in comparison to their opponents, and now made an attempt to wring more performance out of the Buffalo by lightening it. On December 28, "The Shadow's Super Sport Special" made its first flight. "The Shadow" was Squadron Leader Harper, and "The Super Sport Special" was a Buffalo with the ammunition boxes half empty, two of its four guns removed, armor plate removed, the radio equipment lightened, the gun ports faired over, and the airframe otherwise cleaned up. With all this, the "Special" weighed 1,000 pounds less than a standard Buffalo and was 30 mph faster. Unfortunately, there was no time to modify the other fighters.

243 Squadron's Flight Sergeant Fisken claimed his first victory over what he called a "Zero" on December 15; at this point in the war, Allied pilots called every enemy fighter they fought a Zero. He recalled the squadron had almost 20 Buffalos to start with before the war began but only ten pilots. The climate created difficulties for operations, since the Buffalos were ready to fly in the early-morning hours, but as soon as the sun came up, most would become unserviceable due to the heat and humidity. Fisken was fortunate to have a ground crew of Welsh mechanics and a Welsh rigger, who were "the biggest thieves on two legs!" They would steal whatever was needed from other aircraft to keep

his Buffalo operational. "I never asked, and they never told me how they fixed it. All they would say as I climbed into the cockpit was, 'Now give that a try and see if that fixed your problem.'"

Fisken's extra experience in the Buffalo showed up well as combat increased. He shot down his second airplane on January 14. On January 17, he was on patrol with three other Buffalos. They were flying through cloud again; emerging from the clouds, he found two of the others had gotten lost and turned back. He spotted 24 G3M Type 96 twin-engine bombers 4,000 feet below. The two pilots dived straight down on top of them. Fisken began firing at one bomber that was on the outside of the formation. His rounds found one engine, despite the wild defensive fire from the gunners. The bomber began to smoke heavily before bursting into flames and diving straight into the jungle below.

Fisken zoomed through the formation and pulled out of his dive at 2,000 feet, blacking out momentarily. He pulled up underneath the formation and shot down a second one that also burst into flames but didn't blow up, dropping out of the formation and gliding down until it crashed into the jungle. The two pilots were miles from their base, so they turned for home since they were low on gas. On the way home, they spotted another bomber and attacked it, leaving the Nell smoking very heavily and losing altitude. Fisken was credited with the two bombers, giving him four victories in the Buffalo.

The Royal Netherlands East Indies Army Air Force sent reinforcements to Singapore on Christmas Day. The 2e Afdeling (second division) of Squadron 5 (2-VLG-V) arrived with 12 B-339D fighters along with four Martin 139W bombers from the 1e Afdeling (first division) of Squadron 3 (1-VLG-III). Before the Dutch fighters were recalled to Java on January 18, Captain Jacob van Helsdingen had scored two, while First Lieutenant August Deibel was credited with three victories over the island while stationed at Kallang Airport.

The first aerial reinforcements arrived in Singapore on January 3, 1942. Fifty-one crated Hurricane IIb fighters were unloaded from the ship they arrived in and assembled by the 151st Maintenance unit. Twenty-one were ready by January 5 to be flown by the 24 new pilots, several of whom were Battle of Britain veterans, and 232 Squadron was activated on January 8. By January 12, the remaining Hurricanes had been assigned to the New Zealanders in 488 Squadron, which passed its surviving Buffalos to 453 Squadron, which was combined with the survivors of 243 Squadron on January 21. The two Hurricane squadrons were controlled by the newly established 226 Group.

Flight Lieutenant Harry Tweedale, a communications specialist, recalled that on the final two days of their journey to Singapore, they were escorted by two warships for each cargo and troop vessel in the convoy. The convoy was important and represented the last hope of holding Singapore. They were fortunate that the final two days found them in a tropical storm with heavy rain, which saved them from discovery by two formations of enemy bombers sent to attack them that were unable to find the ships. Some of the enemy fighters escorting the bombers were able to inflict some damage, but were driven off by defensive fire from the convoy and the air cover provided by Buffalos from Singapore.

The convoy was welcomed in Singapore with relief. Tweedale remembered that the island itself had hardly been touched and the battle was still raging in Malaya. "Now that we had arrived, though, people thought that Singapore would be safe and the papers were filled with photographs of Hurricanes and news of our squadron." The squadron members had to help with unloading the ship that carried their planes and equipment. One night in particular stood out in his memory. "Bob Robinson and I were working down in the hold of the *Kota Gede* with bright arc lights shining down upon us. The air raid warning sounded. The work couldn't stop which meant that the lights had to remain on." They were unloading ammunition, and Tweedale was scared throughout the raid that they would take a hit, but eventually the all clear sounded.

The unloading was completed in a few days, with the men working continuously in shifts around the clock. They then moved to Seletar to assemble the aircraft and test them. The tropic sun was brutal. "You've no idea how uncomfortable it was climbing on the hot metal of the planes with bare knees." The first morning at Seletar saw a Japanese air raid, which was the first experience of combat for the men, who remained nonchalant and remained in the canteen rather than taking shelter. "We were determined to show the natives there was nothing to be frightened about. In a mere matter of days, we were reaching the shelters ahead of the natives and demonstrating what real running was like."

These Hurricane IIbs were armed with 12, rather than eight, .303 caliber machine guns, and were fitted with the bulky Vokes tropical dust filter under the nose, which reduced their speed to around 305 mph. The additional weight of the guns and drag of the dust filter resulted in the fighters being slow to climb and less maneuverable at altitude, although the increased armament made them more effective bomber killers. 232 Squadron was declared operational on January 22; that day G3Ms of the Genzan Kōkūtai attacked Seletar Airdrome and the Hurricanes took off to intercept them. Unfortunately, the pilots threw away the antibomber capability by engaging in the air combat tactics they had learned in Europe against the Luftwaffe. By the end of January, the two Hurricane squadrons had been as badly decimated as the Buffalo squadrons.

On January 12, 1942, Geoff Fisken claimed another "Zero." Two days later, he scored a third during a fight in which he was lucky to be able to land after being caught in the explosion. He was on patrol with seven other Buffalos at 20,000 feet when they came out of the clouds and spotted 20 enemy fighters a thousand feet below. They immediately dived on the enemy. One Ki-27 turned on him and opened fire. As the two fighters closed, the enemy fighter burst into flames and blew up as it passed beneath him. The force of the explosion put his fighter into a spin. Unable to gain control, he attempted to bale out, but with one foot over the side he was yanked back because his helmet, which was sewn to his oxygen mask, was tangled in the oxygen hose.

Unable to parachute, Fisken climbed back in the cockpit and managed to regain control after spinning another 12,000 feet before he pulled out. "To this day, I have no idea how I got out of that spin. My whole life flashed before my eyes. Things that happened on the farm, the fights I got into at school when I was a kid – all of them were as clear as day to me." Having regained control, he finally landed 30 minutes after the others had returned, angry with himself that he had not thought to simply pull off his helmet and parachute away.

488 Squadron finally was declared fully operational on its Buffalos at the end of December. On January 13, Pilot Officer Noel Sharp claimed a Ki-43 for the squadron's first victory, while Flight Sergeant Ed Kuhn was shot down and crashed. Sharp claimed a second four days later, though he was shot down in the fight and crashed.

On January 15, Japanese bombers flew several raids against airfields on Singapore. The escorting Ki-43s that the 59th Sentai had recently re-equipped with were credited with shooting down six Buffalos, while Ki-27s of the 1st Independent Hikō Sentai ran across 15 Buffalos over the city and claimed seven shot down. Captains Yasuhiko Kuroe and Susumo Jimbo, flying brand-new Ki-44 *Shoki* fighters (Tojo) of the 47th Independent Chutai, engaged in the unit's first aerial combat and shared one Buffalo for a total Japanese claim of 14. 488 Squadron lost three Buffalos, while the Dutch squadron lost one Buffalo. Almost all of the other Buffalos that had engaged in combat returned with varying degrees of damage. 488's Flight Sergeant Kuhn in W8150 reported he attacked a Ki-27, which rolled over into a vertical dive out of control. He was unable to see the final result, since he was attacked by another Ki-27 and his Buffalo was badly damaged; Singapore Air HQ later confirmed the crash. Flight Lieutenant Vanderfield claimed a bomber shot down. 488's first combat loss since the squadron had become operational was Pilot Officer Greville Lloyd Hesketh, a law clerk from Auckland, in Buffalo W8183. His airplane crashed out of control near the oil tanks by the Alexandra Military Hospital.

On January 16, 453's commander, Squadron Leader Frank Howell, claimed a Ki-27 shot down, while Flight Lieutenant Mowbray Garden shared a "Zero" with Flight Sergeant Rex Weber, and Pilot Officer T.B. Marra claimed a Ki-27. Fisken was credited with three G3Ms shared shot down when the 22nd Kōkū Sentai bombed Singapore on January 17. 453's Flight Lieutenant Vanderfield also claimed a Nell shot down in the battle, while Flight Sergeant A.W.B. Clare (RAAF) claimed a Ki-43, and 488's Flight Sergeant P.E.E. Killick claimed a "Zero."

On January 18, 453 Squadron escorted five Australian Wirraway two-seat trainers and the four Dutch Martin 139 bombers in an attack on Japanese troops crossing the Maur River. The formation was intercepted and all the Martins and one of the Wirraways were lost, as well as three Buffalos. As a result, the Dutch fighter unit was evacuated back to Java. On January 19, Flight Lieutenant Read and Flight Sergeant Keith Gorringe each claimed a Ki-51.

Fisken scored his fifth victory on January 21. Five days later, the squadron flew as top cover to escort 12 ancient Vickers Vildebeest torpedo bombers to strike an enemy convoy landing troops at Endau. Those slow biplanes never stood a chance, and were mauled and chewed

Pearl Harbor during the Japanese raid on December 7, 1941, with antiaircraft shells bursting overhead. The largest column of smoke at center comes from the burning USS *Arizona*. (US Navy)

A photograph taken from a Japanese aircraft of Pearl Harbor under attack. (US Navy)

USS *West Virginia* in flames immediately after the raid, with USS *Tennessee* alongside. (US Navy)

Tugs and other ships attempt to keep USS *California* afloat after the attack. (US Navy)

USS *Nevada* aground and burning off Waipio Point following the raid. (US Navy)

A US Army B-17E at Hickam Airfield – smoke from burning ships at Pearl Harbor can be seen in the background. (US Navy)

USS *Cassin*, burned out and capsized against USS *Downes* in the dry dock of the Pearl Harbor Navy Yard. (US Navy)

The remains of USS *Oklahoma*, December 8. (US Navy)

A damaged US Army P-40 at Bellows Field, Oahu, on December 9. (US Navy)

Salvage of USS *California*, April 5, 1942. (US Navy)

Captain Winfield S. Cunningham, USN, commander of US forces on Wake Island in December 1941. (US Navy)

Captain Henry T. Elrod, USMC. The most successful of Marine Fighting Squadron 211 (VMF-211) pilots at Wake, Elrod was the first Marine awarded the Medal of Honor in World War II. (US Navy)

Wrecked Grumman F4F-3 Wildcat fighters of VMF-211, photographed by the Wake airstrip sometime after the Japanese captured the island on December 23, 1941. (US Navy)

Wreckage of a USMC F4F-3, Photographed on Wake by the Japanese on December 23. (US Navy)

Lieutenant John D. Bulkeley, USN, commander of the PT boats used to evacuate General MacArthur from Corregidor, Philippine Islands, in March 1942. (US Navy)

Surrender of American troops at Corregidor, May 1942. (NARA)

HMS *Prince of Wales*, *c*.1941. (Arkivi/Getty Images)

Sinking of HMS *Prince of Wales*, December 10, 1941. (Ullstein Bild/Getty Images)

HMS *Exeter* at sea, *c.*1941. (Arkivi/Getty Images)

HMS *Exeter* sinking during the Battle of the Java Sea, February 27, 1942. (US Navy)

A Bristol Blenheim Mark I of No. 62 Squadron RAF taxies past a line of Brewster Buffaloes of Nos 21 or 453 Squadrons RAAF, at Sembawang, Singapore. (UK Crown Copyright)

USS *Houston*, part of the Allied ABDA fleet, was sunk on the night of February 28, 1942. (US Navy)

Commander in Chief Asiatic Fleet, Admiral Thomas C. Hart, with High Commissioner of the Philippines Francis Sayre. (US Navy)

George H. Gay, Jr., photographed prewar in ROTC uniform. He became a Navy officer after flight training in 1941, serving with Torpedo Squadron Eight (VT-8) on USS *Hornet*. (US Navy)

Part of USS *Enterprise*'s .50-caliber antiaircraft gun gallery fires against attacking Japanese planes during the raid on the Japanese-held Marshall Islands, February 1, 1942. (US Navy)

USS *Enterprise* at Pearl Harbor, March 1942. (US Navy)

A shot of USS *Enterprise*'s new 20mm gun installations, Pearl Harbor Navy Yard, March 19, 1942. (US Navy)

Lieutenant Commander John S. Thach, commander of Fighting Squadron Three (VF-3), in the cockpit of an F4F Wildcat fighter, April 10, 1942. (US Navy)

Lieutenant Edward Henry "Butch" O'Hare in the cockpit of his F4F fighter, spring 1942. (US Navy)

Thach and O'Hare in their F4F-3s near Naval Air Station Kaneohe, Oahu, Hawaii, April 10, 1942. (US Navy)

An SBD Dauntless scout-bomber and five TBD-1 Devastator torpedo planes aboard USS *Enterprise* ready themselves for takeoff, May 4, 1942. (US Navy)

up by the antiaircraft fire from the ships and the enemy fighters that attacked them as they made their torpedo runs. Fisken managed to join up with one of the survivors at the rendezvous point on the return to base, but the Vildebeest flew so slowly he had to fly with full flaps and lower his landing gear and was still faster. The squadron escorted another flight of Vildebeests in the afternoon that ended in a massacre. After this, his squadron was so reduced it was disbanded, with Fisken and the other survivors sent to RAAF 453 Squadron.

Fisken came close to not surviving his final fight on February 1. He and his wingman emerged from the clouds to find 12 enemy fighters a few hundred feet below. Outnumbered six to one, they realized they hadn't been spotted and dived on them. Fisken opened fire at one from 300 yards. It turned into him and opened fire. He managed to knock it down, but was attacked by two more. Taking hits, he ducked back into the clouds, but the enemy hung around and every time he popped out of the cloud he saw an enemy fighter waiting for him. He discovered he'd been wounded in his arm. Finally, he managed to duck out of the clouds and head back toward Singapore. Though the Buffalo had been hit numerous times, it still flew just fine.

Fisken landed and knew there was something wrong when he stood up in his cockpit and one of his mechanics fainted at the sight. His rigger pointed at his leg and he saw his white flying suit was covered in blood from his hip down. A piece of a Japanese cannon shell that had bounced off his armor plate and split in two had torn into his hip. He tried to remove it but couldn't and it eventually had to be cut out. After that, he was unable to fly due to his wounds, as he hobbled around with a walking stick and his arm in plaster.

Three days before Singapore fell on February 15, Fisken was evacuated to New Zealand; it would be a year before he could fly again. Fisken's final battle was one of the last that Commonwealth pilots engaged in, as the RAAF and RNZAF squadrons were evacuated to Sumatra and Java. During the Malayan campaign, over 60 Buffalos of the 167 that had been sent to Singapore before the war were lost in aerial combat, with another 40 destroyed on the ground in bombing and strafing attacks, while 20 were lost in accidents. The last airworthy Buffalo flew out of Singapore on February 10, five days before the surrender, making a total of 20 of the fighters that reached the Dutch East Indies.

In the aftermath of the Malayan disaster and the surrender of Singapore, the Buffalo was a convenient scapegoat. It was outclassed by its opponents both in the experience of the pilots and the quality of the aircraft, but in a fight against the odds the Buffalo pilots faced, a similar number of even the best Spitfires could not have changed the outcome. The fighter's design had peaked with the F2A-2. Every further development reduced its performance as its weight increased without a gain in power.

In truth, the problem at Singapore was not the Buffalo. The British had made the terrible mistake of underestimating their enemy, as had the Americans in the Philippines and the Dutch in the Indies. The Japanese were not, as xenophobically thought, a race of "bucktoothed monkeys" only capable of making poor copies of better equipment invented in the West.

CHAPTER NINE

REINFORCEMENT

American military leaders were aware of how weak their forces were in Asia, and made efforts right up to the outbreak of war to send new units and equipment to the Philippines. Once war broke out, there was a need to find some way to get reinforcements to the beleaguered forces in the Philippines and to Australia and the Dutch East Indies. The fact those places were literally on the other side of the world, with supply routes vulnerable to enemy action, forced extraordinary measures. While medium bombers like the B-25 and fighters could be loaded aboard cargo ships, it was necessary to fly heavy bombers to the war zone.

One last convoy of reinforcements was dispatched to the Philippines before the outbreak of war. Operation *Plum* had been approved by President Roosevelt on November 14, 1941. USS *Pensacola* (CA-24) led what came to be known as "The Pensacola Convoy," which included the Navy transports USS *Chaumont* (AP-5) and *Republic* (AP-33); USS *Niagara* (PG-52), the former civilian yacht *Hi-Esmaro*, which had been converted to a patrol gunboat; the Army transports USAT *Meigs* and *Willard A. Holbrook*; the US civilian cargo ships SS *Admiral Halstead* and *Coast Farmer*, and the Dutch cargo ship MS *Bloemfontein*. Included in the cargo were 48 A-24A "Banshee" dive bombers, the USAAF's version of the Navy's SBD-3 "Dauntless" carrier-based dive bomber intended to replace the obsolescent Douglas B-18 "Bolo" bombers that equipped the 27th Bombardment Group in the Philippines, and 18 brand-new North American B-25B "Mitchell" medium bombers.

On December 5, the convoy crossed the equator. *Pensacola* received the news of the Pearl Harbor attack at 0825 hours on December 7.

The convoy maintained course for Manila until December 9, when the ships were ordered to return to Pearl Harbor. That order was canceled a few hours later and *Pensacola* was ordered to take the convoy to Suva, Fiji Islands, where *Niagara* would be left behind, then head on to Brisbane, Australia.

The first joint operation of the US Navy and Royal Australian Navy in World War II began the afternoon of Monday, December 15, when the cruisers HMAS *Canberra* and *Perth*, under command of Rear Admiral J.G. Grace, RAN, departed Brisbane to meet and escort the Pensacola convoy. At 1155 hours on December 19, north of New Caledonia, *Pensacola* sighted what was soon identified as the light cruiser HMNZS *Achilles*, which joined the convoy. At 1840 hours, *Perth* and *Canberra* joined. The four cruisers launched their scouting planes for air cover during the three-day voyage to Australia, sighting the Free French ship *Cap Des Palmes* on its way from Noumea to Sydney on December 20. Later that day sonar picked up what was thought to be a submarine, which was depth-charged; it was later determined to be a whale.

At 0503 hours on Monday, December 22, 1941, the convoy entered Moreton Bay, and *Pensacola* moored in Brisbane harbor at 1247 hours. What had begun as the last Philippines convoy had become the first reinforcement convoy to arrive in Australia.

There were additional reinforcements on the way.

The 49th Pursuit Group – the "Forty-Niners" as they became known – came into existence when cadre from the 94th Pursuit Squadron under the command of Major Glen Davasher were mustered at Selfridge Airfield outside Detroit, Michigan, on November 20, 1940. The unit was part of the expansion program by the US Army Air Corps to grow itself into the organization everyone knew was going to be needed in the war all saw coming. The three squadrons assigned to the group were the 7th Squadron, who took the name "Screamin' Demons," while the 8th Squadron became known as the "Blacksheep," and the 9th Squadron adopted the name "Flying Knights."

The 49th Group was transferred to Morrison Airfield at West Palm Beach, where the weather was better for the training the pilots needed, in May 1941. Each squadron received a Stearman PT-17 primary trainer, a Vultee BT-13 basic trainer for further instrument work, and three Seversky P-35s and one P-40C for training purposes.

Following the entry of the United States into World War II after the attack on Pearl Harbor, Major Paul "Squeeze" Wurtsmith took command of the 49th on December 12, 1941. Everyone knew they were going into combat; the only question was where they would go and when they would leave. Newspapers were full of desperate struggles by the American forces in the Philippines. Rumors spread through the group when they were notified at the end of December to commence preparation for overseas deployment that they were going to reinforce the Philippines.

The men left Florida on January 4, 1942, heading cross-country by train for California, where they arrived in San Francisco on January 8. Just before leaving Florida, 75 new pilots and 587 more enlisted men arrived to bring the group to full authorized strength. Among the young pilots were second lieutenants George E. Preddy and John D. Landers, who had both graduated from flight training on December 12, the same day Major Wurtsmith had taken command. After arriving in San Francisco, the officers were put up in a downtown hotel while the enlisted men were billeted in the County Livestock Pavilion, affectionately known as the "Cow Palace."

On January 10, embarkation orders arrived and on January 12 the men went aboard the former Matson Line luxury liners *Mariposa* and *Coolidge*, now converted to troop transports, while their heavy equipment was loaded aboard the freighter *Luckenbach*. The ships sailed under the Golden Gate Bridge at mid-day; two hours later, out of sight of land, they rendezvoused with the light cruiser USS *Phoenix* and set course toward the western Pacific.

The rumors had been right; they were headed for the Philippines. On January 28, their destination was changed to Melbourne, Australia. Cape Howes was sighted on January 31 and the convoy dropped anchor in Melbourne on February 1. Once ashore, they moved into tent bivouacs at Camp Darley, 30 miles outside Melbourne.

Reporting to MacArthur's headquarters, Major Wurtsmith learned he'd been promoted to lieutenant colonel and his squadron commanders had all been promoted to captain. The Forty-Niners were the first Americans to arrive in Australia as a complete unit. Over the next three days, after Australian longshoremen refused to unload the ships, the officers and men unloaded all their supplies and equipment by hand. On February 15, they were moved by train to Bankstown Airfield outside Sydney.

All eyes were now on the Dutch East Indies, the newest front against the Japanese with the fall of Singapore. P-40s and B-25s, originally headed for the Philippines, had been diverted to Townsville for assembly. The plan was that, once assembled, they would be flown to Brisbane on the east coast, then on to Charleville, then to Cloncurry in Queensland, and finally on to Darwin, whence they would fly direct to Java. The route was known as "the Brereton Route" and was 3,600 miles long. It followed the Australian coast, and was the equivalent of flying from Boston to Houston, around the US coast, without navigation aids or reliable maps. It was later described to a pilot of the 49th: "You won't have any trouble finding your way to Darwin. Just follow the trail of crashed P-40s; you can't go wrong."

By now, the Japanese had landed in Sumatra and Java was under attack. The situation was desperate, but there was still hope the island might be held if enough fighters could be sent there. The only USAAF unit to make it from Melbourne to Java via the "Brereton route" was a few P-40s of the 17th Pursuit Group (Provisional). Formed from evacuated survivors of the Philippines debacle, 34 P-40Es set out to fly to Java; only 17 made it all the way. In the face of this, the decision was made to ship other P-40Es with their pilots and ground crews aboard the seaplane tender USS *Langley* (AV-3).

Originally the Navy's first aircraft carrier, *Langley* was obsolete by 1936. She went into the Mare Island shipyard, where the forward half of her flight deck was removed; conversion to a seaplane tender was completed in mid-1937. She arrived in Manila on September 24, 1939, assigned to the Asiatic Fleet. *Langley* was anchored off Cavite Naval Station in Manila Bay the day the war broke out. Since the old ship was not capable of surface combat, she was sent to Balikpapan, in the Dutch East Indies, where it was planned she would operate seaplanes for patrol and reconnaissance. With Japanese advances continuing, she headed for Australia and arrived in Darwin on New Year's Day, 1942. At Darwin, she supported RAAF seaplanes until January 11, when she departed for Fremantle.

The 49th Group contributed 32 P-40Es for the reinforcement, flying them to Perth, where they were towed over the main roads to Fremantle and loaded aboard *Langley*. Twenty-seven crated P-40Es assigned to the 13th Pursuit Squadron (Provisional) were loaded aboard the cargo ship *Seawitch* while the assigned pilots went aboard *Langley*. Fifty-nine fighters were not really enough to meet the threat hanging over Java, especially since half would have to be assembled after arrival, but it was all there was available.

On February 22, *Langley* and *Seawitch* departed Fremantle as part of convoy MS5, composed of the US Army Transport *Willard A. Holbrook* and the Australian transports *Duntroon* and *Katoomba*, escorted by the light cruiser USS *Phoenix*. Three days later, Dutch Admiral Helfrich, now the ABDACOM chief of the Allied naval command, ordered *Phoenix* to detach *Langley* and *Seawitch* from the convoy and divert them directly to Java. *Langley* separated from the convoy late in the night of February 26, several hours ahead of *Seawitch* and rendezvoused with the destroyers USS *Whipple* (DD-217) and *Edsall* (DD-219).

While it would have been better for *Langley* to go to Batavia or Surabaya, where her planes could have been easily unloaded and moved to nearby airfields, both ports were now too dangerous due to enemy air attacks; thus, she was ordered to make for Tjilatjap. There was no flying field there, and lighters would have to be provided to move the planes ashore and ramps built for unloading them, while the streets were cleared to permit the P-40s to pass through the town. Many in Tjilatjap knew the date of her expected arrival, and Japanese intelligence agents quickly learned of this too. The Takao Kōkūtai, which had recently arrived on the island of Bali from Formosa, was ordered to find *Langley* and sink her.

The morning of February 27 was fair, with only a few high, scattered clouds and a light northeast wind. At 0800 hours two ML-KNIL Catalina flying boats arrived to provide escort. An hour later, an unidentified plane was sighted. Captain McConnell radioed a request for fighter escort. There were fewer than 15 fighters in all of Java, and none could be sent. *Langley's* remaining flight deck was too short to launch the P-40s she carried. At 1140 hours, *Edsall* reported "aircraft sighted." As *Langley* zig-zagged, nine G4M Betty bombers of the Takao Kōkūtai, led by Lieutenant Jiro Adachi, approached at about 15,000 feet. The nine bombers, and a second flight of seven, made three passes; on the first two they dropped partial bomb loads. *Langley* was able to evade the first two attacks, but the bombers changed their tactic on the third pass and the ship took five hits from a mix of 550- and 130-pound bombs in addition to three near misses. One hit forward, two hit the flight deck near the elevator, a fourth hit the port stack sponson, and a fifth penetrated the flight deck aft and set her afire. This one salvo was fatal.

Aircraft on the flight deck caught fire and there were fires below; the fire mains were broken. *Langley* listed 10 degrees to port, but her engines were running despite rising water. Captain McConnell maneuvered to obtain a zero wind and the fires were put out. The planes on deck were pushed overboard and McConnell ordered counterflooding in an attempt to correct the list. Water continued to rise in the engine room and her list increased.

When McConnell passed the order to prepare to abandon ship, his order was misunderstood and men began to jump overboard. The explosions had blown some off the ship and others had been forced to jump to escape the fire. Fortunately, the attackers withdrew to the east after their escorting Zeros attacked one of the Dutch flying boats.

At 1332 hours, Captain McDonnell gave the order to abandon ship. *Edsall* and *Whipple* skillfully picked up survivors with the result that there were only six killed and five missing. *Whipple* fired nine 4-inch shells and two torpedoes into *Langley* and the old carrier sank approximately 74 miles south of Tjilatjap.

The oiler USS *Pecos* (AO-6) had departed Tjilatjap for Ceylon that morning. That afternoon, she was ordered to proceed to Christmas Island and take on the *Langley* survivors from *Whipple* and *Edsall*.

Pecos arrived at Christmas Island the next morning. Just as a boat from *Whipple* with *Langley's* Lieutenant Commander Thomas A. Donovan aboard came alongside to arrange the transfer, three Japanese bombers appeared in the distance. *Pecos* and the two destroyers headed into a rain squall east of the island. The Japanese dropped six bombs that hit near the docks. Following this, it was decided to transfer the survivors at sea, which was accomplished the morning of March 1. *Whipple* and *Edsall* departed to join the remaining ships of ABDACOM and *Pecos* set course for Fremantle.

At about 1000 hours, *Pecos* was spotted by a Japanese search plane. At 1115 hours, six dive bombers from the carrier *Akagi* appeared overhead. They attacked, scoring three hits and *Pecos* took on an 8-degree list to port. A second wave of six arrived at 1210 hours and scored four hits and a damaging near miss. One hit blew out a section of hull 20 feet long above the waterline and started a fire; a second hit destroyed the radio antenna shortly after a distress call was sent; the list increased to 15 degrees, while the third hit destroyed two boilers and reduced the oiler's speed. After the attackers departed, a rumor spread that the order to abandon ship had been given; two boats and several life rafts were put over the side while several men jumped overboard before the error was corrected.

A third wave of nine planes attacked at about 1545 hours. No hits were scored but one of two near misses that exploded forward on the port side started the ship settling slowly. The attackers departed before *Pecos* finally plunged bow-first into the sea at 1548 hours. The abandon ship order had been passed at 1530 and the men went overboard with anything that floated.

Fortunately, *Whipple* had heard the distress call and she arrived on the scene at 2000 hours. Casualties were high; *Whipple* was able to pick up 220 survivors, 149 from *Langley* of a crew of 430, and 71 from *Pecos*, which had left Tjilatjap with 242 aboard. That wasn't all; *Edsall* was spotted by the Japanese fleet that had just successfully fought the Battle of the Java Sea the night before and was sunk with a loss of 31 of 33 pilots and 12 crew chiefs of the 13th Pursuit Squadron she had picked up following the sinking of *Langley*. All of the 32 P-40s were lost.

Seawitch was luckier, arriving at Tjilatjap unharmed, but too late, on the morning of February 28. The Japanese landed on Java the next day, so rather than assemble the crated planes, they destroyed them in their crates to prevent the enemy acquiring them when Tjilatjap was abandoned. Fifty-nine precious P-40s had been lost without inflicting any damage on the enemy, and the 32 dead pilots were a significant number of the fighter pilots still left in Southeast Asia.

While all this was happening, the 19th Bombardment Group also became involved in the Java battle.

On December 30, Major Walsh took off from Batchelor Field at 0800 hours, leading six B-17Ds and the sole surviving B-17C on an eight-hour flight covering 1,300 miles to the Dutch base at Singosari Airfield outside Malang, arriving at 1600 hours. The next day, three more B-17Ds arrived at 1730 hours.

The 19th Group was reinforced by the 7th Bomb Group, newly equipped with B-17Es. Getting reinforcements to Australia and the Dutch East Indies was difficult. Two air routes had been developed. The first was the Trans-Pacific Route, which stretched from Hamilton Field north of San Francisco to Australia. With the fall of Wake Island, the route now changed once the aircraft reached Hawaii. On January 6, Major Hobson, CO of the 22nd Bombardment Squadron of the 7th Group, led three B-17Es on the first leg of the new route. The bombers headed south-southwest to Christmas Island, 1,400 miles distant and only 50 miles north of the equator. The next stop was Canton Island, 1,500 miles to the southwest, a narrow ribbon of land around a lagoon with a total area of 40 square kilometers. One pilot later recalled, "Canton Island is a small coral strip in the Pacific, with one tree and one landing strip. The one tree had a lookout tower built around it so they could take advantage of the height of the tree looking for anybody who might be coming in unexpectedly." The island was also home to 23 bird species, including a large population of albatrosses, known colloquially as "gooney birds." The ground crews had to do their best to chase the nesting birds off the runway prior to each takeoff, after which the birds returned to claim ownership.

Nandi Field on the island of Veti Levu in the Fiji Islands was the next stop, 1,100 miles further southwest. From there, the aircraft pointed their noses south-southwest again to arrive at Tontouta Field on New Caledonia. There were no servicing facilities at the 5,000-foot strip, which meant aircraft had to be refueled by hand from 55-gallon drums using a hand pump, a process that took about four hours to accomplish per B-17. From there, the bombers flew on to Townsville in Queensland, Australia, then on to Darwin, where the three B-17s arrived on January 13. The next day, Major Hobson flew B-17E 41-2417 "Monkee Bizz-Ness" the 1,400 miles to Singosari. The bomber had flown 13,000 miles to get to its war.

Back at Hamilton Field, it was decided that the next reinforcement mission would fly to Java across what came to be known as "The Southern Ferry Route." Three Consolidated LB-30s, which were British "Liberator II" versions of the B-24 Liberator bomber that had been repossessed by the Air Corps before their delivery to Britain, would lead the way. This was the first part of what had originally been a plan to reinforce the Philippines, involving 15 LB-30s and 65 B-17Es.

The Southern Ferry Route took advantage of the short distance from Brazil to Africa across the South Pacific, which was a little more than one-third the distance from the US to Britain across the North Atlantic. It had been developed before the US entry into the war by Pan American Airways, with a series of airfields constructed in the Caribbean and across Amazonian Brazil. Once in West Africa, the route crossed sub-Saharan Central Africa before turning at Khartoum up the

Nile to Cairo. With the advent of war in the Far East, an additional route extending east from Cairo to Palestine and Iraq to India allowed aircraft to be delivered to the forces in Southeast Asia. Heading south to Sumatra, the end of the line was in Surabaya, Java. The three LB-30s arrived on January 11. The flight from Tampa, Florida via Africa to Java was just over 21,000 miles. The aircraft arrived in desperate need of overhaul after such a flight, but there was no time for such work.

On January 14, an hour after Major Hobson had arrived at Singosari Airdrome via the Pacific route, Major Conrad Necrason and Captain John "Duke" Dufrane, Jr. of the 7th Group's 9th Bomb Squadron touched down in B-17Es 41-2461 "El Toro" and 41-2459, having flown the African route. The next day, Captain Fred M. Key of the 19th Group's 30th Squadron that had remained in the United States when the rest of the group flew the Pacific to the Philippines and First Lieutenant Charles Hillhouse of the group's 32nd Squadron arrived via Africa. During the course of the next 30 days, the rest of the 19th Group's missing squadrons and all of the 7th Bomb Group would fly both routes around the world to Java. Despite the herculean effort, it was once again too little, too late.

B-17s were not the only reinforcements. The 22nd Bombardment Group (Medium) had been established on December 22, 1939 and activated on February 1, 1940, flying B-18s. In the summer of 1941, they moved to Langley Field outside Washington DC, where they received the first Martin B-26 Marauders to come off the production line.

The group was ordered to Savannah, Georgia in November, 1941, and were mobilized for operational service by the end of the day when they received word of the attack at Pearl Harbor. By the end of the month the unit was at Muroc Field in California, where they re-equipped with 44 brand new Marauders. In late January they flew to Hamilton Field, where they were partly dismantled and put aboard ship for transport to Hawaii. From there, the group's 18th Reconnaissance Squadron (Medium) was sent on to Australia, arriving in Brisbane on February 25, 1942. They moved to Townsville on April 7, and then to nearby Reid River on April 12. On April 22, the unit was redesignated the 408th Bombardment Squadron (Medium). A second squadron of the group, the 33rd Bombardment Squadron (Medium), arrived in mid-April, while the third squadron, the 19th Bomb Squadron, arrived at the end of the month. The 22nd Group was the first complete medium bomber group to reach Australia, and would be the only Pacific-based medium bomber unit to fly the Marauder in combat.

The 408th Squadron flew the Marauder's first combat mission of the war on April 5, 1942, a mission to Rabaul by six bombers that flew from Townsville to Port Moresby. The group flew several other Rabaul missions in April and May, with their last happening on May 27. A Rabaul mission took three days to complete. On the first day, the bombers flew from their main base at Townsville in Queensland to Seven Mile 'Drome, which was named for the fact it was 7 miles outside Port Moresby, where the crews refueled the planes by hand from 55-gallon drums. The second day saw the Marauders fly the mission to Rabaul on New Britain, across the Bismarck Sea from New Guinea, without fighter escort. On the third day, they would refuel at Seven Mile 'Drome and return to Townsville. Losses on these daylight raids averaged one plane per mission, an unsustainable 17 percent loss. Weather in the area of the equator where these missions were flown was unpredictable, with the planes frequently flying through massive tropical thunderstorms to get to the target.

Following the Japanese occupation of Lae and Salamaua on the northern coast of New Guinea in March 1942, the 22nd Group's Marauders were among the first US aircraft to fly missions against the bases beginning in April; the Marauders flew low-level unescorted daylight attacks on the two Japanese bases. Saburo Sakai, who by then was based at Lae, recalled that the Marauders were fast and hard to catch, but easily set afire. He admired the crews for their bravery in flying missions where they had no fighter escort.

On March 6, 1942, the 8th Pursuit Group, composed of the 35th, 36th, and 80th pursuit squadrons, arrived in Brisbane. Due to congestion in Brisbane and Sydney harbors, the ships carrying the group's 48 Bell P-39D Airacobras were sent to Adelaide to unload. Once reassembled the fighters were flown to Brisbane, and the new group, who called themselves "Cyclone's Flying Circus" in honor of their commander, Captain Emmett "Cyclone" Davis, assumed responsibility for the air defense of Brisbane while they underwent further training. Among the pilots assigned to the 36th Squadron was brand-new Captain George Welch, the hero of Pearl Harbor. Despite the fact the RAF had turned down the Airacobra in October 1941 after flying four missions with the aircraft and sent it on to the Soviets, the Airacobra was the only other modern fighter in the USAAF inventory besides the P-40E Warhawk; great things were expected of the airplane.

The 35th Pursuit Group departed San Francisco as a skeleton organization on January 31, 1942 aboard the US Army Transport *Ancon* and arrived in Brisbane on February 25, 1942. Second Lieutenant Teddy W. Hanks of the 40th Pursuit Squadron later recalled his memories of arriving in Brisbane:

> After our arrival at Brisbane, we were immediately trucked to Ascot Race Track. I vividly remember the week we spent there. Our tents were small, white and low to the ground; too low to stand erect. Our first meal was curry, prepared by Aussie army cooks. Fortunately, we soon found outside sources of more appetizing food such as fresh pineapple, solid chocolate candy from Tasmania and other goodies.

Still low on personnel and without aircraft, the unit sailed from Brisbane on March 4, arriving in Melbourne four days later, where they were then taken to be billeted in civilian homes at Ballarat until they left for Mount Gambier, South Australia, on March 16. Here, more pilots arrived and the 39th and 40th squadrons received their new P-400 Airacobras. The three squadrons had been among the first in the Air Corps to fly the P-39 when it first appeared in late 1940. The "P-400" was the export version of the P-39 and had been built for the RAF, with the 37mm cannon replaced by a 20mm weapon. When the RAF found the aircraft did not live up to Bell's claims and the service's expectations, the remaining Airacobra Is at the Bell factory were taken over by the USAAF since they were immediately available; most ended up in the South Pacific.

The 100 P-400s the 35th Pursuit Group took on had been originally intended for delivery to the Philippines by the *Pensacola* convoy, but after the convoy was diverted to Australia the aircraft were assembled at Amberley Airfield west of Brisbane. The new pilots who arrived in late April and early May were all recent flight school graduates with virtually no training or experience in fighters. All three squadrons were forced to institute advanced training for the new pilots, with a busy flight schedule since the group expected to be sent into combat soon.

Both the 8th and 35th groups were designated as "interceptor," because of the Airacobra's heavy armament of a 37mm cannon and two

.50-caliber machine guns in the nose, as well as its high rate of climb to 12,000 feet. In the event, the units would never fly in the interceptor role, being sent on to Port Moresby in June, where they were badly outclassed by the Japanese fighters that opposed them.

Most of the 52 Douglas A-24A Banshee dive bombers that had arrived in Australia in the Pensacola convoy were found to be in poor condition due to previous use in training in the United States and were missing various parts, including solenoids, trigger motors, and gun mounts. The reconditioned A-24s were issued to the 16th, 17th, and 91st bombardment squadrons that were formed in Australia in preparation for the defense of Java. Fifteen A-24s from the 91st set out for Java in early February, though only seven were combat worthy by the time of their arrival at Surabaya. The seven A-24As fought against the odds. Referring to themselves as "Blue Rock Clay Pigeons," the crews attacked Bali and damaged or sank several ships. By the time the Japanese invaded Java, two of the bombers had been shot down and three others damaged so badly they could not be used. The 91st was evacuated from Java in early March. The small number of aircraft with their limited operational range and the lack of crew training for the dive-bomber role had kept the bombers from living up to expectations.

Back in Australia, the remaining Banshees were issued to the 8th Bombardment Squadron of the 3rd Bombardment Group (Light). The squadron was sent to New Guinea in June 1942. On July 26, seven A-24s attacked a Japanese convoy off Buna, but the enemy shot down five and damaged the sixth so badly it crashed on the return flight. The Banshees were regarded by their crews as too slow, too short-ranged, and poorly armed. Following this disastrous mission, the remaining A-24s in Australia were assigned to non-combat missions.

Throughout the first six months of the war, the USAAF battled distance and weather more than the enemy itself in the effort to hold the line against further Japanese advance. By the summer of 1942, sufficient force had been gathered to change over from a strict strategy of defense to more offensive operations.

CHAPTER TEN

THE TIGERS OF BURMA

While the Buffalos of 67 Squadron were solely responsible for the defense of Rangoon following their arrival three months before the outbreak of war, they were joined a few days before the Japanese attack by a strange aerial unit that had been training throughout the fall at Kyedaw Airdrome in the Burmese up-country. The unit was officially known as the 3rd Squadron of the American Volunteer Group of the Republic of China Air Force. Unofficially, the American pilots called themselves "The Hell's Angels."

The pilots were all former fliers in the US Army Air Corps, the Navy, and the Marine Corps. One of the ex-Marines was 24-year-old Charles Older, a third-generation native Angeleno who joined the Navy Aviation Cadet program in 1939 following his graduation from UCLA, and was commissioned a second lieutenant in the Marine Corps in 1940. After winning his wings at Pensacola, he was assigned to VMF-1, based at Quantico, Virginia, flying the Grumman F3F-2; to his disgust, squadron pilots were graded more on their ability to fly a "parade ground" formation than on any combat skills. In early 1941, the squadron re-equipped with the new Grumman F4F-3 Wildcat. While flying his Wildcat back to Quantico from the Grumman factory on Long Island, Older first met the P-40. "One of the squadrons from Mitchell Field was up, and two of them decided to jump me. The P-40 struck me as quite an airplane, since it was faster and more maneuverable than what I was flying."

A few weeks later, Older learned recruiters were looking for fighter pilots to fly combat in China. He and squadron-mate Ken Jernstedt took a weekend trip to New York City and paid a visit to the recruiting agency. "They told us President Roosevelt had authorized reserve officers to resign their commissions and take a position with the CAMCO [Central Aircraft Manufacturing Company] corporation for service in China." The next week, the two young lieutenants submitted their resignations to their commanding officer. "He said no. We appealed his refusal, and he was very surprised when it came back from the Secretary of the Navy, approved."

Once accepted, the pilots found their leader was former Army Air Corps Major Claire A. Chennault, a fighter pilot's fighter pilot who had been the leading advocate of fighter aviation in the Air Corps. He had resigned his commission in the late 1930s and taken a position as air advisor to Generalissimo Chiang Kai-Shek, leader of the Republic of China, who had been at war with Japan since 1932. In early 1941, Chennault convinced Chiang, who in turn convinced Roosevelt, that a volunteer group of American pilots trained by Chennault in what he considered "proper tactics" could help change the nature of the war in China. In April, President Roosevelt signed an unpublicized executive order authorizing recruitment of enlisted men and reserve officers on duty with the US armed forces; the British released 100 Lend-Lease Curtiss H-87-A2 "Tomahawks" for transfer to China.

With US–Japanese relations in a delicate position, the recruiting officers had to offer contracts that were "legally consistent" with official US policy. While the operation had the unofficial blessing of the government, it was officially organized by the Central Aircraft Manufacturing Company (CAMCO), run by Edward D. Pawley; he was later described by *Life* magazine as "always able to be at the right place a few minutes before the right time." The contracts the men signed made no mention of the true nature of their service, stating that the signatories were hired to "manufacture, repair and operate aircraft."

The original plan included three groups: two fighter groups and one bomber group. The first group was equipped with Curtiss P-40s, while the next would be equipped with Seversky P-43s; the third was to be equipped with Lockheed Hudsons as a bomber group. The Japanese attack on Pearl Harbor forced the cancelation of the second and third groups.

Along with 100 other pilots and 150 ground personnel, Older boarded the Dutch passenger liner *Jagersfontein* on July 7, 1941, for the trip to the Far East. One of the other pilots, former Army Air Corps pilot Erik Shilling, recalled that he realized shortly after the ship was at sea that there was more going on than they had been told.

In fact, we were an official undercover operation of the American government. We were not mercenaries, though that cover story was so good everyone believed it afterwards. We were escorted to the vicinity of Australia by two US Navy heavy cruisers, the USS *Salt Lake City* and the *Northampton*, because there was a real fear the Japanese had heard about the operation and would attempt to intercept us.

Once arrived at Kyedaw, the training base the British provided for the AVG north of Rangoon, Older, Shilling, and the others were introduced to the P-40 and Claire Chennault's ideas of how to fight the Japanese. Older liked the tactics Chennault taught. "The P-40 was a heavier fighter than the others, and it could dive faster than anything else around at the time. Staying in the vertical plane, using dive and zoom tactics against an enemy whose best performance was in the horizontal plane, made perfect sense to me."

During training that fall, three squadrons were organized: the "Adam and Eves" (the 1st Pursuit Squadron), the "Pandas," and the "Hell's Angels." There were no ranks, though "squadron leaders" and "flight leaders" were named from the more experienced pilots and a military-style organization was followed. Erik Shilling ended up creating the insignia that would forever be linked with the AVG. Forty years later, he recalled:

It's always been said that the tiger mouth came about after we saw a picture of a P-40 being flown by 112 Squadron of the RAF in North Africa. That's not true. I was looking through a British magazine one day and saw a photo of a Me-110 with a shark face on it. They were the *Haifisch Gruppe*. I thought it looked perfect for our squadron insignia.

Shilling chalked a sharkmouth on his P-40 and thought it looked right for the airplane's sharp-nosed shape. When he asked Chennault for permission to use it as a squadron marking, the commander saw it as the group marking. Shilling ended up chalking the sharkmouth on all of the P-40s at Kyedaw before they were painted. "That's why there were no two of them with the same mouth." When Chennault was informed of the possibility of pending war, only the "Hell's Angels" airplanes had their machine guns boresighted. The "Adam and Eves" and the "Pandas" flew to Kunming, China, to complete equipping. The "Hell's Angels" took their airplanes to Mingaladon Airdrome, north of Rangoon, on December 3, 1941.

Following the news of the outbreak of war on December 8, and with air battles raging over Malaya, the Allied force in Rangoon wondered when the Japanese would strike. Among those waiting was former USAAC 57th Pursuit Group armorer Staff Sergeant Charles E. "Chuck" Baisden, who had been among the most experienced P-40 ground crew in the Air Corps when the CAMCO recruiters arrived at Mitchell Field in late April, 1941. They hadn't had to work hard to get Baisden.

> I had just turned 21, I was making $72 a month as a Staff Sergeant, and these guys were offering $350 a month to do the same job. That was more money than the Group CO made! I saw this as an opportunity to travel and work at my trade. There's guys who say they joined for patriotism, and I'm sure there were since anybody who could read could see things were getting worse with the Japanese, but the truth is most of us were a bunch of adventurous kids who saw a chance to make good money and see the world.

When Baisden and the other crewmen had arrived in Rangoon back in July, they discovered life in the tropics was not what they'd been led to believe. "The P-40s were already there in crates when we arrived." With construction of the Burma Road to Kunming on hold till the end of the monsoon season, which prevented the group's move to China, Chennault managed to obtain British approval to use a jungle base at Kyedaw, just outside Toungoo, a jungle outpost 170 miles north of Rangoon where the Americans were unlikely to attract unwanted attention. Baisden and the other ground crewmen arrived in August.

> I've been in worse places since, but Toungoo at the time was the absolutely worst place I'd ever been. It was in the middle of the jungle, and hot and wet and dirty. There were the biggest bugs I'd ever seen in my life everywhere, in your mattress, in the ceilings, they'd even end up in your food.

The one thing Kyedaw had going for it was a paved runway that allowed operations even during the monsoon.

"Our first job was to get the airplanes assembled, and everyone worked on that. We had no tools or forklifts. We used an A-frame to raise a fuselage and a wing would be walked into position. They'd bolt the wing on and lower the gear, then push it out." With his experience on the P-36 and P-40, Baisden became a senior armorer in the squadron, officially a technical officer, responsible for installing and boresighting the guns.

In November, Technical Officer Baisden was given a truck and driver and ordered to drive to Maymo, where the British had 55,000 rounds of .30-caliber ammunition in a warehouse. After a daylong drive, they arrived in Maymo and loaded the ammo. Driving back the next day, they stopped at noon to get gas and food. "A Burmese policeman stopped us. He'd been chasing us all morning to protect us, since there was already a lot of robbery going on in the back country." Baisden arrived with enough ammunition for the Hell's Angels to go to war.

During the training days at Kyedaw, Erik Shilling, who had been involved in Army Air Corps long-range photo reconnaissance experiments before joining the AVG, convinced Chennault to let him modify his airplane with a Fairchild F-24 camera mounted behind the cockpit in the baggage compartment to give the AVG an air reconnaissance capability. He reduced the plane's armament by removing the four .30-caliber wing guns to save weight and improve performance so that he might outrun any interception. On the morning of December 10, it was time to put the new capability to use.

Shilling, escorted by AVG Group intelligence officer Allen Christman and future ace Ed Rector, departed Toungoo before dawn, dropping into the British base at Mingaladon Airdrome at first light to refuel, then stopping one last time to top off at Tavoy Airdrome, on the Burmese–Thai border, so they could fly to Bangkok and return directly to Toungoo. Japanese intelligence had discovered the mission; 20 minutes after the trio left Tavoy, Japanese fighters arrived and strafed everything in sight.

Shilling left Christman and Rector behind when they reached a point 20 miles west of Bangkok and climbed to 26,000 feet, where the sound of his engine would be inaudible to anyone on the ground. Minutes later, he flew over Don Muang Airport outside Bangkok and photographed the 48 Mitsubishi Ki-21 bombers of the 60th, 62nd, and 98th sentais.

After making that pass, he photographed two other airfields and then the Bangkok docks before turning back to the west to rendezvous with his escorts. Back at Toungoo, his developed film revealed 90 aircraft – 50 bombers and 40 fighters – ready to strike Rangoon.

The Japanese Fifteenth Army was ready to begin the invasion of Burma by mid-December, but first the Allied air forces in Rangoon had to be destroyed. The air war over Burma began on December 23, 1941.

Charles Older remembered his first combat with more clarity than any other mission:

> Ed Overend and I had been waiting to see if the Japs were coming that morning. When they didn't, we decided to bicycle into Rangoon. Just as we got to the front gate, we heard the sirens go off. When we got back to the squadron, everyone had already taken off, but we found two P-40s still there. We got them started and took off. We didn't know where the others had gone, didn't have any idea where the enemy was, but we headed southeast after we flew over the city, since we figured that was most likely.

Headed their way were 40 Ki-21 "Sally" twin-engine bombers, escorted by 12 Ki-27 fighters. They arrived 40 minutes after the first warning. The 62nd Sentai, led by Lieutenant Colonel Hiroshi Onishi, headed for Mingaladon Airdrome, followed at some distance by the slower Ki-30 "Ann" single-engine bombers of the 31st Sentai, led by Lieutenant Colonel Junji Hayashi. The 12 Ki-27s of the 77th Sentai were led by Major Hiroshi Yoshioka. The Ki-21s of the 60th Sentai, led by Colonel Kojiro Ogawa, and 98th Sentai, led by Colonel Shigeki Usui, headed toward Rangoon separately.

Older recalled, "We finally spotted the others ahead of us and higher. At about the same time, we saw the Japanese bombers heading for the city, and they were just about at our altitude. The others attacked and we didn't think we had time to climb higher, so we just poured the coals to our planes and went at them."

The pair each exploded a Ki-21 on their first pass.

> What I should have done then was dive to gain speed, then zoomed back up for another pass. But in the heat of battle you don't always remember orders. We turned and made another pass at them at their

own level, but this time the gunners were ready for us, and they let us have it good. As the tracers were flying past, I realized this wasn't how we were supposed to do it, so we both dived away and then zoomed back above.

As Older and Overend positioned themselves for a second attack, a Japanese gunner took aim at the P-40 flown by Hank Gilbert, who at 21 was the youngest AVG pilot, and exploded the airplane, killing Gilbert. While that happened, Older attacked and claimed another Ki-21. At this point, the battle broke up in confusion.

The conclusion of the first fight in the Battle of Rangoon saw the Hell's Angels claim six bombers and four fighters, though only six bombers were actually shot down and the 77th Sentai's Ki-27s suffered no loss. All the 98th Sentai's bombers returned damaged, with many aircrew casualties as well as the loss of their commander. The 60th and 62nd Sentais lost six Ki-27s between them. The 67 Squadron Buffalo pilots also claimed six, with four "probables." Actually, Flying Officer John Lamber and Flight Sergeant Vic Bargh each shot down a Ki-21. The Americans lost three P-40s and two pilots, while the RAF squadron lost four Buffalos with their pilots. With a few more such "victories," the defenders of Rangoon would be decimated.

The Japanese, stung by the unexpected resistance, called on the 3rd Joint Air Group in Malaya for help. The wait for reinforcement meant they did not return for two days, which gave the defenders time to ready themselves.

On Christmas Day, 71 Ki-21 bombers were escorted by 25 Ki-43 *Hayabusas* of Major Takeo Kato's 64th Sentai that had flown to Thailand from Khota Bharu in Malaya, along with 15 Ki-27s from Major Yoshioka's 77th Sentai. The first wave comprised 20 Ki-21s from the newly arrived 12th Sentai led by Major Yoshikuma Oura, while Colonel Kumano Kitajima led the second wave of seven 12th Sentai Ki-21s escorted by Major Kato leading ten Ki-43s. Colonel Ogawa led 36 Ki-21s from the 60th Sentai in the third wave; in the event, they outdistanced their escort and attacked without fighter cover.

Older recalled:

We had noticed the first time that the bombers sped up as they headed into their runs, and the escort fell behind at that moment.

We decided we would hit the escorts first and break them up, so they couldn't catch up to the bombers and defend them. We would hit them in a dive, then use our speed to catch the bombers.

The Japanese force flew out over the ocean, then turned so they would be headed for home when they finished their bomb runs. Only 12 P-40s and 18 Buffalos were able to take off, but with the extra time the enemy took flying around the city, they managed to climb to 18,000 feet.

We dove just about vertically on the fighters. I hit one that exploded, and went on through the formation. We used our speed to catch up to the bombers, then zoomed up and dove on them. I got one bomber on each of two runs. I was pulling out of my second attack when I saw another Jap fighter and exploded him.

With these four victories atop the two scored on December 23, Second Lieutenant Charles H. Older, Jr. became the Hell's Angels' first ace.

The Christmas Day battle saw the Hell's Angels officially credited with 28 victories, while at least eight more Japanese aircraft crashed on the way home from damage suffered in the attacks; the RAF claimed seven. The Japanese admitted "heavy losses," which amounted to five Ki-21s of the 12th Sentai, three of which were brought down over the city while the other two crashed returning to base due to damage, as well as two Ki-43s and three Ki-27s. The Japanese claimed 17 defenders shot down by fighters and 19 by bomber gunners. Five Buffalos and two P-40s were lost in combat, though their pilots were saved, while Parker Dupouy's P-40 was damaged beyond repair, though he made it back to Mingaladon; eight Buffalos on the field were destroyed by bombing. That night, United Press correspondent Charles McGrath first used the name "Flying Tigers" in his report of the battle filed the following day and published throughout the United States on December 27, 1941.

The tactic of gaining height, then diving through the enemy formation and refusing to enter combat with more maneuverable opponents on their own terms had been proven. However, the RAF Air Officer Commanding in Rangoon, Air Marshal Donald "Butcher" Stevenson, who had gained his sobriquet from his sacrifice of Blenheim crews on mostly unsuccessful antishipping strikes in the English Channel during the year before he was posted to the Far East in October 1941, refused to recognize the soundness of the strategy and declared that any RAF pilot seen "diving away from the enemy" would face court-martial for "lack of moral fibre." By mid-February 1942, 67 Squadron had suffered such losses that it was withdrawn to India. Older recalled, "the Buffalo was even heavier than the P-40, and it had a heavier armament, so the diving attack would have been even more successful for them than it was for us. That British air marshal was a fool."

The day after the Hell's Angels became "The Flying Tigers," the Japanese returned, determined to destroy the Rangoon defenders. Flight Leader Dupouy had six P-40s available, while 67 Squadron's A Flight, led by Flight Lieutenant Colin Pinckney, had eight Buffalos and Flight Lieutenant Jack Brandt's B Flight had six.

The attackers had 35 bombers escorted by 32 fighters. They sent a small force of eight Ki-21s from the 62nd Sentai led by Lieutenant Colonel Hiroshi Onishi toward Rangoon as a diversion. The Tigers and their RAF allies scrambled, but the Japanese turned and ran when the Allied fighters approached. They pursued the Japanese until they were forced to return to base. While the P-40s and Buffalos were being refueled, the main Japanese force was spotted inbound. This second wave comprised 27 Ki-30 "Ann" single-engine bombers of the 31st Sentai led by Lieutenant Colonel Hayashi, escorted by 32 Ki-27s of the 77th Sentai led by Major Yoshioka.

Only four P-40s were able to scramble alongside 12 Buffalos, but the defenders were unable to stop the attackers. Armorer Baisden remembered the raid well:

I was working on R.T. Smith's airplane when the sirens went off. I looked up and they were on their bomb run! We ran for the trenches and I jumped in just in time to see them pass over. I saw the bombs come down. I was so scared I couldn't take my eyes off them. Somebody whacked me and I dropped down just before the first one exploded.

With no antiaircraft defense, the Ki-30s systematically attacked the helpless aircraft, hangars, workshops, and fuel storage tanks, leaving the Tigers and their RAF allies a battered force with half their aircraft destroyed. "It seemed forever before they flew off. Everything was blown to hell. We spent the night putting planes back together."

The exploits of the "Hell's Angels" squadron over Rangoon had provided the only good war news to be found in an American newspaper during the first month of the war, with the result that the Flying Tigers rapidly achieved a legendary status in US military history.

The "Hell's Angels" flew north to the AVG base at Kunming in southern China after 18 "Panda Bears" P-40s of Jack Newkirk's 2nd Squadron relieved them at Rangoon two days after the devastating attack on Mingaladon, on December 30. On January 3, 1942, Squadron Leader Newkirk, along with Tex Hill, James O. Howard and Bert Christman, took off before dawn to attack the Japanese airfield at Tak in Thailand. Christman was forced to turn back with a bad engine, while the other three circled around the Japanese base to attack from the east with the rising sun at their backs. There was a crowd on the field to welcome the return of the 77th Sentai's Ki-27s from an attack on Moulmein when the three Tigers appeared overhead.

Tex Hill spotted three Ki-27s on the ground with three others in the landing pattern. Suddenly he realized the American formation had grown – three enemy fighters were close astern, and one had already opened fire on Howard as he took aim at the planes on the ground. Hill banked behind the Ki-27 shooting at Howard and exploded it with a well-aimed burst from his .50-caliber guns, then turned on a second and opened fire on it just after Newkirk did so, the squadron leader having just shot down the leader. Suddenly, Hill felt his plane vibrate as he took hits from yet another enemy fighter that had latched onto his tail. He later recalled, "If those guys had .50-caliber guns, I'd have gone down for sure." He turned and the two planes headed for each other. A lucky hit nicked a propeller blade, knocking it out of balance, and the P-40 began vibrating so badly Hill thought it would go down.

Howard completed his strafing run and came around again. He opened fire, but at that moment he was hit by enemy ground fire and his engine stopped! He pulled up to try to glide away from the field before baling out, but suddenly the Allison sprang to life; he turned and fled west, not knowing how far the damaged engine might take him.

As it turned out, all three were able to make it back to Rangoon, where they claimed four Ki-27s shot down and three destroyed on the ground. Hill's plane had 33 bullet holes in it, while Howard counted 11 in his. The Japanese admitted a loss of two.

On January 8, Newkirk led another strafing mission at sunset to Tak, leading seven P-40s and six 67 Squadron Buffalos. The attackers divided themselves into three flights: Newkirk's foursome attacked out of the sun from the west while the second AVG flight came in from the southwest and the RAF fighters struck from the northwest. Newkirk hit one Ki-27 during his pass and set a truck afire that slammed into the burning fighter, causing both to explode. Behind him, John Petach spotted an antiaircraft emplacement and knocked it out. Landing back at Mingaladon at 1830 hours, they claimed three planes destroyed, though the Japanese only recorded the one Ki-27 and the truck destroyed.

After the Bangkok mission, Erik Shilling's adventures were far from over. In late January, he led a flight of three Curtiss-Wright CW-21 "Demons" from Chungking to Kunming. In heavy weather, he suffered engine failure and crashed in the mountainous jungle, while one of the others flew into a mountainside and was killed.

Shilling climbed out of the wreck and was immediately surrounded by tribal villagers who had seen the crash. "I'm an American," he explained. It meant nothing to these people, who in the middle of the 20th century were unaware there was a white race. All they knew was their country was at war with the Japanese, who flew in metal birds, and that this man who flew a metal bird was not Chinese. As far as they were concerned, this was proof he was Japanese and they treated him accordingly. Shilling was imprisoned in a hole, from which it was made clear to him he would not leave alive. However, his luck held when a Chinese Army patrol happened along a few days later. "The boys in Kunming were very surprised when the Chinese brought me in," he recalled. "They'd already listed me as dead." Shilling's experience prompted the group to sew the famous "blood chit" on the back of their flight jackets; it was a branding to ensure indigenous people in the remote areas over which they flew and fought would know an American when they found one, and know they would be well-rewarded for helping him.

On January 20, the Americans escorted six RAF Blenheims on a mission to bomb Mae Sot in Thailand. Newkirk led six P-40s, three "Panda Bears," and three others from the newly arrived "Adam and Eve" 1st Squadron. Just before they got to the target, they ran across a formation of Ki-27s. In the ensuing battle, Newkirk shot down two to run his aerial score to five, while future leading AVG ace Bob Neale scored his first victory. The Blenheims bombed the target in a shallow dive and set several buildings on fire. They all returned without loss.

The Japanese struck again at Mingaladon on January 23. Eight P-40s and three Buffalos took off to intercept the raiders. The Ki-30s were separated from their escort in the poor weather when the defenders first found them. They hit the bombers from all sides and three went down before the fighter escort arrived. In the battle, Newkirk evaded two Ki-27s by diving away, then climbed back and caught one of them. "After one burst his wing came off and he went down. Another bunch of fighters had been shooting at me while I fired on that one. My engine cut out and heated up and lost power, so I returned to the field, where I crashed due to the fact that my flaps would not come down." Bert Christman's P-40 was shot up and he had to bale out. He was strafed in his parachute and hit in the neck. The Japanese claimed seven, while the Allies lost only a Buffalo and the two P-40s. The Americans claimed 11 shot down while the RAF claimed one. The Japanese reported one Ki-30 shot down and ten more damaged.

Reporting on another fight that happened on January 28, Newkirk wrote:

> The planes that we have here now are beginning to look like patchwork quilts for the holes in them. The engines are also getting tired. There are not sufficient ground crews for the job and there is not enough time for them to teach the Chinese or other helpers which they steal from our neighbors, the RAF. I am firmly convinced that the AVG does not need anything from the army or any other organization, as far as we are concerned.

The Japanese Army began their advance into Burma on January 12, 1942. By the end of February, they were 20 miles from Mingaladon, and Chennault ordered the AVG to evacuate. They moved north to Magwe with the survivors of the 1st and 2nd squadrons, where they were able to hold out until early March. By then, there were only 20 P-40s left. Following Bill Reed's and Ken Jernstedt's attack on Moulmein on March 19, Magwe was hit by Japanese attacks from March 21 to 28. On March 29, Chuck Baisden was assigned to drive a truck filled with salvaged gear. "I drove that truck from Magwe to Kunming over the

Burma Road, which was every bit as difficult and dangerous as history says it was."

While Baisden and the others tempted fate on the Burma Road, Shilling, Charles Older, and four others were ordered to pick up six new P-40Es for replacements – in Africa! Older remembered, "In early April, a Chinese airliner took us over the Hump and on to Bombay, where we caught a British flying boat that got us to Cairo, and then an Army Air Forces C-47 crew flew us across to Accra." After checking out the USAAF fighters, the six pilots set off on an odyssey back to China, flying across Africa to Khartoum and then on to Cairo. Older recalled "We managed to keep company with the same C-47 that brought us across Africa." From Cairo, they flew to Jerusalem, then Baghdad, across the desert to Karachi, and on to Bombay, then across India to Assam, where they took the six fighters over the Himalayas to Chungking. They arrived at about the same time Baisden and the rest of the ground unit made it up the Burma Road to Kunming in late April.

The epic tale of the Flying Tigers was nearing its end. As Baisden remembered, "The monsoon came in early May, which stopped the Japs just as they'd gotten strong enough to wipe us out." The group was officially taken into the Army Air Forces on July 4, 1942, though only five of the pilots, including Tex Hill, elected to remain in China and continue flying in the new 23rd Fighter Group. Several of the others, including Erik Shilling, remained in China for the rest of the war, flying C-47s for the China National Airways Corporation on flights over the Himalayas, known as "The Hump," to bring supplies to China. Charles Older and James O. Howard returned to the United States, where former naval aviator Howard joined the USAAF and was assigned to the 354th Fighter Group, with whom he would see combat in Europe as the first unit to fly the P-51 Mustang. Former Marine Older also joined the USAAF and returned to China in late 1944 to be executive officer of the 23rd Fighter Group, by then led by Tex Hill. R.T. Smith returned to Southeast Asia in 1944 as executive officer of the 1st Air Commando Group led by the legendary Colonel Phil Cochran. Armorer Baisden, by then a USAAF Master Sergeant, returned with his friend and flew as flight engineer and top turret gunner in Smith's B-25H, "Barbie III."

CHAPTER ELEVEN

THE GREAT ESCAPE

In the United States, in the spring of 1942, MacArthur was seen as "The Hero of Bataan" in the American press. This was because there were few independent American correspondents in the Philippines, which meant that most reports printed in the newspapers were rewrites of the press releases coming from MacArthur's headquarters. It had been a joke in the prewar Army that half the personnel in MacArthur's headquarters were devoted to public relations – a situation that would continue throughout the war and after, up until MacArthur was ultimately fired by President Truman in 1951. The only name in the press releases was the general's.

On February 11, MacArthur informed President Roosevelt that he intended to "share the fate of the garrison" with his family. With MacArthur's public star as hot as it was with the political opposition in Washington, it was considered politically inexpedient that the general be left in the Philippines to surrender to the Japanese, especially after the fall of Singapore four days later. Brigadier General Dwight D. Eisenhower, now chief of the Army War Plans Division who had served as MacArthur's chief of staff in the Philippines during the 1930s, wrote in his diary: "I cannot help thinking that we are disturbed by editorials and reacting to 'public opinion' rather than to military logic… Bataan is made to order for him. It's in the public eye; it has made him a hero; it has all the essentials of drama." He continued his entry presciently: "If brought out, public opinion will force him into a position where his love of the limelight may ruin him."

On February 23, MacArthur received the order to leave the Philippines, which had been drafted by the President, Secretary of War Henry L. Stimson, and General Marshall. It read: "The President directs that you make arrangements to leave and proceed to Mindanao. You are directed to make this change as quickly as possible… From Mindanao you will proceed to Australia where you will assume command of all United States troops… You are authorized to take your chief of staff General Sutherland."

On March 1, MacArthur and his wife visited Motor Torpedo Boat Squadron 3, and took a ride on PT-41, commanded by Lieutenant John D. Bulkeley, who also commanded the squadron. The general informed Bulkeley that he wanted to travel the 580 miles to Mindanao aboard MTBRon 3's PT boats. Bulkeley remembered that he responded with the suggestion that it would be safer for MacArthur and his party to escape via submarine. MacArthur, who had a lifelong flair for the dramatic act, told the young lieutenant that the Japanese wouldn't be expecting him to escape aboard the torpedo boats. Lieutenant Robert D. Kelley, the squadron executive officer, later remembered, "MacArthur's decision to use the PT boats for the evacuation of his party dramatically emphasized to the American public the overwhelming odds against which the United States was fighting in the Philippines."

Bulkeley was forced to leave behind 32 of the squadron's crewmen, who were sent to Bataan as infantry, to make room for MacArthur's party aboard the four boats. MacArthur took his long-serving staff with him, including chief of staff Major General Richard K. Sutherland, Brigadier General Spencer B. Akin, Brigadier General Hugh J. Casey, Brigadier General William F. Marquat, Brigadier General Harold H. George, Brigadier General Richard J. Marshall, Colonel Charles P. Stivers, Colonel Charles A. Willoughby, Colonel Allison Ind, Lieutenant Colonel Joe R. Sherr, Lieutenant Colonel LeGrande A. Diller, Lieutenant Colonel Francis H. Wilson, Lieutenant Colonel Sidney L. Huff, Major Curtis L. Lambert, Major Charles H. Morhouse, and Captain Joseph McMicking. These men would serve MacArthur until 1951, when he was fired as UN Supreme Commander in Korea by President Truman. They would become known throughout the Army with contempt as "the Bataan Gang," primarily perceived as the general's sycophants.

PT-41, carrying MacArthur, pulled out of Corregidor at 1945 hours the night of March 11, 1942. The other three departed from Bataan and the formation joined together at 2000 hours. MacArthur later recalled:

> The weather deteriorated steadily, and towering waves buffeted our tiny, war-weary, blacked-out vessels. The spray drove against our skin like stinging pellets of birdshot. We would fall into a trough, then climb up the steep water peak, only to slide down the other side. The boat would toss crazily back and forth, seeming to hang free in space as though about to breach, and would then break away and go forward with a rush. I recall describing the experience afterward as what it must be like to take a trip in a concrete mixer.

The four boats hid during the daylight hours of May 12. Lieutenant Kelly recalled the voyage the night of March 12–13:

> Big foaming waves 15 or 20 feet high thundered over the cockpit, drenching everybody. Our binoculars were full of water and our eyes so continuously drenched with stinging salt that we couldn't see, in addition to which it was pitch-black. We were making good speed through strange waters with islands all around us. We could see the outlines of the big ones – Negros and Mindanao – very dimly against the horizon through the storm. But there were dozens of small ones and probably hundreds of reefs. You had to keep one hand in front of your eyes to avoid the slapping force of the water and yet you needed both to hold on.

Bulkeley spotted what was identified as a Japanese cruiser and managed to outrun it. Having been slowed by the heavy seas, the boats crossed the Mindanao Sea by daylight on March 13. Intelligence chief Charles A. Willoughby recalled:

> We were behind schedule and reached the north coast of Mindanao in broad daylight. It was a clear, dazzling day. Fortunately, no Japanese planes cut across the blue sky, though the enemy was known to make regular flights from Mindanao to Luzon. We were pretty conspicuous as the hours dragged on.

On March 11, three war-weary B-17Es and their crews from the 19th Bomb Group and one from the 7th Group were sent from Melbourne, where they had evacuated after escaping from Java, to Batchelor Field outside Darwin. Captain Godman, who led the mission, recalled that they were given no idea what they would be doing other than "a mission to the north." He also remembered that "The airplanes were in really terrible shape." Once at Batchelor, they learned the mission involved flying supplies to Del Monte Airfield on Mindanao, and returning with General MacArthur and his staff. The four planes took off shortly after noon on March 12, intending to reach Del Monte after dark. Lieutenant Casper's 7th Group airplane developed engine trouble and did not attempt takeoff. Captain Adams in the 19th Group's "Lady Lee" lost an engine 30 minutes after takeoff and aborted the mission. Godman and Lieutenant Harl Pease continued individually. Pease's B-17 lost its hydraulic system halfway to Mindanao, which killed the superchargers and meant there were no brakes for landing; he continued on at a lower altitude. Four hours into the mission, Godman's flight engineer began transferring gas from the bomb bay tank to the wing tanks; by mistake, he did the opposite, suctioning gas from the wings to the full tank in the bomb bay. Godman reported seeing "gasoline cascading in Niagara proportions out of the overflow, down the sides of the tanks and into the bomb bay and out into the atmosphere." Having passed the point of no return, Godman flew on, praying the remaining fuel would get him to Del Monte.

As night fell, Godman flew lower. He finally spotted Mindanao and started a descent. With the altimeter reading 1,200 feet, the bomber hit the water at 170 mph! It bounced back into the air, then slammed back into the water nose-first, killing two gunners in the rear. Godman later described the crash: "We hit so hard my co-pilot's parachute burst open." Navigator Second Lieutenant Carl E. Epperson was knocked out and came to as water cascaded into the nose; he swam up to the cockpit. Godman and co-pilot Second Lieutenant Carlisle had already crawled out onto the wing. Godman managed to pull Epperson out of the plane and they deployed their Mae Wests. "We turned around and saw the tail going perpendicular and then the plane slid out from under us as it sank. The radioman and another gunner managed to get out." They were a mile offshore in shark-infested waters. Godman remembered, "We were all scared to death. We realized that at any moment the sharks

could hit and that our stroking, kicking and bleeding weren't helping."
After a four-hour struggle, they made it to shore.

Pease managed to find Mindanao, but without brakes he had to
ground loop the B-17 before it went off the runway end. Once shut
down, he learned MacArthur wasn't expected for another 12 hours.
Reluctant to expose the airplane to daylight discovery by the enemy, he
suggested he take evacuees back to Australia and another plane be sent.
He left with 16 19th Group ground crewmen, and had to ground loop
again on reaching Batchelor Field.

When MacArthur arrived to find there was no transport, he sent off
a dispatch to Washington demanding the best plane and crew in the
Pacific be sent to Del Monte as soon as possible. Four newer B-17Es
of the 14th Reconnaissance Squadron that had just been attached to
the 19th Group flew to Batchelor Field, where the new crews took on
experienced 19th Group pilots as co-pilots to assist them in finding
Del Monte successfully. Again, things went wrong from the beginning.
Two bombers had engine trouble and didn't take off, but Captain
Lewis's "Why Don't We Do This More Often" and 1st Lieutenant
Bostrom's "San Antonio Rose II" successfully took off. Bostrom's tail
gunner, Private 1/c Herbert Wheatley, remembered that the crews were
not informed of the purpose of the mission until they were airborne.
"It is always nice to know when one is designated as a volunteer. We
knew how the war in the Philippines was going. To me, it looked like
a one-way trip."

When the two bombers arrived the night of March 17, they were met
by Captain Godman, who had managed to get to Del Monte after a
two-day struggle through the jungle. Afraid of being left behind, he told
his story to MacArthur. "He looked at me and paused for a moment with
that long corncob pipe held in his hand, and then he said, 'Godman,
anybody as lucky as you, who can crash into the sea at 170 miles an hour
and live to tell about it, can work for me.'" A month later, Godman
became MacArthur's personal pilot for the rest of the war.

Everyone was forced to leave their baggage behind to crowd aboard
the two planes. Godman managed to sneak his co-pilot into the tail-
gunner's position of Lewis's airplane. Knowing the weight in the tail
would affect the takeoff, he whispered the news to Lewis, who adjusted
the trim tabs accordingly. On start-up, Bostrom's No. 3 engine refused
to start. Afraid of exhausting the battery, he sent gunner Weathley and

another crewman to start the engine using the long-handled inertia crank. Weathley remembered, "On the second try, the engine caught and we dropped the crank and ran for the door." They were airborne at 0230 hours on March 18.

En route to Australia, they learned the Japanese had attacked Darwin. Diverting to Batchelor Field, they then flew on another 1,000 miles to Alice Springs, where the party split up. MacArthur and his family, Sutherland, Morhouse, and Huff took a special train that General Brett had borrowed from the Australians, while the rest of the staff flew down to Melbourne via Adelaide in two Australian National Airways DC-3s. Changing trains at Terowie Railway Station in South Australia on March 20, MacArthur made his famous speech, in which he stated, "I came through and I shall return."

On March 18, Lieutenant Chaffin finally managed to fly out from Batchelor Field to Del Monte; his return flight with 21 evacuees was memorable. Colonel Allison Ind, one of MacArthur's staff, was among those awaiting a ride out from Mindanao. He remembered the night takeoff at 2230 hours. "From the tiny cubby of the tail gunner to the glass nose, the bomber was an unbroken mass of men and baggage." The flight back to Batchelor Field took eight hours. Once refueled, Chaffin took off and headed for Melbourne, 1,900 miles away across the forbidding Australian "outback." Just after passing the point of no return, Chaffin's navigator informed him that they were struggling with strong headwinds; Chaffin began watching his gas gauges. Thirty minutes later, the navigator informed him that his gear was faulty and they were 40 miles off course. Once the course correction was made, the bomber flew into a heavy rainstorm that affected the radio compass they were using to home in on Melbourne.

Low on fuel and flying through a black night in lashing rain, the B-17 finally made it to Melbourne. The city was blacked out and in the storm it was nearly impossible to find the airfield. Once he was over the field, Chaffin missed lining up for the runway and had to go around twice, narrowly missing trees and buildings. Finally, he set down only to discover he had missed the runway again. Colonel Ind described what happened: "The big B-17 heels, rights, and seems for all the world to be trying to pitch herself over on her nose." Chaffin finally brought the bomber to a stop and killed the engines; the gas gauges had stopped registering. Crew and passengers tumbled out into the mud.

Only then did they realize their luck. Chaffin had landed dead center in the middle of a wide deep ditch; had he landed ten feet to either side, he would have hit the side of the ditch with a wingtip. The next morning a ramp was built and the B-17 was towed out by a team of horses.

On March 17, President Roosevelt had stated:

> I know that every man and woman in the United States admires with me General MacArthur's determination to fight to the finish with his men in the Philippines. But I also know that every man and woman is in agreement that all important decisions must be made with a view toward the successful termination of the war. Knowing this, I am sure that every American, if faced individually with the question as to where General MacArthur could best serve his country, could come to only one answer.

Not everyone agreed with the President. Men back on Bataan and Corregidor were dismayed by the news. Josef Goebbels labeled MacArthur "the fleeing general," and Mussolini called him a "coward." Nevertheless, MacArthur's public image loomed larger and larger in the American press, with Republican senators demanding that the general return to the United States to take over supreme command of the entire US war effort. General Eisenhower recorded in his diary, "The public has built itself a hero out of its own imagination."

In the face of this, President Roosevelt and General Marshall agreed that he should be awarded the Medal of Honor for his leadership of American forces in the Philippines. The medal is normally awarded for "bravery on the field of battle, above and beyond the call of duty." MacArthur had never visited the front lines, and only visited the men on Bataan once, on February 10, 1942. Otherwise, following his departure from his penthouse headquarters suite in Manila, he was seldom seen on Corregidor outside of the Malinta Tunnel. Nevertheless, the award went through. The accompanying citation read:

> For conspicuous leadership in preparing the Philippine Islands to resist conquest, for gallantry and intrepidity above and beyond the call of duty in action against invading Japanese forces, and for the heroic conduct of defensive and offensive operations on the Bataan Peninsula. He mobilized, trained, and led an army which has received

world acclaim for its gallant defense against a tremendous superiority of enemy forces in men and arms. His utter disregard of personal danger under heavy fire and aerial bombardment, his calm judgment in each crisis, inspired his troops, galvanized the spirit of resistance of the Filipino people, and confirmed the faith of the American people in their Armed Forces.

The general became the first of two sons of a Medal of Honor recipients to be given the award (the other being Theodore Roosevelt Jr., for his heroic leadership at Omaha Beach on D-Day). His father, Arthur MacArthur, had been awarded the medal as a young officer when he took the flag from a dying colorbearer and led the Union Army charge at Missionary Ridge during the American Civil War.

At the same time General MacArthur was being nominated for and awarded the nation's highest honor for non-existent personal military valor in combat, morale among the American and Filipino troops had dropped and the men began singing a song written by sergeants Bernard Fitzpatrick and Jerry Lundquist of the 194th Tank Battalion, titled "Dugout Doug" and sung to the tune of "The Battle Hymn of the Republic":

> Dugout Doug MacArthur lies a-shaking on the Rock
> Safe from all the bombers and from any sudden shock
> Dugout Doug is eating of the best food on Bataan
> And his troops go starving on.
>
> Dugout Doug's not timid, he's just cautious, not afraid
> He's protecting carefully the stars that Franklin made
> Four-star generals are rare as good food on Bataan
> And his troops go starving on.
>
> Dugout Doug is ready in his Kris Craft for the flee
> Over bounding billows and the wildly raging sea
> For the Japs are pounding on the gates of Old Bataan
> And his troops go starving on…

Behind his back, MacArthur was known by the men who served under him as "Dugout Doug" for the rest of the war, and many would fault him for leaving his men to the mercies of the Japanese.

On April 5, all 38 crew members of the five B-17s were awarded the Distinguished Flying Cross. Navigator First Lieutenant Bob Roy Carruthers wrote in his diary, "We had delivered our precious cargo safe and sound and we all felt pretty swell about it."

For his role in MacArthur's escape, the general subsequently nominated Lieutenant Bulkeley for the Medal of Honor. Admiral Ernest King, Commander in Chief, US Fleet (COMINCH), wrote the citation for Bulkeley himself on behalf of the Navy and President Roosevelt presented it to the young lieutenant at an Oval Office ceremony on August 4, 1942. Author W.L. White wrote a book, *They Were Expendable*, about Bulkeley and his PT boats that fall, which became a wartime best-seller. Excerpts were serialized in *Reader's Digest* and *Life* magazines before it was adapted in 1944 as a movie starring Robert Montgomery playing a character based on Bulkeley, while John Wayne played one based on Kelly, with Donna Reed as an Army nurse who had a brief affair with Kelly. Postwar researchers have found most of the claims made in the book to be exaggerated.

With MacArthur now in Australia, there were calls from Republicans in Congress that he be brought back to the United States. Realizing that doing so would put irresistible political pressure on President Roosevelt to name him supreme commander, General Marshall and the other chiefs of staff developed a command reorganization in the Pacific that provided the general with a suitable position while keeping him overseas. On March 30, 1942, the Pacific Theater command was cut in two. MacArthur was named commander in the South West Pacific Area (SWPA), which included the Philippines, the Netherlands East Indies, New Guinea, the Bismarck Archipelago, the Solomon Islands, and Australia. Admiral Chester Nimitz was named commander of the Pacific Ocean Areas, which included the Hawaiian Islands, the Gilberts, Marshalls, Marianas, and the Japanese Home Islands. Creation of the two commands was a violation of the sanctified American military belief in the unity of command, but it satisfied both the political needs of the President and the fact the Navy would never have acceded to command of the naval forces in the Pacific by a general as unaware of the basic requirements of seapower as MacArthur. The decision ensured there would be interservice bureaucratic infighting and a political struggle between MacArthur and Nimitz throughout the Pacific War.

Both commanders were ordered to commence preparations for offensive operations to drive the Japanese back from their conquests. MacArthur's forces were few and the rest of 1942 would be spent in the Southwest Pacific fighting to prevent further Japanese gains. Nimitz's naval forces were stretched thin, but the aircraft carriers that had not been present at Pearl Harbor now presented what possibility there was of offensive operations in the Pacific.

CHAPTER TWELVE

INDIES FINALE

The Japanese South Seas offensive hit so fast it left the Allies reeling. Japanese forces invaded the Malay Peninsula on the war's first day. Eight days later, on December 16, they struck northern Borneo, which outflanked the Americans on Luzon and set the stage for further advances. Four days later, on December 20, an invasion fleet landed troops at the port of Davao on the south coast of Mindanao, the major island at the southern end of the Philippine archipelago. On Christmas Day, Jolo Island, between Mindanao and Borneo, was occupied. Possession of these southern bases allowed movement of air units from the north to support further advances against the Indies.

Celebes was next, with Japanese forces landing on the northeast corner of the island on January 11. By January 24 they were able to land at Makassar, completing their conquest of the island and giving them control of the vital Makassar Straits. Native troops that had defended a bridge into the city and surrendered were forced to remove their puttees. Japanese soldiers then used the puttees to tie the surrendered troops together in groups of three and four; they were then thrown from the bridge to drown. The event was one of many Japanese atrocities committed during the South Seas campaign that would lead to the Pacific War becoming a fight with no quarter asked or given by either side.

With the conquest of Malaya well in hand and the American forces on Luzon retreating to the Bataan Peninsula, the Japanese were able to turn toward the Netherlands East Indies earlier than originally planned. The battle for the Indies began when the Japanese 35th Infantry Brigade, led by Major General Kiyotake Kawaguchi, landed at Miri, Sarawak, in British Borneo on December 16, 1941. Seizing the oilfields of Borneo was the primary Japanese goal of the South Seas campaign. The four northern territories – Sarawak, Brunei, the island of Labuan, and British North Borneo – were administered by Britain, while the remainder of the island was part of the Netherlands East Indies. The 2nd Battalion of the 15th Punjab Regiment, stationed in Kuching, was the only Allied infantry unit on the island. The Allied forces in both parts of Borneo were no match for the invaders. Governor Charles Robert Smith surrendered British North Borneo the morning of January 19, 1942.

In mid-January, the three sentai of the JAAF 5th Air Corps left Malaya and returned to Thailand to reinforce the Burma campaign, while the 3rd Air Corps turned its attention to the Netherlands East Indies. With the capture of Tarakan and Manado, the last week of January 1942 saw the Japanese forces ready to strike hard. Rather than wait for the fall of Singapore, the Japanese took aim at Sumatra.

Sumatra itself was little developed, being still covered in a thick triple-canopy rainforest. At Palembang, the Sumatran capital, there were two airfields that had been surveyed in mid-December and found acceptable for use by bombers. "P1" was a civilian airfield with a concrete runway, but no way to disperse aircraft on the field. "P2" was a secret military airfield that was never discovered by the Japanese during the campaign. It had a grass runway, and aircraft could be dispersed under the trees. In early January 1942, the surviving British bombers were evacuated from Singapore to Palembang.

Fifty Hurricane IIb fighters of the RAF's 232 and 258 squadrons were flown off of the carrier HMS *Indomitable* on January 27. Five were written off on landing at P-1, while 15 from 232 Squadron were flown on to Singapore. The Hurricane IIb was armed with 12 .303 machine guns; the outer two in each wing were quickly removed from the aircraft to make them more maneuverable in light of the air combat reports from Singapore. Most of the pilots had been sent straight from operational training, and their inexperience showed with the loss of the first five at P-1. Servicing the Hurricanes was difficult since there were few spares and no toolkits, while most of the ground crews were from the Buffalo squadrons in Singapore and had no experience with the Hurricane. Additionally, there was no radar on Sumatra, with what passed for early warning being organized ground observers. The ML-KNIL withdrew all their serviceable aircraft from Sumatra at the end of January, leaving the RAF fighters as the sole air defense of the island.

On February 5, 232 and 258 squadrons reported they had 33 Hurricanes between them. By the time of the Japanese invasion two weeks later, only 15 Hurricanes would still be serviceable.

Palembang itself was seen from the outset as a primary invasion target for the Japanese, due to the fact that the oilfields were considered the best in Southeast Asia, supplying two major refineries at nearby Pladjoe and Sungei Gerong operated by Royal Dutch Shell with the sweetest crude oil available. Having failed to capture Balikpapan before it could be blown up by the Dutch, Palembang was an even more important target than it had been.

While all Allied eyes were on Sumatra, the Japanese mounted a surprise attack on Java on February 3, 1942. The Tainan Air Group had moved from Formosa to Jolo in the Sulu Islands midway between Mindanao and Borneo on December 30, then moved on to Tarakan in Borneo a week later; on February 2, they moved to Balikpapan Airfield on Borneo. The day after they arrived at Balikpapan, 17 Zeros of the Tainan Air Group led by a Mitsubishi C5M Command Reconnaissance Plane, the Imperial Navy's version of the Army's Ki-15, known to the Allies as "Babs" for navigation assistance attacked an airfield near Surabaya. The Zeros caught an airborne B-18 and shot it down, then strafed aircraft on the field and shot down a Dutch-flown Buffalo.

On February 4, 72 G3M Nells and 22 Zeros of the 22nd Air Flotilla and an additional 22 Zeros from the Kaiohsung Air Group that had recently moved south from Formosa attacked several airfields on Java. By the time the Japanese departed, 16 Allied fighters had been shot down or crash landed, three Catalinas and two B-17s were claimed shot down, and several flying boats and floatplanes had been destroyed on the water; four B-17s on the ground had been hit with varying degrees of damage. A force of G4Ms of the Tainan Air Group found and attacked the cruisers USS *Houston* and *Marblehead*. Both ships were hit but remained afloat and escaped to Tjilatjap; *Houston*'s aft 8-inch main turret was no longer operable as a result of damage.

On February 5, a sweep of Tainan Air Group Zeros caught four ML-KNIL CW-21Bs and two Hawk 75A-4s in the air. The Zero pilots claimed two CW-21Bs and both Hawks shot down.

At 1100 hours, February 6, 1942 the Japanese mounted their first air raid on P-1 Airfield at Palembang. During the attack, two Blenheims were shot down by the 59th Sentai's Sergeant Major Hiroshi Onozaki, with loss of all six crewmen. Six 232 Squadron Hurricanes took off to oppose the raid. Two were shot down with one pilot dead, while two more were listed missing. Of the two survivors, South African Sergeant Pilot Dick Parr in BG678 lost the little finger of his left hand after a 20mm shell exploded in his cockpit; he landed with the severed digit in his shirt pocket. Pilot Officer Reg Bainbridge in the other surviving Hurricane claimed a Ki-43 shot down. Two ML-KNIL Buffalos were destroyed on the ground. The body of American Pilot Officer Cardwell Kleckner, pilot of one of the missing Hurricanes, was found in the jungle two days later, while New Zealand Pilot Officer Campbell-White, pilot of the other Hurricane, arrived back at P-1 on February 10 after being rescued from the jungle by Sumatran natives. The raids continued on a daily basis. Over February 7, 8, and 9, the JAAF 3rd Air Corps mounted all-out attacks on Palembang and the P1 airfield. On February 10, there were only 20 Hurricanes still serviceable.

The main battle to take the Indies began on February 14, when Lockheed Hudson reconnaissance bombers from 1 Squadron RAAF spotted a Japanese fleet in the South China Sea, headed toward Sumatra shortly after dawn on February 14. Twenty Hudsons and 35 Blenheim bombers were based at the Dutch airfield known as P2. They were launched at 0700 hours, with the 15 surviving Hurricanes as escort, tasked with attacking the fleet. When an attack was mounted, the bomber crews discovered to their dismay that the fleet was supported by the light carrier *Ryūjō*, with a squadron of Zeros aboard. The defending Japanese fighters made short work of the outclassed bombers and shot down five Hurricanes.

At 0800 hours on February 14, the ground observers warned of the approach of a large formation of hostile aircraft. The Ki-21s hit P-1 with the only opposition being six Bofors 40mm cannon and six 3.1-inch antiaircraft guns that could not reach their altitude of 12,000 feet. When the bombers departed, the Ki-43 fighter escorts from the 59th Sentai strafed the airdrome. Minutes later, a low-flying formation of Mitsubishi Ki-56 transports, a license-built version of the Lockheed Model 14 airliner, appeared out of the skies filled with smoke from the burning refineries, and 180 paratroopers of the 2nd Parachute Regiment of the 1st Airborne Division, commanded by Colonel Seiichi Kume, were dropped on the field, while a second group of 100 paratroopers were dropped on the oil refineries. Eighteen Ki-21 bombers from the 98th Sentai then dropped supplies for the paratroopers. It was the first major airborne operation of the Pacific War and the Japanese capability came as a surprise to the defenders.

The defenders – 150 British soldiers manning the antiaircraft defenses, 110 Dutch soldiers, and three officers and 72 men from the RAF Regiment, all under the command of Wing Commander H.G. Maguire – were able to hold the field against repeated attacks by the paratroopers, firing their 40mm and 3.7-inch antiaircraft cannon over open sights. Incorrectly warned of a Japanese landing some 15 miles away, and now low on ammunition for the antiaircraft weapons, the defenders retreated from the airfield to Palembang town that afternoon. The paratroops dropped on the refineries were able to hold out overnight by fortifying the air raid shelters. The next morning, 100 more paratroopers were dropped near the refineries.

After a battle that lasted all day, the Dutch defenders were unable to set fire to the Pladjoe Refinery before being pushed out. At Sungei Gerong, the defenders were able to set demolition charges that damaged the refinery. Pladjoe's damage was slight, allowing the Japanese to quickly make it operational; the damage at Sungei Gerong, while not enough to shut down production, nevertheless meant the refinery would not operate at its prewar level at any time before it was finally leveled by British Fleet Air Arm raids two years later.

At dawn on February 15, the same day the Commonwealth forces at Singapore surrendered, Japanese troops disembarked into landing craft from the transports of the invasion fleet that had arrived off Palembang overnight and proceeded up the Moesi, Telang, and Salang rivers toward Palembang. The Dutch forces made no attempt to stop them on the invasion beaches, since the enemy enjoyed overwhelming aerial and naval superiority. The landing decided the issue, but the fighting was not over. Surviving RAF Blenheim and Hudson bombers attacked the invasion fleet and the transport *Otawa Maru* was sunk. The Hurricanes, now operating from the still-secret P2 airfield, strafed the landing craft, but there was no stopping the enemy. By early afternoon, Palembang town was occupied and Allied forces retreated into the surrounding jungle. That afternoon, all surviving aircraft were ordered to fly to Java. The Japanese fully occupied Palembang by sundown. The next day, the RAF headquarters that had been established at Palembang on February 2 escaped in the last planes to leave P2 Soekaboemi on Java. The fighting on Sumatra had confirmed the brutality of Japanese warfare. JAAF after-action reports of battles over Sumatra made no attempt to hide the practice of shooting parachuting Allied pilots and aircrew.

In Australia, on January 21, 1942, General Brereton told a group of fighter pilots in Melbourne, "You are a task force and are going to Java to delay the Japanese in their offensive movement. Do your best and when the time comes we'll see that you get out."

Forty-nine combat-experienced fighter pilots had managed to make it to Australia from the Philippines. Five provisional pursuit squadrons were organized: the 3rd, 13th, 17th, 20th, and 33rd. The 17th Squadron, which would play the major role in the fighting in Java, was activated on January 10, 1942, under the command of Captain Charles A. "Bud" Sprague. By the time the squadron was ordered to fly to Darwin on January 16, Sprague had been promoted to major. Thirteen Philippines survivors, including first lieutenants W.A. Sheppard, E.B. Gilmore, George Kiser, and Joe Kreuzel – the pilot who had stolen Lamar Gillet's P-40 at Clark Field back on December 10 – along with four fresh flight school graduates, made five stops on the 2,000-mile flight from Brisbane to Darwin, where they expected orders that would send them island-hopping back to the Philippines. By then, however, the enemy had taken northern Borneo and Celebes, which prevented such a flight and they were ordered to Java.

The flight to Java was largely over water: 540 miles across the Timor Sea to Koepang; 250 miles to Waingapoe on Soemba Island; with a final leg of 500 miles to Surabaya on Java. On January 30, 13 of the 17 pilots completed the 3,300-mile journey and took residence at Blimbing. The airfield had two 4,000-foot sod runways; taxiways led into the jungle around the field where the P-40s could be hidden from aerial observation. In fact, the field was so carefully camouflaged an experienced Dutch pilot had to guide them to the base. In order to keep the location secret, pilots would hedge-hop after takeoff to a town 15 miles away before they formed up and climbed to altitude. Landing approaches were flown at low altitude, with a pilot "popping up" only long enough to lower his wheels before landing.

Lieutenant Kiser remembered:

The enlisted men assigned to this squadron consisted of a crew chief and an armorer for each plane, plus three radio technicians and a first sergeant. The enlisted men brought their tool kits, an extra aileron or two, a couple spare tires and nuts and bolts of assorted sizes. This, together with what we could salvage from accidents and losses, was the extent of our maintenance during the six weeks we were there. The ground crews proved themselves past masters at improvising and worked constantly to keep the few P-40s we had flying. Our successes were attributed to their ingenuity in maintaining the planes with practically nothing.

The Dutch assisted us in every way possible, furnishing guards on the field, food and medicine. Living conditions were not too bad. We had nice quarters, the food was not good but sufficient and altogether everything was as good as could be expected considering the supply situation at this stage of the war.

Once at Blimbing, the squadron was responsible for the defense of Surabaya on the northeast coast, while the RAF and ML-KNIL squadrons based in western Java defended the port of Tjilatjap on the south coast.

On February 10, Japanese reconnaissance spotted some 60 Allied fighters at Surabaya, including P-40s of the 17th squadron and most of the remaining Dutch Hawk 75s and Buffalos. They were the largest Allied fighter force in Southeast Asia.

Five flights of P-40s had left Australia for the Indies by February 11. The fighters had limited navigation equipment and the inexperienced pilots were accompanied by LB-30s carrying mechanics to service the planes at intermediate stops and provide navigational assistance. On February 11, 22 P-40Es of the 20th Provisional Squadron set off for Java in two formations; nine of 13 in the first flight were lost to weather, while all nine in the second flight crashed at Timor attempting to land in a rainstorm. The survivors of these flights that reached Java were incorporated in the 17th Provisional Squadron. Altogether, 34 of 58 P-40s successfully flew to Java from Australia. The squadron had a chance to catch its breath before entering sustained combat, since bad weather and a need on the part of the Japanese to consolidate the position on Sumatra led to a partial lull in air action over Java.

More importantly, most of the pilots were inexperienced. Lieutenant Sheppard later recalled:

By February 1, 1942 there were about 30 airplanes and 45 pilots in Java. Three-fourths of the pilots had just graduated from flying school and had never flown a pursuit ship until they landed in Australia. After about three hours of transition instruction, they started up toward Java. The first time they ever fired a machine gun was at a Japanese aircraft. In 30 or 40 hours of combat flying, however, they grew very proficient in flying ability. A few of them were killed. Almost every time it was a case of not looking around.

On February 19, 23 Zeros from the Tainan and Kaiohsung air groups flew the 430 miles from Balikpapan to attack the Allied fighters at Surabaya. Saburo Sakai was one of the Japanese pilots. He remembered the fight that ensued as the largest fighter battle in the Pacific War to that date.

We arrived over Soerbaja [Surabaya] at 1130 hours, at 16,000 feet. Below us, at least 50 Allied fighters flew in a large counter-clockwise formation of at least three waves of Vs over the city at 10,000 feet. They outnumbered us at least two to one. As we dropped our belly tanks they spotted us and broke their circular path as they climbed toward us, eager for a fight. Less than a minute later, the orderly formations of Japanese and Allied fighters disintegrated into a wild, swirling dogfight.

I watched a Hawk scream toward me, then flicked into a left roll, waiting his reaction. Foolishly, he maintained his course. I snapped around into a sharp right turn, standing my Zero on her wing, and came out directly on his tail. I checked my tail, then closed the distance. Slight control movements kept me glued on his tail. Fifty yards away, I opened up. Almost immediately, his right wing broke off and snapped away; then the left wing tore loose. Spinning wildly, the enemy plane broke up into wreckage as it plummeted. The pilot failed to get out.

Sakai spotted six other Allied fighters falling out of the sky as he flew back into the battle. "To my left, a P-40 closed in on the tail of a diving

Zero and I turned desperately to head him off. Suddenly the other Zero whipped up and around in a loop that put him on the P-40's tail. With a single burst of cannon fire, it burst into flames."

Sakai had to dodge a P-40 that flashed by trailing a streamer of flame, while a Dutch Hawk flipped past, its pilot dead at the controls. He spotted the Babs that had led them from Balikpapan, pursued by three Dutch Hawks. Before he could intervene, another Zero dived on them, shooting down one, then looping around to come up behind the other two and shoot them down.

A Hawk flew past overhead and Sakai slammed his throttle forward, and looped onto the surprised enemy's tail. "I cut inside his turn and dove after him. Less than fifty yards back, I opened fire and the shells exploded in his fuselage. Thick black smoke belched back and I pulled out as a sheet of flame enveloped the Dutch fighter."

Climbing back to 8,000 feet, Sakai spotted 20 Zeros circling as the few surviving Allied fighters turned into specks disappearing into the distance. "The battle was over, six minutes after it started." He then spotted another Hawk flying over the city. He turned to attack but opened fire too soon and the enemy pilot dived away. Unfortunately, he was too low to make a long dive and escape the Zero that couldn't keep up in such a maneuver with the heavier airplane. "He pulled out and I used my superior speed to catch up. He hedgehopped and zigzagged frantically. Every time he turned I cut inside him and closed the distance. Finally, with Malang Airfield in sight, I opened fire but my cannons were out of ammo. I still held him with my nose machine guns. He crashed into a rice paddy just short of the field and flipped over."

Sakai rejoined the others. "We had lost Lieutenant Asai, our chutai leader, and two other pilots." Back at Balikpapan, the pilots submitted claims for 40 enemy fighters. "I have always reduced the claims by 30 percent, but here there seemed to be little overclaiming. From that day on, we met practically no opposition."

While Sakai and his fellow pilots were wiping out Dutch aerial resistance over Surabaya, 18 G3M Nell bombers, escorted by 18 Zeros, bombed Semplak on Java. Eight Buffalos of 2-VLG-V were based on the nearby airfield. The Dutch pilots took off to intercept the approaching enemy formations. First Lieutenant August Gerard Deibel went after an escorting Zero and managed to get on its tail, but a second Zero got on his tail and he was wounded by a 20mm shell that forced him to break off and land. Eleven G3Ms were shot down, while the Zero escorts shot down four Buffalos, killing two pilots. Three RAF Hudsons and two ML-KNIL Martin 139 bombers on the airfield were destroyed.

The air battles on February 19 saw the beginning of the end for Allied forces in Java. Sakai and his fellow pilots shot down seven 17th Provisional Squadron P-40s for the loss of one of their own, while the two Dutch squadrons involved ceased to exist as effective units. Over all of Java that day, the Allies lost 15 irreplaceable fighters. At Singosari Airdrome, three B-17s were destroyed by strafing Zeros while two more were badly damaged.

The morning of February 19, 500 Japanese troops landed at Samur Beach on Bali and marched unopposed into Denpasar. The Bali garrison of 600 Indonesian militia offered no resistance, and the airfield was captured intact by the end of the day. Possession of the Bali airfield gave the Japanese a position from which they could attack all of Java. It also shut down the aerial ferry route from Australia since the Japanese could now intercept incoming aircraft over the sea before they landed at Surabaya, sealing the fate of the Indies.

On February 17, eight P-40Es armed with Dutch 20-kilogram bombs attacked ships of the Sumatra invasion fleet off the Moisi Delta near Palembang. They were intercepted by eight JAAF Ki-27 fighters over the target. The Americans claimed four Japanese aircraft destroyed with three probables. The Japanese admitted to the loss of one Ki-27, while claiming three P-40s shot down, though all eight returned from the mission.

Major Sprague was killed in combat over the Bali invasion fleet on February 20. Lieutenant Gilmore later wrote of Sprague's loss:

> The morale of the squadron was very high, in no small part due to the fine leadership of Major Sprague. He was one of the most eager pilots I have ever known. He would always listen to suggestions by the pilots. His experience in fighter type aircraft was somewhat limited, because he had held a staff job from the time he graduated from flying school. However, his outstanding personality was a driving force in the 17th Pursuit Squadron. With enlisted men, whether they were staff sergeants or buck privates, the man who worked the hardest would get the promotion and the man who wouldn't would get busted. Under his command, the 17th Pursuit Squadron was the hardest-working outfit I served in.

During three weeks of combat over Java, the pilots claimed quite a bit of success. Lieutenant Sheppard wrote, "During our stay in Java, the United States Navy and the Dutch authorities gave us credit for shooting down 71 Japanese aircraft, at a loss of 11 pilots." Lieutenant Kiser wrote, "At all times we were out-numbered, at the least ten to one, but still we managed to get official credit for in excess of 65 victories with only a loss of about nine pilots." However, Lieutenant Gilmore recalled, "There is no reliable source for the number of victories. There was no means set up for confirmations of our kills." Confusion resulted in both sides recording spurious victory claims. On February 23, pilots of the 17th Squadron claimed they shot down six enemy bombers and fighters, though Japanese records for both Army and Navy air units recorded no losses that day. At the same time, pilots of the Tainan Air Group claimed three P-40s, though none were lost.

The top-scoring pilot in Java was Second Lieutenant William J. Hennon, who claimed five victories between February 2 and 26. "King" Kiser, who had shot down two enemy aircraft in the Philippines flying with "Buzz" Wagner, added three to his score, claiming his fifth enemy plane shot down on February 24, 1942. Other future aces who scored in the Java campaign included Joe Kreuzel, who would later command the 361st Fighter Group of the Eighth Air Force in England in 1944–45 and Grant Mahoney, who would command the 51st Fighter Group in China during 1943.

Also on February 19, the Allies lost the use of Darwin as a point of resupply and reinforcement when the Japanese attacked the port. Kido Butai, the Japanese carrier force that had struck Pearl Harbor, had moved into position in the Indian Ocean at the end of January to provide support for the invasions of Sumatra and Java. Commander Mitsuo Fuchida, air group commander on the carrier *Akagi*, led 81 B5N "Kate" bombers and 71 D3A "Val" dive bombers, escorted by 36 Zeros, launched from *Akagi*, *Kaga*, *Sōryū*, and *Hiryū* at 0845 hours. An Australian coastwatcher spotted the inbound formation at 0935 hours, but the RAAF in Darwin mistakenly considered them to be an expected formation of ten P-40Es due in that morning. When the alarm was finally given at 1000 hours, the attackers were already overhead.

Sixty-five ships were in Darwin Harbor. HMAS *Gunbar* was the first attacked when she was strafed by several Zeros. The Kates and Vals attacked over the next 30 minutes, sinking the destroyer USS *Peary*

(DD-226); gunboat HMAS *Mavie*; and US Army transports *Meigs* and *Mauna Loa*. The transport MV *Neptuna* was docked at the main wharf and exploded with 21 dead ashore; the troop ship *Zealandia* and tankers *British Motorist* and *Karaloo* were also sunk. The cargo ships *Portmar*, *Barona*, and *Tulagi* were damaged and beached to be later refloated. All but one of the P-40Es at Darwin Airfield were shot down or destroyed on the ground. The Japanese bombed and strafed the base and civil airfield, as well as the army barracks and oil storage facility, seriously damaging all. Japanese losses were five aircraft, with 34 returning to their ships with varying degrees of damage from the thoroughly inadequate AA defenses.

Just before noon, the second attack, composed of 27 G3M2 Nell and 27 G4M1 Betty bombers, was sighted flying at 18,000 feet. The two formations attacked Darwin Airfield simultaneously from the southwest and northeast. AA was ineffective and the bombers departed at around 1220 hours without loss. The bombing destroyed six Hudsons, a USAAF B-24A Liberator, and two P-40s, while badly damaging another Hudson and a Wirraway trainer. The town of Darwin was badly damaged, including most essential services such as water and electricity. Fear of an imminent invasion spread and the majority of the town's civilian population fled inland. For the Allies, the raid destroyed most of the available shipping to continue reinforcement of the Indies, and the damage suffered at the airfield meant that it was no longer useable for aerial reinforcement. The campaign to save the Netherlands Indies was now doomed; the best Allied forces could do would be to slow the Japanese advance and give time for supplies, new equipment, and men to arrive in Australia. Allied military leaders had no expectation that the meager forces available could hold the islands against Japan.

General Brereton was relieved of his duties as deputy air commander of ABDACOM on February 23. He later wrote of the decision that led to his departure:

> I felt it necessary to request General Wavell to relieve me of my duties. The morale of my own air force was low and my presence was required with it. I was criticized by General Wavell and General Brett for what appeared to them to be a somewhat unwarranted and pessimistic attitude.

Brereton also admitted to differences with Air Marshal Sir Richard Peirse, the ranking RAF officer. With the general's departure, the 19th Bomb Group's Lieutenant Colonel Eugene L. Eubank became commander of the USAAF forces in Java. On February 24, the survivors of the 19th and 7th groups began to depart Java for Australia. That day, Brereton flew to Ceylon on his way to take his new post as commander of the Tenth Air Force in India. Captain Grant Mahoney, who had taken command of the 17th Squadron following Sprague's death, accompanied the general. General Wavell departed for India on February 25, which essentially ended ABDACOM.

Perhaps the most surprising British mission of the Java campaign occurred on February 28, when six ancient Vickers Vildebeest and a single Fairey Albacore torpedo bombers of 36 Squadron RAF attacked the Java invasion fleet. The Vildebeest had first entered service with 100 Squadron in 1932 and had been based at Singapore since that squadron arrived with its airplanes in 1933. Following heavy losses in attempted attacks on the Malaya invasion fleet in December and January, 100 and 36 squadrons had been combined following their evacuation to Java at the end of January. With open cockpits and a speed of 140 mph, the obsolete biplanes were sitting ducks for the enemy. Since there were no torpedoes available, they were loaded with 250-pound bombs. They set off at 1700 hours and found the fleet two hours later at dusk. Flying low-level attacks in the face of the ships' antiaircraft fire, they were credited with sinking an amazing nine ships. Japanese records listed two transports seriously damaged and a cruiser damaged. Unfortunately the attackers suffered four losses, including 36 Squadron's second commanding officer, who had taken command when the squadron was evacuated from Singapore after losing their first commander.

The 19th Bomb Group's surviving bombers also took part in the battle for Java. Lieutenant Frank Kurtz recalled General Brereton's visit on December 29:

> He told us that the United States Army Air Force of the Far East was moving all its bombers to Java. The main base would be on a field outside the city of Malang. From there we could operate out of advance bases already prepared by the Dutch on the outlying islands of Borneo and the Celebes, from where we could break up

the immense concentration of Japanese shipping at Davao Bay that was gathering for the invasion of the Indies.

Elated at the thought they must be receiving reinforcement to be worthy of such a new title, morale quickly sank when the men realized that the "bombers of the United States Army Air Forces of the Far East" were the 11 worn-out Flying Fortresses sitting on the airfield. "We didn't know whether to be sorry for ourselves or for General Brereton for having such a pitifully small command."

Beginning the first week of January, bombers were flown up to Java. On January 10, they moved to Malang Airfield, which would be their primary base. The war-weary B-17Ds were reinforced by four LB-30 Liberators and six B-17s of the 7th Bomb Group that arrived in Java on January 15 via the South Atlantic ferry route; by the end of January, 15 B-17Es and four LB-30s had arrived, all but three via the South Atlantic route; soon after, the 7th Group moved to a new base at Djokjakarta, 150 miles west of Malang.

The 7th Group's crews were inexperienced; one LB-30 pilot received only a 20-minute briefing on the plane before he took off from McDill Field in Florida. Many crewmen had never flown in a four-engine bomber before they were assigned to the group.

Both groups attacked targets in Malaya, the southern Philippines, and the Dutch East Indies. Few missions were successful, though each took a toll in men and machines just by the distances involved. Bad weather and enemy opposition created losses of aircraft and crew, while aborted and failed missions saw morale sink among the survivors. General Brereton visited both groups on February 17. He wrote about what he found:

Combat replacement crews did not exist. Fatigue and combat weariness had worn men to their last ounce of resistance. Pilots returned from attacks crying with rage and frustration when a crew member was killed or when weather or mechanical failure prevent successful completion of the mission. A flight commander, a fine leader, committed suicide. Boys were on the verge of mental and physical collapse.

In late January, IJNAF fighter units moved to northern Borneo. While Saburo Sakai would later report that the pilots were frustrated by the difficulty of shooting down the heavy bombers, some missions ended in real success for the Japanese. Nine B-17s from both groups attempted an attack on Kendari Island in the Celebes, where the IJNAF now based most of its bombers. Nine Zeros happened upon the bombers when they were halfway to the target. By this time, the Japanese fighter pilots had learned the B-17 was most vulnerable to head-on attacks. Using this tactic, they shot down six Fortresses. The survivors claimed to have shot down five Zeros, but only two took hits and both returned to base. These missions demonstrated that the B-17E's upper turret was not effective in defending the forward area, while the single .30-caliber weapon in the nose did not have the range or the hitting power to deter an attacker. The early B-17E's remotely controlled belly turrets proved completely unusable, with gunners experiencing extreme vertigo when they attempted to use the mirror gunsight.

Most operations were flown with only 4–6 bombers, some with only a single aircraft able to reach and bomb the target. Most attacks were against shipping. In 60 missions during the Indies campaign involving over 300 individual sorties, one destroyer, eight transports, and two unidentified ships were claimed sunk, while 23 enemy aircraft were shot down. Postwar examination of Japanese records revealed that only three minesweepers and four troop transport or cargo ships were sunk by high-altitude level bombing.

In the end, the 17th Provisional Squadron lost all its P-40s. The unit was disbanded on arrival back in Australia on March 5, 1942, with the surviving pilots assigned to new pursuit groups arriving from the United States. Kiser wrote: "I am convinced that each man, though he may serve in numerous other squadrons in this war, will always feel that the 17th Pursuit Squadron (Provisional) came closer to upholding the true traditions of the AAF than any other group of fighting men."

Following the Java campaign, Lieutenant Gilmore wrote about the two lessons that were learned in the squadron's first fight: "First, it is very foolish to attack Jap fighters without superior altitude unless it is necessary. Second, when Jap fighters are operating in pairs, if you attack the leader, always be on the watch for his wing man. The wing man will try and get on your tail after he has broken from formation." He continued:

The P-40 gave a good account of itself – it could outdive the Japanese fighters, was faster in level flight, and was better armored. But the

Zero seemed to have more range, could outclimb the P-40, and was more maneuverable. For the American pilot to risk a dogfight was to flirt with suicide. Indeed, by no means least among the lessons learned was a new respect for the foe.

Independently of the pilots of the AVG in Burma, the pilots of the 17th Provisional Squadron learned quickly to keep their speed up and fight in the vertical plane, diving on the enemy and not sticking around to dogfight their more capable foe.

The last line of defense for the Indies was destroyed when ten ships of the Allied ABDA fleet were sunk in the Battles of the Java Sea on February 27 and Sunda Strait the night of February 28–March 1. The losses included the heavy cruiser USS *Houston*, which had served in the mid-1930s as "President Roosevelt's yacht," becoming one of the most famous and beloved ships in the Navy. With only her forward turrets operational, and out of ammunition as she took repeated hits from the enemy ships, the gunners aboard *Houston* fired the star shells that were all they had left at the enemy as her bow slipped beneath the waters of the Sunda Strait. The Japanese had clearly demonstrated that their more realistic prewar training and emphasis on night combat gave them superiority to their opponents. Java was now completely open to invasion, which came in the afternoon of February 28.

Early on the morning of March 1, the ABDA air force flew its last mission of any importance when all surviving fighters – nine American P-40s, six RAF Hurricanes, and four Dutch Brewsters – were pitted against the landing forces. A strafing attack was made at low level, but shore-based AA shot down three of the P-40s. The last six P-40s, all damaged, returned to Blimbing. Before they could be rearmed and refueled, Zeros swept over the previously undiscovered airfield and destroyed the aircraft. The surviving pilots and ground personnel managed to get to Djokjakarta in trucks after an all-night drive just ahead of the advancing Japanese. The airfield had been strafed, leaving wreckage behind, but three 19th Group B-17s arrived at 2100 hours the night of March 1. The last bomber, filled with evacuees who had nothing but the clothes on their backs, departed at 2330 hours on March 2.

Another group of Americans waited for pickup at Andir Airfield outside Badoeng, but the B-17 sent for them was unable to find the field in the darkness and returned to Australia. While most of those awaiting evacuation gave up hope they would escape Java, B-17 crew chief Tech Sergeant Harry Hayes was determined to avoid becoming a Japanese prisoner. Three shot-up B-17Es were still on the field, and Hayes determined that 41-2460, which had managed to make it back after being shot up over Balikpapan on January 25, was salvageable. Over the next two days, working with native laborers, he rebuilt two engines out of parts from the other wrecks and managed the engine changes. Declaring the airplane flyable, Hayes went in search of pilots. He managed to convince American civilian Gerald L. Cherymisin and Dutch Lieutenant Sibolt J. Kok, neither of whom had ever been near a B-17, that the airplane was easy to fly and they could do it. The night of March 4, with Cherymisin and Kok at the controls and Hayes as flight engineer, with 18 evacuees aboard including Cherymisin's pregnant Dutch wife, the Fortress got airborne despite losing an engine shortly after takeoff. Over the next eight hours, they flew the bomber 1,500 miles over the Indian Ocean to Port Hedlund, Australia, the last B-17 to escape Java.

The remaining Dutch forces continued the fight on Java for a week. On March 7, Captain Jacob van Helsdingen led the last four airworthy Buffalos in an interception of Japanese bombers attacking Batavia. The two survivors who returned reported he had shot down a Zero before being shot down in turn by the wingman. Van Helsdingen had scored two victories over Singapore in January; his three victories tied him with Lieutenant August Deibel as the most successful Dutch pilots of the campaign. Altogether, the ML-KNIL had lost 17 pilots killed and 30 fighters shot down, with 15 destroyed on the ground, against claims of 55 enemy aircraft destroyed. On March 8, Dutch forces in the Indies surrendered.

Following the Dutch surrender, the Japanese air forces reported their claims against the Allied air forces for the Indies campaign: the JAAF claimed 33 aircraft shot down, 53 destroyed on the ground, and 150 damaged on the ground for a total JAAF loss of three aircraft. The IJNAF reported 32 aircraft shot down and 11 probables, with 48 burned on the ground. Whatever the real numbers, the fact was the Allied air forces, which had been inadequate from the beginning, had been eliminated in one of the most effective air campaigns of the war, given that the IJNAF never committed more than 70 Zeros in the entire campaign, while the JAAF fighter force had been limited to two sentais.

Following the surrender of Singapore on February 15 and the occupation of the Andaman Islands on March 23, Japanese forces had easy entry into the Indian Ocean. If Japan could solidify its control of the Bay of Bengal with the capture of Ceylon, British supply lines to India and Australia could be disrupted or blocked. In the face of this threat, Ceylon was hastily reinforced by Australian troops withdrawn from North Africa. The carrier HMS *Indomitable* was taken off operations in the Mediterranean to ferry aircraft to the island.

Following the destruction of the ABDA naval forces in the battles of the Java Sea and Sunda Strait in late February, Kido Butai, the Imperial Navy's carrier striking force, was ordered to move into the Indian Ocean and Bay of Bengal to destroy the Royal Navy and support the invasion of Burma, as part of Operation *C*. The striking force, commanded by Admiral Chūichi Nagumo, was composed of the carriers *Akagi*, *Hiryū*, *Sōryū*, *Shōkaku*, and *Zuikaku*. Admiral Gunichi Mikawa's 3rd Battleship Squadron, composed of his flagship *Kongō*, *Haruna*, *Hiei* and *Kirishima*, and Rear Admiral Hiroaki Abe's 8th Cruiser Division with his flag aboard *Tone* accompanied by *Chikuma*, provided cover to the carriers with ten destroyers of destroyer divisions 17 and 18.

Vice Admiral Jisaburo Ozawa, with his flag aboard the heavy cruiser *Chokai*, commanded the Malay Force that had so recently destroyed the ABDA Fleet, with Rear Admiral Takeo Kurita leading the 7th Cruiser Squadron from his flagship *Kumano* with *Mikuma*, *Mogami*, and *Suzuya*, supported by the light carrier *Ryūjō*.

The combined fleet departed Staring Bay, Celebes, on March 26 and entered the Indian Ocean on March 31.

The Royal Navy had moved their main base from Singapore to Addu Atoll in the Maldive Islands. British Far Eastern Fleet commander Admiral Sir James Somerville learned of the Japanese move into the Indian Ocean on April 1. Somerville led Force A aboard his flagship, the battleship *Warspite*, with the carriers *Indomitable* and *Formidable*, heavy cruisers *Cornwall* and *Dorsetshire*, and light cruisers *Emerald* and *Enterprise*, with six Australian and British destroyers. Force B was led by Vice Admiral Willis aboard the old battleship *Resolution* with *Ramilles*, *Royal Sovereign*, and *Revenge*, supported by the old carrier *Hermes*, and light cruisers *Caledon*, *Dragon*, and the Dutch *Jacob Van Heemskerck*, supported by eight Royal Navy, Australian Navy, and Netherlands Navy destroyers.

Force A sortied from Addu Atoll on April 1, followed by Force B's older ships. Somerville expected to meet the Japanese the next day. However, Admiral Nagumo delayed his strikes. When the Japanese failed to attack Ceylon, Somerville sent the old carrier *Hermes* to Trincomalee, Ceylon, for repairs escorted by the Australian destroyer HMAS *Vampire*, while *Cornwall* and *Dorsetshire* were sent to Ceylon to meet a troop convoy. The rest of Force A returned to the Maldives base on April 3.

Admiral Ozawa's Malay Force made the first move of Operation *C* on April 4 with an air attack on Ceylon that sank 23 ships in and around Trincomalee Harbor. That evening, Kido Butai was spotted 400 miles south of Ceylon by a Catalina from 413 Squadron, Royal Canadian Air Force, flown by Squadron Leader Leonard Birchall. Birchall managed to make a report before he was shot down by a Zero fighter from *Hiryū*. Somerville immediately sortied, but Force A was too far west to intercept the Japanese before Nagumo struck Ceylon.

The naval base at Colombo, Ceylon was attacked on Easter Sunday, April 5, by 36 D3A dive bombers and 53 B5N torpedo bombers, with an escort of 36 Zeros led by *Akagi*'s Commander Mitsuo Fuchida, who had led the Pearl Harbor attack. Despite the fact the strike force flew up the coast for 30 minutes in full view, there was no warning at Colombo and most RAF fighters were still on the ground at Ratmalana Airdrome when the enemy appeared overhead.

The armed merchant cruiser HMS *Hector* and the old destroyer HMS *Tenedos* were sunk in the harbor, while 18 attackers were claimed shot down by antiaircraft fire. Twenty-seven Fleet Air Arm and RAF aircraft were destroyed on the ground. An hour later, *Cornwall* and *Dorsetshire* were discovered 200 miles southwest of Ceylon. An attack force of dive and torpedo bombers sank both with a loss of 424 sailors.

Seaman Walter Fudge, who was on board HMS *Dorsetshire*, later remembered that at 1100 hours on April 5, a single Japanese plane was spotted astern and at 1340 hours the ship was attacked by some 80 planes. In less than ten minutes *Dorsetshire* was sunk and within five minutes more *Cornwall* went down too.

Two of Fudge's shipmates went down to the mess and refused to leave because they were non-swimmers. Fudge saw the ship's new captain, giving a salute standing on the forecastle and intending to go down with the ship, but his shipmate Seaman Cassier grabbed the captain and got him over the side. Fudge and another lookout scrambled down a rope to the water. By that time only the bow was out of the water. Once he was in the water, Fudge was surprised that there was no vortex from the sinking ship. As he and others swam away from the sinking cruiser, Japanese planes strafed the survivors. Fudge was grazed by one of the bullets.

Between the two sunken cruisers, there were 1,222 survivors who were in the water for over 30 hours. The ships had taken 425 down with them. Tropical sun and thirst were problems, but the wounded had the worst time. The wounded and the badly burned were moved into the only surviving ship's boat while the rest clung to the Denton rafts and Carley floats.

Engineering officer Lieutenant E.A. Drew only just managed to get out of the engine room before the order to abandon ship was given. He remembered that once he was in the water he had no lifebelt and was soon covered in thick fuel oil and could only barely open his eyes. As he swam away from the ship, he found he was being drawn back due to the fact the starboard outer propeller was still rotating with the shaft at water level; as it churned the water it drew him to it. As Drew approached the propeller, the ship lurched over to port, the propeller came out of the water and he sailed under it. He then found Sub-Lieutenant (E) Dougall, a Royal Canadian Navy Volunteer Reserve officer, who managed to get a lifebelt off one of the corpses and helped Drew get it on, which wasn't easy with both covered in oil and swimming in an oil-covered sea. They then were attacked by the strafing Japanese planes and he never saw Dougall again. Minutes later, he saw the ship's Walrus spotter plane float off the catapult and sink when it was hit by the ship's wireless aerials.

Drew was half a mile astern of *Dorsetshire* when she went down by the head and her stern came right out of the water. "About half of her length stood out of the water as she went straight down into the Indian Ocean which is about a mile deep at that point – it is hard to believe but I heard a faint cheer as the survivors, spread along a line about a mile long, watched it all happen." He then found a messdeck tabletop, about 3 feet wide and 10 feet long, which he was able to cling to.

In the late afternoon at 1655 hours and just before sunset at 1800 hours, two Fleet Air Arm Albacores from *Indomitable* spotted the Japanese carriers. The first was shot down before it could send a sighting report, while the other was damaged. Admiral Somerville's plan to make a night torpedo attack with radar-equipped Albacores was frustrated and the Royal Navy's only opportunity to launch a strike faded away.

The next day, the heavy cruisers *Kumano* and *Suzuya* and destroyer *Shirakumo* sank the British merchant ships *Silksworth, Autolycus, Malda,* and *Shinkuang* and the American *Exmoor*. The Indian Navy sloop *Indus* was discovered off the coast of Burma and sunk by air attack.

Three days later, on April 9, the Japanese attacked Trincomalee Harbor at 0700 hours. The British were warned of the attack by radio intelligence; *Hermes, Vampire,* and the corvette *Hollyhock* had left the night before. Eight defending Hawker Hurricanes and a Fairey Fulmar were shot down in the attack. The ships were discovered at 0855 hours. *Hermes* was defenseless with no aircraft aboard when she was attacked at 1035 hours by 70 dive and torpedo bombers off Batticaloa. After taking 40 hits, *Hermes* sank with a loss of 307. *Vampire* and *Hollyhock* were also sunk, though 590 survivors were later rescued by the hospital ship *Vita*. Japanese losses in the Trincomalee strike and attack on *Hermes* were five bombers and six fighters.

Nine Blenheim IV bombers from 11 Squadron attacked the Japanese carriers. Bombing from an altitude of 11,000 feet, they scored no hits and lost four bombers over the fleet shot down by *Zuikaku*'s Petty Officer Kaname Harada. A fifth Blenheim was shot down by a Zero returning from the strike on *Hermes*, while one Zero was shot down by a Blenheim gunner.

Nagumo's strikes at Colombo and Trincomalee created such a dire situation in South Asia that Prime Minister Churchill feared a successful invasion of Ceylon would allow the Japanese to link up with the Germans, but the Japanese did not have the troops, shipping or air power for a successful invasion and occupation. Ceylon never faced a real threat of invasion at any time during the war. However, Royal Navy surface forces could no longer operate in the central Indian Ocean, and the Far Eastern Fleet was forced to retreat to the east coast of Africa and operate from Mombasa, Kenya. *Formidable* and *Indomitable* returned to Britain. The Royal Navy would not appear in force again in the region for two years.

In the United States, the public response to the loss of *Houston* was one of determination. An emotional enlistment campaign, "Avenge the Houston!" was sponsored by the city of Houston, Texas. Residents built an 80-foot replica of the cruiser to attract recruits, and less than three months after the Battle of the Sunda Strait, on Memorial Day 1942, 1,400 men were sworn into the Navy in a mass ceremony. On October 12, 1942 the light cruiser *Vicksburg* (CL-81), then under construction at the Newport News Shipbuilding & Dry Dock Company in Newport News, Virginia, was renamed *Houston*. President Roosevelt declared: "Our enemies have given us the chance to prove that there will be another USS *Houston*, and yet another USS *Houston* if that becomes necessary, and still another USS *Houston* as long as American ideals are in jeopardy."

CHAPTER THIRTEEN

THE GUARANTEE OF VICTORY

The original Japanese plan of attack had foreseen a 50-day battle to take the Philippines. By mid-March, 1942, Lieutenant General Masaharu Homma's campaign was 45 days over that goal and there was no end in sight. The Americans and their Filipino allies were resolute in their continuing battle against the invaders.

Reinforced by the 14th Division that was transferred from Malaya, along with air and artillery units, Homma began his final offensive on March 28 with a wave of air strikes and artillery assaults on the Allied lines. On April 3, Homma sent a message to Lieutenant General Jonathan M. Wainwright, who was now in command of Allied forces in the Philippines, suggesting that the men on Bataan and Corregidor follow the example of "the defenders of Hong Kong, Singapore and the Netherlands East Indies, in the acceptance of an honorable surrender." Receiving no reply, Homma ordered the final attack on Bataan. The breakthrough was achieved later that day when a battalion managed to cross Mount Samat, which the defenders had considered impassable. The Philippine Division, its troops exhausted by five days of nearly continuous combat and no longer a coordinated unit, was unable to counterattack effectively, while the 57th Infantry Regiment of the Philippine Scouts and the Philippine Army's 31st Division were overrun near the Alangan River on April 8. At the time, 80 percent of the defenders had malaria, 75 percent were suffering from dysentery, and 35 percent had beriberi; they were existing on less than 1,000 calories a day.

The end came for the defenders of Bataan on the night of April 8, when Major General Edward P. King, who commanded the defense of the peninsula, after speaking with his corps commanders who told him they could not hold further, concluded that his force could no longer delay the enemy advance, let alone stop it.

Corporal Sidney Stewart, who would survive the Bataan Death March and three years of Japanese captivity, wrote of his experience of the fighting in his highly praised postwar memoir *Give Us This Day*:

> We could hear the shelling up on the hillside and the crashing and whining as the shells went through the air. But at least we were having a break. There was only an occasional zinging of snipers' bullets whizzing and biting at the leaves of the trees
>
> Suddenly a shell shattered alarmingly close over our heads. We ducked down into the trench again and then stood up when no more came. Just a momentary fright. I couldn't help comparing that fright to the greater, overall fear.
>
> Fright is a thing of the moment, attacking as a cornered animal does, on a second's notice. But fear is an ulcerous growth, pulsating and alive, attached to you like a jungle leech. No fire under the exploding heavens can burn it free. Sometimes it is not so bad, but then again it grips you and binds you as though it will not allow you the smallest movement. Again, at other times, through absolute weariness, you feel you can be free from it. But no, you can only hope to control it.
>
> It is always there. It lives with you, whispering sounds easily heard above the crashing world around you, and you are two people, yourself, and the fear that lives within you. When a man is blown to pieces beside you, it hammers in your brain and makes you smell the warm, sickening blood, a smell which even the acrid powder smoke cannot drive away.
>
> Oh dear God, give us rest. Not rest from weariness, for gladly we would never close our eyes if only that gnawing fear would die.

For 2nd Lieutenant Lamar Gillet and the others on Bataan, the end came on April 9, 1942, when they were ordered to surrender. The surrender meant 76,000 Americans and Filipinos were now at the mercy of an army that believed there was no worse fate for a warrior than surrender. To the Japanese, their opponents had lost all honor and had no claim on their captors for any kind of decent treatment as called for in the Geneva

Conventions regarding the treatment of prisoners of war. The true test of Gillet's personal moral courage now began. He was among the 10,000 starving Americans marched from Bataan to Camp O'Donnell in what would become known as the Bataan Death March. Once in the prison camp, "there were more dead and dying Americans to bury and care for than there were those of us well enough to care for them." That summer, he was moved to Cabanatuan prison camp, in central Luzon. "We were able to smuggle vegetables into the camp, which cured the scurvy we all suffered." In December 1942, Gillet and several hundred other POWs were placed aboard Japanese freighters and sent to Japan as slave laborers. The ship was attacked but not sunk by an American submarine and it survived a typhoon on the four-week voyage.

Lamar Gillet survived the next two and a half years as a slave laborer in the Japanese coal mines on Shikoku Island and later in a small metal-working factory. Recalling his wartime experience, he said:

> It's better to be lucky than good. I was lucky I was behind the Zero instead of in front of him. I was lucky when I landed back at Clark that the guys who were shooting at me didn't give enough lead. I was lucky when my CO on Bataan sent me to Corregidor to get the chewing out he was in for so I wasn't there for the shelling that killed him. I was lucky that the Japanese family whose factory I worked in were willing to feed and care for us when others wouldn't.

Evacuation from Bataan had been hit and miss. Lieutenants W.A. Sheppard and E.B. Gilmore recalled being members of a group of six pilots ordered to evacuate from Bataan on December 28, 1941. They discovered higher-ranking officers had stolen their airplane and run off. On New Year's Eve, they climbed aboard a Philippine Airlines Beechcraft 18 flown by civilian Louis J. Connelly. The plane left Bataan Field at 1500 hours and hedge-hopped down the archipelago to Del Monte Field on Mindanao, landing shortly after 2200 hours. At 0400 hours on New Year's Day, Connelly took off from Del Monte; he and Gilmore traded off flying on instruments. "We were in very poor weather, with very poor maps," Gilmore recalled. They arrived over Tarakan Airfield on Borneo in a light rain. "Just by chance, we spotted a clearing – that was the airfield." There were barricades strewn across the runway and they were not certain of the nationality of the soldiers below. However,

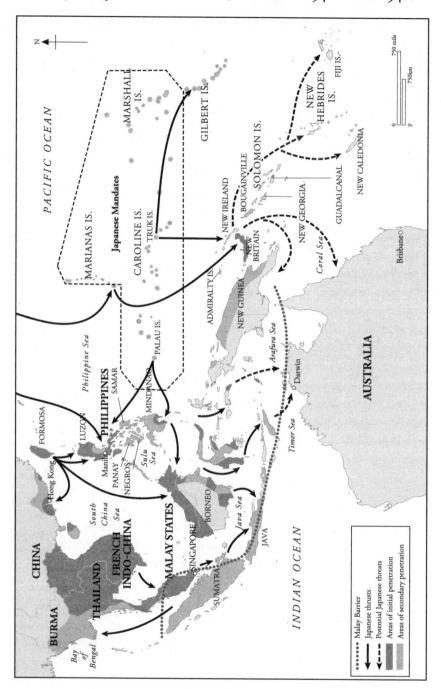

View of B25B bombers from the island of USS *Hornet* as it heads toward the Doolittle Raid's launching point. (US Navy)

Lieutenant Colonel James H. Doolittle (front left), and Captain Marc A. Mitscher, Commanding Officer of USS *Hornet*, during ceremonies on the vessel's flight deck. (US Navy)

Doolittle attaches a Japanese medal to a bomb, ready for its return to the Japanese Home Islands.
(US Navy)

Doolittle lifts off from *Hornet*, April 18, 1942. (US Navy)

Hornet arrives in Pearl Harbor after the Doolittle Raid, April 30, 1942. (US Navy)

Hornet at Pearl Harbor, May 26, 1942, just before she departed for the Battle of Midway. (US Navy)

Pilots of the Flying Tigers, American volunteers flying and fighting in China, March 1942. (Corbis/Getty Images)

Flying Tiger pilots run to their fighters at an advanced US base in China. (Corbis/Getty Images)

USS *Yorktown* in the Coral Sea, April 1942. (US Navy)

Japanese aircraft carrier *Shōkaku* endures a bomber attack from *Yorktown*, during the morning of May 8, 1942. Flames are visible from a hit on her forecastle. (US Navy)

Another view of *Shōkaku*, showing splashes from dive bombers' near misses off her starboard side. (US Navy)

Damage to *Yorktown*'s third and fourth decks from a 250-kilogram bomb dropped during the Battle of Coral Sea, May 8, 1942. (US Navy)

Firefighters at work on board *Yorktown*. (US Navy)

Crewmen escape using lines suspended from *Lexington*'s stern. (US Navy)

An explosion aboard *Lexington*, probably at 1727 hours as the carrier's abandonment neared its end. (US Navy)

A mushroom cloud rises from *Lexington*, probably from the great explosion from the detonation of torpedo warheads stowed in the starboard side of the hangar. (US Navy)

Lieutenant John A. Leppla (right) shakes hands with Radioman 3rd Class J.A. Liska in front of an SBD scout-bomber. During the Battle of the Coral Sea they were credited with shooting down five Japanese planes during one air action from *Lexington*. (US Navy)

Douglas SBDs and Grumman F4Fs on *Enterprise*'s flight deck as the ship operates in the Coral Sea, May 15, 1942. (US Navy)

Enterprise's air group commander, Clarence W. McClusky, Jr., receives the Distinguished Flying Cross from Admiral Chester W. Nimitz, Pearl Harbor, May 27, 1942. (US Navy)

USS *Yorktown* being repaired at Pearl Harbor after the Battle of Coral Sea, May 29, 1942. She left Pearl Harbor the next day, headed for Midway. (US Navy)

Grumman F4F-4 Wildcat Fighters of Fighting Squadron Three (VF-3) being serviced at Naval Air Station, Kaneohe, Oahu, May 29, 1942, shortly before VF-3 joined *Yorktown*. (US Navy)

Two crewmen play acey-deucey on board *Yorktown*, on the morning of June 4, 1942. (US Navy)

A junior officer poses with one of *Yorktown*'s 20mm guns on the morning of June 4, 1942. (US Navy)

An attack aircraft from the Japanese carrier *Hiryū* flies past *Yorktown* during the mid-afternoon torpedo attack, June 4, 1942. (US Navy)

Two of *Hiryū*'s aircraft fly past *Yorktown* amid heavy antiaircraft fire, after dropping their torpedoes. (US Navy)

Far Left: Lieutenant Joichi Tomonaga, *Hiryū*'s air group commander during the Battle of Midway, was killed in action leading the torpedo attack on *Yorktown* on June 4, 1942. (US Navy)

Left: *Hiryū*'s bomber unit commander, Lieutenant Michio Kobayashi, was killed in action leading the dive-bombing attack on *Yorktown* at Midway. (US Navy)

An SBD-3 scout bomber, probably flown by Lieutenant Commander Maxwell F. Leslie, ditches alongside USS *Astoria* at about 1348 hours on June 4, 1942. (US Navy)

Yorktown is hit by a Japanese Type 91 aerial torpedo during the June 4 attack by *Hiryū*'s planes. (US Navy)

Men on *Yorktown*'s flight deck prepare to abandon ship shortly after it was hit by two Japanese aerial torpedoes, June 4, 1942. (US Navy)

Yorktown aflame, and with a serious list. (US Navy)

A destroyer picks up survivors from the now-abandoned *Yorktown*. (US Navy)

Japanese heavy cruiser *Mikuma* after being bombed by planes from *Enterprise* and *Hornet* on June 6, 1942. (US Navy)

I-168 torpedoed *Yorktown* on June 6, 1942, causing damage that sank the carrier the following morning. (US Navy)

Yorktown capsizes to port, exposing the turn of her starboard bilge, with a large torpedo hole amidships severing the forward bilge keel. (US Navy)

Yorktown disappears beneath the waves just after dawn on June 7, 1942. (US Navy)

the barricades were pulled away and they were greeted by "Dutch native troops" when they landed. They discovered the ML-KNIL Buffalos that had been stationed there had been shot down and the Japanese were bombing daily.

After refueling, they decided to press on. The airfield was very muddy and in poor condition. Gilmore remembered:

On takeoff from Tarakan, Captain Connelly gave the airplane full throttle. It accelerated very slowly, and looked as if it would not get off the ground. A fence loomed in front of us, but the experience of an old airline pilot saved the day. In one operation, he pulled up the wheels and put down full flaps. The airplane leaped over the fence and almost settled to the ground, but finally caught and eventually was safely air-borne.

Connelly stopped for more fuel at Balikpapan, then headed for Makassar on Celebes Island. Landing there, the airplane skidded on the mud and came to rest in a hole, undamaged. The next morning, he flew to Koepang on Timor, arriving shortly after noon. They managed to land at dusk at Darwin, having flown over 1,800 miles of long over-water flights in bad weather, with poor maps and the limited navigation aids available in 1941, and arrived in an undamaged aircraft.

Another escape from Bataan was even more eventful. On January 2, 1942, Buzz Wagner's wingman, Lieutenant George E. "King" Kiser, and six other pilots were able to repair a twin-engine Beech Model 18 airliner that had been bombed and strafed, with over 130 bullet holes in it. The damaged leading edge of the left wing was replaced by a piece of sheet tin roofing material. Kiser recalled dramatically that "We wired the wing back on with baling wire."

When they landed at Del Monte, "the right wheel brake barely worked, the left didn't work at all, and the tailwheel could not be locked." Ground crews at Del Monte worked on the plane overnight, but could not fully repair the brakes. "They successfully rigged a hose and funnel arrangement from inside the cabin to a wing gas tank and loaded ten 5-gallon cans of gas in the cabin to assure enough fuel to reach Tarakan."

Taking off before dawn, they climbed into the overcast at 400 feet and flew on instruments for an hour before breaking into clear skies.

Continuing on, the weather again turned bad, with a 200-foot ceiling and a half-mile of visibility by the time they reached Borneo. Kiser was pouring the last can of gas into the funnel when the pilot spotted the airport. Despite having lost a magneto on one engine, Kiser took off that afternoon for Balikpapan in weather that forced him to fly at 100 feet. "Halfway to Balikpapan, oil pressure fell to zero on one engine. The engine survived and adding oil at Balikpapan restored it to normal operation."

On January 5, they departed Balikpapan for Banjermasin, New Guinea, where they refueled. The battered airplane finally gave out, but with the assistance of the Dutch they contacted the US Navy at Surabaya; a PBY was dispatched to pick them up, and they were flown from Surabaya to Darwin in a B-17.

At the end of March, General MacArthur attempted to launch a counteroffensive in the Philippines. On April 11, two days after the surrender at Bataan, a special force of ten brand-new North American B-25C Mitchell medium bombers and three B-17Es manned by crews of the 19th and 7th groups, commanded by Brigadier General Ralph Royce, departed Batchelor Field headed for Del Monte on Mindanao. Known as "the Royce Special Mission," it was the first American aerial counteroffensive against Japan. Named Operation *Plum*, Royce's mission had originally been requested by Lieutenant General Jonathan Wainwright in late March, in hopes that bombing raids from Mindanao could lift the Japanese blockade of American forces on Luzon. With the fall of Bataan, MacArthur decreed the Royce Special Mission should continue, though now the mission involved shipping attacks and bombing Japanese bases in the southern and central Philippines.

General Royce was the senior Air Staff officer at Allied Air Force Headquarters for the newly created South West Pacific Area theater command. He had arrived in Australia in early February from London, where he had been the air attaché. He was one of the most senior pilots in the USAAF, having received his wings in 1915 and flown in France as a squadron and group commander during World War I.

The planes arrived at Del Monte the night of April 11. First Lieutenant John P. Burns noted in his diary that everyone on the field was startled by the unannounced arrival and that no one had ever seen a B-25 before. The B-25s were hidden at the nearby airstrips at Valencia and Maramag while the B-17s remained at Del Monte. The next day,

Japanese bombers raided Del Monte in the morning and afternoon. Following the morning raid, which caused no damage, the B-17s flew a mission with the B-25s; the enemy's afternoon raid caught all three heavy bombers on the field, where they were all damaged, one seriously.

Over the next three days, the Japanese were caught completely by surprise as the bombers attacked targets throughout the Philippines. The operation ended on April 14, with the aircraft and crews returning to Australia the next morning after departing before dawn. General Royce was awarded the Distinguished Service Cross. Unfortunately, the mission never received the recognition it was due, as the B-25 flew into history four days later on April 18, 1942, when Lieutenant Colonel James H. "Jimmy" Doolittle led 15 other Mitchells off the flight deck of the USS *Hornet*, to strike Japan.

Fortunately for the air war to come in the South Pacific, General Royce took an evacuee with him back to Australia, a gifted self-taught troubleshooting engineer and "tinkerer extraordinaire," Paul Irvin "Pappy" Gunn, who had retired from the Navy in December 1939 as a naval aviation pilot, an enlisted naval aviator, after 21 years' service and founded Philippine Airlines. Gunn had received a wartime commission as captain in the USAAF following the Japanese attack. By the time Royce arrived with his B-25s, Gunn was in charge of maintenance at Del Monte, and his expertise was crucial to the success of the Mitchells in their Philippine debut. He would become even more important in the Southwest Pacific air war as the inventor of the "gunship," B-25s and A-20s heavily modified with an intimidating number of heavy machine guns for ground attack.

MacArthur sent official word to the War Department on April 15 that Royce's command had

> attacked the enemy in the Philippines at Nichols Field, Batanga, Cebu and Davao with the following results: at Nichols destruction of hangars and damage to runways; at Davao one bomber destroyed and several damaged, two transports hit with one probably sunk, two seaplanes damaged, one shot down, troop concentrations dispersed, docks and warehouses damaged; at Cebu three transports sunk, two others hit and several close misses, shot down three planes, damaged several on the ground, and damaged docks; at Batanga one freighter sunk. One of our planes was lost but the crew saved.

Sadly, there would be no more offensive missions flown in the Philippines. The two P-35As that escaped from Bataan to Del Monte were among the last four American fighters to fly combat in the Philippines. The last mission was flown on April 22 by First Lieutenant John Brownewell, who picked up two Americans surrounded by the Japanese on Negros Island, squeezing them into the baggage compartment for the return to Del Monte. On April 30, when he was evacuated to Java, Brownewell turned over the P-35A Gillet had been flying when he shot down the Zero over Lamon Bay to Captain Ramon Zosa of the Philippine Army Air Corps. Zosa flew the final P-35 sortie, accompanying a P-40 on a strafing attack of Japanese landings at Mindanao's Macajalar Bay, on May 3, 1942.

Japanese artillery on Bataan shelled Corregidor for the three weeks following the Bataan surrender, during which parts of the island were literally blown into the sea. The morning of May 8, 1942, two assault battalions attempted to land near the narrow tip of the island. The "Old China Hands" of the 4th Marine Regiment, the last Americans to leave China the previous summer, were waiting; the Marines were reinforced with several hundred sailors, Philippine Scouts, artillerymen, and service troops. The second attacking battalion's boats were spotted in the moonlight; less than half the attackers survived to reach land. At the same time, the first battalion managed to establish a beachhead and move inland, capturing "Battery Denver." By dawn, several pieces of artillery and a few tanks had been landed. By 1030 hours, the defenders were forced back within a few yards of the entrance to Malinta Tunnel. Most of the artillery was out of action and the reserves had been committed; ammunition was nearly exhausted and there was only a two-day water supply left.

During the siege of Corregidor, five submarines of the Asiatic Fleet which had moved down to Australia ran the Japanese blockade, arriving at night and leaving before dawn. Several important officers and enlisted men who had been left behind were evacuated, in addition to as many surviving aircrew as possible. USS *Seawolf* (SS-197), commanded by Lieutenant Commander Fred Warder, took 12 army pilots and 13 enlisted men to Surabaya, Java. *Seadragon* (SS-194), commanded by Lieutenant Commander Peter Ferral, took four officers including lieutenants Harl Pease and "Pinky" Hoevet, and 20 enlisted men of the 19th Bomb Group to Darwin.

Lieutenant Commander Tyrrel Jacobs' *Sargo* (SS-188) took the Army code breakers and all their information to Melbourne, Australia, to join MacArthur's headquarters. Lieutenant Commander Chet Smith brought *Swordfish* (SS-193) to the island twice. The first time, he brought out Philippines Commonwealth President Manuel Quezon and United States Ambassador Francis Sayre and his wife, and the gold reserves of the Commonwealth; the second, which was the next-to-last mission to "The Rock" before its fall, took as many remaining pilots as had managed to make their way to Corregidor, and several staff officers. On May 2, *Spearfish* (SS-190), commanded by Lieutenant Commander James Dempsey, took the last evacuees to Australia. Four Army nurses who refused evacuation, 173 officers, and 2,317 soldiers, sailors, and Marines were left behind.

General Wainwright sent a last message to Washington the night of May 3: "Please say to the nation that my troops and I have accomplished all that is humanly possible and that we have upheld the best traditions of the United States and its Army. With profound regret and continued pride in my gallant troops, I go to meet the Japanese commander."

That evening, General Eisenhower wrote in his diary: "Poor Wainwright! He did the fighting, another got such glory as the public could find in the operation. But he's a hero! Yah."

The American forces in the Philippines had held out for 142 days, rather than the 50 the Japanese had expected. MacArthur's defenders claimed afterwards that the "prolonged defense" of the Philippines disrupted the Japanese timetable and delayed their operations against Australia, New Guinea, and the Solomons, despite the fact that the Japanese never had a plan to invade Australia, and had not yet considered operations in either New Guinea or the Solomons.

The fighter pilots in the Philippines had given their all in the battle. Of 165 pilots in the four squadrons, 33 were killed in action or accidents between December 8, 1941, and June 20, 1942, when the last air force personnel on Mindanao finally surrendered. Forty-nine were evacuated to Australia; they would continue the fight in the Dutch Indies where several more would pay the ultimate price, while 83 pilots including Lamar Gillet, surrendered and became prisoners of war. Of the 27 officers and 1,444 enlisted men in the ground echelons, one officer and 20 men – all wounded – were evacuated. Of the 1,504 officers and men who surrendered in the Philippines, 900 – 60 percent – died in captivity. During the campaign, they were credited with 37 aerial victories against their Japanese opponents.

The importance of the battle in the Philippines was psychological and moral. In the United States, "Colin P. Kelly, the pilot who sank a battleship," "the battling bastards of Bataan," "the Rock," the doctors and nurses in Malinta Tunnel who served to the last and refused evacuation, and MacArthur's dramatic escape, became part of wartime folklore. There was little exaggeration in President Roosevelt's last message to Wainwright: "You and your devoted followers have become the living symbol of our war aims and the guarantee of victory."

CHAPTER FOURTEEN

"GO FORWARD, FIGHT WELL, AND DO US HONOR"

The week after Pearl Harbor, newly minted Ensign John Bridgers found his assignment to the Atlantic Fleet changed, with orders that sent him to Pearl Harbor to join Bombing 3 at the Ford Island Naval Air Station. Thirty minutes after the train left the station bound for San Francisco, he realized he had left his suitcase behind, which contained his orders and pay records. Just before Christmas, Bridgers and 50 other naval aviators went aboard the transport SS *President Hoover* along with 2,000 construction workers, and headed for Pearl Harbor. His group bunked in what had been the liner's luxurious cocktail lounge.

Diamond Head came into view after a week at sea. Bridgers later recalled:

> As we pulled into Pearl Harbor, I recalled having seen a newsreel with Secretary of the Navy Frank Knox maintaining that little substantial damage had been done to the Pacific Fleet by the Pearl Harbor attack. We looked out and saw that the waters were still uniformly oil-covered, and we passed the grounded battleship USS *Nevada* in the channel. In the harbor itself were more derelicts, including the capsized USS *Oklahoma*, the sunken USS *West Virginia*, and the remains of the blasted USS *Arizona*. It was evident there had been grievous hurt inflicted by the enemy.

Like many others who came through Pearl Harbor until 1944 and saw the results of the Japanese attack, Bridgers took a personal oath of vengeance on the enemy. *Saratoga* had departed two days before his arrival to patrol off Midway, taking Air Group 3 with her, so Bridgers waited at Ford Island for her return to join his new squadron.

While John Bridgers traveled across the Pacific to Hawaii, Admiral Ernest J. King was promoted by President Roosevelt from command of the Atlantic Fleet to the revived position of Commander in Chief, US Fleet on the last day of 1941. The official title at the time was Commander in Chief US Fleet, with the unfortunate military acronym of CINCUS; King quickly changed that to COMINCH. On New Year's Day 1942, Admiral Chester Nimitz became Commander in Chief, Pacific Fleet. King's first order to Nimitz was a directive to protect US shipping between the United States and Australia, as far south as Samoa.

At their first meeting on January 2 to plan how to accomplish this, Nimitz's staff recommended strikes against the Japanese air bases in the Gilberts and Marshall Islands to at least delay any potential attacks against Samoa. A convoy carrying 5,000 Marines to garrison the naval base on Tutuila Island at Samoa was already forming, which would be provided cover by Admiral Fletcher's Task Force 17 centered around his flagship, the newly arrived *Yorktown* (CV-5). Vice Admiral William S. Pye, who had briefly commanded the Pacific Fleet before Nimitz's arrival, raised the possibility of the Japanese expecting reinforcement of Samoa, which they might use as an opportunity to engage in a battle with the depleted Pacific Fleet. He suggested, and Nimitz agreed, that two carriers should cover the arrival of the Marines in Samoa. Once the Marines were ashore, the two carriers would strike the Japanese bases as the staff recommended. The staff, however, was opposed to risking two carriers in a possible fleet action.

Admiral Halsey returned to Pearl Harbor aboard *Enterprise* on January 7. He immediately approved Admiral Pye's plan and volunteered to lead the operation. On January 9, Nimitz ordered Halsey to give support to Task Force 17 with *Enterprise*'s Task Force 8; the two carriers would then strike the Gilberts and Marshalls bases while Admiral Wilson Brown aboard *Lexington* with Task Force 11 would strike Wake to divert Japanese attention. *Saratoga*'s Task Force 14 would guard Hawaii.

Enterprise's working parties provisioned the ship all day and into the night on January 10 and stood out past Diamond Head at 1200 hours on

Sunday, January 11. Rear Admiral Raymond A. Spruance's flagship, the heavy cruiser *Northampton*, in company with the heavy cruisers *Salt Lake City* and *Chester* and six destroyers, provided protection for the carrier.

The plan changed drastically shortly after noon. *Saratoga*, returning from her Midway patrol, was 480 miles southwest of Oahu when she was hit by a torpedo fired by the Japanese submarine *I-6*. Three boiler rooms were flooded, six crewmen were killed, and her speed was reduced to 16 knots. Listing to port, *Saratoga* limped toward Pearl Harbor. She would soon depart for repairs and modernization in Bremerton, Washington, keeping her out of action until she arrived in Pearl Harbor just too late to participate in the Battle of Midway in June. The overall plan of attack now changed, with *Lexington* remaining off Hawaii.

When *Saratoga* departed a week later, she exchanged her Wildcat-equipped Fighting 3 for *Lexington*'s "Flying Chiefs" of Fighting 2 and their F2A-3s, which had proven too fragile for sustained carrier operations. Bombing 3 was left behind at Ford Island, where John Bridgers now joined an "orphan" squadron.

Enterprise's voyage to Samoa was plagued by accidents and bad news. On January 13, a patrolling pilot broke radio silence, potentially putting the whole mission at risk. The next day a sailor was washed overboard from the destroyer USS *Blue* and lost. Two days later, a sailor was accidentally killed aboard *Salt Lake City* while a Dauntless crash-landed aboard *Enterprise*, killing a chief petty officer. To finish off a bad day, the Torpedo 6 TBD-1 flown by Chief Naval Aviation Pilot Harold Dixon with crewmen Tony Pastula and Gene Aldrich disappeared while on anti-submarine patrol. Fortunately, the three fliers survived a 750-mile sea voyage over 35 days at sea in their raft, washing ashore March 22 on Puka-Puka Island, an uninhabited atoll, where they were later rescued.

Regardless of the accidents, Task Force 8 arrived at Samoa on January 18 and took up a defensive station 100 miles to the north. The convoy arrived on January 23. On January 25, *Enterprise* and *Yorktown* and their supporting task forces set course to the northwest. Halsey's chief of staff, the irascible Commander miles Browning, was in charge of planning the raid. *Yorktown* would strike Makin in the Gilberts, and Jaluit and Mili atolls in the southern Marshalls. *Enterprise* would hit Wotje and Taroa in the Maloelap Atoll in the northern Marshalls. The submarine *Dolphin* reconnoitered the targets and reported on January 27 that they were not as heavily fortified as thought, and that there was significant enemy air and shipping activity at Kwajalein Atoll, 150 miles west of Wotje. Browning convinced Halsey to add the atoll to the target list, despite the fact that striking Kwajalein would require *Enterprise* to operate closer to Wotje and Taroa. However, the air forces based on Kwajalein represented a threat to both carriers; not striking those airfields was the more dangerous option.

The afternoon of January 28, Task Force 8 conducted underway refueling with the oiler *Platte* (AO-24). Heavy seas slowed the operation and *Enterprise* did not come alongside *Platte* until 1600 hours; the two ships steamed in formation until 2130 hours, the first time a capital ship had refueled underway at night.

At dusk on January 29, the two task forces parted company to conduct their strikes; at dawn they crossed the International Date Line into January 31. While *Enterprise* steamed on to her combat debut, the men of Air Group 6 worked feverishly to install boiler plate armor in each of the aircraft. Halsey ordered all ships rigged for towing or being towed, in preparation to give assistance to any ship damaged by the enemy.

At 1830 hours, *Enterprise* began her run into the launching point, her engines answering to the command "all ahead flank" and her speed increased to 30 knots. At 0220 hours, the officer of the deck reported sand blowing in his face. Halsey ordered their position be checked, since they were using old maps of questionable accuracy and there was fear they could run into one of the numerous small islands at top speed. Moments later, the OOD realized the "sand" tasted sweet; the source was soon traced to a watch stander who was stirring sugar in his coffee. At 0300 hours, reveille was sounded and the ship went to general quarters. Taroa and Wotje were less than 40 miles distant. On the flight deck, plane captains made last-minute inspections of their charges. Shortly before 0400 hours, the command "Pilots! Man your planes!" echoed through the ship. Minutes later, engines began coughing into life and soon the entire task force could hear the steady thrumming sound of aircraft engines warming up.

At 0430 hours, *Enterprise* turned into the wind. At 0445 hours, six Fighting 6 F4F-3 Wildcats were launched. They were followed minutes later by the 18 SBD-3 Dauntlesses of Scouting 6 and 17 SBD-2s of Bombing 6, the strike force led by Enterprise CAG Commander Howard L. "Brigham" Young. One SBD-2 suffered an engine problem that delayed its takeoff. Shortly after 0500 hours, that Dauntless climbed into the dark sky, followed by nine TBD-1 Devastators from Torpedo Six. The 46 aircraft took several minutes to complete the difficult task of joining up in the darkness, then headed for Kwajalein Atoll, 155 miles distant. Each SBD carried one 500-pound bomb on the centerline rack and a 200-pound bomb under each wing, while three 500-pound bombs hung beneath each Devastator rather than a torpedo.

Sunrise was still an hour off when 12 Fighting 6 Wildcats were launched to hit Wotje and Taroa. Ensign David W. Criswell apparently became disoriented in the darkness; shortly after takeoff, his Wildcat stalled and plunged into the sea, taking him with it in its dive to the bottom. The five surviving Wildcats, each armed with a 100-pound bomb under each wing, headed for their target. All aircraft were to arrive over their respective targets at 0700 hours, as sunrise came in the Central Pacific. While the aircraft droned through the darkness, Admiral Spruance's cruisers closed on Wotje, target of *Northampton* and *Salt Lake City*, and Taroa, which would be shelled by *Chester* and two destroyers.

At approximately 0655 hours, Torpedo 6 commander Lieutenant Commander Gene Lindsey led his nine Devastators toward Kwajalein anchorage, 44 miles to the south, while the SBDs set up to hit Roi. Darkness, low-lying fog, and inaccurate old maps delayed identification of the target, and it was not until 0705 hours that the VS-6 SBDs began winging over into their dives. The defenders on the ground had been alerted to their presence by the delay.

Scouting 6's commander, Lieutenant Commander Halstead L. Hopping, led a division of six SBDs that dived through increasing defensive fire and hit the airfield, where they could see enemy fighters on their takeoff rolls below. Hopping drew much of the AA fire; he and gunner Aviation Radioman 1/c Harold Thomas were lost when their Dauntless was set on fire and plunged into the sea. Lieutenants Earl Gallaher and Clarence E. Dickinson followed Hopping with their divisions, their bombs destroying an ammunition dump, two hangars, and a radio station. Swinging back to strafe the field, three more SBDs went down, two to ground fire and one to a defending A5M4 Claude fighter. The dive bombers claimed three Claudes in return.

Roi was now a burning shambles. At that moment, Gene Lindsey radioed his discovery of several merchant ships and the cruiser *Katori* at the Kwajalein anchorage. Seven VS-6 Dauntlesses that had not yet attacked Roi joined the 18 VB-6 dive bombers led by squadron commander Lieutenant Commander William R. Hollingsworth and his Annapolis classmate and newly promoted executive officer, Dick Best. Lindsey's Devastators had achieved complete surprise, damaging several ships in glide-bombing attacks against poorly directed defensive fire. The Dauntlesses attacked from 14,000 feet. After making their attacks, they reported the transport *Bordeaux Maru* and subchaser *Shonan Maru* were sinking, while six other ships were damaged.

Those aboard *Enterprise* could see the attack on Wotje carried out by Fighting 6 commander Lieutenant Commander C. Wade McClusky as his six Wildcats made two high-speed bombing runs over the sleeping island, hitting the under-construction airfield, then strafing the island.

Fighting 6 executive officer Lieutenant James S. Gray's five Wildcats found the most action at Taroa. Gray and his wingman, Lt(jg) Wilmer Rawie, had mistakenly bombed the unoccupied island of Tjan, which Gray misidentified as Taroa, at 0700 hours. They found Taroa 15 miles away, and already alert. The Wildcat pilots had been briefed to attack what was thought to be a lightly defended seaplane base. Instead, they found a fully operational air base with two new 5,000-foot runways and at least 30–40 G3M2 Nell bombers on the ground. After dropping their remaining bombs on the airfield, the five Wildcats turned back to strafe. With no incendiary ammunition, they were only able to set one airplane on fire, but several others were rendered inoperable from hits.

Gray's wingman Rawie recovered from his pass and identified two A5M4 Claude fighters a mile ahead. Staying low, Rawie crept up on them unawares and crippled one with a long burst of fire. The wingman turned on him and he turned back to face the attacker. The enemy pilot didn't turn away and Rawie clipped the Claude with the belly of his Wildcat, knocking the lighter and less rugged fighter out of the sky. Six more Claudes managed to get airborne. Rawie's four guns jammed on his second pass, as did Ensign Ralph Rich's guns. Moments later, the guns on two more Wildcats jammed and the four pilots turned back for the carrier.

Gray was suddenly alone, the center of attention for the more maneuverable enemy fighters. Three of his guns jammed as he maneuvered to get away. He turned and fired at each Claude with his one gun as they streaked past. Finally, Gray was able to break away from the enemy at 0720. When he landed back aboard *Enterprise*, the airedales counted 30 bullet holes in his fighter, making him the first of many pilots to owe his life to the Grumman Iron Works.

At 0715 hours, *Northampton* and *Salt Lake City* opened fire on Wotje. After several salvos they turned their fire on some merchant ships spotted slipping out of the anchorage. *Chester* and the two destroyers opened up on Taroa minutes later and came under attack from defending Japanese airplanes. *Chester* was hit aft by a small bomb and came under attack from eight G3Ms that made a level bombing run on her at 0830 hours. At that point, Spruance ordered his force to break off and retire.

After interviewing returning pilots, Halsey and Browning determined Taroa would require additional strikes. The other nine TBD-1s of Torpedo 6 had been armed with torpedoes and sent to hit the shipping reported by Lindsey. The Dauntlesses were hurriedly refueled and rearmed. They would have to attack without escorts, since the Wildcats were now needed for Combat Air Patrol. At 0930 hours, Bombing 6's Lieutenant Commander Hollingsworth led nine SBDs, two from Scouting 6 and the other seven from Bombing 6, to hit Taroa. Arriving over the field, they found most enemy aircraft on the ground being refueled. Their attack knocked down two hangars and set at least nine aircraft afire. As they turned away, five A5M4s engaged them but were chased off by the Dauntless gunners and the attackers returned safely to the ship.

Enterprise launched a third strike at 1030, led by Bombing 6's XO, Lieutenant Dick Best. The bombers wrecked a radio tower, fuel tanks, and other airfield installations, while CAG Young led a second strike to Wotje. The defending fighters engaged Best's Dauntlesses, whose pilots and gunners claimed two. Ensign John Doherty and his gunner, Aviation Ordnanceman 3/c Will Hunt, became involved in a sustained aerial combat as they turned back and sought to keep the enemy away from the others as they made their escape. Doherty and Hunt failed to return to the carrier; his last words over the radio were: "These goddamn Japs will never get me."

Doherty's roommate, Lt(jg) Tony Schneider, had been on a different mission when Doherty was lost. He later remembered:

> Johnny was a good man. He never swore much, was always considerate, very kind, he and I became fast friends. You could say he was typical of the kind of people we had as pilots. On duty, he was studious, attentive,

dedicated. I learned about Johnny when I got back to the ship. I cursed, I cried a little, then I calmed down. There was no time for allowing a period of grief. Johnny, I know, would understand. If you allowed yourself to go numb over the deaths of your friends, you'd join them. After the war, there was time to sit and finally give them proper due. The way he died was true Johnny, right down to his radio call as he stayed behind to tangle those three Japs. At least he killed one of them. We held a memorial service for him and the others who were killed on that day. We said our goodbyes, then we got back into the war.

While *Enterprise*'s raiders had shot down 15 Japanese aircraft and sunk two ships, the simultaneous *Yorktown* raid had been less successful. Air Group 5 sent 11 TBD-1s of VT-5 and 17 SBD-3s of VB-5, led by CAG Commander Curtis W. Smiley, to hit shore installations and shipping at Jaluit. The mission ran into severe thunderstorms, and five planes were lost to the weather while two Devastators were hit by enemy defensive fire and crashed into the Jaluit lagoon. Other *Yorktown* planes attacked installations and ships at Makin and Mili atolls without the success enjoyed by *Enterprise*.

With the Dauntlesses safely back aboard, Admiral Halsey judged he had taken as many chances with the raid as was prudent, and he ordered the fleet to head north. At 1330, a "bogey" appeared on *Enterprise*'s radar, closing at high speed. The CAP was sent to investigate and identified five G3M2 Nell bombers 15 miles out. The four Wildcats tried to attack, but jammed guns and cloud cover allowed the Nells to escape. Minutes later, the bombers burst out of the clouds 3,500 yards off the carrier's bow, approaching in a shallow dive at 250 mph. The gunners opened fire with the 5-inch mounts, but inexperience and battle stress led to the enemy evading the defenses. Captain George Murray ordered a hard left rudder, followed quickly by hard right. *Enterprise* responded nimbly and "stepped aside" the oncoming bombers. As the 1.1-inch "Chicago pianos" opened up, the five bombers dropped three bombs each. All but one fell harmlessly in the sea to port, but the last exploded close aboard, severing a gas line, starting a small fire, and mortally wounding Boatswain's Mate 2/c George Smith, the first member of *Enterprise*'s ship's company to die in the war.

The Nells recovered from their dives 1,500 feet above the ships and four sped away. The Nell flown by flight leader Lieutenant Kazuo Nakai turned sharply left and then circled back toward the carrier. Every gun that could bear opened fire but Nakai came on, clearly intending to crash the ship. At the last moment, Captain Murray ordered a hard right turn and the Nell, whether due to damage or a wounded pilot, failed to match the turn. Flashing mere feet above the flight deck aft, the bomber's right wing clipped the tail of a parked VS-6 Dauntless whose rear gunner, Aviation Machinist's Mate 2/c Bruno Gaido, was firing at the enemy. The Nell's wing snapped off and drenched the island and flight deck with gasoline before it fell into a port catwalk. Nakai and his crew went into the sea off *Enterprise*'s port quarter and quickly disappeared. Gaido jumped out of the Dauntless with the fire extinguisher and fought the fire. With the flames extinguished, he realized he was in trouble for having left his battle station to man the Dauntless's guns, and promptly disappeared back into the ship. Halsey ordered that the runaway be found and brought to him. When Gaido was presented to the admiral sometime later, he was given a spot promotion to first class petty officer by Halsey, who told him, "By God, sailor, we need men like you!"

Enterprise and her escorts again took up a course to the north and increased speed to 30 knots as they sped away from the Marshalls. A wag aboard the carrier recorded in the logbook that they were "Haulin' ass with Halsey."

An hour after Nakai's attack, two Wildcats on CAP intercepted a snooping H6K "Mavis" and played cat-and-mouse with the big flying boat in the clouds before finally shooting it down. At 1600 hours, two more G3Ms popped out of the clouds and made a level bombing run. Fighting 6 CO McClusky gave spotting assistance to the ship's gunners, and one Nell broke off its attack after being hit. McClusky and the other three pilots sent the other Nell crashing into the sea in flames.

Sunset came at 1835 hours, finding all 14 Fighting 6 Wildcats still on patrol, with several pilots weary as they flew their fifth mission of the day. The last Wildcat landed at 1902 hours, aided by a full moon that illuminated the fleet's wakes. To throw off enemy snoopers, Halsey briefly turned on a northwest course and was grateful to find shelter under a damp cold front. Under cover of what would become known as "Enterprise weather," *Enterprise* turned northeast shortly before midnight and the task force headed for Pearl Harbor.

Task Force 8 returned to Pearl Harbor on February 5 to celebration. The daring raid was the Navy's first significant victory of the Pacific War and the publicity surrounding it saw the beginning of Halsey's public reputation as "America's fightin'est Admiral."

Despite newspaper accounts that called the raid "Japan's Pearl Harbor," it was soon known that the damage actually inflicted fell far short of initial estimates. One transport and two smaller vessels were sunk, with eight other ships damaged at Kwajalein, half the number originally reported sunk. Nine aircraft were destroyed on the ground at Taroa and Roi, with three A5Ms shot down at the cost of one Wildcat and five SBDs.

The true significance of the Marshalls raid was in the lessons learned. Halsey's action report repeatedly noted the poor performance of the ship's antiaircraft defenses:

> The inability of the 5-inch AA battery to knock down the formation of enemy twin-engine bombers is a matter of grave concern. AA Gunnery practices should be scheduled when opportunity offers, with ship steaming at not less than 25 knots. If adequate safeguards can be introduced, ship should be required to make radical changes of course.

Both the air group and ship's company gained valuable combat experience that would prepare them for the battles to come.

Though hardly enough to stall the Japanese South Seas offensive, Halsey's raid served notice that the Navy's striking arm did not lie broken in the mud at Pearl Harbor.

While *Enterprise* and *Yorktown* made their presence known in the Central Pacific, *Lexington*'s Task Force 11 was ordered to strike the new Japanese base at Rabaul. On the day *Enterprise* returned to Pearl Harbor, Task Force 11 was spotted by Japanese snoopers before they could launch their strike. The task force was soon under attack by land-based Japanese bombers from Rabaul. During the air battle over the fleet, Fighting 3's Lieutenant Edward H. "Butch" O'Hare and his wingman, Lt (jg) Marion F. Dufilho, intercepted one group of seven attacking G4M1 "Betty" bombers and shot down all of them before they could attack the task force. O'Hare scored five of the bombers to become the Navy's first ace of the Pacific War, for which he was awarded the Medal of Honor. *Lexington* withdrew back into the Coral Sea, where she was joined by *Yorktown* and the two task forces commenced patrolling the South Pacific.

On February 20, *Enterprise* departed Pearl Harbor to strike Wake Island. The morning of February 24, the carrier launched what would be the first of many strikes by carriers against Wake over the course of the rest of the war, when the "Alamo of the Pacific" was turned into a training target with live ammunition for newly arrived air groups. Aviation Radioman 2/c Ronald W. Graet, who had joined VT-6 in August 1941, remembered the mission:

> The flight from the ship to the island sure stands out. The old TBD had a cruising speed something like 110 or 115 knots. We were carrying 12 100-pound bombs under the wings and had to attain the altitude of 12,000 feet before we got to the island. I can't imagine what our actual forward speed was, but, since all planes were to arrive over the target at the same time, the fighters and bombers had to wait for us. I remember looking up at the formations of SBD aircraft over us, flying a big zig-zag pattern to maintain the same forward speed as us.
>
> We made our first run over the island at 12,000 feet then turned and climbed about 500 feet for the next run. Each pass we made, we adjusted our altitude by about 500 feet. The bursts of antiaircraft fire were close enough to make the plane bounce around like we were in turbulent air. As we turned away from the island and started back toward the *Enterprise*, our bombardier climbed back up from the bombsight position below the pilot's feet to the middle seat and said over the intercom, "Boy, the air was sure rough up there this morning!" When Mr Rombach and I both chimed in and told him that was because of the exploding antiaircraft shells nearby, he said, "Damn, if I had known that, I would have got out and walked back!"

Enterprise headed west and on March 4, Air Group 6 attacked Marcus Island, only 1,148 miles southeast of Tokyo. Following this attack, the closest any American aircraft carrier had yet come to Japan, she returned to Pearl Harbor.

The Japanese offensive in the South Seas continued. With the conquest of the Indies, Operation *MO* – the capture of Port Moresby on the southern coast of New Guinea – was the next move. The preliminary move came on March 5, when an invasion fleet departed Rabaul and crossed the Bismarck Sea, planning to offload 3,000 troops to capture Lae and nearby Salamaua on the northeast coast of New

Guinea. The airfields at each location had been used to launch Allied attacks on Rabaul after it had been taken by the Japanese in February. Possession of these airfields would allow Japanese aircraft to attack Port Moresby in preparation for the main attack, while preventing further Allied attacks on Rabaul. The invasion fleet was spotted by an RAAF Hudson the afternoon of March 7 as the ships approached their targets.

For the invasion of Salamaua and Lae, the Japanese 4th Fleet, under the command of Admiral Shigeyoshi Inoue, and Admiral Tomitarō Horii's South Seas Detachment established a landing force built around the 2nd Battalion, 144th Infantry Regiment, under the command of Major Horie Masao, and a battalion of the Kure Special Naval Landing Force.

The Imperial Japanese Navy formed an escort group to support the operation, under Rear Admiral Kajioka Sadamichi's command, and using the heavy cruisers of the 8th Cruiser Division, *Aoba*, *Kinugasa*, *Furutaka* and *Kako*; the light cruisers *Tenryū* and *Tatsuta*; the destroyers *Mutsuki*, *Mochizuki*, *Yoyoi*, *Asanagi*, *Oite*; and *Yūnagi*, with the light cruiser *Yūbari*.

The invasion fleet left Rabaul on March 5. The troop transports *Yokohama Maru* and *China Maru* sailed for Salamaua with Horie's troops, while the transports *Kongō Maru*, *Kokai Maru*, and the auxiliary minelayer *Tenyo Maru*, sailed for Lae with the naval landing party. Air support operations were flown by the 24th Air Flotilla.

The first of the Special Naval Landing Force troops went ashore at Lae at 0100 hours on March 8 in the middle of a heavy rainstorm. Simultaneously, troops of the elite SNLF South Seas Detachment that had taken Wake Island landed at Salamaua. At both locations, the small Australian garrisons withdrew into the jungle after demolishing everything they could at the airfields. The two towns and their airfields were secured by mid-day and the Japanese set to unloading the ships and fortifying the beachheads. Zero fighters of the Tainan Air Group were set to arrive the next day from Rabaul when the weather cleared. To cover the landings, missions were flown from Rabaul to hit the Australian airfields at Port Moresby, Bulolo, and Wau, where the fact they met no Allied fighter opposition gave the Japanese confidence they had achieved surprise.

Lexington and *Yorktown* and their respective escorts had remained in the Coral Sea following the Marshalls strike and the attempted attack at Rabaul. The two air groups were set to attempt a second attack on Rabaul and the airstrip at Gasmata on New Ireland when word came of the landings at Lae and Salamaua. The planned strikes were immediately changed to strike the Japanese while they were still unloading the transports. For the Americans, the most direct route, across the Solomon Sea and up the New Guinea coast, posed a risk that the American fleet would be detected by Japanese air patrols from Rabaul.

The decision was made to launch the strike from the Gulf of Papua south of New Guinea. This would require the aircraft to cross the island's backbone, the Owen Stanley Mountains, which presented some of the most difficult flying conditions anywhere, with mountains as high as 15,000 feet, covered in triple-canopy jungle and frequently obscured by clouds and mist. With the available charts providing scant guidance, *Lexington*'s CAG, Commander William B. Ault, flew to Port Moresby, where he was able to obtain the guidance necessary to fly the mission from experienced Australian bush pilots.

Admiral Wilson Brown, the senior officer present, sent Australian Admiral J.G. Crace's four cruisers and their accompanying destroyers to the Louisiade Archipelago off the eastern end of New Guinea, from where they could both cover his flank and also cover the arrival of a US troop convoy at Noumea. Wilson's move into the Gulf of Papua precluded discovery of the two carriers and the Japanese proceeded with their unloading at Lae and Salamaua in the belief they had the time to accomplish this without any Allied intervention.

At 0400 hours on March 10, reveille sounded aboard the American ships as they stood off the southern New Guinea coast and the crews went to general quarters. *Lexington* began launching Air Group 2 at 0749 hours, composed of 18 SBDs from VS-2, 12 from VB-2, 13 TBDs of VT-2, and eight VF-3 Wildcats led by Lieutenant Commander John Thach. *Yorktown*'s 17 VB-5 SBDs, 13 from VS-5, 15 TBDs from VF-5, and 10 VF-42 Wildcat escorts were launched at 0803 hours. Because of the difficulty crossing the mountains, only VT-2 carried the heavy Mark XIV torpedoes, while VT-5's Devastators carried two 500-pound bombs each. *Lexington*'s CAG Bill Ault flew ahead to scout the pass he had been told was the only route to the northern coast, as the 104 aircraft commenced their climb to cross the Owen Stanleys.

The slow TBDs struggled at the high altitude necessary to transit the pass; the torpedo-armed Devastators of VT-2 had to turn back from their first attempt to get through and find upcurrents that would lift them through the rocky narrow pass at an altitude of 13,000 feet.

Air Group 2 arrived over the Huon Gulf shortly after 0900 hours to find there were no Japanese fighter patrols over the invasion fleet. Scouting 2's Dauntlesses pushed over into their dives from 16,000 feet at 0922 hours, aiming for three transports tied up at the Lae pier and two transports anchored offshore. Two pilots had to pull out when their aiming telescopes fogged over in the dive from colder air into warm air over the target; they spotted the cruiser *Kinugasa* and made a glide-bombing attack, hitting her stern and setting the warship afire. Another pair attacked a destroyer and hit the ship's stern, setting it afire. Defensive AA caught the VS-2 SBD flown by Ensign Joseph Philip Johnson and set it afire; he and his gunner, Aviation Radioman 3/c J.B. Jewell, were lost when their plane crashed into the water. Thach's Wildcats went after the AA guns and put them out of action.

At 0938 hours, VT-2 and VB-2 commenced a coordinated torpedo and bomb attack. Three TBDs attacked two transports anchored close to shore off Salamaua. One transport later identified as *Kongō Maru* was hit and began to sink, while the other two torpedoes ran too deep and exploded when they hit the shore. Five other TBDs went after another transport but only two torpedoes exploded when they hit, although they sank the *Yokohama Maru*. Three other TBDs attacked two other transports; two scored hits while the third exploded ashore. Another Devastator went after Rear Admiral Kajioka's flagship, the light cruiser *Yūbari*, damaging the ship.

The six VB-2 SBDs carrying 1,000-pound bombs went after the heavy cruiser *Furutaka*, but were only able to inflict light damage with one direct hit, while the others landed close enough that the pilots reported their belief the ship had been sunk on their return to *Lexington*. The other six SBDs, armed with one 500-pound and two 100-pound bombs, went after other transports and scored hits. The Japanese warships made smoke to cover the transports and the invasion fleet fled to sea as the *Lexington* attackers flew off.

Air Group 5 commenced their attack at 0950 hours. VB-5's SBDs went after the fleeing Japanese warships. Three attacked *Yūbari* and claimed three hits, while another division attacked the destroyer *Asanagi*, knocking out her boilers, while three others damaged the destroyer *Yūnagi*'s engines. Other SBDs strafed a gunboat, setting it afire.

Scouting 5 pushed over at 1005 hours, scoring hits on three transports that were left on fire and beached. Torpedo 5's Devastators found the seaplane carrier *Kiyokawa Maru* and an escorting destroyer north of Lae. Unfortunately, the Devastator crews lacked experience in level bombing and all the bombs missed, though a near miss on *Kiyokawa Maru* let water into the engine room and the ship was left dead in the water.

As the planes flew off, they left three transports beached on fire at Lae, with *Kiyokawa Maru* dead in the water, *Yūbari* so heavily damaged she would require dockyard repair in Japan, and the destroyers *Asanagi* and *Yūnagi* dead in the water. Off Salamaua, one transport listed heavily and another sank. The Tainan Air Group's Zeros arrived too late to give any cover.

The two air groups had lost one SBD and had 11 others damaged by enemy fire. *Lexington* and *Yorktown* had all 103 aircraft back aboard by noon. Admiral Fletcher aboard *Yorktown* advocated a second strike, but Admiral Wilson considered it was time to withdraw before the fleet was found by Japanese search planes. The carriers and their escorts retired to the southeast until dark, when they turned east and rejoined Admiral Crace's cruisers. The raid had given the aircrews their first combat experience against warships and ground targets defended by AA. While the accuracy of some squadrons left a great deal to be desired, the deficiencies exposed would be resolved through training by the next time the two air groups entered action. Admirals Brown and Fletcher didn't receive the praise Admiral Nimitz had lavished on Halsey for the Marshalls raid. He expressed disappointment that the Japanese had not been turned away from landing on New Guinea. However, President Roosevelt's report on the raid to Winston Churchill, in which he called it "the best day's work we have had," turned out to be right. The raid had produced alarm at Navy General Staff Headquarters in Tokyo. Plans to advance on Port Moresby were delayed while a larger invasion force was assembled. The General Staff planners now advocated a further advance into the South Seas, with the Solomon Islands now being seen as essential parts of the Japanese defensive screen. Admiral Yamamoto saw the raids by the American carriers as proof that further advance east into the Central Pacific was necessary, to provoke the fleet action that would guarantee victory before the Americans could bring their industrial power fully to bear against Japan. Yamamoto expressed fear that the American carriers might even have the audacity to raid Tokyo.

Two weeks after the Lae–Salamaua raid, HYPO, the Naval Communications Intelligence unit at Pearl Harbor, decoded a message detailing a Japanese plan to establish a seaplane base at Tulagi in the southern Solomon Islands on May 3, to be followed by a seaborne invasion of Port Moresby on May 10. Following these operations, Fiji, Samoa, and New Caledonia would be taken over the summer.

Lexington returned to Pearl Harbor on March 26 and went into the Pearl Harbor Naval yard for a brief refit, during which her four 8-inch gun turrets were removed to provide coastal defense for Hawaii and additional antiaircraft weapons were mounted on the carrier.

The first tentative actions by the Navy's carrier fleet were over.

Ensign John Joseph Doherty was awarded the Distinguished Flying Cross for his action to save his fellow aviators, the first *Enterprise* flier so honored. On January 6, 1943, the USS *John Doherty* (DE-14), an *Evarts*-class destroyer escort, was christened at the Mare Island Navy yard in California. Ensign Doherty's mother Dotty, an Irish immigrant who had given birth to five sons who would all serve in World War II, broke the bottle of champagne on the ship's bow and cried: "I christen thee *John Doherty*, in the name of God, Country, Clan. Go forward, fight well, and do us honor!"

CHAPTER FIFTEEN

THE FORTY-NINERS

Panic spread throughout Australia following news of the devastating carrier raid on Darwin that happened on February 19. Was it a sign of a coming Japanese invasion? Fear was rampant, especially since the vast majority of the Australian armed forces were fighting in North Africa and there was no way of returning them in time to face such an imminent event as was expected. The civilian population of the city was largely evacuated in the aftermath of the first attack, and the port was abandoned as a major base.

In the event, there was no invasion. The Japanese recognized that mounting such an operation to conquer a continent was beyond their capabilities in their wildest dreams. However, they did need to distract the Allied forces in Australia from confronting the expansion of Japanese control of New Guinea and the move into the Solomons. A continued air campaign against Darwin could accomplish that, given the limited resources the Allies had in Australia.

The campaign lasted until November 1943, during which the Australian mainland, offshore islands, and coastal shipping were attacked at least 97 times, primarily by the Imperial Japanese Naval Air Force.

All first-line units of the Royal Australian Air Force were committed to the North African campaign. Until new units could be organized, the only fighter unit in the country capable of offering any defense against further attacks was the 49th Pursuit Group.

Group commander Paul Wurtsmith was a career officer who had been a fighter pilot since graduating from Randolph Field in 1927 and was a graduate of the USAAC Tactical School with 4,800 flying hours. Executive officer Major Don Hutchinson was another experienced pursuit specialist, with 2,500 flying hours. The leaders' experience, however, masked the inexperience of the group as a whole. Of an initial strength of 102 pilots, only seven had more than 600 hours in fighters, nine had 15 hours, and the rest none whatsoever; 95 had never flown a P-40 before.

On February 14, Captain Selman's 9th Pursuit Squadron transferred from Camp Darley to Williamtown Airfield near Newcastle, New South Wales; some of the men stayed in Newcastle while the rest lived in the Williamtown barracks. The next day, the headquarters squadron under Major Hutchinson and the 7th Pursuit Squadron under Captain Robert Morrissey arrived at Bankstown Airfield, west of Sydney in New South Wales. Hutchinson set up his headquarters in the golf clubhouse across the road from the airfield. The following day, February 16, Captain Van Auken moved his 8th Pursuit Squadron to Fairbairn Airfield, near Canberra. The next week, the first P-40E Warhawks arrived in the squadrons and they were fully equipped with 25 each over the next several days.

With the overwhelming majority of the pilots being recent flight school graduates, an intensive training program had been started in February. The experienced pilots the unit had hoped would lead this training had been diverted to Java, which meant that their expertise did not become available until their evacuation back to Australia in early March. Within two weeks of the first arrival on February 22, 30 P-40Es had been wrecked during training, many in ground loops on takeoff but with the majority occurring on landing, proving AVG ace Charles Older right in his description of the P-40 as an airplane one did not want to have to land in the best of circumstances, due to its narrow-track landing gear.

The accidents were due to inexperience and their long layoff from flying since leaving the United States. One pilot ripped up 50 feet of fence before coming to a stop in the kitchen of a civilian home 2 miles from the end of the Fairbairn runway. Another aircraft left the runway without sufficient flying speed, touched down again, put a wheel in a hole filled with loose sand, and flipped over on its back. Fortunately, while the accident level was high, most of the pilots escaped serious injury. However, the number of useable P-40s dwindled, and the squadrons received additional P-40E-1-CU fighters that had been supplied to the RAF as Kittyhawk Ias and were diverted to the RAAF after the outbreak of war. The RAAF was reluctant to give up these aircraft, since it meant delay in organizing three new squadrons, but the fact the 49th was further along in organization and training meant the unit received first priority of equipment.

Buzz Wagner, who had become an ace in the Philippines back in December, had recovered from the injuries that had forced his evacuation to Australia. Assigned to Fifth Air Force Fighter Command and promoted to lieutenant colonel, he instituted a "clobber college" training program to teach the newcomers what he had learned the hard way over Luzon.

Following the large Japanese bombing raid on Darwin on February 19, General Brett sent an advance team from the 49th Group to Darwin. Sergeant Fred Quick and 16 men of the 9th Pursuit Squadron moved from Williamtown to Sydney, and then moved on to Darwin via flying boat.

The Forty-Niners began advancing toward their destiny on March 4, 1942, when group commander Lieutenant Colonel Paul Wurtsmith asked 7th Squadron commander Captain Morrissey how many pilots were combat ready. Morrissey replied that he considered 11 pilots ready. Leaving Bankstown five days later, Morrissey and his 11 men headed for Horn Island, Queensland. The squadron's line chief, Master Sergeant Hays, issued each pilot a small tool kit with spark plugs and simple instructions, since there was no ground support between Bankstown and Darwin, while the armorers also instructed the pilots on how to load the six .50-caliber wing guns.

By 1941, only 1.5 percent of the Australian continent had been completely and accurately mapped. The pilots used road maps to find their way to Brisbane, then switched to maritime maps to find their way up the Queensland coast. Three of the fighters were forced to divert to Charters Towers with mechanical problems. The nine remaining Warhawks remained overnight at Townsville before flying on to Iron Range Airfield on March 8. They finally arrived at Horn Island off the tip of Cape York late that afternoon. There were no facilities at the field, so after parking the P-40s at the southern end of the shorter runway, they set up two-man tents in the bush nearby. The next day, they commenced flying patrols within sight of the base.

The day the 7th Squadron arrived at Horn Island, newly assigned squadron leader Captain James Selman led 25 Warhawks of the 9th Pursuit Squadron from Williamtown to follow "The Brereton Route" to Darwin, over 500 miles to the north. George Preddy thought himself lucky to have been chosen for the mission; he had reminded Selman when he was promoted to lead the squadron that he would like to transfer over, and Selman brought him along. At Brisbane, they stayed at Archer Field where spark plugs were changed using Master Sergeant Hays' instructions and tool kits and the airplanes were fitted out with needed equipment. Taking off March 11, they were forced to return to Brisbane by poor weather, losing two aircraft to mechanical problems. The next day, led by a B-17 to provide navigation aid as they flew over the dangerous "Outback," the 23 remaining Warhawks flew on to Charleville, 400 miles west. On March 14 they headed for Cloncurry, 500 miles northwest, where two more fighters were lost to heavy landings. The 21 airplanes left Cloncurry on March 16, headed for Daly Waters 600 miles further northwest. Lieutenant Sidney S. Woods made a heavy landing at Daly Waters, writing off his P-40 and sending him to the hospital with his injuries. George Preddy had thought Cloncurry was primitive, but he later said of Daly Waters:

> That's the worst place I've ever seen. It's just an airfield stuck out in the middle of nowhere. The heat and flies are terrible. Luckily the mosquitoes weren't bad. I had to sleep on the wing of my airplane that night. They told us we would be living with our airplanes, but I didn't expect it to be this close!

Of the 25 fighters that left Williamtown on March 8, 13 finally arrived at Darwin ten days later, where they were ordered to commence patrols immediately. Darwin Airfield had been so badly damaged on February 19 and in the subsequent Japanese raids that the squadron was forced to land at Batchelor Field, 50 miles south. They arrived shortly after the B-17s that evacuated MacArthur from the Philippines landed. The next day, the four P-40s that had become lost in the rainstorms and had landed at a sheep station arrived in Darwin after the air force had flown in fuel to them.

Over the course of the rest of the month, more Warhawks flew "The Brereton Route" to Darwin; by March 31, 1942, the 9th PS had 21 P-40Es and 25 pilots. George Preddy and the other young pilots now had about 15 hours each in the P-40, experience gained on their flights to Darwin. They were Australia's front-line defense.

On March 14,1942, Japanese raiders were spotted over the Timor Sea. All fighters were scrambled. The 7th Squadron intercepted the formation of G4M1 Betty bombers and their Zero escorts over the sea. In their initial bounce, Lieutenant A.T. House, Captain Robert Morrissey's wingman, had his guns jam when he opened fire on one of the escorting Zeros. He maneuvered above the enemy fighter and dipped his right wing into the cockpit, killing the pilot and sending the Zero into the water below. House then managed a forced landing on Horn Island with 3 feet of his right wing missing – proof of the P-40's toughness. When the others returned to the field, they claimed four Zeros and one Betty.

On March 22, the 9th Squadron opened its wartime score when lieutenants Clyde L. Harvey, Jr. and Stephen Poleschuk managed to shoot down a C5M reconnaissance plane near Darwin. Two days later, the squadron moved from Batchelor Field to the RAAF field at Darwin. With most of the town's population evacuated, the pilots were finally able to move indoors with all the conveniences of home including electricity, running water, and refrigerators as they took up residence in abandoned homes. Their headquarters was the main hotel.

At the end of March, experienced pilots who had fought in Java with the 17th Provisional Squadron joined the group. The Forty-Niners welcomed a number of experienced airmen to their number. Captains Nate Blanton and Bill Hennon, along with Lieutenant Lester Johnsen, became new flight leaders in the 7th Pursuit Squadron, while the 8th Pursuit Squadron was glad to have as flight leaders captains Allison W. Strauss and George Kiser, while lieutenants R.C. Dockstader and Jim Morehead became element leaders. The 9th Squadron welcomed Captain "Bitchin" Ben Irvin and lieutenants Joe Kreuzel and Andy Reynolds.

The 8th Squadron had remained at Melbourne until early April, when the squadron moved to Darwin. Later that month the 7th Squadron left Horn Island and all three squadrons operated from Darwin. Joe Kreuzel became a flight commander and took his new wingman Preddy with him. John Landers joined the flight. A talented local artist painted a fire-breathing green dragon on their right cowls, and they became known as the Dragon Flight.

On March 28, seven Nells hit the RAAF airfield the Forty-Niners had just moved to at 1230 hours. Preddy later remembered that his flight was at Batchelor Field that day and wasn't involved in the fight. "The boys at Darwin intercepted them on the way home and knocked down two for sure and maybe disabled two more that didn't make it home. Nobody was hurt by the bombs." Lieutenant Mitchell Zawista's flight had managed to catch the G3Ms after they dived following bombs away to gain speed and escape. Lieutenants Clyde Harvey, William Sells, and Robert Vaught were credited with one each. The Japanese had learned their lesson; this was the last unescorted raid. On March 30, Preddy's flight made an interception. Preddy remembered, "We went up about 15 minutes before they arrived to intercept them, and got hit by the Zeros at 11,000 feet. Neither side lost anything, but McComsey had to bail out when he got in a spin. I had a perfect shot at a Zero but missed by not having turned the gun switch on." He still had much to learn. McComsey's P-40 had spun out after being badly hit by a Zero, while Lieutenant Porter's tail assembly was shot up. McComsey made it back to base after spending a frightening night in the swamps outside of town.

Not only did the Americans have to fight the enemy, but they were also in a battle with the environment. Being close to the equator, weather forecasting was difficult, since storms could arise quickly over the water. A pilot could take off in clear weather and be forced to find his way back to the field in a driving rainstorm that limited visibility such that he would only see the field when he flew over it and could easily lose it while circling lower to land. The country around Darwin was difficult. There were virtually impassable mangrove swamps, while the tributaries from the Timor Sea extended far inland and were filled with crocodiles. Huge ants lived in enormous colonies that could destroy any aircraft that hit the structure, while the swarms of mosquitoes carried dengue fever, malaria, and yellow fever. Being shot down in this environment was deadly. During the rainy season, the air was hot and muggy at all times.

In April, Japanese raiders returned three times in the first week on April 2, 4, and 5, attacking the RAAF airfield again in the last strike.

Preddy remembered that on April 2, the Japanese couldn't spot the airfield due to the clouds and so bombed the town. On April 4, "We gave the Japs the prettiest surprise they ever had today." There had been sufficient warning that seven P-40s managed to stagger up to 26,000 feet, where Lieutenant Lawrence Smith recalled, "I was indicating 90 miles an hour and walking the stick all over the cockpit to keep from stalling out." Preddy described the fight: "The Japs were at 23,000 feet. When they left, there were only two bombers and one Zero." Lieutenant Gardner was hit by "friendly fire" from the antiaircraft gunners and was forced to bale out. Lieutenant Livingston overshot making a forced landing and was killed when the fighter crashed. Lieutenant John D. Landers opened his wartime score by shooting down two of the Zeros. On April 5, the Japanese came over at 25,000 feet and the defenders were unable to reach them.

In these combats, the pilots came up against the performance deficiencies of the P-40 in comparison to its adversaries. The fighter had only a single-stage supercharger and performance fell off rapidly above 12,000 feet. The Japanese bombers regularly flew at 18,000 feet with their Zero escorts at 20–21,000 feet, meaning they almost always had the altitude advantage.

Bad weather provided a break until a raid on April 25, with the enemy returning on April 27 and 30. During the first raid, 24 bombers escorted by nine Zeros were intercepted by fighters from the 7th and 8th squadrons as they turned away from their bomb runs. The 7th Squadron accounted for one Zero while the 8th scored ten of the bombers and a Zero. None of the Forty-Niners was lost, though Lieutenant Morehead had to crash land. The Americans were getting better.

Preddy's flights had either been on the ground, out of position or unable to make contact in these fights. On April 27, he finally saw combat against the Zeros. The Dragon Flight was scrambled at 0900 hours on a false alarm. They returned and refueled and were scrambled again at 1140 hours with another flight. The eight Warhawks were joined by flights from the other squadrons and the entire group met the 18 G3Ms and a similar number of Zeros flying at 19,000 feet. Preddy engaged two Zeros, recalling "I could not get a decent shot at either of them." Lieutenants Zawista and Taylor each claimed a Zero. The Forty-Niners took losses: Lieutenant Owen Fish of the 8th Squadron was lost when his damaged aircraft stalled and spun into Fanny Bay, while Captain Strauss crashed in the port. The 7th Squadron took two losses when Lieutenant Stephen W. Andrew baled out over the ocean, while Lieutenant Harold J. Martin made a forced landing on the beach; both were rescued. The group claimed three bombers and four Zeros for these losses. Lieutenant Sidney Woods returned from the hospital after having crashed at Daly Waters during the 9th Squadron's first movement to Darwin back in March.

In May 1942, pursuit aviation in the USAAF became fighter aviation, and the Forty-Niners changed their name to the 49th Fighter Group. On May 5, Preddy wrote in his diary:

> … the funny thing about war for us here at Darwin is that for two or three days the Nips keep us busy as hell and fighting like mad; then for two or three weeks we are seemingly forgotten and this is the most peaceful place in the world. We don't have enough to do at these times and get lazy eating, sleeping and lying around. It has been a life of ease for the past week. The weather hasn't been too hot during the day and has been wonderful at night.

The enemy were concentrating their activity in New Guinea during May and the Forty-Niners saw little action. In early June, the group posted its scores since arriving at Darwin: 13 Zeros, with the 7th Squadron leading for a claim of six; 24 bombers, with the 8th Squadron claiming 13 and the 9th ten. They had lost seven P-40s and three pilots.

The combat lull ended on June 13 with the heaviest raids since January, when 27 Nells escorted by 12 Zeros raided Darwin. The P-40s were unable to climb to their altitude in time and the Zeros shot down four P-40s from the 8th Squadron and one from the 7th. Lieutenant Clarence T. Johnson, Jr. of the 7th was found alive after five days without food in the mangrove swamps, while the 8th's Captain Van Auken landed on Melville Island and was returned by native Australians four days later.

The next day, 27 bombers and 12 Zeros were intercepted by Preddy's Dragon Flight.

> Our flight went in to attack just before they reached their target but we were attacked from above by several Zeros. We were forced to

dive out, but Manning's flight then hit them from above. Manning and McComsey got one each while Peterson and Fowler shared one. My ship was hit in three places, but the squadron suffered no other damage.

Again, 27 bombers and 12 escorts came the next day. Preddy's flight chased them 50 miles over the ocean. John Landers scored his third victory. Reynolds and McComsey both crash-landed back ashore, while the 8th Squadron lost three pilots.

After another two-week lull, July 12, 1942 was a slow day at Darwin. When no strikes had materialized by noon, flight leader Kreuzel decided it was a good day for training. That afternoon, lieutenants John Sauber, George Preddy, Jack Donaldson, and Deems Taylor were assigned to the mission. Sauber instructed Preddy that he would simulate an attack, in which Preddy would show the appropriate escape maneuver. Sauber dove on Preddy, but misjudged his separation and the two collided. Sauber was killed on impact after Warhawk number 87 broke up and fell to the ground. Badly injured, Preddy managed to bale out of "Tarheel" and parachute to safety, while the two P-40s hit west of Manton Reservoir. Evacuated to Brisbane, Preddy spent two months in hospital recovering from his injuries. On release, he received orders back to the United States.

He later wrote,

The Army now finds it was a great mistake to send green pilots just out of flight school into combat. I am thankful I lived through the first stage as I feel I am now a little better prepared having learned from actual experience how to take care of myself up there. There is something to be learned on each combat mission, and I am just a beginner.

In the five months the Forty-Niners spent on operations in the Northern Territory of Australia, they claimed 64 Japanese aircraft shot down for the loss of 16 of their P-40s, a 4:1 victory ratio set by young, inexperienced pilots in an outclassed airplane, flying against some of the best enemy pilots of the war. Their Japanese opponents admitted a loss of 19 aircraft in raids on Darwin between March and August, comprising one C5M "Babs" reconnaissance aircraft, seven Zero fighters, and 12 G3M and G4M bombers, plus several more damaged. When the group moved to Port Moresby that fall, they were relieved by 77 Squadron RAAF, which arrived at Darwin in August, and 76 Squadron, which was brought back from New Guinea in October.

CHAPTER SIXTEEN

"OUR TARGET IS TOKYO"

Over the three months since John Bridgers had arrived at NAS Barber's Point, he had trained hard to become a dive bomber pilot. He recalled:

> Bombing 3 provided the Navy a handy place to familiarize a group of newly-hatched replacement scout-bomber pilots with the Douglas SBD Dauntless, which none of us had previously seen, much less flown. The veteran *Saratoga* pilots resented the idea of having to take us on familiarization flights, sitting in the rear seats of their planes while being piloted by fellows several years their junior in age and experience. Their headquarters and ready room were in a beach house alongside the airfield, left over from the beachside holiday spot the area had been before it was converted to an air station shortly before hostilities started. In their mind we unnecessarily cluttered their living and work place, and it was frequently suggested that we spend more time outdoors. There were worse places to be than outdoors in Hawaii.

Saratoga had left a landing signal officer behind, and he trained the "nuggets." Bridgers recalled that he was given orders to join Bombing 5 in late March, pending the return of *Yorktown* from the South Pacific. However, in early April, things changed:

> Suddenly I was in a hybrid air group made up of *Enterprise* and *Saratoga* pilots, at sea and bound for what none of us knew. We sailed northwest and, in the vicinity of Midway Island, our group was joined with another task group including the USS *Hornet* (CV-8), an Atlantic

fleet carrier which had been transferred to the Pacific. Her flight deck was fully loaded with Army Air Force B-25 medium bombers. As was typical for wartime operations we embarked with sealed orders, operational plans that were unseen by the ship's commander. These were carried in the skipper's safe and not opened until a given time or at a given location out at sea. In this case ours were opened and made known to all hands when we rendezvoused with the *Hornet* group. We learned that we were going to sail within several hundred miles of Japan. Then the B-25s on *Hornet*'s deck, under the leadership of Colonel Jimmy Doolittle, an aviator whose exploits all of us knew, would take off from the *Hornet*, bomb targets in Tokyo, and fly to China. At best, it would be a perilous undertaking.

Dick Best had assumed command of Bombing 6 when his Annapolis classmate Bill Hollingsworth had left the squadron at Pearl Harbor to take up an assignment in Training Command. "I will always remember that I was floored to see *Hornet* rendezvous with us with all those Army bombers on her deck. It was obvious to anyone that we were now involved in the most important mission of the war to date. I knew they were going to hit Japan, and I only wished it was we who could do it, but such was impossible."

The mission Ensign Bridgers and Lieutenant Best now found themselves part of had been in planning since early January, a month after the Pearl Harbor attack. On December 21, 1941, President Roosevelt met with the Joint Chiefs of Staff at the White House. At that meeting, he told his military leaders that he believed Japan should be bombed as soon as possible to boost public morale following the Japanese attack.

On January 10, 1942, Captain Francis Low, assistant chief of staff for Antisubmarine Warfare, submitted a memorandum to Chief of Naval Operations Admiral Ernest J. King, expressing his belief that twin-engine Army bombers could be launched from an aircraft carrier and that they could then strike Japan. The memo was the result of research by Captain Donald B. Duncan, King's air operations officer, to whom Low had first taken his idea; he had concluded such an operation was technically feasible. King passed the Low Memorandum on to General Henry H. "Hap" Arnold. Arnold called in his new special projects officer, Lieutenant Colonel James H. "Jimmy" Doolittle, America's most famous test and race pilot, who had given up his position as a Shell Oil vice-president in charge of aviation fuel development (where he had been responsible for the prewar development of 100-octane aviation fuel that would eventually guarantee American technological superiority in the coming war), to return to military service; Doolittle was ordered to investigate the feasibility of such a proposed mission.

Doolittle and Captain Duncan were assigned project responsibilities for their respective services on what was called "The Tokyo Project." Doolittle studied the available USAAF bombers and concluded that the only one that could carry out such a mission was the North American B-25 Mitchell. This was primarily due to its weight and wingspan, which would allow it to take off from the deck of a *Yorktown*-class aircraft carrier. Doolittle and Duncan successfully demonstrated the concept when they flew two B-25Bs off the deck of *Hornet*, the latest *Yorktown*-class carrier, in Chesapeake Bay on February 3, 1942. While the bombers could take off, it was obvious it would be impossible for them to land back on board after the mission.

Doolittle expressed hope in his first report that the attackers might land at the Soviet Pacific Fleet base at Vladivostok just across the Sea of Japan, with the bombers given to the USSR as Lend-Lease. When secretly queried, the Russians refused, since the Soviet Union had signed a neutrality pact with Japan in April 1941 and could not afford a two-front war, given they were only holding on against the invading Germans. Doolittle changed the plan, with the B-25s landing at airfields in eastern China following the raid. From there, they would continue on to western China and enter service in the Republic of China Air Force. Chiang Kai-Shek's government was eager to agree.

With the decision made to use the B-25, at this point Lieutenant Colonel Robert D. Knapp, a man with a lifelong involvement in Army aviation as the 137th Army aviator, who had met the Wright Brothers at age ten when they stayed with his family for ten days in 1907, was brought into the project. Having served in the interwar period as the chief of flight training for the entire Air Corps, he had been assigned in 1941 to organize the new bomb groups that were being equipped with the B-25 as the new medium bomber began to come off the North American production line that summer.

By the spring of 1942, Knapp personally knew every B-25 pilot in the USAAF and was intimately aware of their individual abilities.

He recommended that Doolittle work with the 17th Bombardment Group (Medium), composed of the 34th, 37th, and 95th bombardment squadrons and the 89th Reconnaissance Squadron, since the 17th was the first unit to take delivery of the B-25 in September 1941 and they were now the most experienced Mitchell crews in the air force. Knapp accompanied Doolittle to visit the 17th Group, where he told the men of a special "extremely hazardous mission" in which the rewards reflected the hazards. Pilot Ted Lawson, who would later write *Thirty Seconds Over Tokyo*, the definitive first-hand account of the mission, remembered, "When Jimmy Doolittle stepped onto that stage to address us, everyone knew this was something we didn't want to miss."

The only hint they got of where they were going came when they landed at Eglin Field, Florida, to meet Navy Lieutenant Henry L. Miller, a naval aviator who instructed them over the next few weeks on how to take off in a fully loaded B-25 after a takeoff run of only 450 feet, lifting off only slightly above stalling speed. The pilots accurately concluded they were going to hit a target in the Pacific, though they wrongly guessed the Philippines. Doolittle ordered them to venture no guesses and keep their mouths shut about anything they saw or did, lest any spies piece things together.

The B-25Bs were highly modified for the mission. The retractable ventral turret was removed, saving 600 pounds, which allowed more fuel to be carried. After the modifications, the total fuel load came to 1,243 gallons: 646 gallons in the wing tanks, 227 gallons in the bomb bay tank, 160 gallons in the collapsible crawlspace tank above the bomb bay, another 160 gallons in the ventral turret space, and ten 5-gallon cans for refills carried in the rear fuselage. The mission would be flown at low level, so there was no need for the still-secret Norden bombsight; it was replaced by a makeshift bombsight that proved more satisfactory for low-level operation. Each bomber would carry four 500-pound bombs other than Doolittle and the first four, who carried three 500-pound bombs and a 500-pound incendiary to Mark the targets. The only defensive armament was the Martin power-operated turret located aft of the wing amidships in the fuselage. Two wooden broomsticks painted black were positioned to stick out through the Plexiglass tail cap to deter enemy fighters attacking the rear. Thus modified, takeoff weight was 31,000 pounds, the maximum allowable for the B-25. Additionally, each aircraft's engine carburetors were individually modified for lean operation in order to extend range.

On March 25, 22 B-25s of the original 25 flew from Eglin to McClellan Field in Sacramento, California, flying across the continent at 500 feet the entire distance to allow the crews to practice low-level navigation. A major problem arose at McClellan, when the crews discovered as they prepared to leave that mechanics on the base, unaware of the mission, had re-set the carburetors for standard operation. Ted Lawson later remembered that it took everything he could muster to not punch the master sergeant who gave him this news as he told Lawson, "I don't know what those mechanics you've been working with think about this airplane, but they've put you in real trouble." There was no time to fix the damage. The raiders departed McClellan for Alameda Naval Base across the bay from San Francisco, where the crews first saw *Hornet* tied up at the dock. Only 16 of the bombers could be loaded aboard, though all crew members who were trained for the mission went aboard as backups. *Hornet* and her escorts steamed under the Golden Gate Bridge headed west at dawn on April 2, 1942 and disappeared into a foggy Pacific Ocean.

Eleven days later on April 13, northwest of Hawaii, *Enterprise*'s Task Force 16 rendezvoused with *Hornet*'s Task Force 18 to provide escort for the mission. Doolittle called his men to *Hornet*'s wardroom and finally told them: "Our target is Tokyo."

John Bridgers recalled the voyage westward:

The *Enterprise* was along to provide scouting, antisubmarine and air defense for the force. My days were marked by tedium. The flight deck was kept ready with a coterie of planes, prepared for a deck-load launch at any time.

Aircraft were launched repeatedly throughout the day with search and patrol flights kept airborne from sun up to sun down; one flight was launched and then the one in the air brought aboard every four hours. This necessitated taxiing all the unused planes forward to clear the landing area. When the pilots manned their plane for this 15-minute exercise, they had to go with up-to-date navigational material, prepared to immediately launch rather than taxi if enemy contact occurred during this brief but critical time.

Lieutenant Commander Max Leslie was the skipper of Bombing 3 and I was his "taxi" pilot. I sat in the ready room most of the day, reworking my chart board every four hours or so and then taxied the skipper's plane forward. I was not allowed to fly on any of the patrol missions because I had not yet been carrier qualified in the SBD and Admiral Halsey, the task force commander, said he could not risk a plane for this purpose before our mission was complete. I wasn't unhappy that I had been brought along, but I couldn't exactly figure why that was.

The original plan called for the B-25s to be launched at dusk when the fleet was 400 miles from Japan, so that they would attack at night, flying on across the Yellow Sea to land in China in daylight. However, at 0738 hours on April 18, when the fleet was 750 miles from Japan, a Japanese picket boat was spotted; before it was sunk by Admiral Spruance's *Northampton*, radiomen aboard *Enterprise* detected that it sent a warning. Doolittle and *Hornet*'s Captain Marc Mitscher decided to launch immediately, ten hours early and 200 miles farther east from Japan than planned. Even knowing that they were unlikely to successfully make it to China in this situation, members of the back-up crews who attempted to buy their way aboard the attackers were unsuccessful.

The men aboard *Enterprise* watched the raiders take off. John Bridgers remembered:

We watched the launch. It was a hairy business for all of them, most of all for Colonel Doolittle who went first. They seemed unprepared to cope with the rough weather. In a fully-loaded condition and with the wind across the deck standardized to 20-or-so knots largely obtained from the ship's headway, this was no trouble. However, when the seas were high and the wind was strong, as it was now, extra air speed was easily attained in the deck run. All of them rushed into the air, having pulled up early. Fortunately, none were hit by the rising bow. It was some time before they were all airborne and on their way, each plane alone as it disappeared into the murky skies. After the launch, the fleet immediately turned back east toward friendly waters while Doolittle's brave band flew west to only God knew what.

By 0919 hours, the 16 bombers were flying west toward Japan.

The raiders arrived over Japan around noon. Their targets in Kobe, Yokohama, Nagoya, and Tokyo were successfully bombed and no planes were lost over Japan. However, bad weather in eastern China prevented the fliers finding their landing fields that night, since the Chinese had not received word of their arrival. The bases maintained radio silence, expecting a Japanese attack. Eleven crews baled out over the dark countryside while four others crash-landed, with seven crewmen injured and three killed. The crew of one bomber (40-2242) flew to Vladivostok because they were very low on fuel; the Soviets interned both aircraft and crew.

Eight raiders were captured by the Japanese and tortured to reveal where they had come from; none of them ever revealed the facts of the mission, with four dying under torture. The Japanese response to the raiders having been sheltered and assisted by the Chinese was an orgy of death and destruction as the Imperial Army initiated Operation *Sei-go* to punish the Chinese for helping the raiders. Chinese peasants found with American equipment were shot immediately. Villagers were beheaded with samurai swords. Bodies were stuffed down village wells to poison them and fields were plowed up and salted. Germ warfare and other atrocities resulted in approximately 250,000 Chinese villagers being killed throughout eastern China over the next three months.

Doolittle believed at first that the mission had been a complete failure and told his crew when they rejoined after parachuting from their plane in the darkness that he expected a court-martial on his return to the United States. Such was not to be. On his return, Doolittle was promoted to brigadier general and awarded the Medal of Honor for his leadership. By the end of the year he was named commander of the USAAF Twelfth Air Force in Tunisia and he was later named commander of the Eighth Air Force in England in January 1944, which he led to victory over the Luftwaffe that spring, as American bombers and fighters obtained the air superiority necessary for the invasion of Europe.

President Roosevelt himself made the official announcement about the raid, exercising his love of myth and mystery by stating that the planes had taken off from "Shangri-La," the mythical Himalayan kingdom that author James Hilton had immortalized in his novel *Lost Horizon*.

The Tokyo Raid gave an incalculable boost to American home front morale when nearly every piece of news from the Pacific was of another defeat. The Japanese now knew their country was vulnerable to attack and they kept four first-line JAAF fighter groups in the Home Islands over the next two years, despite the losses incurred during the fighting in the South Pacific.

More importantly, Admiral Yamamoto, who was in the midst of planning the next Japanese offensive in the Pacific, decided that an invasion and occupation of Midway Island to secure the western Pacific approaches to Japan would protect the empire from further attack and lead to the crucial naval battle all members of the Imperial Navy knew was necessary to guarantee Japanese victory.

Originally, it was planned that *Enterprise* would conduct a strike against Marcus Island during the return to Pearl Harbor to insure the Japanese were unable to mount an attack on the fleet. However, Admiral Nimitz now knew of the Japanese plans in the South Pacific and he ordered the two carriers to expedite their return so they could reinforce *Lexington* and *Yorktown* in the Coral Sea.

On April 20, 1942, Ensign John Bridgers was finally able to become a "carrier qualified" naval aviator.

Earlier, my qualification landings had been scheduled repeatedly only to be scuttled each time by Admiral Halsey due to his concern that no plane should be risked while further offensive action was in the offing. So now the fateful day finally came. The plan was for this to occur between the launching of one scouting and patrol flight and the landing of the preceding one. To add to my confidence, the oldest airplane in the group was chosen, and it was decreed that everything of value would be removed from the aircraft and it would be ballasted with sandbags. I was to make two approaches with the LSO to "wave off," and then, if my third approach was decent, I would be given a "cut" and land. All went as planned. With a larger than usual crowd of onlookers gathered on the walkways and in the gun sponsons on the island, I made one of the best carrier landings I would ever make. That done, I didn't get to fly again until I was launched on an antisub patrol just before we entered Pearl Harbor.

When *Enterprise* returned to Pearl Harbor, Bombing 6 was finally able to replace their SBD-2 Dauntless bombers with new SBD-3s. Dick Best remembered that when he saw the airplanes his squadron was to re-equip with on the flight line at Ford Island, "they were the cleanest airplanes I had ever seen in my flying career to date, right out of the factory." The old SBD-2s were quickly rehabilitated and their national insignias were repainted with white paint over the red circles in the center. The well-worn Dauntlesses were flown to the Marine air station at Ewa, where new graduates of Pensacola received ten hours of transition training before they took off on May 25, escorted by a B-17 assigned to provide navigational assistance, as reinforcements for VMSB-241 at Midway.

The Doolittle Raid would assume an outsized importance in the United States for the rest of the war, with books and movies made about it to inspire the public with the devotion to duty and sacrifice of the raiders.

Ted Lawson lost his leg as a result of injuries suffered when his bomber, "The Ruptured Duck," crashed in China. His book was published in time for Christmas 1943 and became an instant bestseller; the rights were bought before publication by Warner Brothers. The movie made from the book during the spring of 1944 was directed by Mervyn LeRoy from a screenplay adapted by Dalton Trumbo and starred Van Johnson as Ted Lawson, Spencer Tracy as Jimmy Doolittle, and introduced Robert Mitchum in his first major role as pilot Bob Gray. The film won the Oscar for Best Special Effects and was nominated for Best Cinematography of 1944.

Released on New Year's Eve 1943, six months before the release of *Thirty Seconds Over Tokyo*, *Destination Tokyo*, a fictional account of a submarine sent to penetrate the defenses of Tokyo Bay and land crewmen to Mark targets for the raiders, starred Cary Grant as the skipper and John Garfield as the medic who performs an appendectomy, which was based on an actual event aboard the submarine *Silversides*.

Following closely the release of *Thirty Seconds Over Tokyo*, *The Purple Heart*, a fictionalized account of the imprisonment and torture of a crew of raiders captured and put on trial by the Japanese, was also released in 1944. Directed by Lewis milestone from a screenplay by Jerome Cady with story by Twentieth Century Fox head Darryl Zanuck and based on unofficial Swiss reports of the actual trial of the captured Doolittle raiders, the film starred Dana Andrews, Richard Conte, and a young Farley Granger in his first role. The film concludes with a speech by Dana Andrews as Captain Harvey Ross, in which he declares that he now knew that he had understood the Japanese less than he had thought, and that they did not know Americans if they thought this trial would frighten them.

Like some other American propaganda films made during World War II, such as *Casablanca* and *Action in the North Atlantic*, these three Doolittle Raid movies stand the test of time and are eminently watchable today.

CHAPTER SEVENTEEN

RAMSEY'S LAMBSIES

The port of Rabaul, administrative capital of Australian New Guinea, a territory that included the eastern, Australian-controlled part of the island of New Guinea, and the main islands of New Ireland and New Britain, where Rabaul and its port, Simpson Harbor, was located, fell to the Japanese on January 25, 1942. It would become the main Japanese base in the South Pacific and the objective of a two-year Allied campaign to capture or neutralize.

The Australians had sought in the summer of 1941 to turn Rabaul into a "secure fleet anchorage," hoping to establish a radar station and provide a strong defensive minefield. However, Australian planners determined that fall that they lacked the capability to expand the Rabaul garrison beyond the 1,400-man "Lark Force" commanded by Lieutenant Colonel John Scanlan or to increase the defensive combat force beyond the 700 infantrymen of the Australian Imperial Force 2/22 Battalion commanded by Lieutenant Colonel Howard Carr, due to the nation's inability to reinforce the base should it come under attack, since most of their armed forces were committed in North Africa.

The Japanese saw Rabaul as the main harbor in the South Pacific other than their base at Truk Atoll in the Carolines to the north. Its strategic location would allow the Imperial Navy an advanced base from which to protect Truk, and to take control of the rest of Australian New Guinea and the Solomon Islands to the southeast, which would cut the main supply routes from the United States to Australia. Thus, their campaign to take the base began on January 4, 1942, with bombing raids from Truk and Yap in the Carolines.

Ten days later, the invasion force went aboard ship at Truk and departed for Rabaul, covered by the Mobile Fleet carriers *Kaga* and *Akagi*, seven cruisers, and 14 destroyers. The two carriers launched strikes against Rabaul on January 20, flying over 100 sorties to hit the base in multiple waves. After a second day of strikes against Rabaul and the port of Kavieng on New Ireland, 4,000 invading troops of the 144th Infantry Regiment of the 55th Infantry Division, supported by a battalion of the 55th Mountain Artillery Regiment and a company of the 55th Engineer Regiment, landed at Blanche Bay on New Ireland and took Kavieng without opposition. The next day, 5,000 troops landed in Simpson Harbor. Within hours, the invaders had captured Lakunai Airfield. Colonel Scanlan considered the situation hopeless and ordered "every man for himself." The Australian defenders split into small groups, and retreated through the jungle, losing two officers and 26 enlisted troops killed. By the time the Japanese landed at Gasmata on the south coast of New Britain on February 9, approximately 1,000 Australians had surrendered.

When Saburo Sakai and the other pilots of the Tainan Air Corps arrived in early March, they were struck by the terrific sulfuric stench from the volcanoes that surrounded Rabaul and the overall primitive state of the airfield. Their Zeros would provide cover for the further moves to New Guinea that led to the strikes by *Lexington* and *Yorktown* at Lae and Salamaua. By late March, the Tainan Air Group had departed Rabaul and was based at Lae in New Guinea.

Shortly after the invasion, MacArthur's air force determined to attack Rabaul. In February 1942, there were very few B-17s in Australia, even with the arrival in late January of the new 43rd Bombardment Group. Flying from the main B-17 base at Cloncurry in southern Queensland, the bombers operated in small groups from the forward airfield at Horn Island and from Seven Mile 'Drome at Port Moresby to mount raids against Rabaul. There were never more than six B-17s able to mount an individual mission, but over the next three months they would create enough damage at Rabaul to force the Japanese to divert more resources to defending the base and replacing losses. The raids were flown primarily at night, since the Japanese had no effective night defense, lacking radar and specially equipped night fighters. Despite a relative lack of enemy opposition, the bombers found that their main enemy was weather. Enormous storm fronts could quickly develop over the Bismarck Sea that separated New Guinea from New Britain, and weather over New Guinea itself could quickly change, leading to difficulty in airplanes getting over the barrier of the Owen Stanley Mountains. Nevertheless, the bombers persisted.

In late April, the Allies learned the details of the plan for the next Japanese offensive in the Southern Seas from an intercepted message decoded by HYPO, the Pacific Fleet radio intercept operation at Pearl Harbor. The operation would begin with the occupation of the small island of Tulagi, near Guadalcanal in the southern Solomons, on May 3, to establish a seaplane base from where IJNAF flying boats would be able to attack Allied supply convoys in the Coral Sea headed to Australia. The Tulagi invasion force, commanded by Rear Admiral Kiyohide Shima, consisted of the transport *Azumasan Maru* with 400 men of the 3rd Kure Special Naval Landing Force (SNLF), supported by the minelayers *Okinoshima* and *Kōei Maru*, and destroyers *Kikuzuki* and *Yūzuki*, with a support group commanded by Rear Admiral Kuninori Marumo of the light cruisers *Tenryū* and *Tatsuta*, and the seaplane tender *Kamikawa Maru*, operating 12 A6M2-N floatplane fighters developed from the Zero, soon to be known to the Allies as "Rufe," along with 12 A6M2-Ns of the *Kiyokawa Maru* Air Group, escorted by the gunboats *Keijo Maru*, *Seikai Maru*, and *Nikkai Maru*.

The Port Moresby Invasion Force was commanded by Rear Admiral Sadamichi Kajioka aboard the light cruiser *Yūbari* with the destroyers *Oite*, *Asanagi*, *Uzuki*, *Mutsuki*, *Mochizuki*, and *Yayoi*. The Transport Unit was led by Rear Admiral Kōsō Abe aboard the minelayer *Tsugaru* with 11 transports, the Imperial Navy's *Mogamigawa Maru*, *Chōwa Maru*, *Goyō Maru*, *Akiba Maru*, and *Shōka Maru*, and the Imperial Army's *Asakasan Maru*, *China Maru*, *Mito Maru*, *Matsue Maru*, *Taifuku Maru*, and *Hibi Maru* carrying 500 troops of the 3rd Kure SNLF and 5,000 army troops to take Port Moresby.

The invasion force was covered by Rear Admiral Aritomo Gotō aboard the heavy cruiser *Aoba*, with the other heavy cruisers of the 8th Cruiser Division: *Kako*, *Kinugasa*, and *Furutaka*, escorting the light carrier *Shōhō*, which carried an air group composed of eight A6M2 Zero and four A5M4 Type 96 fighters, and six B5N2 Type 97 torpedo bombers.

In Hawaii, Fighting 2 returned to Ford Island in early April. The squadron was no longer "The Flying Chiefs," as nearly all the highly experienced chief petty officers had been transferred to Training Command when they arrived in Bremerton, Washington aboard *Saratoga* in late February. The squadron was now "Ramsey's Lambsies," in honor of their new CO, Lieutenant Commander Paul Ramsey, who had taken command on arrival in Bremerton and led the unit through the absorption of newly commissioned ensigns straight from flight school and the transition from the Brewster F2A-3 to the Grumman F4F-3 Wildcat. They expected to be reunited with *Lexington* when the carrier completed the brief modernization work at the Pearl Harbor Naval yard that saw her 8-inch guns removed and additional antiaircraft weapons installed.

On April 13, the British intercepted and deciphered a message from the Imperial Navy General Staff informing overall theater commander Admiral Inoue that the Carrier Striking Force commanded by Vice Admiral Takeo Takagi aboard the heavy cruiser *Myōkō*, with Rear Admiral Chūichi Hara's Carrier Division 5 composed of Hara's flagship, *Zuikaku*, with an air group of 25 A6M2s, 22 D3A1s, and 20 B5N2s and her sister, *Shōkaku*, with an air group of 21 A6M2s, 20 D3A1s, and 19 B5N2s, had been assigned to cover the Port Moresby invasion. In addition to *Myōkō*, Takagi's force included the heavy cruiser *Haguro* and destroyers *Ushio*, *Akebono*, *Ariake*, *Yūgure*, *Shiratsuyu*, and *Shigure*. This was the Imperial Navy's "first team."

It took Admiral Nimitz two days to prepare a response once the message was passed to the Americans. Rear Admiral Aubrey Fitch had taken command of Task Force 11 on April 1, as *Lexington* came out of the yard. The carrier was protected by the cruisers *Minneapolis* (CA-36) and *New Orleans* (CA-32), and seven destroyers. The newly returned Fighting 2 was ordered back aboard *Lexington* on April 15, along with Scouting 2, Bombing 2, and Torpedo 2.

Since "Ramsey's Lambsies" lacked pilots with combat experience, the squadron was "fleshed out" with experienced pilots from Fighting 3 on April 12. Squadron strength was increased from 18 to 27 Wildcats. Lieutenant Albert O. "Scoop" Vorse became the second division leader, with Ensign Edward L. Sellstrom as his wingman and Lieutenant (jg) Robert J. Morgan as element lead with Ensign John H. Lacket as wingman. Lieutenant (jg) Marion F. Dufilho, who had been O'Hare's wingman in the epic fight against the bombers off Rabaul, took over the 3rd Division with Ensign Newton H. Mason as his wingman. Lieutenant Noel A.M. Gaylor, who had scored three victories with

Fighting 3 during the battle off Rabaul, became 4th Division leader with Lieutenant (jg) Howard F. Clark as element lead and Ensign Richard H. Rowell as wingman. Ensigns Willard E. "Bill" Eder and Leon W. Haynes joined the 5th Division.

Task Force 11 sortied from Pearl Harbor on the evening of April 15, headed for the Coral Sea, where they would join forces with Admiral Frank Jack Fletcher's *Yorktown*-based Task Force 17.

On 29 April, Nimitz ordered Admiral Halsey's Task Force 16, composed of *Enterprise* and *Hornet*, which had just returned to Pearl Harbor the day before from the Doolittle Raid, to leave in haste and reinforce *Lexington* and *Yorktown*. Nimitz was going "all in." John Bridgers and the rest of VB-3 found themselves again headed for possible action. Bridgers recalled, "Now that I was finally a carrier-qualified naval aviator, I was able to admit to myself in private that I did indeed hope we would meet the enemy."

The Imperial Navy had intercepted radio traffic from Task Force 16 during their return from the Tokyo strike, and believed that all but one of the four American carriers were in the central Pacific. Thus, they did not expect a response by American carriers to the Moresby operation until it was well underway. Admiral Takagi's Carrier Strike Force sortied from Truk on May 1 to take up position north of the Solomons and then move as necessary to support the invasion.

During the voyage south from Hawaii, "Ramsey's Lambsies" trained hard. The Fighting 3 veterans were now experienced in the use of the new "Thach Weave" maneuver developed by their former commander, and the squadron's inexperienced pilots worked with the veterans to learn the maneuver. Essentially, the "Thach Weave" utilized the basic formation of a section of two airplanes: when attacked, they would turn toward each other, placing each Wildcat in position to meet a Zero that had commenced its attack on them from the rear head-on. This would throw off the opponent while giving either Wildcat the chance to bring its four heavy machine guns to bear. By the time they got to the Coral Sea, everyone knew how to fly the maneuver.

The morning of May 1 saw Task Forces 17 and 11 rendezvous 300 nautical miles northwest of New Caledonia. Fletcher ordered *Lexington* and her escorts to refuel from the oiler *Neosho* (AO-48), while his ships refueled from the oiler *Tippecanoe* (AO-21). Task Force 17 completed fueling the next day, but heavy seas delayed Task Force 11 until May 3.

The morning of May 3, Fletcher ordered *Yorktown* toward the Louisiades Islands off New Guinea and ordered Admiral Fitch to meet Australian Rear Admiral John Crace's Task Force 44, a joint Australia–US force composed of the cruisers HMAS *Australia* and *Hobart*, and USS *Chicago* (CA-29) with three destroyers, which was en route from Sydney and Noumea.

The Japanese invasion force arrived on schedule at Tulagi on May 3 and found the island undefended, since the small garrison of Australian commandos and a Royal Australian Air Force reconnaissance unit had been evacuated just before their arrival. Aircraft from *Shōhō* covered the landings until the early afternoon, when Admiral Gotō's force turned northwest toward Bougainville to refuel in preparation for the Port Moresby invasion.

Admiral Fletcher learned of the Japanese arrival at Tulagi at 1700 hours on May 3. He was not aware that Task Force 11 had completed fueling earlier that morning as the sea calmed, and was only 60 nautical miles east of him as he turned north toward Guadalcanal with the intention of launching strikes the next morning. *Yorktown* arrived 100 miles south of Guadalcanal at dawn on May 4, and launched 60 aircraft in three consecutive strikes against Tulagi. The Americans surprised Admiral Shima's ships, sinking the destroyer *Kikuzuki* and three minesweepers, damaging four other ships, and destroying four seaplanes. The strikes cost Air Group 5 one TBD and two F4Fs, whose fliers became the first Americans to arrive on Guadalcanal, where they were rescued by the local Australian coastwatchers. With her aircraft back aboard, *Yorktown* retired south. Despite the losses suffered, Shima's force continued their construction of the seaplane base. H6K Mavis flying boats of the Yokohama Air Group flew down to Tulagi from their base in the Shortland Islands on May 5 and began flying reconnaissance missions on May 6.

Admiral Takagi's Carrier Striking Force was fueling 350 miles north of Tulagi when the admiral received a message late that afternoon informing him the Americans had attacked Tulagi. Knowing now that at least one enemy carrier was in the Coral Sea, the fleet stopped fueling and headed southeast while remaining to the north of the Solomons chain.

Task Forces 11 and 44 joined Task Force 17 at 0816 hours on May 5, 320 miles south of Guadalcanal. A few minutes later, four VF-42 Wildcats from *Yorktown* intercepted a Yokohama Air Group H6K flying boat operating from the Shortlands base, and shot it down 11 miles from

Lexington. While the flying boat failed to send a report before it went down, its failure to return alerted the Japanese that American carriers were in the Coral Sea. Later that day, Admiral Fletcher was informed by Pearl Harbor that radio intelligence had determined the Japanese planned to land at Port Moresby on May 10, and their carriers would likely cover the invasion convoy. Ever concerned about his fuel state, Admiral Fletcher immediately ordered his ships to refuel from *Neosho* and notified Admiral Fitch that once fueling was completed on May 6 the fleet would head toward the Louisiades, with the expectation of a fleet action on May 7.

Throughout the rest of the day of May 5, both fleets sent out scout patrols that failed to discover the enemy, since each was just out of range of the other.

Admiral Takagi's Carrier Striking Force continued down the east side of the Solomons chain through the day, then turned west that evening to pass south of San Cristobal, entering the Coral Sea after transiting between Guadalcanal and Rennell islands in the early morning hours of May 6. Having not spotted the Americans, but knowing they were present, Takagi met his oilers and refueled 210 miles west of Tulagi while his crews prepared for the carrier battle the admiral expected the next day.

At 1000 hours on the morning of May 6, an H6K flying from Tulagi sighted the American carriers. When Admiral Takagi received the report at 1050 hours, his fleet was 300 miles north of the reported American position, maximum range for a strike. The admiral concluded the Americans were heading south, which increased the range. Additionally, he knew from the snoopers that the enemy carriers were under a heavy overcast, which he believed would create difficulties for his fliers in finding their targets. Since Takagi's surface force was still refueling, he detached Admiral Hara with *Zuikaku* and *Shōkaku* to head south at 20 knots toward the estimated American position, to be in position to attack at dawn.

Admiral Takagi's belief that battle was imminent was confirmed when Admiral Gotō's fleet was spotted by B-17s staging through Port Moresby. The American bombers attacked the approaching invasion force several times during the day, but without success. Admiral Fletcher received the reports of the attacks and the locations of the Japanese. When he received the spotting report that located "at least one carrier" (*Shōhō*) 489 miles northwest of Task Force 17, Fletcher too was convinced action was imminent.

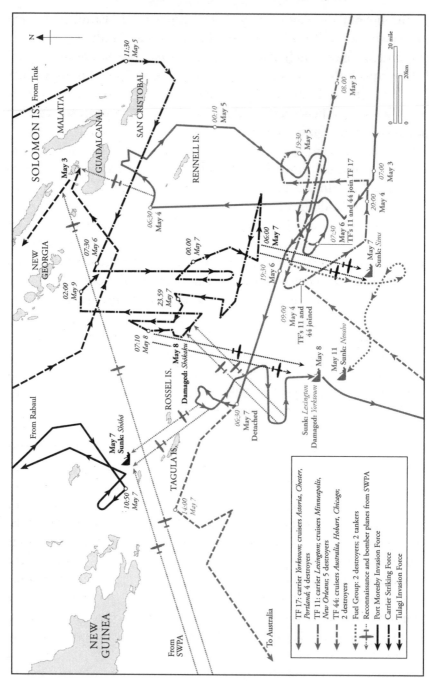

Throughout the day of May 6, the Combat Air Patrol protecting *Lexington* and *Yorktown* was vectored through the cloudy skies to chase and find Japanese search planes. Four Wildcats from *Yorktown*'s VF-42, led by squadron commander Lieutenant Commander Jimmy Flatley, and four VF-2 Wildcats, led by Lieutenant Noel Gaylor, were sent after one shadower. When Flatley found the enemy flying boat, he reported the discovery to *Yorktown*, which requested its position. Flatley replied, "Wait a minute and I'll show you." The *Mavis* blew up under his fire and pieces of it fell through the clouds, narrowly missing Gaylor, who radioed, "That almost hit me!" to which Flatley replied, "That'll teach you not to fly underneath me."

At 1800 hours, the American ships completed fueling and Fletcher detached *Neosho* with an escorting destroyer, *Sims* (DD-409), to head further south to the fleet's prearranged rendezvous. Fletcher then turned the fleet northwest toward Rossel Island in the Louisiades.

Neither side was aware that at 2000 hours, they passed within 70 miles of each other.

The morning of May 7 dawned with *Lexington* and *Yorktown* steaming under the low clouds of a warm tropical front. At 0615 hours, *Yorktown* launched ten SBDs to search the Louisiades. At 0655 both *Zuikaku* and *Shōkaku*, which were 300 miles east of Task Force 17, launched 12 B5N2s to search for the enemy. Believing the Americans were south of their force, the searchers flew east of Task Force 17 and failed to sight the enemy in the poor weather.

At 0722 hours, a Japanese scout found *Neosho* and *Sims*, and mistakenly identified *Neosho* as an aircraft carrier. At 0800 hours, Admiral Hara launched 78 aircraft from both *Zuikaku* and *Shōkaku*:18 A6M2 fighters, 36 D4Y1 dive bombers, and 24 B5N2 torpedo bombers. Twenty minutes later, an H6K from Tulagi found the American carriers and reported the sighting to Admiral Inoue at Rabaul, who forwarded the message to Admiral Takagi. The sighting was confirmed at 0830 hours by a scout launched from the cruiser *Kinugasa*. Now confused by the conflicting reports, Admiral Hara decided to continue the strike on the first ships spotted, while he ordered *Zuikaku* and *Shōkaku* to head northwest to close the distance with *Kinugasa*'s reported contact. Hara reported to Takagi that he considered the conflicting reports might mean the enemy was operating in two separate groups.

At 0815 hours, Scouting 5's Ensign John L. Nielsen sighted the invasion screening force; after a few minutes, he spotted *Shōhō*. He reported sighting "two carriers and four heavy cruisers" 225 miles northwest of Task Force 17. On receipt of Nielsen's message, Admiral Fletcher ordered both carriers to launch all available aircraft. The 93 planes were on their way by 1013 hours: *Lexington's* 40 planes included ten VF-2 Wildcats led by Paul Ramsey, who placed four fighters led by Lieutenant Fred Borries as close escort to the 28 SBDs from VB-2 and VS-2, with two others as high cover for Air Group Commander William B. Ault, while Ramsey's division covered the 12 TBDs at low altitude. Unlike *Yorktown's* strike that organized themselves en route, *Lexington's* air group formed up into an organized unit before heading out.

Fletcher received a report at 1012 hours from the B-17s that they had spotted an aircraft carrier, ten transports, and 16 warships 30 miles south of Nielsen's sighting location; this was actually the same fleet Nielsen had spotted, since his position report had been inaccurate, plus the transports of the invasion force. Believing the B-17s had spotted the main enemy carrier force, Fletcher directed the strike force to hit this target.

At 0915 hours, the Japanese strike spotted *Neosho* and *Sims*. Correctly identifying the two ships, the planes then searched in vain for the American carriers. At 1051, the *Shōkaku* scout realized his mistake and corrected his identification. Admiral Hara now realized the enemy was further west, between him and the invasion convoy, which put the invasion force in extreme danger. The strike was ordered to attack *Neosho* and *Sims* and return as soon as possible. At 1115 hours, the 36 dive bombers attacked and in four minutes sank *Sims* and left *Neosho* badly damaged with her main deck awash, while the B5Ns and their Zero escorts headed back with their ordnance.

At 1020 hours, Paul Ramsey spotted an E7K Type 94 "Alf" twin-float biplane near Misima Island; he dispatched Lieutenant (jg) Paul Baker, a former NAP and veteran of "The Flying Chiefs," who caught the ancient biplane at 500 feet and forced it down.

Shōhō was spotted at 1040 hours and the *Lexington* strike deployed to attack. Six A6M2 Zeros and two A5M4 Type 96 Claude fighters were airborne as fleet CAP. The rest of *Shōhō's* air group was aboard ship, preparing for a strike against the Americans.

At 1045 hours, Air Group 2 CAG Commander Ault deployed his dive and torpedo bombers for a classic coordinated attack. Bombing 2 commander Lieutenant Commander William L. Weldon deployed his squadron of dive bombers as the TBDs went in low to drop their torpedoes. Weldon later reported, "As Bombing 2 made its attack, the carrier was completing its second circle. There was no evidence of antiaircraft fire. Five minutes later the ship was a flaming wreckage rent by tremendous explosions." The Dauntlesses had hit *Shōhō* with six 1,000-pound bombs, creating a smoke screen that protected the TBDs. When the Devastators bored in, the two A5M4s swooped down on them, but were intercepted by Paul Baker's Wildcat section. Maintaining his speed and refusing to engage the nimble Claudes in dogfights, Baker claimed both. However, he apparently only damaged them, since two Claudes were also claimed by VF-42, one by Jimmy Flatley; *Shōhō* only launched two Claudes. Torpedo 2 CO Lieutenant Commander James Brett dropped the first torpedo at 1048 hours, with the last dropping into the water at 1052. The Devastators claimed five hits and the slow torpedo bombers escaped without loss.

Lieutenant Commander Robert E. Dixon's Scouting 2 followed Bombing 2's attack. Dixon reported, "It was obvious we had caught them by surprise. They had a number of planes on deck, and one was coming up from the hangar deck on the elevator. I could see them all clearly as I kept my eye on them through my sight." Dixon's Dauntlesses went low before pulling out and they scored two hits. Dixon radioed *Lexington*: "Scratch one flattop! Dixon to carrier. Scratch one flattop!"

Air Group 5 arrived overhead shortly after Air Group 2 and initiated their attack on the almost-stationary carrier shortly after 1100 hours, scoring hits with 11 more 1,000-pound bombs and at least two torpedoes. Torn apart, *Shōhō* slipped beneath the waves at 1135 hours, the first aircraft carrier lost in a carrier-vs-carrier battle. Fearing more attacks, Admiral Gotō withdrew his warships to the north while the Port Moresby invasion force turned back toward Rabaul. The admiral sent the destroyer *Sazanami* back at 1400 hours to rescue survivors, but only 203 of the carrier's 834-man crew were saved. Three SBDs were lost in the attack – two from *Lexington* and one from *Yorktown*. The Americans had stopped the New Guinea invasion.

Takagi and Hara were still unsure of the American location, and *Shōkaku* launched eight B5N2s at 1515 hours to sweep west 200 miles. Shortly before 1615 hours, the eight scouts reached the end of their search legs and turned back without spotting anything in the thick overcast. With the opportunity for a daylight attack narrowing, Admiral Hara chose his most experienced crews to attempt an attack. At 1615 hours, 12 D3A1s and 15 B5N2s were launched from *Zuikaku* with orders to fly bearing 277 degrees to a distance of 280 miles.

At 1747 hours, the Japanese strike was spotted on *Lexington's* CXAM radar. Eleven Wildcats were flying CAP. Fighting 2 CO Paul Ramsey's division was sent out to hit the raiders first, since his Wildcats were equipped with the new IFF gear. As the four F4F-3s turned toward the enemy, both carriers began launching a total of 18 more Wildcats. Minutes later, Ramsey spotted nine B5N2s. His division was perfectly positioned for a bounce. Ramsey and his wingman took one side of the formation while Lieutenant (jg) Paul Baker and his wingman took the other. Flying a high side gunnery pass, Ramsey hit the first B5N2 from 700 yards and it exploded. He then hit a second from a distance of 300 yards that burned all the way until it disappeared in the dark sea below. Baker shot down a third B5N2 while his wingman repeatedly hit a fourth that finally caught fire and went down. When Baker gave chase to a fifth, he disappeared into the darkening sky; a moment later, an explosion lit the clouds. Ramsey reported that Baker must have collided with his second victim. "Ramsey's Lambsies" had completely broken up the Japanese attack, shooting down five of the deadly torpedo bombers while the surviving attackers jettisoned their ordnance and turned for home as the sun set on the horizon at 1830 hours; with the upper sky still lit, they had the misfortune to run into two divisions from VF-42, which promptly shot down two more B5N2s and a D3A1.

The surviving dive bombers were briefly confused regarding the identity of the ships below and mistakenly circled in preparation for landing before they were driven off by antiaircraft fire from the escorting destroyers. Noel Gaylor's division returned to *Lexington* at that moment and briefly came under American fire as they entered the landing pattern. Gaylor recalled:

They had a whole bunch of .50-caliber machine guns independently operated on the catwalk. Somebody started shooting and in those days the fire discipline was not very good, so everyone started shooting. The landing signal officer realized what was happening because he knew who he had in the landing pattern. He turned around and hit the nearest guy across the face with his signal flags and knocked him away from his gun. Gradually the word went up the line and they realized who we were. Christ, I had my wheels down and my flaps down when they opened up!

The opposing fleets were now 100 miles apart. During the night, the warm frontal zone with low-hanging clouds that had hidden the American carriers so well the first day moved north and east. At dawn, the front covered the Japanese fleet and visibility was between 2 and 15 miles in heavy cloud.

Lexington and *Yorktown* launched 18 Dauntlesses at 0635 hours to search for the enemy. At 0820 hours, *Lexington* SBD pilot Lieutenant (jg) Joseph G. Smith looked down through a hole in the thick clouds and spotted *Shōkaku* and *Zuikaku*. Two minutes later, *Shōkaku's* Lieutenant Kenzo Kanno looked down from the cockpit of his B5N2 and sighted the American carriers. The opposing forces were approximately 210 miles apart. Both now raced to launch their strikes.

Shōkaku and *Zuikaku* launched a combined strike of 18 A6M2 fighter escorts, 33 D3A dive bombers, and 18 B5N2 torpedo bombers led by *Shōkaku* Air Group commander Lieutenant Commander Kakuichi Takahashi at 0915 hours. At the same time, *Yorktown's* six F4F-3s, 15 SBDs, and nine TBDs were on the way. Ten minutes later, *Lexington* launched seven F4F-3s, with Noel Gaylor's division flying escort for the 12 TBDs, and Lieutenant Albert O. Vorse's three-plane division, which included Ensign Bill Eder, escorting the 15 SBDs. All four carriers now increased speed as they headed directly for each other's location to reduce the distance their aircraft would have to fly when they returned.

The *Yorktown* SBDs arrived over the Japanese carriers at 1032 hours; the dive bombers circled to allow the slower TBDs to position themselves in order to conduct a simultaneous attack. *Shōkaku* and *Zuikaku* were about 4 miles apart, with *Zuikaku* hidden beneath a rain squall. The American strike was hampered by the poor weather and the 16 Zero fighters of the Japanese CAP. VF-42 shot down two Zeros while losing two Dauntlesses. The *Yorktown* dive bombers were able to hit *Shōkaku* with two 1,000-pound bombs that tore open her forecastle, causing major damage to the flight and hangar decks. Unfortunately, the TBDs scored no hits.

An hour later, *Lexington's* strike arrived. The towering cumulus clouds they had been forced to fly through had broken up their formations and the strike group was unable to form up for a coordinated attack. Vorse's three Wildcats had been forced to abort. The Dauntlesses immediately came under attack from the defending CAP. Gaylor's Wildcats and the Zeros tangled as the dive bombers attempted to attack. Gaylor's division was flying low and slow with the torpedo bombers when four Zeros attempted to attack, exploding Gaylor's wingman on the first pass. Gaylor was immediately involved with a *Zero*. He later recalled:

> I think the guy I tangled with was a much better pilot than I. He got on my tail pretty promptly, and he was a very good shot. His wingmen went by on both sides. As soon as I saw them, I took the stick with both hands and pushed into a dive but there wasn't enough altitude to gain speed. I came around on another Jap and made a big hairy climbing turn, taking a long shot at him, and fell out for lack of airspeed just as I saw him starting to burn. It was just such an incredibly confusing, mixed-up situation, poor visibility and people yelling on the radio.

Gaylor managed to flame a Zero that flew in front of him. However, the two Wildcats in the other element of his division were lost in the melee.

One *Lexington* dive bomber managed to hit *Shōkaku* with a third bomb, causing more damage, while two SBDs made unsuccessful attacks on *Zuikaku*. Unfortunately, the rest of the *Lexington* force were unable to find the enemy in the poor weather; if they had managed to stay together in the weather, it is likely *Shōkaku* would have been sunk.

As it was, *Shōkaku* suffered 223 of her crew killed or wounded, while her flight deck was heavily damaged. With the ship unable to conduct further air operations, Captain Takatsugu Jojima requested permission to withdraw, to which Admiral Hara agreed. At 1210, *Shōkaku* retired to the northeast, escorted by two destroyers.

At almost the same time that the American planes arrived over the Japanese fleet, *Lexington*'s radar detected the inbound enemy strike 68 miles distant and vectored nine Wildcats to intercept. Paul Ramsey's three-plane division was at 10,000 feet when wingman Ensign Ed Sellstrom spotted the 63 aircraft, with torpedo bombers at 9,000 feet, dive bombers at 14,000 feet, and Zeros at 18,000 feet.

Due to the heavy losses suffered the previous night, the Japanese could not execute a full attack on both carriers. *Zuikaku*'s air group commander Lieutenant Commander Shigekazu Shimazaki sent 14 B5Ns to attack *Lexington* and four to attack *Yorktown*. As the speedy torpedo bombers dived toward the task force, Ensign Sellstrom dived after them and found they were fast enough that it was hard to catch up. With his speed increased in the dive, Sellstrom caught the rear of three and flamed the last B5N 5 miles from the ships. He was then caught by the Zero escort and later reported he managed to damage two before he escaped in a dive.

Wildcat losses the previous day and the need to send escorts on the strike meant the defending fighters were supplemented by 23 Dauntlesses, including six from Scouting 2. Twelve Zeros attacked four VS-2 SBDs led by Lieutenant Stanley "Swede" Vejtasa; his rear gunner shot down a Zero while he managed to score three others with his twin .50-caliber nose guns. Lieutenant (jg) John Leppla and his rear-seater, Aviation Radioman 3/c Donald K. Liska, added three more Zeros to the four they claimed from the previous day. VF-42's Lieutenant (jg) Richard Crommelin managed to score two Zeros before being hit and ditching his Wildcat in the ocean below.

The American defenders mistakenly expected the Japanese torpedo bombers would attack in a similar manner to the TBD – low and slow. Because of this, the six VF-42 Wildcats were too low at 1,000 feet and could only watch the B5Ns swarm overhead at speeds over 200 mph, dropping their deadly Type 91 torpedoes at an altitude of 1,500 feet. The four that attacked *Yorktown* all missed as the carrier turned away from the incoming torpedoes, but the other 14 successfully employed a "hammer and anvil" attack on *Lexington*, which had a much larger turning radius than *Yorktown*. At 1120 hours, the carrier was hit by two torpedoes. The first hit buckled the port aviation gasoline stowage tanks while the second ruptured the port water main; this reduced water pressure to the three forward firerooms, forcing the associated boilers to shut down. As thousands of tons of water poured in, damage control was forced to counterflood to maintain an even keel. As the attackers sped away, four were shot down by *Lexington*'s gunners.

The 33 dive bombers circled to attack from upwind, and did not enter their dives until shortly after the torpedo bombers attacked. Nineteen *Shōkaku* D3As led by Lieutenant Commander Takahashi lined up on *Lexington* while *Zuikaku*'s Lieutenant Commander Tamotsu Ema led 14 on *Yorktown*. Four VF-2 Wildcats led by Fred Borries attacked

Takahashi's force, but were swarmed by escorting Zeros and were forced to dive away to save themselves. Two VF-42 Wildcats above *Yorktown* disrupted Ema's formation and damaged two enemy planes in their dives, while throwing off the others' aim.

Takahashi's attack damaged *Lexington*, scoring two hits and several near misses. *Yorktown* was hit in the center of her flight deck at 1127 hours by a single 550-pound semi- armor-piercing bomb that penetrated four decks before exploding. The explosion caused severe structural damage to an aviation storage room and killed or seriously wounded 66 men. Twelve near misses damaged her below the waterline. Two of the attackers were shot down by a VF-42 Wildcat during the attack.

As the bombers attempted to escape, they ran a gauntlet of defending Wildcats and SBDs. Vorse's division had just returned from aborting the strike and were immediately involved in a fight. Bill Eder recalled:

> My wingman and I headed for two Jap planes, but lost them in the clouds. Then we became separated and I turned and saw this fighter below me. He turned up toward me as I headed down toward him and we met head on. I was firing four .50-calibers on a down slant and he was firing on an up slant. I could see his 20 millimeter stuff was falling short, though his 7.7.s were doing better. Then my .50 calibers began hitting him. Almost immediately he sort of snap-rolled, then spiraled downward, uncontrolled. My emotion was "scored," and I'm glad my .50 calibers were more adequate than his guns.

The ensuing fight saw three SBDs, three Wildcats, three B5Ns, one D3A, and Eder's Zero lost. *Shōkaku's* Lieutenant Kanno and Lieutenant Commander Takahashi were both shot down and killed.

The American and Japanese strike formations ran across each other on their return flights to their respective fleets. VF-42 Wildcats shot down a B5N2 and two D3As, while Noel Gaylor became the leading Navy ace of the time with eight victories when he shot down two D3As.

Lexington's fires were out by 1233 hours and the carrier was still able to operate despite the torpedo hits. When the surviving planes from her strike returned, Noel Gaylor did not notice any damage as he approached for landing. "She was making 25 knots and operating airplanes. She looked okay from the air. It was only after I landed, when I noticed nobody paid any attention to me, contrary to before, then I looked around and noticed some of the faces were looking sort of strange. I saw flecks of fire-fighting foam all over the deck and knew she had been hit."

Vorse's division also recovered aboard. Gaylor tried to organize another strike against *Zuikaku* while *Lexington* still seemed able to function. Unfortunately, there was no way to fuel the planes. Bill Eder remembered, "We were to refuel, rearm and relaunch. However, before that was accomplished the below-decks fires reached the hangar deck."

Admiral Fletcher assessed the situation while Task Force 17 recovered aircraft. The fliers reported they had damaged one enemy carrier heavily but that the other had escaped. Both American carriers were badly damaged and their air groups had lost many fighters. With the loss of *Neosho*, fuel was a concern for the escorts. At 1422 hours, Admiral Fitch notified Fletcher of reports there were still two undamaged Japanese carriers, which was supported by radio intercepts. In the belief he faced overwhelming Japanese superiority, Admiral Fletcher decided to withdraw.

At 1430 hours, Admiral Hara informed Admiral Takagi that there were only 24 Zeros, eight D3As, and four B5Ns operational aboard *Zuikaku*. Admiral Takagi was also worried about fuel, since his cruisers were at 50 percent and some destroyers were down to 20 percent. At 1500 hours, Takagi notified Admiral Inoue his force had sunk two American carriers – a "*Yorktown*-class" and a "*Saratoga*-class" – but he could not continue to provide air cover for the invasion due to heavy aircraft losses. In the face of this, Admiral Inoue recalled the invasion convoy to Rabaul and postponed Operation *MO* to July 3. *Zuikaku* and her escorts turned toward Rabaul while *Shōkaku* headed for major repair in Japan.

Sparks from unattended electric motors ignited gasoline fumes near *Lexington*'s central control station at 1247 hours; the resulting explosion killed 25 men, starting a large fire. A severe fire began after another large explosion occurred at 1442 hours. At 1525 hours there was a third explosion. Damage control reported the fires were uncontrollable at 1538 hours. The order to abandon ship was given at 1707 hours. Noel Gaylor recalled:

We were driven to the extreme stern by the fire. The ship's service ice cream plant was in the extreme port stern quarter. Some clown passed the word that there was free ice cream and sailors who were abandoning ship lined up for it. Of course they puked it up afterwards as soon as they had been swimming in salt water a while. There was no panic, no worry about being picked up. The water was warm and the destroyers moved in with cargo nets.

Gaylor was picked up by a destroyer after 90 minutes in the water. Bill Eder remembered:

After the abandon ship order was given, I waited my turn and descended a knotted line to the warm water. I found an inflated life raft with three older chief petty officers aboard. Since I had a life jacket, I stayed alongside in the water. Pretty soon the destroyer *Dewey* came along and picked us up. They threw us a line and I, being the young 'un, held it for the chiefs to climb. When it was my turn I was too exhausted to climb and a sailor had to come down and put a line around me so they could winch me up.

At 1915 hours with the sun setting over the Coral Sea, the destroyer *Phelps* (DD-360) fired five torpedoes into the burning *Lexington* and the carrier sank in 2,400 fathoms at 1952 hours, taking 216 of the 2,951-man crew and 36 aircraft down with her. *Phelps* and the other warships that had picked up survivors immediately departed to rejoin *Yorktown*, and Task Force 17 withdrew from the Coral Sea to the southwest.

The experienced Japanese carrier aircrews had put in a better performance than the Americans, but had suffered much higher losses, losing 90 killed compared with 35 for the Americans. The cadre of highly skilled carrier aircrews was irreplaceable, since an institutionalized limitation in the IJNAF training programs and the absence of a pool of experienced reserves or expanded advanced training programs for new airmen meant there were no ready replacements of equal skill. The Battle of the Coral Sea marked the beginning of a trend that would result in the irreparable attrition of Japan's veteran carrier aircrews during the Solomons and Rabaul campaigns.

While the Battle of the Coral Sea – the first fleet action in which the opposing ships never saw each other – was a tactical victory for the Japanese because of the loss of *Lexington*, it was a strategic victory for the US Navy, since the Imperial Navy never engaged in another offensive operation in the South Pacific. The previously unstoppable enemy had been rocked back on his heels with an unexpected body blow from his bloodied but unbowed opponent.

CHAPTER EIGHTEEN

VICTORY DISEASE

When he received orders to implement his Pearl Harbor attack plan, Admiral Yamamoto informed his superiors, "I will run wild for six months, after that I can promise nothing." For the next five months and 27 days, he kept his word as the Imperial Navy swept across the Pacific and even went as far as Ceylon in the Indian Ocean. The admiral's ultimate goal was to provoke a fleet action with the US Navy while the Combined Fleet still had technological and material superiority, to achieve that decisive victory in which the United States would be forced to recognize the power of Imperial Japan and allow the empire to be consolidated.

The Doolittle Raid on April 18, 1942 had a much greater effect on Japanese military planning than the Americans expected. While little military damage was inflicted, the raid provoked a major response from the Imperial Army and Navy. The Home Islands had been defiled by the enemy! Such a thing must never happen again! While the Army promoted a consolidation of the conquered areas of the South Seas in order to ensure a defensive barrier, and the Navy advocated further expansion in the South Pacific to cut off Australia from American support that could lead to an invasion of that continent, Admiral Yamamoto advocated expansion eastward past Wake Island to prevent the American Navy from approaching Japan again. Yamamoto went so far as to intimate he would resign if his plan was not adopted, leading the Navy's General Staff finally to support him on the grounds that taking Midway would make the operations planned for the summer of 1942 against Fiji and Samoa more secure since the Americans would not be able to intervene in force. The Imperial Army acceded to the plan when Yamamoto included an operation to establish Japanese bases on islands at the western end of the Aleutians chain, which would prevent the Americans establishing air bases from which they could mount bombing missions against the Home Islands.

The result was a plan to attack and occupy Midway, the last American base in the western Pacific between Japan and the Hawaiian Islands, with an operation to deceive the Americans as to the main Japanese goal by a secondary strike against the Aleutians. Japanese occupation and control of Midway would make it difficult for the Americans to approach Japan again without discovery in time to counter the move. Yamamoto hoped that the invasion would provoke the American fleet to respond, and the decisive mid-Pacific battle every Japanese naval officer knew must happen to assure victory would occur under conditions advantageous to Japan.

Discovered in 1859 and annexed by the United States in August 1867, Midway Atoll consisted of Sand and Eastern islands, surrounded by a coral reef less than 6 miles in diameter. The atoll had been used as a cable station and way station for Pan American Airways' China Clipper from 1935 until March 1941, when the US Navy began construction of a naval air station on Eastern Island. Completed that August, NAS Midway had a 5,300-foot runway on Eastern Island. The Japanese destroyers *Sazanami* and *Ushio* had shelled the airfield on December 7 in an attempt to prevent its use for reinforcing Wake Island.

The Midway invasion and occupation plan was known as Operation *MI*. It was typical of almost all Japanese naval plans of the Pacific War, being extremely complex and requiring careful and timely coordination of many different units over a vast area of open sea. It also depended on the enemy playing his role in accordance with the Japanese script. This kind of plan stemmed from the games of *botaoshi* and *kendo* that Japanese officers played as midshipmen during their days at Eta Jima in the same way that American naval plans stemmed from the football and baseball games played at Annapolis.

Kendo is an individual martial art combat sport in which the victor is able to knock down his opponent with a single blow or thrust with a 4-foot bamboo stick. *Botaoshi* is a team sport in which the winners are able to confuse their opponents with feints and other distractions that allow the winner to capture and lower the opposing team's pole. To a Westerner, *kendo* looks like precise choreography in which every move has a scripted countermove, while *botaoshi* resembles organized chaos on the playing field. All senior Imperial Navy officers were recognized masters of both games from their days at Eta Jima. Thus, their concept of strategy was based on highly intricate individual and group maneuvers relying on deception, diversion, and division of the opponent's force to open a path that gave victory through one powerful, victorious blow.

American football and baseball, on the other hand, involve the cumulative wearing down of the opponent through a series of confrontations that dissipate the opponent's resources to the point at which the only path left is surrender, a cumulative victory.

The necessary deception would be provided by the strike at the Aleutians, conducted shortly before the main operation at Midway. It was designed to lure the American fleet from Hawaii north to Alaska, placing the US force out of position to oppose the Midway thrust when it materialized. The operating assumption was that the enemy would not deploy from Pearl Harbor prior to their learning of the Aleutians attack and would run across a line of Japanese submarines deployed west and north of Hawaii to intercept and sink as much of the enemy fleet as possible.

As with a game of *botaoshi*, the Midway force was dispersed in such a way that its full size and power would be concealed prior to the battle. Critically, the four carriers of Kido Butai were only directly supported by two battleships and six cruisers, while the main force of battleships and cruisers accompanied by two light carriers was several hundred miles distant and unable to quickly respond with support if the fleet action failed to go as set by the Japanese plan. Admiral Yamamoto intended that the main force would engage what was left of the American fleet once it had been weakened by attacks from Admiral Nagumo's carriers, so that a night battle in which the Japanese were superior would lead to the American defeat. Critically, Kido Butai was operating at only two-thirds strength with four fleet carriers, since *Shōkaku* was undergoing repair from the damage suffered at Coral Sea, while *Zuikaku* was engaged in rebuilding her air group from the losses suffered in the battle. Overconfident, the Japanese had given no thought to combining the survivors of the two air groups to go aboard *Zuikaku* and thus provide a fifth carrier, which might have been the deciding factor in what happened.

Not only was the carrier force not at full strength, but what force it had was constrained by the fact that production of the D3A dive bomber had been drastically reduced, while production of the B5N2 torpedo bomber had ceased; thus there were no replacement aircraft to send to the carrier air groups without removing them from other units. Additionally, most of the aircraft aboard the four carriers had been in extended operational use since the previous November with little opportunity for overhaul or extended maintenance; while the aircraft were well maintained, many were nearly worn out and were increasingly unreliable. All this meant that the air groups of Kido Butai had fewer reliable operational aircraft than their normal complement, with almost no spare aircraft or parts.

Much of Yamamoto's plan was the result of a general feeling among the Japanese leadership that American morale was low following the string of Japanese successes since Pearl Harbor, as well as their optimistic belief that the Americans had lost both *Lexington* and *Yorktown* at the Coral Sea, leaving only *Enterprise* and *Hornet* in the Pacific. They were further mistaken as to the location of the two American carriers, since *Enterprise* had not been spotted by the Japanese since May 15 when Admiral Nimitz had ordered Admiral Halsey to allow a Japanese snooper in the northern Coral Sea to make its spotting report. Yamamoto was convinced the Americans were unaware of Japanese intentions.

The Japanese, aware of the fact that all available United States carrier strength had been present in the distant Coral Sea only three weeks before, designated June 6, 1942 as the date of occupation of Midway Island, and made the following estimate of the United States situation:

> Relying on the line determined by our initial operational advance as his first line of defense, the enemy is growing desperate to check his decline as his outer shell crumbles under our successive blows, and as India, Australia and Hawaii become directly threatened. By strengthening and giving an active role to both his aircraft in the Australian theatre and his submarines, roaming under the seas which we command, he conducts guerrilla operations against us. With a striking force he reconnoitered the South and Southwest Pacific Ocean Area. Comparatively speaking, he is displaying remarkably vigorous activity. His morale was not at once shaken by his crushing defeat in the Coral Sea on May 7–8, 1942; and the last 10 days of May saw the sudden return of lively activity throughout enemy areas after our fleet sortie from Hashira Jima; he is paying singular attention to the Australian Area; the time is ripe to strike at Midway and the Aleutians.

CHAPTER NINETEEN

"A NEW AND SHINING PAGE"

Had it not been for the fact that the US Navy had broken the Japanese naval codes, history might have recorded Yamamoto's operation victorious as planned. Even knowing the Japanese plan and its target, the American response was incredibly close-run. While the cryptanalysts at HYPO were confident that "AF" in the Japanese messages referred to Midway, higher commanders demanded confirmation that "AF" did in fact refer to Midway. Using the undersea cable that connected Midway to Hawaii in order to prevent the possibility of the Japanese intercepting the order, the island was directed to send an uncoded message that the water purification system had broken down. Amazingly, no one in Japanese intelligence questioned that such an important piece of information would be broadcast in "clear," while none seemed to remember that the island had access to secure undersea cable for communications. HYPO soon decoded a message to Japanese forces that "AF" was short of water. With that, Admiral Nimitz went "all in" and bet the family homestead on the outcome of battle.

Seven of the F4F-3As that *Enterprise's* Fighting 6 had traded for F4F-4s before leaving on the Doolittle Raid, as well as the 18 war-weary Bombing 6 SBD-2s Dick Best had replaced with factory-new SBD-3s, were sent on to the Marines at Midway as reinforcements for VMSB-241's obsolete SB2U-3 Vindicators and VMF-221's F2A-3s. The aircraft were given quick overhauls by the Fleet Replacement Unit, then loaded aboard the aircraft transport *Kitty Hawk* on May 22, 1942. VMF-221 received the seven Wildcats and VMSB-241 took the SBD-2s when they were offloaded four days later, along with 12 brand-new second lieutenants right out of flight school who were divided up between the two units. The squadrons had only nine days to familiarize themselves with the new airplanes before being launched against the Japanese fleet.

B-17s were flown from California to Pearl Harbor to increase the island's offensive force, and other Flying Fortresses flew on to Midway. The six brand-new TBF-1 Avengers with which Hornet's VT-8 had been re-equipping when the carrier was rushed to the Pacific in March had arrived in Hawaii while their carrier was launching Jimmy Doolittle's B-25s, and had been sent on to Midway as a separate detachment. By the end of May, VMF-221's Captain Marion Carl, who was very happy to be the recipient of one of the well-worn *Enterprise* F4F-3s, recorded that the airfield on Midway Atoll's Eastern Island was filled beyond capacity with Marine fighters and dive bombers, Army Air Force B-17s and six B-26 Marauders armed with torpedoes, as well as Navy PBY Catalinas that ceaselessly patrolled to the north, west, and south.

When Task Force 16 returned from their unsuccessful attempt to reinforce *Lexington* and *Yorktown*, Admiral Halsey was suffering from what some called dermatitis and others called shingles, most likely caused by the stress he had been under since the beginning of the war. "America's fightin'est Admiral" would be unable to lead anyone into combat. In an act of generosity, Halsey recommended to Nimitz that he be replaced by his surface force commander, Rear Admiral Raymond A. Spruance. To the argument that Spruance lacked experience in naval aviation, Halsey pointed out that he would be working with chief of staff Captain miles Browning, a naval aviator whose history went back to the first group of pilots to operate from the *Langley*, who had been intimately involved during the 1930s with all the planning that went into the development of the Navy's strategy and tactics for fighting the Pacific War. Nimitz assented, and Raymond Spruance, a very different admiral from the man he replaced, moved into the flag stateroom aboard *Enterprise*.

Yorktown returned to Pearl Harbor from the Coral Sea on May 27, and entered dry dock the next day. The damage she had sustained at Coral Sea was so extensive that the yard inspectors initially estimated she would need a minimum of two weeks for the necessary repairs. Admiral Nimitz replied that she had to be ready to depart with *Enterprise* and *Hornet* in three days. Further inspection revealed the aircraft elevators were undamaged, and that the damage to the flight deck and hull by the bomb that had penetrated several decks before exploding could be temporarily repaired sufficiently to allow her to operate.

Yorktown's air group for the battle would combine squadrons of her regular Air Group 5 with those from Air Group 3, which had been sidelined by the torpedoing of *Saratoga* back in January. Lieutenant Commander John S. "Jimmy" Thach, who had spent the previous six weeks training new aviators assigned to Fighting 3 in how to fly his "Thach Weave," brought 25 new F4F-4 Wildcats to the carrier, where 11 of VF-3's most experienced pilots and 16 VF-42 Coral Sea veterans would man the fighters. Lieutenant Commander Max Leslie, for whom John Bridgers had acted as "taxi pilot" during the Doolittle Raid, brought 18 SBD-3 Dauntlesses of Bombing 4, while Air Group 5's Lieutenant Wallace C. Short, Jr. brought 19 Scouting 5 SBD-3s to round out the carrier's dive-bomber force. Lieutenant Commander Lance E. Massey's 18 old TBD-1 Devastators from Torpedo 3 completed the temporary *Yorktown* air group. John Bridgers remembered, "When we members of Bombing 3 went aboard *Yorktown* after she came out of dry dock, there were still construction workers aboard busily finishing their repairs. In fact, they would accompany us to battle in their effort to get the ship ready for war."

Saratoga had just come out of the Bremerton Navy yard after completing repairs from her torpedoing. Unfortunately, there were not enough escorts available to bring her to Hawaii, where there was now a shortage of air units to deploy aboard her if she did arrive in time.

Task Force 16, with *Enterprise* and *Hornet*, sortied from Pearl Harbor on May 29, followed by Admiral Fletcher's Task Force 17 with *Yorktown* on May 31. The picket line of Japanese submarines had been delayed in taking up its patrols north and west of Hawaii, and did not arrive on station until June 1, thus completely missing the American departure. The lack of reported American movement by the submarines contributed to Japanese complacency that their operation remained undiscovered as they had expected and planned for. Operation *K*, a planned flight over Pearl Harbor by two H8K flying boats that would depart their base at Kwajalein and be refueled by a submarine at French Frigate Shoals, was aborted when the submarine reported the presence of American warships, sent there to patrol following the "second Pearl Harbor" raid by flying boats that had used the same tactic back in March. Thus, the two American task forces were able to rendezvous at "Point Luck" northeast of Midway on June 2 completely undetected by their opponents. Admiral Fletcher assumed tactical command of the combined force. Both he and Spruance were surface officers, but Fletcher had experience of having fought the battle in the Coral Sea.

While American codebreakers had been reading the Japanese JN-25 code successfully since early 1942, the Japanese had issued a new code book on May 24; however, it was not uniformly in use until May 27, which marked the last date the US Navy would ever "read the enemy's mail" for the rest of the Pacific War. Fortunately, HYPO had been able to obtain all needed information, including the Imperial Navy's order of battle and the expected attack date: June 4, 1942. While the Americans knew everything they needed to know about their opponent, the Imperial Navy had no warning, and no idea, of what lay in wait.

Just before dawn on June 3, Ensign Jack Reid. flying Catalina 44-P-4 on a west/southwestern search leg, came to the end of his search leg. Reid and navigator Robert Swan decided to push the search a few miles further west. Suddenly, far out on the horizon, Reid spotted wakes of ships in the pre-dawn greyness. "Do you see what I see?" he asked co-pilot Gerald Hardeman. Hardeman took a look and replied, "You're damn right I do." VP-44's Crew 4 had just found the Japanese invasion force, composed of transports, destroyers, and cruisers. While the fleet looked impressive, it was not the carrier striking force. Reid promptly radioed Midway "Sighted Main Body. Bearing 262. Distance 700." Midway responded: "Amplify." Diving low over the water on the assumption the enemy had air cover, Reid turned north for 15 minutes, then turned west for 10 minutes, at which point he figured he was behind the enemy fleet. Using thin cloud cover, Reid climbed high enough to identify what he thought were two small carriers and other ships, unaware this was a separate task group from what he had first spotted. Upon sending the supplementary contact report, he was ordered to return. Though he hadn't sighted the main force, Reid had made the first sighting of Japanese ships headed to Midway. Shortly after receiving his report, the B-17s at Midway were launched to bomb the invasion force. The most important battle of the Pacific War began.

An hour later, the Japanese launched an air strike from the aircraft carrier *Ryūjō* to strike Harbor in the Aleutians. The attack was exactly as had been planned and the Americans took Reid's spotting of the attack as proof their intelligence regarding what the enemy would do was correct. Unknown to both sides at the time was that the A6M2 Zero flown by 19-year-old Petty Officer 1/c Tadayoshi Koga, wingman to Chief Petty Officer Makoto Endo, would be damaged by .50-caliber antiaircraft fire when they and Petty Officer 3/c Tsuguo Shikada attacked a PBY-5 Catalina, flown by Lieutenant (jg) Bud Mitchell, over the harbor and shot it down. The Zero's return oil line was severed by one fatal bullet. As the Zero immediately began trailing oil, Koga reduced his speed to prolong ultimate engine failure as long as possible.

Uninhabited Akutan Island, 25 miles east of Dutch Harbor, had been previously designated for emergency landings, and a Japanese submarine was ready to pick up any downed pilots. Once over the island, the three Zeros circled what appeared to be a smooth area of grass about half a mile inland from Broad Bight. As Koga lowered his gear to land, wingman Shikada noticed water glistening through the tundra vegetation as he made a second low pass. Before he could warn Koga to make a belly landing, the young pilot touched down. The landing gear immediately mired in the tundra and the Zero flipped upside down and skidded to a stop.

From the air, it was impossible for the two pilots to know that Koga had been killed instantly on impact from a broken neck as his fighter flipped over. Orders had been given to destroy any aircraft that crash-landed in enemy territory; not knowing if their fellow pilot was still alive, neither could bring himself to strafe the plane and they left without firing on it. Before the submarine stationed off Akutan could land a party to rescue Koga and destroy the airplane, it was driven off by the destroyer USS *Williamson* (DD-244). Thirty-seven days later, on July 10, Lieutenant William "Bill" Thies, who had become lost in the poor Aleutians weather, happened to fly over Akutan Island as he tried to return to Dutch Harbor. His plane captain, Aviation Machinist's Mate 1/c Albert Knack, spotted the wreckage. The Catalina circled the crash site and noted the position on a map. On his return to Dutch Harbor, Thies persuaded his commander to let him return to the island with a salvage party. The next day, the US Navy came into possession of Koga's flyable, almost-undamaged Zero, one of the greatest prizes of the war. Writing of the event following the war, Commander Masatake Okumiya called it "no less serious for the fate of Japan than the outcome of the Battle of Midway."

While Koga and the other Japanese pilots attacked Dutch Harbor, John Bridgers took off from *Yorktown* on a search flight.

My first operational sortie from a carrier at sea, other than my brief qualification flight from the *Enterprise*, was a 150-mile two-plane search flight from the *Yorktown*. As fate would have it, this was also my only active contribution to what became the Battle of Midway. What I remember the most about that particular mission was that the thin parachute cushion on which I was sitting caused me inordinate discomfort during that four-hour flight, a good part of which we spent circling the ships waiting to come back aboard. I was hurting so much that I thought little about my pending second carrier landing in an SBD. I just wanted to be able to stand up and ease the pain in the seat of my pants.

Dawn came to the Central Pacific the morning of June 4, 1942, revealing clear weather over the four carriers of Kido Butai, with building clouds of a storm front to the east and northeast. The carriers began launching the strike mission at 0430 hours. Thirty-six D3A1 bombers, accompanied by 36 B5N2 bombers loaded for level bombing rather than torpedo attacks, were escorted by 36 Zero fighters. At the same time, eight floatplanes were launched from the cruisers *Tone* and *Chikuma* to conduct a search for the unlikely presence of enemy forces. *Tone* was able to launch three of four of her Aichi E13A Type 0 Reconnaissance Seaplanes (Jack) on time, but engine problems delayed the launch of *Tone* Number 4 for 30 minutes. Crucially, the eight seaplanes were an insufficient force to adequately cover their assigned search area, particularly with the bad weather to the northeast.

At almost the same time, 11 PBY Catalinas took off from the Midway lagoon to search to the north, west, and south of the atoll. At 0534 hours, a PBY sighted two Japanese carriers through the scattered clouds and radioed a report. Ten minutes later, another Catalina spotted the inbound air strike and reported it. Fifteen minutes later, Midway's radar screen picked up the first returns identifying the attackers. The report went out: "Many planes, 93 miles, 310 degrees, altitude 11,000 feet."

At 0555 hours, the wail of Midway's air raid siren sent the defenders scrambling. VMF-221's duty officer, Second Lieutenant John C.

Musselman, Jr., raced along the line of revetments in the command post pickup truck, yelling "Get airborne!" At 0600 hours, the order was given for VMF-221 to scramble. As soon as the 23 fighters were airborne, VMSB-241's commander, Major Lofton R. Henderson, led his mixed formation of SBD-2 Dauntlesses and SB2U-3 Vindicators to the runway. His orders were to attack the carriers reported by the Catalina.

The 23 fighter pilots of VMF-221, known as the "Fighting Falcons," were a mixed lot. Eight were recent graduates of flight school who had only arrived on the island nine days earlier; another five had been recent flight school graduates when they arrived on the island in March, while the rest had arrived on the island in December 1941 when they had flown off *Lexington* after failing to get to Wake Island as reinforcement. Only four had seen aerial combat of any kind, back on March 10 when Captain John Neefus' division was vectored to intercept a Mitsubishi H8K "Emily" operating from Kwajalein, which they had managed to shoot down after a prolonged battle that saw one of the American fighters badly damaged by gunfire from the heavily armed flying boat.

The squadron's leader, 31-year-old Major Floyd B. "Red" Parks, had enlisted in the Navy in 1928 and won an appointment to Annapolis in 1930. Graduating with a commission as a Marine second lieutenant in 1934, he had commenced flight training at Pensacola in May 1936 and pinned on his Wings of Gold as a Marine aviator on June 12, 1937. Following a year as an instructor at Pensacola, he joined the First Marine Air Wing at Quantico in May 1941 and trained as a dive-bomber pilot. He had arrived on Midway in March; promoted to major, he was given command of VMF-221 on May 8 after the original squadron commander, Lieutenant Colonel Ira L. Kimes, had been promoted from major and become commander of Marine Air Group 22 (MAG-22). The night before, Captain Kirk Armistead had found his normally extroverted commander moody and distracted. When Armistead tried to cheer him up, telling him "By this time tomorrow, it'll all be over," Parks had replied, "Yeah, for those of you who get through it."

Parks had divided his force, assigning the 13 F2As of 2nd and 3rd division leaders, captains Daniel J. Hennessy and Armistead, to orbit north of the island as reinforcement until it was known whether the incoming attackers were flying as one formation or two. Parks led the four F2A-3s of the 1st Division and Captain Robert E. Curtin's two 4th Division F2As, along with Captain John F. Carey's three F4F-3 Wildcats; Carey's wingmen were Captain Marion E. Carl and Second Lieutenant Clayton M. Canfield. Two remaining Wildcats were airborne on dawn patrol while the sixth and seventh of the war-weary fighters were grounded with mechanical problems.

Twenty-one of the Marine fighters were Brewster F2A-3s. While the F2A had been the first all-metal monoplane fighter ordered by the Navy in 1938, by the time the 108 F2A-3s were ordered in January 1941, the Navy was thoroughly disgusted with the inability of Brewster to deliver the airplanes on schedule due to poor management and a factory not designed for aircraft production. Difficulties in sealing the wing fuel tanks and the seeming never-ending problems with the delicate landing gear had soured the Navy on the F2A.

The F2A-3's fuel capacity was increased to 240 gallons, resulting in CG problems in handling, while an increase in armor and ammunition capacity pegged the fighter's gross weight at 6,518 pounds, 1,400 pounds heavier than the F2A-2 with no increase in engine power. Maximum speed decreased from the F2A-2's 340 mph to 321 mph; rate of climb and service ceiling were also worse, though the fuel increase gave a range of 1,680 miles, better than any other contemporary US fighter.

Parks' three divisions were vectored on a bearing of 320 degrees, directly toward the incoming strike, now reported by radar at 11,000 feet. Captains Hennessey and Armistead took a heading of 310 degrees to allow for radar error and the chance the attackers might split and attack from different directions.

At 0612 hours, Captain Carey's three Wildcats were at 14,000 feet when he sighted the enemy formation 40 miles north of Midway, below his altitude. The B5N2 level bombers were in a "vee of vees" formation at 11,000 feet, followed by the dive bombers at a slightly higher altitude, while the escorting Zeros were stepped up behind the dive bombers; the disposition gave the Marines a clear shot at the bombers for at least the first pass. At 0614 hours, Canfield saw Carey make "a wide 270-degree turn, then a 90-degree diving turn." Canfield then heard the electrifying "Tally-ho! Hawks at angels-twelve," and, after a slight pause, "accompanied by fighters."

Carey put his Wildcat into a steep dive for a "high side pass" and caught the lead bomber in his gunsight. He waited until it filled his gunsight and then fired a long burst, shredding the enemy plane and setting it afire, while its gunner's return fire cracked his windshield with a bullet. An instant later, the bomber blew up, filling the air with debris. Carey made a high wingover to repeat the attack on the next when suddenly his fighter was raked by a burst of fire that hit his right knee and left leg. On the verge of passing out in excruciating pain, "I dove at about a 40-degree angle and headed for a large cloud about five miles away."

Lieutenant Canfield followed his leader through the enemy formation, recalling, "I fired at the number three plane in the number three section until it exploded and went down in flames." An instant later, the Zero escort hit him. "My Wildcat was hit on the right elevator, left wing and flap and just ahead of the tail wheel by three 20mm cannon shells. There was also a .30-caliber hole through the tail wheel and one that entered the hood on the right side about six inches up, passing just over the left rudder pedal and damaging the landing gear."

Canfield sought refuge in nearby cloud. Emerging moments later, the enemy was gone. "I went around the cloud in the opposite direction and joined up with Captain Carey again." The two flew unsteadily toward Midway as Carey kept losing altitude and falling behind. "I kept throttling back so he could keep up. His wounds kept him from working the rudders, and his plane was all over the sky."

They reached Midway while it was under attack, and prepared to land, at which point Canfield discovered his flaps were gone. "When the wheels touched the ground the landing gear collapsed and the plane slid along the runway. When it stopped, I jumped out and ran for a trench just as a Jap strafed my abandoned plane." Carey landed right behind and remembered, "I ended up in a ground loop, as I had a flat tire and could not control the plane because of the wound in my leg." Carey crashed into a revetment and was pulled out and dragged to safety with the bombs falling.

Marion Carl had been left behind by Carey and Canfield. As he rolled into an overhead pass against the bombers, "I caught sight of these damn Zeros... the air was full of them!" He made a high-side firing pass on one; when he looked back, "I was surprised to see several Zeros swinging into position on my tail, so I dived straight down at full throttle, then zoomed back up to 20,000 feet." As he headed back toward Midway, he spotted three Zeros below him:

They didn't see me drop astern and to the inside of the circle made from one of the fighters. I gave him a long burst, until he fell off on one wing… out of control, and headed almost straight down with smoke streaming from the plane.

I looked around and couldn't find a friendly airplane any place… and the next thing I know, I've got a Zero on my tail that's shooting away. I headed for a cloud, chopped the power, and threw the plane into a skid. When I came out of the other side, the Zero had overrun me. I pulled the trigger on my guns – and got nothing! My guns had jammed, but the maneuver scared him so badly that he gave up the fight.

Despite being badly shot up, Carl was able to limp back and land safely.

5th Division leader Kirk Armistead remembered:

At about 0620 hours, I heard Captain Carey transmit "Tally-ho." I started climbing, and sighted the enemy at approximately 14,000 feet five to seven miles out from Midway and approximately two miles to my right. I was at 17,000 feet when I started my attack. The target consisted of five divisions, flying in division "Vs." I estimated there were 30–40 dive-bombers. I was followed in column by five F2A-3s and one F4F-3 that had joined up with us from its patrol. I made a head-on approach from above at a steep angle and at very high speed on the five planes of the fourth enemy division. I saw my incendiary bullets travel from a point in front of the leader, up through his plane and back through the planes on the left wing of the "V." I continued in my dive, and looking back, saw two or three of those planes falling in flames.

After my pull-out, I zoomed back to an altitude of 14,000 feet. I noticed another group of the same type bombers. I looked back and saw three fighters climbing toward me about 2,000 feet below and behind. At first I thought they were from my division, but when the nearest one was about 500 feet below and behind me, I realized it was a Zero. I kicked over in a violent split-S and was hit by three 20-mm shells, one in the right wing gun, one in the right wing root tank, and one in the top left side of the engine cowling. I also received about 20 7.7-mm rounds in the left aileron, which mangled the tab and sawed off a portion of the aileron. I continued in a vertical dive at full throttle, corkscrewing to my left due to the effect of the damaged aileron. At about 3,000 feet, I started to pull out, and managed to hold the plane level at an altitude of 500 feet.

Armistead decided it was time to nurse his damaged fighter back to Midway.

Captain William C. Humberd rolled into a high-side approach behind Armistead and shot down one bomber, then climbed back up and attacked again from the other side. "I was halfway through another run when I heard a loud noise and turning around, saw a large hole in the hood of my plane, and two Jap Zeros on me about 200 yards astern." He pushed over in a steep dive to escape. "But one of the enemy planes kept on my tail. I stayed at water level with full throttle until I gained enough distance to turn into him. We met head on. I gave him a long burst when we were about 300 yards distant, and he caught fire and dived into the water, out of control."

Humberd managed to land shortly afterward. "My hydraulic fluid was gone, and my flaps and landing gear would not lower, so I used my emergency system to lower my wheels." Once stopped and out, he discovered the plane "had three or four holes in the left fuel tank and two 20mm holes in the fuselage." Regardless, Humberd refueled, rearmed, and took off again, staying a distance from Midway until all planes were ordered to land.

Second lieutenants William V. Brooks and William B. Sandoval followed their leader, Armistead, and made a pass down the right side of the enemy formation. Brooks remembered that "One of us got a plane from the right side of the Vee. When I pulled out, two Zeros came at me. I could not out-dive these planes, since my landing gear had partially locked in the down position, but I managed to dodge them and fire a burst or so into them as they swept past." Brooks was now close enough to Midway that AA fire from the island drove his opponents off and he stayed in the fight. "I saw two planes dog-fighting and decided to go help. My plane was working very poorly, and my climb was slow. As I neared the fight, both planes turned on me!

I turned and made a fast retreat, collecting a goodly number of bullets on the way." With his fighter badly shot up, he decided to land. "As I circled the island, I saw two Japs on a Brewster. Three of my guns were jammed, but I cut across the island, firing as I went with my one gun." He was too late to save the Marine from being shot down. When he finally landed his tattered fighter, the ground crew counted 72 bullet and cannon holes in it.

Sandoval was not as lucky. Another pilot reported that he leveled off on his firing run and was shot down by a rear gunner. He failed to return and was listed as killed in action. Brooks requested that "Lieutenant Sandoval, deceased, be logged up with the bomber which one of us got in our first run."

The last surviving pilot in Armistead's division was Second Lieutenant Charles M. Kunz. He made a pass and shot down two torpedo bombers. "I saw tracers go by my cockpit and bullets ripping my wings. I immediately dived for the water in an attempt to shake the Zero off my tail. I made radical turns at full throttle hoping the pilot couldn't get steadied on me." Bullets, which would crease his scalp, skimmed above his ears on both sides of his head. Close to passing out, Kunz managed to land safely. That night, the flight surgeon had to give him several "stiff shots" before he could sleep. Kunz later returned to combat in the Solomons, where his two Vals combined with five other victories made him the only American ace to score any victories in the F2A-3.

4th Division leader Captain Curtin's wingman, Second Lieutenant Darrel D. Irwin, had most of his left aileron shot away and was pursued back to Midway by two Zeros, but he managed to land his crippled fighter at 0650 hours in the middle of the dive-bombing attack. No one saw how Curtin died and he was listed missing in action when he failed to return.

Captain Phillip R. White of Hennessy's 2nd Division escaped a Zero after making a run on the formation.

> After the first pass, I lost my wingman and the rest of the division. I made a long, low, fast climb and made a second above-side pass, and started for a third, when I saw a Zero fighter climbing up on my tail very rapidly. I pushed my stick forward as hard as I could and went into a violent dive. When I recovered and looked around, I had lost the Zero fighter.

He then spotted a dive bomber. "I made a long fast side pass and it made an easy left turn into the water." White regained altitude and found another dive bomber that he made two passes on before running out of ammunition. He returned to Midway. In his after-action report, he complained bitterly: "The F2A-3 is not a combat aircraft. It is inferior to the planes we were fighting in every respect. It is my belief that any commander that orders a pilot out for combat in a F2A-3 should consider the pilot as lost before leaving the ground."

White's division-mate, Captain Herbert T. Merrill, was hit by defending Zeros and he lost partial control when the F2A caught fire. He stayed with the burning fighter in an attempt to reach Midway and was badly burned. When the fire finally forced him to bale out at 8,000 feet and very close to Midway, he delayed opening his parachute for fear of being strafed by the enemy. He landed in the lagoon near the reef and inflated his Mae West. One of the Navy PT boats spotted him, and Seaman 3/c E. J. Steward dived into the turbulent water and hauled him to safety.

Major Parks wasn't as lucky as Merrill. The squadron commander was hit by the swarming escorts early in the fight. As his fighter fell toward the ocean, Parks baled out and his parachute was seen to open. An enemy fighter then strafed him and then continued to strafe his body when it fell on one of the outer reefs. All six pilots of Parks' 1st Division were shot down in the battle.

Not only were the 23 Marines outnumbered by the 36 Zeros, they were completely outclassed by the faster and more agile enemy fighters, whose experienced pilots quickly shot down 16 Buffalos and a Wildcat, as well as putting Carey's and Canfield's Wildcats out of action.

Fourteen pilots were killed in action. Of the survivors, four crash-landed on Eastern Island and six managed to evade the enemy and land after the air raid was over. Only two planes were fit to fly again. VMF-221 was out of action. The 23 pilots were each awarded the Navy Cross, all but nine posthumously. For Marion Carl, it was the first of two he would be awarded for his prowess in combat. Their opponents that morning were seasoned veterans of what was at the time the most effective naval air arm in the world, flying the best carrier-based fighter in the world. Against these losses, the Japanese admitted the destruction of seven B5N2 torpedo bombers and two A6M2 Zeros.

For his heroic leadership, Major Parks was one of those posthumously awarded the Navy Cross. The citation reads as follows:

> For extraordinary heroism and conspicuous devotion to duty as Squadron Commander for Marine Fighting Squadron TWO TWENTY-ONE, in action against enemy Japanese forces during the Battle of Midway, June 4, 1942. Leading his squadron in a dauntless and aggressive attack against a vastly superior number of Japanese bomber and fighter planes, Major Parks aided in disrupting the plans of the enemy and lessening the effectiveness of their attack, thereby contributing materially to the success of our forces. As a result of his courageous and daring tactics and because of the circumstances attendant upon this engagement, there can be little doubt that Major Parks gallantly gave up his life in the service of his country. He displayed the characteristics of a fine leader and excellent airman in keeping with the highest traditions of the United States Naval Service.

On March 31, 1945 USS *Floyd B. Parks* (DD-884) was launched by Parks' widow and commissioned on July 31, 1945. The destroyer served in both the Korean and Vietnam wars before being decommissioned in 1974.

The commanders at Midway knew that any strike against the Japanese must be made before the arrival of the attackers. The torpedo-armed Army Air Force B-26 Marauders and the six Torpedo Eight TBF Avengers were ordered to take off and attack the enemy fleet as soon as the Marine dive bombers waiting at the runway departed.

At 0605 hours, just after the 23 fighters had climbed into the morning sky, Major Henderson gunned his SBD-2 down the runway and lifted off. As he circled the island, the others joined up. The enemy carriers were "180 miles out, bearing 320 degrees, enemy course 135 degrees, speed 20 knots." Because his pilots were all inexperienced in actual steep-angle dive bombing, he had briefed them before takeoff that when the enemy carriers were found, they would execute a glide-bombing attack. Such a tactic would expose the attackers to defensive fire for longer than would be the case in a dive-bombing attack, but it was the only maneuver Henderson knew his pilots were capable of that afforded any chance of success.

The Dauntlesses and Vindicators had such different performance that it was not possible to maintain one formation. With Henderson leading the 18 SBD-2s, VMSB-241's executive officer, Major Benjamin W. Norris, led the SB2U-3 Vindicators.

The squadron had originally been ordered to Midway before Pearl Harbor, taking their 24 SB2U-3s aboard *Saratoga* during the week before the Japanese attack. Following the attack, which found *Saratoga* still some distance from Midway, the carrier was recalled to Hawaii.

On December 23, 1941, 18 Vindicators, accompanied by a PBY for navigation, demonstrated their long-range capability when they made the 1,135-mile flight from Oahu to Midway in nine hours and 45 minutes.

Marine Second Lieutenant Sumner H. Whitten had been at Pearl Harbor when the Japanese attacked. In late December, he and 14 of his fellow brand-new Marine aviators were assigned to MAG-22 at Midway, seven to VMF-221 and seven to VMSB-241. They had shipped out for Midway the first week of January, 1942, on the only troop-carrying destroyer the Navy had.

Whitten later recalled the Vindicator:

The SB2U-3 was a slow plane, as far as speed went, and a lousy bomber. They didn't know much about dive brakes when they built the SB2U. Up until then, dive bombers had been biplanes, and they produced enough drag to keep down the speed in a dive, but with a cleaned-up monoplane like the SB2U series, you'd easily see 390–400 knots on your airspeed indicator in a dive from 8,000 feet. It was like riding a rock! You could hardly maneuver – the ailerons became stiff as a board. We would drop our landing gear, which slowed us down a bit – 15 to 20 knots – but you still had to be very strong to operate an SB2U in a dive.

Whitten had been assigned SB2U-3 BuNo 2054, number 11 in the squadron.

My crewman was Sergeant Frank E. Zelnis. Me being from outside Boston, and he from a very recently immigrated Latvian family, we could hardly understand each other, but finally – a couple of weeks later – we could interpret each other over the intercom. Frank was a good ordnance man who taught me about the guns on the plane. He cleaned his own gun, while my job was to clean the fixed .50s. I was also responsible for cleaning inside the cockpit, as well as the brakes and wheels, including the tail wheel. Keeping the brakes clean was important because the coral dust we kicked up during takeoff and landing wore out the brakes in no time.

At the time they were sent to Midway, the Vindicators were due for an overhaul that would have included replacing the wing and fuselage fabric covering the airframe. Suffering from heat, sunlight, and salt air on Midway, the fuselage fabric went from bad to worse, and the squadron was reduced to wrapping 4-inch medical tape over the worst areas to keep the fabric in place, which was then doped over, resulting in all the dirt on the airplane at the moment being preserved under the dope. These became the famous "white stripes" seen in photos of Vindicators at Midway. No two airplanes had similar taping.

During the first five months of 1942, the Vindicators would take off at 0400 hours for a morning antisubmarine patrol, with an evening patrol taking off at 1730 hours. Whitten recalled:

In between, we'd practice bombing during the day. There was a barge out in the lagoon, but we got no practice in hitting a moving ship. Meanwhile, Japanese submarines were watching us; they knew what we had. Every Friday night they surfaced and shelled us, but the three or four rounds they fired were not too effective considering that the island was no more than 4 feet above sea level. We'd sit on top of our dugout on Friday night, wondering where the shells would come from and where they would go. Most went right over the island and into the lagoon. They sometimes hit, making a hole 15 feet long, and we'd just fill it in.

In February 1942, several VMSB-231 personnel were sent back to MCAS Ewa to form new squadrons, and on March 1, 1942, the squadron was redesignated VMSB-241, calling themselves "Sons of Satan."

Whitten remembered the morning of June 4:

Major Benjamin W. Norris led 12 SB2Us, though one had to drop out with mechanical problems. Japanese carrier planes were attacking Midway; as we were taking off, bombs were falling on the island. All aircraft were to rendezvous 40 miles east of the island, but when our SB2Us got there the SBDs were long gone, so we climbed at 200–300 feet per minute until we reached 8,000 feet, just above the clouds.

The weather over Midway on June 4 was clear, with scattered clouds. However, as we proceeded northwest toward the Japanese fleet the cloud cover became more complete. By the time we were within 25 miles of the projected attack point, the cloud cover was solid to broken, heavy clouds, extending up to 8,000 feet. We could see elements of the Japanese fleet between breaks in the overcast. I can remember seeing a carrier going on a course of say 120 degrees, with flames coming out of it and a destroyer alongside, along with a couple of other wakes. Then, suddenly, we came under attack. Zelnis said three Zero fighters came at him; they were joined after two or three runs by more.

The Vindicators were in three four-plane sections, in a step-down formation. Whitten recalled what happened when the Japanese Combat Air Patrol came in:

Zelnis was a damn good gunner, and I was greatly relieved by that. He was firing almost continuously, in two to three-round bursts so as not to waste the 90 rounds in his drum, which he would then have to change. You had to be awfully adept at doing this in a slipstream, with fighters firing at you. During the fight, a Zero went under my right wing with black smoke pouring from the junction of the engine and fuselage and wing. That is probably the one with which he was officially credited. Another Zero came down at a 90-degree angle, burning back down the whole fuselage. I personally believe that Zelnis should have been credited with two kills, but for a gunner, one is more than normal, and we lost several gunners before we got to the fleet.

Once above the Japanese fleet, the Vindicators dove down in column formation through cloud breaks, still under attack by Zeros. They emerged into clear air at about 3,500–4,000 feet, in the vicinity of a battleship, which Norris ordered them to attack; going after the carriers would have meant flying across the entire fleet under attack.

Whitten remembered:

I made a lousy attack – from 4,000 feet, I could not get a good approach. Making too shallow a dive, diagonally from starboard aft to forward port, I dropped my bomb off the bow of the ship, but didn't hit it. But we scared 'em! Major Norris, Second Lieutenant George T. Lumpkin and Second Lieutenant Kenneth O. Campion dived on the battleship, too. Norris managed to score a near miss that caused it some damage. I think there was a direct hit made amidships. I then made a sharp right turn and started home at 100 feet. We made it back okay. Ours was the only plane in the squadron that was not damaged during the battle.

The two SB2Us of Lieutenant Andrew Campion and Private Anthony J. Maday, and Second Lieutenant James H. Marmande and Private 1/c Edby M. Colvin, did not come back. Second Lieutenant Allan H. Ringblom ditched after running out of fuel. He and his gunner, Private E. L. Webb, were rescued by PT-26. After ditching a few miles short of Midway, Lieutenant Cummings was rescued by PT-20.

The survivors of the morning strike were refueled and rearmed. They spent until 1900 hours waiting to go out, at which time they were ordered to find and attack two burning Japanese carriers.

Major Henderson's SBD formation was faster than the Vindicators'. The 16 Dauntlesses arrived over Kido Butai just before 0800 hours, some 50 minutes after the Marauders and Avengers had made their attacks around 0710 hours. Without fighter cover, five of the six Avengers and two of the four Marauders were shot down, with no damage to the enemy.

The Dauntlesses and Vindicators had become separated when the Japanese Combat Air Patrol found the Vindicators and concentrated on them. Henderson and his bombers spotted the carrier *Hiryū* through the cloud cover while the bombers were at 8,000 feet. Henderson gave the signal for the formation to spread out for the glide-bombing attack just as the Zeros fell on them.

When Henderson pushed his control stick forward to send the Dauntless into its glide, two enemy fighters hit him and set the bomber afire. The others in the formation lost sight of him as the Dauntless steepened its dive and disappeared into the clouds below. Three other SBDs went down on fire shortly after Henderson disappeared. The survivors continued on as the Zeros circled for new attacks. Antiaircraft fire from the ships below exploded other dive bombers as the fighters cut into their ranks. By the time they were over the carriers and in position to release their bombs, the formation had been cut in half. Those remaining dropped their bombs as best they could and endeavored to escape the cauldron of enemy fire.

Among the survivors were First Lieutenant Daniel Iverson, Jr. and his radioman-gunner, Private 1/c Wallace Reid, in SBD-2 BuNo 2106. Their Dauntless was badly damaged from fighter attacks as they bored in to attack, and both men were wounded. Iverson managed to stagger back to a crash landing on Midway. Those on the ground later counted 259 bullet holes made by the Zeros and the ships below. Iverson was later awarded the Navy Cross while gunner Reid received the Distinguished Flying Cross for their performance in the mission.

Surprisingly, BuNo 2106 was among other SBD-2s shipped back to Pearl Harbor in August 1942, where they were then shipped on to the west coast and completely overhauled for use in training. BuNo 2106 ended up at the Carrier Qualification Training Unit at NAS Glenview, Illinois, where fledgling naval aviators learned to land on the training carrier *Wolverine* in Lake Michigan. On June 11, 1943, little more than a year after the battle, Second Lieutenant Donald A. Douglas, Jr. stalled out on his approach and spun into the water. Douglas survived, but BuNo 2106 settled to the lake bottom in 170 feet of cold fresh water, where she remained until she was discovered and recovered in October 1993, covered in Z mussels. Over the next ten years, BuNo 2106 was restored and she is currently on display at the National Museum of Naval Aviation at Pensacola, Florida, one of four aircraft still in existence known to have been present at the attack on Pearl Harbor, and the only survivor of the aircraft that flew in the Battle of Midway.

While the efforts of the Marines on June 4 may seem to have been in vain, the truth is that they made quite a contribution to the ultimate American victory. Postwar analysis of Japanese records shows that, at 0810 hours on June 4, damaging hits were scored on *Akagi* and *Sōryū*; with the damage quickly brought under control. However, the

Dauntlesses had a greater effect on the enemy than a few bomb hits. Admiral Nagumo and the rest of the officers on the bridge of *Akagi* were deeply impressed by the determination of the Americans in their Marauders, Avengers, and Dauntlesses, none of whom turned away from their attacks despite the heavy opposition they faced in making their attacks without any diversionary support. One burning B-26 had dropped its torpedo and lifted over the carrier's deck, missing the island where the admiral stood on the bridge by a matter of yards. Nagumo's new-found respect for his enemy's determination to fight had a major effect on subsequent events.

The six surviving SBDs still flyable, now led by Captain Marshall A. Tyler following the death of Major Henderson, joined with Major Norris's five surviving SB2Us in an attempt to attack two burning enemy carriers still afloat north of Midway at the end of the day. Lieutenant Whitten was part of the strike force and later remembered:

The weather was bad, and we never found a target. It became dark – the flames from the exhaust stacks of the plane on whose wing I flew were the only lights I could see. We zigzagged around some clouds, and suddenly nobody was there. I made a square search for two minutes, then said to myself, "I'm going home."

After a 15-minute search, Whitten jettisoned his 500-pound bomb.

After another square search, I found Pearl and Hermes, a coral outcropping southeast of Midway, so I knew where I was. I turned around and headed for Midway, but Midway didn't turn up. I did a two-minute square search, then another for four minutes, then turned back. Then Zelnis told me, "Make a 180, I see flames." I didn't see anything, but I turned in that direction for a minute or so, and then I saw the fire, an oil tank that the attacking Japanese planes had hit on Sand Island.

Whitten was fired on by the Marine defenders as he entered the landing pattern, but number 11 was still lucky and wasn't hit. "After I landed, they took half a pail of fuel out of my tanks. Major Norris never came back, but everyone else did. By the time I'd finished my debriefing, it was about 0230 in the morning."

On June 5, Whitten was allowed to sleep in since the squadron had more crews than planes. He later remembered:

> At 0430 hours, the squadron took off to attack two enemy cruisers, *Mogami* and *Mikuma*, which had collided during the night. My airplane was flown by Second Lieutenant Robert W. Taylor. Captain Tyler's six SBDs failed to finish off *Mogami*, but the SB2Us, led by Captain Fleming, got a couple of hits on *Mikuma*, one a solid hit forward, and another a bouncer off the stern.

Fleming's SB2U was hit by antiaircraft fire early in the attack and burst into flames. He flew his plane into the ship, killing himself and his gunner, Private 1/c George A. Toms. The executive officer of *Mikuma*, who survived the battle, said after the war he thought Fleming was a very brave man because he hit the after turret and put it out of action. He also caused a fire that was sucked into *Mikuma's* starboard air intakes, suffocating her engineers.

For carrying on his attack at cost of his life, ensuring VMSB-241's attack was successful, Captain Richard A. Fleming was recognized with the posthumous award of the Medal of Honor.

Recalling the missions he flew at Midway, Whitten said:

> We did what we could with what we had. I'd like to add, though, that I have always admired the guts of those rear-seat gunners. Especially those in the Vindicators who had to change ammo cans in the face of enemy attacks. Those kids – and most of them were kids – were a trusting lot. They rode along backwards, most of the time, not having a say about where or why or how or when. They died when their pilots died, far too many times. And their recognition has never equaled their devotion to duty.

Sumner Whitten was sent back to Pearl Harbor that September to become executive officer of an SBD squadron that arrived on Guadalcanal in December, where they fought through the Solomons campaign until August 1943, when he returned to the United States to work on developing the system of forward air controllers the Marines would use with such devastating effect in the Marianas, Iwo Jima, and Okinawa.

VMSB-241 remained on Midway until September 1943, when they returned to Pearl Harbor. Among the aircraft they left behind were three surviving SB2U-3s; by that time they were the last Vindicators in use by any American unit anywhere.

For their actions at Midway, the Marines of MAG-22 were awarded the Presidential Unit Citation.

> For conspicuous courage and heroism in combat at Midway Island during June 1942. Outnumbered five to one, Marine Aircraft Group 22 boldly intercepted a heavily escorted enemy bombing force, disrupting their attack and preventing serious damage to island installations. Operating with half of their dive-bombers obsolete and in poor mechanical conditions, which necessitated vulnerable glide-bombing tactics, they succeeded in inflicting heavy damage on Japanese surface units of a large enemy task force. The skill and gallant perseverance of flight and ground personnel of Marine Aircraft Group 22, fighting under tremendously adverse and dangerous conditions, were essential factors in the unyielding defense of Midway.

Admiral Nimitz recognized the Marines' contribution to victory at Midway as follows:

> Please accept my sympathy for the losses sustained by your gallant aviation personnel based at Midway. Their sacrifice was not in vain. When the great emergency came, they were ready. They met, unflinchingly, the attack of vastly superior numbers and made the attack ineffective. They struck the first blow at the enemy carriers. They were the spearhead of our great victory. They have written a new and shining page in the annals of the Marine Corps.

CHAPTER TWENTY

SIX DEADLY MINUTES

With the failure of the strikes launched by the defenders at Midway, Admiral Nagumo was faced with a quandary. Would he order a second strike against the atoll, as recommended by the strike leader who reported significant damage but considered that a second strike would be necessary to knock out the defenses, or would he hold his aircraft in readiness for an attack against the American Navy? The fact that the submarines had reported no deployment from Hawaii gave cause for optimism among the staff that Operation *MI* was proceeding according to plan. Yet Nagumo was nagged by the worry that an enemy who had shown himself as determined as had the men who attacked the fleet regardless might yet have another surprise in store.

The first report of the Midway strike came at 0640 hours, when the *Kaga* strike group commander reported "Great results obtained." Thirty minutes later at 0710 hours, the overall strike group commander, Lieutenant Joichi Tomonaga, radioed, "There is need for a second attack…" Moments later, Kido Butai came under attack by the first of the Midway strikes, as the six Torpedo 8 Avengers and the four torpedo-carrying Marauders came into sight. Five of the Avengers were shot down by Zeros and shipboard antiaircraft fire; the sixth, with its control surfaces shredded, the gunner dead, and the pilot and radioman wounded, managed to drop its torpedo and then turn away to return to Midway. The four B-26s were equally unsuccessful, losing two to the defenses, though they killed five *Akagi* crewmen by strafing. The attempt by one of the two Marauders that were hit to crash into *Akagi*'s bridge had left Nagumo convinced that Tomonaga was right – there was indeed a need for a second strike.

Of the 108 aircraft that had attacked Midway in Kido Butai's first strike, 11 had been lost, including three damaged aircraft that ditched during their return to the fleet; of those that returned, 14 were heavily damaged, and 29 were damaged in some degree. Nagumo was unaware of the losses suffered by VMF-221, and was further convinced that Midway was dangerous. The fleet's first strike had not succeeded in neutralizing Midway, since American aircraft could still refuel and rearm to attack the Japanese fleet, while most of the land-based defenses were still intact. The leaders of the first strike agreed that a second attack was necessary if troops were to successfully land on June 7.

Japanese carrier doctrine for such a situation had dictated that Nagumo keep half his aircraft in reserve, which in this case comprised a squadron of dive bombers on *Kaga* and one of torpedo bombers on *Akagi*. While the dive bombers were unarmed, the torpedo bombers had been armed with torpedoes in expectation of launching an immediate attack if any enemy warships were discovered.

Following the attack by the Avengers and Marauders, at 0715 hours Nagumo ordered the torpedo bombers be rearmed with general-purpose bombs for another level bombing strike, and the dive bombers be loaded with high-explosive bombs. Down in the carrier hangar decks, the crews began the arduous task, which involved removing the ordnance already loaded, returning it to the ship's magazine, then rearming with different ordnance.

The changeover had only just begun when the *Tone* No. 4 scout, whose launch had been delayed earlier, sent a message at 0728 hours that it had sighted an enemy naval force to the east, but gave no indication of the force's composition. Nagumo and his staff were thunderstruck – how could this be? The admiral weighed his options, before giving the order at 0745 hours that *Akagi* and *Kaga* stop rearming and directed the force to prepare for an attack against ships. As the crews began reloading their charges, Nagumo ordered the scout to "ascertain ship types."

Before the scout could reply, Major Henderson's Marine dive bombers were sighted over the fleet at approximately 0755 hours.

While the survivors of Henderson's attack departed, having scored two minor hits on *Akagi* and *Kaga*, the *Tone* scout radioed at 0809 hours that the enemy force was five cruisers and five destroyers. As Nagumo was reading the message, eight B-17s from Midway appeared overhead and bombed *Hiryū* from 20,000 feet; once again, the ships evaded the high-altitude bombing. Within minutes of that attack, seven more B-17s that had been inbound to Midway from Hawaii when they had been diverted to attack the newly discovered enemy fleet bombed from an altitude of 7–8,000 feet, with equally unsuccessful results. The B-17 crews returned to Midway, claiming hits on two carriers. As the Flying Fortresses turned away, Major Norris's 11 Vindicators appeared out of the clouds and targeted the battleship *Haruna*, which they bombed ineffectively.

Nagumo was now badly rattled. If the American ships that the scout had spotted were operating without a carrier, they didn't constitute a threat. Midway, on the other hand, was throwing punches that had so far missed, but what might result from the next one? Another strike was definitely required and the order was again passed to rearm. The crews in the hangars didn't have time to take the armor-piercing ordnance below, and stacked the bombs and torpedoes to the side as they began loading the bombers with the high-explosive bombs. Within moments of giving this order, Nagumo received a third message from the *Tone* No. 4 scout: "Enemy is accompanied by what appears to be a carrier."

Coral Sea had demonstrated that the lesson of prewar carrier exercises was right: the side that landed the first blow would win. The sweating ordnance crews were once again ordered to change their loads. Rear Admiral Tamon Yamaguchi, leading Carrier Division 2 with *Hiryū* and *Sōryū*, recommended an immediate strike with the forces at hand: 18 bombers each on *Sōryū* and *Hiryū*, and half the ready Combat Air Patrol about to be launched. The opportunity to launch an immediate strike was limited by the imminent return of the Midway strike force, which needed to land immediately or be forced to ditch at sea. Spotting the decks and launching aircraft would take at least 30 minutes and would mean that some of the planes launched to strike the enemy carriers would not be properly armed and might not have fighter escort. Nagumo had just seen what happened to unescorted American bombers. The admiral decided to wait and recover his planes, then launch a proper maximum-effort strike against the enemy.

At approximately the same time, USS *Nautilus* (SS-168) came to periscope depth and her captain, Lieutenant Commander William Brockman, raised his periscope to find his vessel in the middle of the Japanese fleet while he observed "ships moving across the field at high speed and circling away to avoid the submarine's position." The prewar "cruiser" submarine was one of 11 US submarines dispatched to Midway to find and attack the enemy. She had already been strafed and depth-charged. As Brockman attempted to maneuver to bring her torpedo tubes to bear on a target, *Nautilus* was attacked by the cruiser *Nagara* and destroyer *Arashi*, which depth-charged her for 20 minutes while the fleet steamed on. When the attack ended, Brockman again raised his periscope, to discover *Arashi* was waiting for him. The destroyer dropped more depth charges until she broke off at 0918 hours. *Arashi* then increased speed, leaving on the calm sea a brilliant white streak, reminiscent of an arrow pointing at Kido Butai.

Aboard the three American carriers cruising at "Point Luck," the crews had been awakened at 0130 hours and fed between 0300 and 0400 hours to give them time to prepare. Surprisingly, *Yorktown*, the only carrier of the three whose leaders had direct combat experience, was held back in reserve, while *Enterprise* and *Hornet*, which had yet to engage an enemy carrier, were assigned to make the maximum-effort strike. At approximately 0430 hours, *Yorktown* launched ten SBD-3s from Scouting 5 to search north of the fleet for a distance of 100 miles. While Admiral Fletcher expected the Japanese to make their approach to Midway from the northwest, he wanted assurance his flank was secure. Point Luck was approximately 200 miles north-northeast of Midway; the admiral expected the enemy would not launch their strike from more than 300 miles north of the island, which would put them some 100 miles north of the American carriers.

A bit over an hour since the SBDs had departed, the electrifying news "Carriers sighted" was received from the Catalina search plane at 0534 hours. At 0553 hours came the report, "Many planes heading Midway." Finally, at 0603 hours, the Catalina reported "Two carriers and battleships bearing 320 degrees, distance 180, course 135, speed 25." Quick calculations placed the enemy fleet 175 miles west-southwest of the Americans. In fact, the position report was incorrect; the enemy was now 200 miles away. Those extra miles would matter.

The pilots and crewmen of all three carriers manned their planes on the flight deck in preparation of immediate launch. On board *Yorktown*, John Bridgers remembered that "One repair made after we left Pearl was a large metal plate covering a hole in our ready room deck, through which a bomb had penetrated to the lower decks during the Coral Sea

Battle." Bridgers was disappointed that morning to find he was among the group of less-experienced pilots who would be held back from the initial strike, in case there was a need for a second strike. "I was on the traveling squad, but not yet on the first team."

At 0607 hours, Admiral Fletcher ordered Spruance's two carriers to launch their attack. "Proceed southwesterly and attack enemy carriers as soon as definitely located." Spruance considered that while the reported range to the enemy was extreme, a strike could succeed. Chief of staff miles Browning determined that because the fleet would have to turn away from the enemy to launch the strike into the light southeasterly breeze that they should launch at approximately 0700 hours, giving them an hour to close the distance a further 25 miles, placing the enemy about 155 miles distant. Spruance agreed and *Enterprise* and *Hornet* began launching their air groups at 0656 hours. Where the Japanese had launched 108 aircraft from their four carriers in only seven minutes, *Enterprise* and *Hornet* required more than an hour to complete their launch of 117. Browning convinced Spruance that the need to attack the enemy at the earliest moment possible was greater than the need of making a coordinated attack, even if it meant that such lack of coordination would lessen the impact of the attacks.

While a student at the Naval War College ten years earlier, Browning had written a prescient paper in which he argued that the most vulnerable moment for an enemy carrier force was when they had recovered one strike and were attempting to launch a second. Knowing of the Japanese attack on Midway and assuming the enemy fleet was within 200 miles of the atoll, Browning determined that a strike as soon as possible had the best opportunity of catching the enemy in just this situation. At first, Spruance demurred and ordered the two air groups should form up before heading out to make their attack.

Hornet CAG Commander Stanhope Ring had graduated first in his Annapolis class in 1923, and pinned on Wings of Gold in 1927. A by-the-book officer who had never shown interest in challenging the rules even when necessary, he was not well respected as an aviator or leader by the air group's pilots, having been known to ground a pilot who failed to rise when he walked into the room. When planning the Midway mission, Ring had informed his squadron commanders that the group would assemble as a whole before they headed out, and that the escorting Wildcats would stay high with the dive bombers. Torpedo squadron commander John Waldron had argued that the fighters should be divided as they had been at Coral Sea, with at least two divisions low to protect the vulnerable Devastators. The argument went as high as *Hornet*'s commander, Captain Marc Mitscher, who sided with Ring and his decision to head directly west toward the reported Japanese position.

Aboard *Enterprise*, the flight deck was spotted first with eight Wildcat fighters to be launched for Combat Air Patrol. Behind them were 37 SBD bombers from Scouting and Bombing 6. Six of the VS-6 bombers carried a single 500-pound bomb, 13 were armed with one 500-pound and two 100-pound bombs. Bringing up the rear of the bomber strike force were the 18 Bombing 6 SBDs, each armed with one 1,000-pound armor-piercing bomb. The air group was led by Lieutenant Commander C. Wade McClusky, a fighter pilot by experience who had only recently assumed the position of CAG. This would be his first mission leading the dive bombers, and his inexperience in proper tactics would affect the battle.

The *Enterprise* Dauntlesses were airborne by 0725 hours, forming up and climbing in circles above the carrier. Below, plane handlers struggled for long, gas-wasting minutes to strike below the four SBDs that had not been launched due to mechanical problems, in order to bring up Torpedo 6's 18 planes. McClusky, who led the entire formation with VS-6, remembered, "things seemed to come to a standstill." Twenty minutes after the dive bombers had launched, the first of the VF-6 Wildcat escorts was launched. They were followed by the slow torpedo bombers. At 0745 hours, Spruance finally acceded to Browning's argument and ordered McClusky and the dive bombers to "proceed on mission assigned." By the time the torpedo bombers were airborne and assembled under the leadership of Lieutenant Commander Gene Lindsey, the dive bombers were distant on the horizon. At this point, the escorting VF-6 Wildcats mistakenly took up position over *Hornet*'s Torpedo 8, which left Torpedo 6 without fighter escort.

Hornet's air group also broke up shortly after Ring took up his westerly heading of 265 degrees at the head of the dive bombers. Waldron, who still believed his course information was correct, signaled his pilots to follow him and took up what he had determined was the most direct course to the enemy, taking a heading of 240 degrees.

Fortunately, Admiral Fletcher decided to commit *Yorktown*'s air group to launch at 0838 hours. The combat-experienced Air Department ordered the squadrons to execute a "running rendezvous." Lieutenant Commander Lance Massey's slow Torpedo 3 TBDs were launched first and headed off at low altitude. Bombing 3 and Scouting 5, led by VB-3's Lieutenant Commander Max Leslie, launched next, while John Thach's eight F4F-4 Wildcats launched last.

Unfortunately, the 36 *Enterprise* Dauntlesses flew a tight, prewar "parade ground" formation. Despite the fact that all pilots had leaned their throttles as well as they could to maximize their range, the Japanese were a crucial 25 miles further away than they believed. The junior and less-experienced pilots had to jockey their throttles to maintain their position in the formation, using more fuel than the leaders; there would be losses due to fuel exhaustion regardless of any action over the Japanese fleet.

By around 0930 hours Midway time, the enemy fleet had not been spotted. *Enterprise* CAG McClusky later recalled:

> With the clear visibility it was certain that we hadn't passed them unsighted. Allowing for their maximum advance of 25 knots, I was positive they couldn't be in my left semi-circle, that is, between my position and the island of Midway. Then they must be in the right semi-circle, had changed course easterly or westerly, or, most likely reversed course. To allow for a possible westerly change of course, I decided to fly west for 35 miles, then to turn north-west in the precise reverse of the original Japanese course. After making this decision, my next concern was just how far could we go. We had climbed, heavily loaded, to a high altitude. I knew the planes following were probably using more gas than I was. So, with another quick calculation, I decided to stay on course 315 degrees until 1000 hours, then turn north-eastwardly before making a final decision to terminate the hunt and return to the *Enterprise*.

The formation droned west for another 25 minutes.

Dick Best flew at the head of Bombing 6, to the rear and below the 18 Scouting 6 SBDs led by McClusky. He remembered:

> Mac flew right over what we had plotted as the likely Japanese course, and then flew on to the limits of range before we got lucky and spotted that destroyer and he made that right turn he should

have made 25 minutes earlier. I knew we'd blown it, because I had it plotted and I was an excellent navigator. Unfortunately, we were maintaining radio silence and there was no way to catch up with Mac and convince him to turn when he should have, without burning too much fuel to make it to the target. Had we done that right, had we not flown wrong for 25 minutes and then spent 15 more minutes getting back to where we should have been, we wouldn't have lost half our crews to fuel starvation when they were trying to get back to the ship afterwards, and we likely could have coordinated the attack with the torpedo bombers.

What had happened was Admiral Nagumo had received the first report clearly stating an American carrier was in the vicinity. Shortly after receiving that message, while he considered whether to strike the enemy immediately or land the planes from the Midway strike, the admiral had ordered a change of course to the northeast to close on the American carriers. While the three American strike forces headed for the Japanese fleet, the Japanese were planning a strike against *Yorktown*, the carrier that had been spotted and identified.

Torpedo 8 commander Waldron was beloved by his pilot as an inspirational leader who had done everything possible to take new pilots just out of flight school and give them the necessary training to have a chance at performing their mission. Just before takeoff, the squadron's pilots had found the following message from their leader posted in their ready room:

> My greatest hope is that we encounter a favorable tactical situation, but if we don't, and the worst comes to the worst, I want each of us to do his utmost to destroy our enemies. If there is only one plane left to make a final run in, I want that man to go in and get a hit. May God be with us all. Good luck, happy landings and give 'em hell.

An hour into their flight, Waldron had spotted a strange plane that had suddenly appeared to the squadron's rear. The strange aircraft made no attempt to close on the Devastators. It was the *Tone* No. 4 scout, and it warned the fleet: "Fifteen enemy planes are heading toward you."

Having taken the most direct course to the enemy, Waldron spotted Kido Butai shortly after his spread-out search formation had spotted smoke on the horizon at 0925 hours. His guess that the enemy would make a turn to the north had been right.

Unfortunately, his call to Stanhope Ring that he had found the fleet came too late. The *Hornet* CAG had taken the dive bombers and their escorting fighters out to their maximum range and missed the Japanese fleet entirely, ending up somewhere to the north. Prewar carrier doctrine called for a strike force in this position to return to the nearest friendly land base. In this case, that meant a turn south to Midway, which was in no condition to receive the strike force. Ring had required a "parade ground" formation, which meant increased gas usage; it was now questionable that the planes had the fuel to get to Midway. Some SBDs and F4Fs tried to return to *Hornet*, while the others headed toward Midway. While most of the dive bombers made it, only two of the ten Wildcats returned. Ring's decision effectively removed the *Hornet* from the battle equation and nearly cost Marc Mitscher his career, had he not already received notice of promotion to rear admiral.

While Torpedo 8 had been accidentally escorted by the fighters from *Enterprise* for part of their flight, when Waldron turned northwest, Lieutenant James Gray, the new CO of VF-6, continued to the west since he was not on the same frequency and had not heard Waldron's change of course order. The Devastators were now completely alone. Waldron waggled his wings and pushed into a dive toward the ocean, followed by the others. They leveled off at 60 feet to take up their attack formation and headed alone toward the enemy carriers.

Approaching from the east, Waldron turned to attack the southernmost carrier of the four. The planes closed to a range of 16,000 yards from the enemy when 30 Zero fighters of the Combat Air Patrol swarmed the formation from behind and above. The first Devastator fell from the left side of the formation in flames. Ensign George Gay later reported he heard Waldron ask his gunner, Aviation Radioman 1/c Horace Dobbs, if the burning plane was a torpedo bomber or a fighter. The radioman in a distant PBY heard his indistinct words, "Watch those fighters!... My two wingmen are going into the water..."

The Zeros turned back from their initial assault and struck the formation again. Waldron was hit in his left wing, rupturing the fuel tank and setting the entire wing afire. He was last seen standing up in his cockpit as he tried to get out, just before the Devastator hit the water on fire, then disappeared into the depths.

Japanese gunners on the cruisers *Tone* and *Chikuma* opened up on the planes when they flew past, still aiming for the carriers. Both ships opened up with their main batteries, in hopes of creating water spouts the Devastators would fly into. By the time the bombers were past the two cruisers, there were only six left. Defensive fire from the fleet increased, putting up a veritable curtain of fire. One by one, five of the six planes were hit and sent crashing into the sea.

One flew on.

George Gay later remembered that just after the last of the five Devastators went down, he heard his gunner, Aviation Radioman 3/c Bob Huntington, call out over the intercom, "They got me, sir." He glanced back and saw his gunner slumped over his guns. Gay turned toward what he identified as the *Kaga*, though later research determined he was headed toward the wildly evading *Sōryū*, which was making a hard starboard turn. He maneuvered to come in on her port bow. A glance over his shoulder revealed a sky full of enemy fighters trying to close on him. Finally, 800 yards from the carrier, he pulled the handle and dropped his torpedo. The plane lifted from the loss of weight and he flew directly over the stern. Once past the targeted ship, he was hit by more fire and the first of five attacking Zeros flashed overhead. A 20mm shell flash-burned his left leg. A second Zero attacked and another shell fragment hit his left hand, while a bullet hit his upper left arm. The stick went slack in his hand and the rudder pedals fell away. With its controls destroyed, the bomber pancaked out of control into the ocean a quarter mile behind the carrier Gay had attacked.

As the plane struck the water, the hood slammed shut over the cockpit. The plane began tipping for its final dive as Gay struggled to open the canopy. "I couldn't hardly get it open. That's when I got scared." Finally the hood slid back and he scrambled out as it took its final dive. He was left bobbing in the sea; a moment later his seat cushion popped to the surface.

At 0930, shortly after John Waldron turned toward the enemy, Torpedo 6's CO Gene Lindsey spotted the smokescreen laid by the defenders on the horizon to his north and turned to investigate. A moment later he identified three carriers and selected the closest, *Kaga*, for the attack. Japanese lookouts spotted the incoming torpedo bombers at 0938 hours, just as they were hit by the defending CAP. *Kaga* turned north to evade, forcing Lieutenant Arthur Ely's seven-plane formation into a stern chase while Lindsey made a wide half-circle turn around the outside of the screening destroyers in an attempt to attack the ship's port bow.

Ely radioed for Gray's Wildcats as Zeros and the antiaircraft fire concentrated on him, but the fighters were not there; Gray had arrived on the far side of the enemy fleet and waited for the call for assistance as they orbited 15 miles on the opposite side of the fleet from the torpedo bombers they were charged with protecting. The seven Devastators continued to chase *Kaga* as the CAP slashed at them, taking them down one-by-one. Finally, only the TBDs flown by NAP Aviation Machinist's Mate 1/c A. Walter Winchell and Chief Aviation Machinist Stephen B. Smith were still in the air, both damaged. At a range of 1,000 yards, they both dropped their torpedoes and managed to escape the fire. Smith and his gunner made it back to *Enterprise*, while Winchell and gunner Aviation Radioman 3/c Douglas M. Cossit were forced to ditch when they ran out of fuel, surviving 17 days in their life raft until they were found and rescued by a Midway PBY on June 21.

Lindsey's section was spared the attention of the CAP as they flew around the enemy formation, but were finally caught by the Zeros as they began their run in. Lindsey and three others were shot down, though Aviation Radioman 1/c William C. Humphrey managed to shoot down one Zero. The remaining three Devastators managed to drop their torpedoes and escape to return to *Enterprise*.

All of Torpedo 8 had been lost and only four of Torpedo 6 returned. No hits were scored.

At 0950 hours, *Enterprise* CAG McClusky was seriously worried as he scoured the sea below through his binoculars, searching for the enemy. At maximum range, he had to do something. Where Ring had followed "standard procedure," McClusky did the opposite. "I knew they had to be north of us," he later explained, "and so I turned north. I could hold the course for 15 minutes before our fuel state would require we turn east." The 37 Dauntlesses turned north, and at 0955 McClusky looked down through a break in the clouds and saw the wake of the destroyer *Arashi* as it hurried to return to the fleet from its battle with the *Nautilus*.

Hoping that the ship below would lead him to the enemy fleet, McClusky turned and followed. Below, the crew of the Japanese destroyer didn't see the flock of tiny dots high above that turned onto their course.

At 1005 hours, that decision paid dividends. Peering through my binoculars, which were practically glued to my eyes, I saw dead ahead about 35 miles distant the welcome sight of the Jap carrier striking force. They were in what appeared to be a circular disposition with four carriers in the center, well spaced, and an outer screen of six to eight destroyers and inner support ships composed of two battleships and either four or six cruisers. I then broke radio silence and reported the contact to the *Enterprise*.

As the *Enterprise* Dauntlesses approached from the southwest, McClusky identified the nearest carrier as *Kaga*, with *Akagi* beyond, and informed the formation they would attack these two ships. As a fighter pilot, he was unfamiliar with dive-bombing doctrine, which called for the lead squadron, VS-6, to fly across and attack the far target (*Akagi*), while the trailing squadron, VB-6, would attack the near target (*Kaga*), thus taking on both in a near-simultaneous attack that had the greatest chance of success. McClusky executed a wingover and centered *Kaga* in his telescopic sight.

The first thing Dick Best knew of McClusky's incorrect attack strategy was when the air group commander's SBD flashed past directly in front of him. He turned and saw all the other VB-6 Dauntlesses execute dives, following VS-6. Rocking his wings violently, Best managed to keep his two wingmen, Lieutenant (jg) Bill Kroeger and Ensign F. T. Weber, with him. In an instant, Best was left alone with his two wingmen over the Japanese fleet; according to Navy tactical doctrine, these three bombers were not only insufficient, they were irrelevant. Best led his two wingmen across the Japanese fleet, where he pushed over in what would be recorded as the single most accurate, devastating dive-bomber attack by any pilot in all of World War II.

"I centered my sights on that big red rising sun painted on the deck. The flight deck was holystoned yellow and made an excellent target. I dropped my bomb at minimum altitude and as I pulled out I looked over my shoulder in time to see it hit just forward of the meatball." Moments later, Kroeger and Weber dropped their thousand-pounders. Kroeger's hit close amidships and Weber's close on the stern. They were almost as damaging as direct hits, as they opened seams in the hull below the waterline.

Best's bomb crashed through the flight deck to explode in the confined space of the hangar below, where fully armed and fueled torpedo bombers stood amidst stacks of bombs set aside that had not been taken below to the magazine while torpedoes were slung beneath the planes. The explosion was devastating. Shrapnel holed the planes and leaking gasoline caught fire; flames spread to the torpedoes and bombs, which exploded, tearing the hangar apart and spreading the fires to the neighboring hangar compartments, which were filled with gasoline-laden aircraft and their extra bombs. "By the time I leveled off," Best recounted, "the carrier was afire from bow to stern."

McClusky remembered his attack on *Kaga*:

I leveled off at masthead height, picked the widest opening in the defending destroyer screen and dropped to deck level, figuring any antiaircraft fire aimed at me would also be aimed at their own ships. All their ships must have been pretty busy because I was well through the screen before I noted bursting shells creeping up behind. With the throttle practically pushed through the instrument panel, I was fortunate in avoiding a contact with death by slight changes of altitude and varying the getaway course to right and left.

McClusky then quickly calculated a return course on his chart.

As I raised my head from the plotting board, a stream of tracer bullets started chopping the water around the plane. Almost immediately my gunner, W. G. Chochalousek, opened fire. Then a Zero zoomed out of range ahead of me. A hurried glance around found another Zero about 1,000 feet above, to the left and astern, about to make another attack. Remaining at 20 feet above the water, I waited until the attacking plane was well in his dive, then wrapped my plane in a steep turn toward him. This not only gave him a more difficult deflection shot, but also enabled my gunner to have free room to maneuver his guns. A 5-minute chase then ensued, first one Zero attacking from the right, then the second from the left. Each time I would wrap up toward the attacker with Chochalousek keeping up a constant fire. Suddenly a burst from a Jap seemed to envelop the whole plane. The left side of my cockpit was shattered, and it felt like my left shoulder had been hit with a sledgehammer. Naturally enough it seemed like the end, we sure were goners. After two or three seconds, I realized there was an unusual quietness except for the purring engine of the old Dauntless. Grasping the intercom, I yelled to Chochalousek, but no answer. It was difficult to turn with the pain in my left shoulder and arm, but I finally managed and there was my gunner, facing aft, guns at the ready and unharmed. He had shot down one of the Zeros and the other decided to call it quits. When we got back to the ship, we found our plane had been hit 55 times.

Among the *Enterprise* Dauntlesses that were shot down attacking the fleet was an SBD flown by Ensign Frank O'Flaherty of Bombing 6. His gunner was Aviation Machinist's Mate 1/c Bruno Gaido, the man who had manned the rear guns of a Dauntless back on February 1 to do battle with Lieutenant Kazuo Nakai during the Kwajalein raid. Their dive bomber took hits in the gas tanks from Japanese AA, and after flying only a few miles away from the enemy fleet, O'Flaherty was forced to ditch. After several hours in the water, they were spotted and rescued by the Japanese destroyer *Makigumo*. Once aboard the destroyer, the two men were interrogated and tortured for the next two weeks as the ship steamed back to Japan, but they gave the enemy no information about their ship. Finally, both men were tied to a gasoline tank by their captors and thrown overboard to drown. The Japanese captain recorded in his logbook that both met their end "with stoic and dignified defiance." Gunner Gaido was posthumously awarded the Distinguished Flying Cross, while the destroyer escort DE-340 was named USS *O'Flaherty* for the pilot.

The 12 TBDs of Yorktown's VT-3, led by their CO Lieutenant Commander Lance "Lem" Massey and escorted by six F4F-4 Wildcats led by Lieutenant Commander John Thach, found the enemy a matter of minutes after the *Enterprise* strike had commenced its attack on *Kaga* and *Akagi*. Above them, Lieutenant Commander Max Leslie led 36 dive bombers, despite the fact he had lost his own bomb when he had accidentally dropped it shortly after takeoff due to his plane's release mechanism being miswired; three other planes in the formation had also lost theirs and turned back, but Leslie felt he was needed as strike

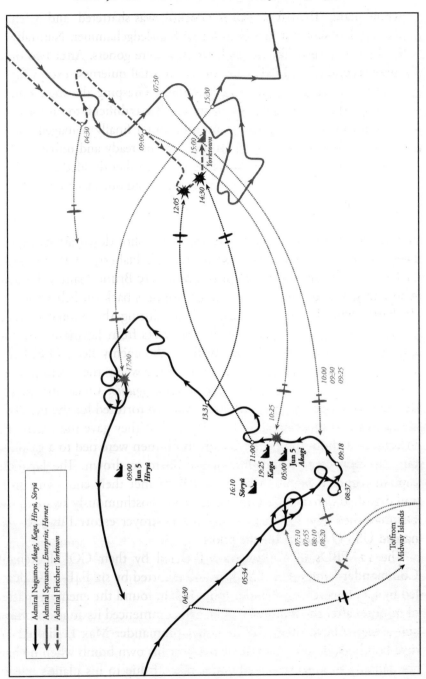

07:50
15:30
04:30
09:06
15:00
14:30
Yorktown
12:05
17:00
13:31
10:00
09:30
09:25
10:25
11:00
09:18
19:25 *Kaga*
05:00 Jun 5 *Akagi*
09:00 Jun 5 *Hiryū*
16:10 *Sōryū*
08:37
07:10
07:55
08:10
08:20
05:34
04:30

To/from Midway Islands

Admiral Nagumo: *Akagi, Kaga, Hiryū, Sōryū*
Admiral Spruance: *Enterprise, Hornet*
Admiral Fletcher: *Yorktown*

leader. *Yorktown's* strike had made their running rendezvous on the way to the fleet and was the only air group to make a coordinated attack.

Thach recalled that the squadron had only a few hops to get used to the new F4F-4 Wildcat with which they had re-equipped just before going aboard *Yorktown*. Jim Adams, one of the VF-42 pilots who fleshed out the squadron for experience, later recalled, "We went from bad to worse when we picked up the F4F-4 for Midway. We had all kinds of extra weight and a real sluggish aircraft; six guns and less firing time. The reduction in rounds per gun with the increase from four to six guns cut the firing time by six seconds. That doesn't sound like much, but it can be a lifetime in combat."

Thach's formation of six included his wingman, Ensign Robert A.M. "Ram" Dibb, with VF-42 Lieutenant (jg) Brainard Macomber as section leader with wingman Ensign Edgar Bassett, also from VF-42. NAP Aviation Machinist's Mate 1/c Tom Cheek and his wingman, Ensign Daniel Sheedy, were just astern of the torpedo planes, all flying about 1,000 feet above the torpedo bombers, which were flying 750 feet above the waves. Thach later remembered that the fighter pilots had to do S turns so they could stay with the TBDs due to the torpedo bombers' slow speeds, while maintaining sufficient speed to be able to maneuver quickly in case they ran into the defending Japanese fighters. The pilots were all trained in the "Thach Weave" and were using it in the combat formation Thach had developed.

Torpedo bomber leader Massey made a small change of course to the right. Thach recalled wondering why he did that, but soon he could see ships through the breaks in the clouds, and realized they had found their target. The formation began their approach approximately 10 miles from the outer screen. The Japanese fleet looked like it was spread over the ocean. Soon colored antiaircraft bursts appeared, one red and another orange, and then no more. Thach soon realized the ships had fired at them to alert the combat air patrol. They were quickly surrounded by some 20 defending Zero fighters.

The fight developed quickly. In an instant, Bassett's plane caught fire and he went down. Thach soon realized this first group of defenders intended to overwhelm his fighters while a second large formation flew past and attacked the torpedo bombers.

Thach's section leader, Macomber, was holding position too close for the two to create an effective weave, and Thach was unable to get any shots at the Zeros. When he called Macomber on the radio with an order to open out more, there was no answer since his radio had been shot out. Thach had spent nearly a year developing his tactic and now he couldn't put it into practice! He quickly called his wingman, Ram Dibb, and told him to move out far enough to weave. The two Wildcats were now able to defend themselves against the enemy.

Several Zeros made a head-on attack on the Devastators and hit Lem Massey's plane, which exploded in flames. A second group attacked the torpedo bombers from the beam. The sky was full of enemy fighters and finally Thach's weave tactic began to pay off. He got good shots at two Zeros and burned them. Suddenly Dibb called that he had a Zero on his tail. Thach got a head-on shot at the enemy fighter as Dibb flew past him and set the Zero on fire. Thach held his maneuver and the burning fighter missed him by only a few feet.

Thach's five Wildcats kept their weave and shot at every enemy fighter that flew in front of them. Thach was convinced he and his pilots and the torpedo bombers were not going to survive.

All but three of the torpedo planes were shot down in the attack. As the last went down, the *Yorktown* dive bombers attacked *Sōryū*. Thach later recalled that he had never seen such superb dive bombing. From where he was, it looked like almost every bomb hit. The *Enterprise* bombers were attacking the *Kaga* and *Akagi*, all of which were now on fire. Thach picked up one of the three surviving Devastators and flew on back to the *Yorktown* with it. Their fight had lasted 20 minutes.

In six deadly minutes, the Japanese had lost *Akagi*, *Kaga*, and *Sōryū*. The serendipitous arrival of 64 dive bombers over Kido Butai at its single most vulnerable moment, after the Japanese had defeated every previous American attack, ranks with the discovery by the Persian commander of the Greek fleet's ambush in Salamis Bay, just when it was too late for him to change course.

One Japanese carrier was left, the *Hiryū*. As the American attackers flew off, she launched 18 dive bombers and six Zeros at 1100 hours. At 1205 hours, they found *Yorktown*.

Aboard *Yorktown*, John Bridgers and the other pilots held back from the morning strike did their best to stay out of the way.

The planes from the fourth Japanese carrier found the *Yorktown* before we found their ship and, in short order, we were under attack.

We pilots had no duties other than to sit in our ready room. Unable to see out, we became more and more tense with no activities to release the tension. This was by far the toughest experience I had during the war. Our antiaircraft guns began shaking the ship, and we figured enemy planes were closing in. In steel ships, there were many plates to rattle and reverberate, so the firing of guns was a noisy din indeed. Most of us gathered around the plate patching the ready room deck after one fellow said, "Surely lightning won't strike twice in the same place!" The response was "But do you think the Japs know that?" Just as quickly, we dispersed to our empty desk-seats, and in short order the ship was struck by a couple of bombs. Since the overhead of our ready room was the underside of the flight deck above, we felt considerable jolts and the lights blinked out, to be automatically replaced by the dim red glare of battle lamps, and smoke was immediately evident. The attack passed quickly. In a few minutes, we were released to move topside and survey the damage. By now, our ship was dead in the water.

Once on the flight deck, Bridgers was immediately confronted with war's cost when he saw bodies covered with tarpaulins. *Yorktown* had weathered the first strike and was soon able get underway and bring planes aboard; then came warning of a second strike.

After the first attack, I observed that many had been injured because they were standing around upright and were either hit by flying debris or knocked up against projecting fittings. This must have been something noticed by the others, for all of us immediately lay down prone on the deck – a precaution well worthwhile. Next, there was a tremendous explosion and I was lifted bodily what felt to be a foot or more off the deck. I now knew what a torpedo hit felt like. Almost immediately, it was evident that the ship was listing to one side and was once again dead in the water. Word was passed to abandon ship. I went back to the ready room and put on my Mae West life jacket. Back topside, knotted life lines had been let down over the low side of the hull and people were beginning to lower themselves into the water. Large life rafts were thrown over the side and the grim business got under way. I walked around the island and across the deck, trying to decide when I would go, secretly hoping someone would change their mind about the whole affair. I passed Captain Buckmaster taking a turn around the deck and he told me to hurry and get off the vessel. In several minutes, I passed him again and he said: "Son, I thought I told you get off this ship. Now get moving!"

Bridgers took a line down as far as it would go and then dropped into the sea below. He soon discovered he had lost his shoes when he hit the water. Several minutes later, he came across a wounded sailor whom he took under tow. After what seemed a long time, the two were picked up by the destroyer USS *Hughes* (DD-410).

The next day, Bridgers and other *Yorktown* survivors were transferred to the submarine tender USS *Fulton* (AS-11) for the return to Pearl Harbor, where his personal problems took a turn for the worse.

Months earlier, when I shipped out from Norfolk, my main suitcase had been left behind in the rush of getting on the train at night. In it were my copies of my orders and pay records. On first reaching Pearl Harbor, the paymaster refused to open a new pay record until he had some confirmation of my orders. I wrote the paymaster in Norfolk and a validated copy along with a reconstructed pay record was waiting for me aboard the *Yorktown* when we sailed for Midway. Unfortunately, these were lost along with my size 14-AA shoes. When we got back to Pearl Harbor after Midway, the paymaster again refused to issue me my back pay on just my say-so. It was another month before I was re-entered on the regular payroll, and it was several years later before I got the back pay I had missed.

Dick Best landed back aboard *Enterprise* shortly before noon, one of four left from the original 17 from Bombing 6 that had left the ship that morning. He went below to his stateroom. "Suddenly, I felt weak and dizzy and the next thing I knew I was coughing up more blood into the sink than I had ever seen." During the flight to the Japanese fleet, Best had experienced an accident that would profoundly change the rest of his life. As the formation climbed above 10,000 feet, the crews went on oxygen; at the time, the SBD was equipped with a cranky rebreather system similar to that used by submarine crews for emergency escapes. Several of the pilots and gunners had suffered failures of the system, and had to drop to lower altitude where they lagged behind the formation.

Best had remained at altitude, where he was breathing with increasing difficulty, but did not connect his problem to that experienced by the others. Once the attack was made, everyone flew back at lower altitude, where the problem did not recur.

Best reported to sick bay, where he was put in bed while he was checked over. Before the doctors could resolve anything, scouts from *Yorktown* found the *Hiryū* at 1330 hours. Following the second Japanese strike that hit the *Yorktown*, a 24-plane strike was put together from the survivors of the *Enterprise* squadrons and the now-homeless *Yorktown* survivors who had landed aboard *Enterprise*. Every pilot who could fly was needed. Best checked out of sick bay and returned to the flight deck, again leading Kroeger and Weber.

The outbound flight to attack *Hiryū* was not flown at high altitude, since the problem with the oxygen rebreathers had been identified. Best and his two wingmen were in the second group to dive on the wildly evading *Hiryū*, which hit the carrier and set her afire. Unfortunately, Weber and his radioman were among those shot down by defending fire, though Bill Kroeger survived the mission; he and Best would not see each other again until both showed up at a 50th year reunion of the *Enterprise* crew.

Best's landing back aboard *Enterprise* would be his last carrier trap, and the flight to strike *Hiryū* would be his last flight as a pilot ever; he spent the return to Pearl Harbor in the sick bay. "Many of my generation had been exposed to tuberculosis as children, though it would remain dormant unless something happened to activate it. In my case, it was activated by the failure of the rebreather," he explained. Once back at Pearl Harbor, he was transferred to the Naval Hospital where the diagnosis of tuberculosis was made. After a promotion to lieutenant commander, the Navy retired him from active service because of the disability, an action he fought hard to stop. "There were all kinds of men with worse problems than I had who remained on active duty during the war. I had participated in all the early war actions from Pearl Harbor to Midway with the exception of Coral Sea, and had experience the Navy could have used."

Spruance's most important decision of his career was made the evening of June 4, when he turned Task Force 16 to the east rather than continue west in search of the remainder of the Japanese fleet, stating that "We've done what we came to do." Had he continued west, he would very likely have run into the ambush Admiral Yamamoto planned with his battleships. A night surface action against a superior force would have completely negated the day's success. Halsey most likely would have continued on, and there is reason to believe that Yamamoto set the ambush in the belief that Halsey was his opponent.

For his actions at Midway, Spruance was awarded the Navy Distinguished Service Medal and cited as follows: "For exceptionally meritorious service… as Task Force Commander, United States Pacific Fleet. During the Midway engagement, which resulted in the defeat of and heavy losses to the enemy fleet, his seamanship, endurance, and tenacity in handling his task force were of the highest quality." Summing up Spruance's performance, naval historian Samuel Eliot Morison later wrote: "Fletcher did well, but Spruance's performance was superb. Calm, collected, decisive, yet receptive to advice; keeping in his mind the picture of widely disparate forces, yet boldly seizing every opening. Raymond A. Spruance emerged from the battle one of the greatest admirals in American naval history."

There is a myth in the US Navy that the Battle of Midway has been replayed many times at the US Naval War College in Newport, Rhode Island, and that each time the Americans lose. Midway appears to have been won as the result of a very fortunate combination of good intelligence, planning, and good luck. Somehow, despite the American fleet having inferior numbers and combat experience when compared to its opponents, it managed to sink all four of the Imperial Navy's aircraft carriers present at the battle.

The root of victory at Midway was the successful cracking of the Imperial Navy's code in early 1942 by Station HYPO, the team of Navy cryptanalysts led by Commander Joseph Rochefort, which led to the discovery of Yamamoto's plan to attack and occupy Midway within a week of the Imperial Navy General Staff's agreement with the admiral to undertake the operation.

Pacific Fleet intelligence officer Lieutenant Commander Edwin "Eddie" Layton recounted in his memoirs how he presented the fruits of HYPO's work at the Pacific Fleet staff conference on May 27 where Admiral Nimitz approved the plans to ambush the Japanese at Midway.

"Summarizing all my data, I told Nimitz the carriers would probably attack on the morning of June 4, from the northwest on a bearing of 325 degrees. They would be sighted at about 175 miles from Midway at around 0700 local time." That morning, as the initial sighting reports began arriving at Pacific Fleet headquarters, Nimitz remarked to Layton , "Well, you were only five minutes, five degrees, and five miles out." The assessment, the last that would be made through direct knowledge of Imperial Navy communications for the rest of the war, allowed Nimitz to take the "calculated risk" of putting into the battle all three of his aircraft carriers. Anything less would have been insufficient to gain victory.

While the initial Japanese victories in the Pacific War were the result of Western – and particularly American – underestimation of Japanese capabilities, the victory at Midway was the result of Japanese underestimation of American capabilities. The entire course of the Pacific War through to the end would be the result of this continuing failure on the part of the Japanese to fully comprehend the nature, ability, and power of their opponent. Admiral Yamamoto had understood his opponent sufficiently well to tell his superiors, "I will run wild for six months. After that, I can promise nothing."

Midway marked the end of the beginning. Two months after the battle, the bloody, relentless island-hopping advance across the Pacific would begin at Guadalcanal, leading to complete Japanese defeat three years later.

CHAPTER TWENTY-ONE

THE CORNERSTONE OF VICTORY

Following the victory at Midway, Japan would never undertake another offensive operation in the remainder of the Pacific War.

The men who had survived the first six months of war would become the cornerstone of final victory, as their experience placed them in positions of leadership, not only in the Pacific but around the world.

Jimmy Doolittle, who had thought on the morning of April 19, 1942 that he would likely be court-martialed for failure on his return to the United States, found instead that he was lionized by the public for leading the epic mission. He was promoted directly to brigadier general and that fall became commander of the Twelfth Air Force during the North African invasion. In January 1944, he was promoted to command the Eighth Air Force in Britain, leading it during the final 15 months of the war. His first assignment was to make a success of Operation *Argument*, the campaign to break the Luftwaffe and establish Allied air superiority over Western Europe in anticipation of the Normandy invasion.

Richard H. Best, Jr., who had sworn the night of December 18, 1941 that he would "make the bastards pay" put paid to that oath on June 4, 1942 when he changed the course of the Battle of Midway by sinking the *Akagi*. He battled tuberculosis for the next ten years. Eventually, he became the librarian of the RAND Corporation in California. In 1971, he "turned a blind eye" to Daniel Ellsberg and Anthony Russo when they removed what came to be known as "The Pentagon Papers" and copied them for later publication. In later years, he always said he believed he had done a greater service to his country in that instance than he had over the Japanese Fleet. "The American people deserved to know the truth, to know what had been done in their name."

John Bridgers survived the next year after Midway in combat in the Solomons. Promoted to lieutenant, he returned to the United States in 1943 and was assigned to Bombing 15 of Air Group 15, which would become the top-scoring carrier air group of the Pacific War. Twenty-eight months after he was fished out of the water following the sinking of the *Yorktown*, as a 24-year-old lieutenant commander and executive officer of the squadron, he led the Task Force 38 strike of over 400 aircraft that sank the last of the Japanese aircraft carriers off Cape Engaño on October 25, 1944. His squadron's bombers were responsible for sinking *Zuikaku*, the last surviving carrier of the six Pearl Harbor attackers. As he flew back to land aboard USS *Essex*, "I thought to myself that I had put paid to the Navy's investment in me." After the war, he finally went to medical school, then served as a U.S. Navy Flight Surgeon. As a hospital administrator afterwards, he was known for developing plans to provide medical care to underserved communities throughout the United States. He raised four children to think for themselves, "a decision he later regretted," as his eldest son put it, and died in 2007.

Frank Kurtz became well known in 1942 as the pilot of "The Swoose," the last of the B-17Ds that had flown in the Philippines, which he salvaged by grafting the rear fuselage and tail of B-17D 40-3091 to the wings and forward fuselage of 40-3097, resulting in a hybrid B-17D. It received its nickname from 9th Bomb Group pilot Captain Weldon Smith because it was "half swan and half goose," reminiscent of the lyrics in the then-popular novelty song "Alexander, the Swoose." The bomber was used as a transport and became the most well-known airplane of the Pacific War other than the "Enola Gay." When "The Swoose" was scheduled for scrapping and smelting down for its aluminum, Kurtz convinced the City of Los Angeles to retrieve the by-then famous bomber as a World War II memorial. Today, it is the sole surviving early B-17 and is under restoration at the National Museum of the US Air Force. Kurtz himself was later promoted to colonel and ended the war as commander of the 463d Bombardment Group (Heavy), Fifteenth Air Force, where he flew 60 missions and became the most-decorated Air Force combat pilot of World War II, awarded the Croix de Guerre, three Distinguished Flying Crosses, three Silver Stars, three Air Medals and five Presidential Unit Citations. His daughter, well-known Broadway and Hollywood actress Swoosie Kurtz, was named for the airplane.

Major Emmet "Rosie" O'Donnell, who led the first B-17s on a 7,000-mile flight to the Philippines, survived the fighting in the Philippines and Java, and became operations officer of the Far East Air Force. Evacuated to India after the fall of Java, he became assistant chief of staff for operations of the newly organized Tenth Air Force. Returning to the United States in 1943, he was promoted to brigadier general in January 1944 and assigned as commander of the new 73rd Bomb Wing (Very Heavy), the first operational unit to take the B-29 Superfortress to the Pacific. On November 9, 1944, he led the first B-29 mission against Tokyo. Following the outbreak of the Korean War in June 1950, O'Donnell became commander of Far East Bomber Command until his return to the United States in January 1951. He became Commander in Chief Pacific Air Forces in August 1959, holding that position until his retirement in July 1963.

The Forty-Niners' experience as the first USAAF fighter group to arrive in Australia and enter combat in the early days over Darwin and later New Guinea provided a cadre of fighter pilots who would become leaders throughout the Air Force as they completed their Southwest Pacific tours and returned to the United States.

Once back in the United States, George Preddy ran across another 49th Group veteran who helped him join the 487th Fighter Squadron of the newly minted 352nd Fighter Group. Sent to England in late 1943, the 352nd traded in their P-47s for P-51s in April, 1944. George Preddy proceeded to become the top-scoring Mustang pilot of history, with 26 victories, including five in one day in August, 1944, and rose to command the 487th Squadron before he was accidentally shot down and killed by American flak units while chasing an Fw-190 at low altitude over the Ardennes forest on Christmas Day, 1944. He had just turned 25. His group commander, Colonel John C. Meyer, said of him, "He was a man with a core of steel in a largely sentimental soul."

Among other virtues, Preddy showed a typically American attitude toward air-to-air fighting, once saying, "I'm sure as hell not a killer, but combat flying is like a game, and a guy like me likes to come out on top."

John D. Landers left the group in January 1943 and returned to combat that October, flying P-38s with the 55th Fighter Group in England, later moving on to command the 357th Fighter Group and fly the P-51 Mustang in 1944, having finished his combat tour with the 55th; he flew a third ETO tour in 1945 as group commander of the 78th Fighter Group, taking them through their conversion from the P-47 Thunderbolt to the Mustang and commanding to the end of the war. He was the only USAAF pilot in World War II to score victories in all four of the major Air Force fighters flown during the war.

Sidney S. Woods flew 112 missions with the Forty-Niners, scoring a Betty and a Zero, before returning to the United States in early 1943. In November 1944, he revitalized the 4th Fighter Group, following the departure of their legendary commander Don Blakeslee, and led the former Eagles to become the top-scoring American fighter group of history in the last six months of the war.

Joe Kreuzel, who stole a P-40 from Lamar Gillet at Clark Field on the second day of the war, then managed to escape from the Philippines and survive the fall of Java, returned to the United States in early 1943, and was assigned as executive officer of the 361st Fighter Group. In addition to 3.5 victories scored over Java and Darwin, he scored three more flying out of England and took command of the 361st Group following the death of Colonel Thomas J. J. Christian in combat in August 1944. He led the group through to V-E Day.

Paul Wurtsmith, the Forty-Niners' first group commander who took them to Australia, was promoted to command Fifth Air Force Fighter Command in January 1943 by General George Kenney, commander of the Fifth Air Force. In 1945, at age 38, he assumed command of the Thirteenth Air Force in the Philippines and Okinawa campaigns. He was killed in a flying accident on September 13, 1946, a month after he turned 40.

"Ramsey's Lambsies" also made major contributions to the US Navy in the years following the Battle of the Coral Sea. With the sinking of *Lexington*, the squadron was disestablished on July 1, 1942. A year later, Fighting 2 returned to life, the only prewar Navy squadron to be re-established during the war. Flying the Hellcat, VF-2 entered combat in November 1943 aboard *Enterprise* during the invasion of the Gilberts. The squadron went aboard the new USS *Hornet* (CV-12) in March 1944. They participated in the Battle of the Philippine Sea that summer and in Admiral Halsey's Philippines rampage in September. When they returned to the United States, they were the top-scoring carrier fighter group, an honor they would lose two months later to

VF-15. Under Commander William F. Dean, the squadron produced more aces than any other Navy squadron in the war.

Lieutenant Commander Paul Ramsey was awarded the Navy Cross for his actions at Coral Sea. He became CAG of Air Group 14 aboard the USS *Ticonderoga* (CV-14) in 1943, and commanded USS *Philippine Sea* (CV-37) during the Korean War, operating with Task Force 77. Promoted to vice admiral, he was appointed Commander in Chief US Pacific Forces in 1964. In 1955, he was the first veteran of the Battle of the Coral Sea to attend the annual celebration in Sydney, Australia. He retired as Deputy Chief of Naval Operations for Air in 1972.

Lieutenant Noel Gaylor, who had won his first Navy Cross for his actions in February in defense of *Lexington* and his second for defending the ship that March, was awarded a third for his actions at Coral Sea. He was appointed head of the National Security Agency in 1972 and was appointed Commander in Chief, US Pacific Forces in 1975. He retired in 1981.

Lieutenant Albert O. "Scoop" Vorse was awarded the Navy Cross for his actions at Coral Sea. That summer he transferred to Fighting 10, commanded by Jimmy Flatley, and fought at Guadalcanal in October and November 1942. He commanded VBF-80 aboard USS *Ticonderoga* in 1945, fighting in the Okinawa campaign and the final strikes against the Home Islands that summer. He retired as a rear admiral in 1962.

Ensign Willard E. "Bill" Eder was awarded the Navy Cross for his actions at Coral Sea. In April 1944 he took command of VF-29. The squadron deployed aboard USS *Cabot* (CVL-28) from October 12, 1944 to April 11, 1945, taking part in the Battle of Leyte Gulf, the Philippines campaign, Admiral Halsey's South China Sea strikes, and the first two carrier strikes on Tokyo. On November 5, 1944, Eder became CAG Air Group 29. During this deployment he added 6.5 victories to the 1.5 he scored at Coral Sea. In the last months of the war, he led the "Victory Squadron," an assemblage of 16 aircraft that toured the United States promoting war bonds in 52 cities.

The pilots of the American Volunteer Group also made major contributions following the disbandment of the organization on July 4, 1942.

James O. Howard returned to the United States and took a commission as captain in the USAAF. In 1943, he was assigned to the 354th Fighter Group, then training at Hamilton Field, and promoted to major as commander of the 356th Fighter Squadron. The group arrived in England in November 1943 and became the first to take the P-51 Mustang into combat. On January 11, 1944, Howard led the group on a target support escort mission to Oschersleben and Halberstadt. Arriving on station, the bombers were already under heavy attack. Fewer than 40 Mustangs had to provide cover for over 500 bombers. Moments later, 36 Bf-109s, Bf-110s, and Fw-190s dove through the Mustangs. Howard latched onto a Bf-110 and exploded it. He became separated from the rest of the group, and was now the sole defender of the bomber box, in lone battle against more than 30 enemy fighters. Howard's account of the action states, "I was so busy in my constant pursuit of the enemy fighters, I may not have seen the presence of other enemy aircraft that were out of my visual range." Major Allison Brooks, leader of the 401st Bomb Group that Howard defended, later recalled, "For sheer determination and guts, it was the greatest exhibition I've ever seen. It was a case of one lone American against what seemed to be the entire Luftwaffe." Howard was awarded the Medal of Honor for this mission, the only fighter pilot in the ETO so honored.

Charles Older returned to the United States and entered the USAAF as a major. He returned to China in early 1944 as deputy commander of the 23rd Fighter Group, the descendants of the AVG. By the time he left in February 1945 he had added eight victories to the 10.5 he scored with the AVG to become the leading surviving ace of the China-Burma-India Theater; six of the eight were Ki-84 "Franks," scored in one low-level mission over Hankow in September 1944. He was the only Flying Tiger to see combat in a second war, flying B-26 Invaders in Korea with the 452nd Bomb Group. Following the Korean War, he finally attended UCLA law school. On January 23, 1972 – 30 years and one month to the day after scoring his first victories over Rangoon – Los Angeles Superior Court Judge Charles H. Older, Jr., who had only been appointed to the bench by Governor Ronald Reagan one month before being assigned the case, sentenced Charles Manson and his followers to death for the sensational Tate–LaBianca murders.

Tex Hill was one of only five pilots of the group to remain in China after the end of the AVG, activating and commanding the 75th Fighter Squadron and later rising to command the 23rd Fighter Group, the AVG's successors. On Thanksgiving Day 1943, he led a force of 12 B-25s, 10 P-38s, and eight new P-51s from Saichwan, China, for the first strike against Formosa. Of 100 bombers and 100 fighters at Shinchiku Airfield, the raiders destroyed 42 and probably destroyed 12 more in the attack, for no American losses. In 1944, Hill returned to the US and took command of the 412th Fighter Group, the Air Force's first operational jet fighter group, first flying the P-59 Airacomet and later the P-80 Shooting Star.

Erik Shilling, who was considered by his fellow Tigers to be the best flyer in the group, spent the next 30 years in Asia, flying in America's wars. After flying "The Hump" an amazing 59 times during World War II, he became one of the founders of Continental Air Services, which later became better known as Air America. In 1951, he flew a C-54 from Clark Field in the Philippines to Kadena Air Base in Okinawa – via Chungking! – making the flight across Red China at 500 feet in daylight to drop supplies to anticommunist guerillas. In 1954, he led the aerial resupply missions for the French forces at Dien Bien Phu, and later flew in the secret war in Laos. One of the founders of Flying Tiger Airlines, he was an organizer of the orphan airlift from Saigon in 1975.

BIBLIOGRAPHY

Bartsch, W.H., *Doomed at the Start* (College Station: Texas A&M University Press, 1992)

Bartsch, W.H., *December 8, 1941: MacArthur's Pearl Harbor* (College Station: Texas A&M University Press, 2003)

Bridgers, John D., *Naval Years, A Memoir* (self-published, 2002)

Burton, John, *Fortnight of Infamy: The Collapse of Allied Airpower West of Pearl Harbor* (Annapolis: Naval Institute Press, 2006)

Busha, James P., *Wings of War: Great Combat Tales of Allied and Axis Pilots During World War II* (New York: Zenith Press, 2015)

Camp, Richard, "A Shattered Command," *Aviation History Magazine* (May 11, 2017)

Casius, Gerard, "CW-21: The St Louis Lightweight," *Air Enthusiast*, Issue 16 (August–November 1981), pp.14–28

Casius, Gerard, "Batavia's Big Sticks," *Air Enthusiast*, Issue 22 (August–November 1983), pp.1–20

Clark, J.J., *Carrier Admiral* (New York: David McKay Co., 1967)

Cleaver, Thomas McKelvey, *F4F Wildcat and F6F Hellcat Aces of VF-2* (Oxford: Osprey Publishing, 2014)

Cleaver, Thomas McKelvey, *Air Combat Annals* (Pacifica: Pacifica Press, 2011)

Colledge, J.J. and Warlow, Ben, *Ships of the Royal Navy: The Complete Record of all Fighting Ships of the Royal Navy*, rev. edn (London: Chatham Publishing, 2006)

Cull, Brian, *Hurricanes Over Singapore: RAF, RNZAF and NEI Fighters in Action Against the Japanese over the Island and the Netherlands East Indies, 1942* (London: Grub Street, 2004)

Cull, Brian, *Buffaloes over Singapore: RAF, RAAF, RNZAF and Dutch Brewster Fighters in Action Over Malaya and the East Indies 1941–1942* (London: Grub Street, 2008)

Dull, Paul S., *A Battle History of the Imperial Japanese Navy, 1941–1945* (Annapolis, Maryland: Naval Institute Press, 2007)

Evans, David and Peattie, Mark, *Kaigun: Strategy, Tactics and Technology in the Imperial Japanese Navy, 1887–1941* (Annapolis: Naval Institute Press, 1997)

Ford, Daniel, *Flying Tigers: Claire Chennault and his American Volunteers, 1941–42* (Warbird Books, 2016)

Franks, Richard B., *Guadalcanal: The Definitive Account of the LandMark Battle* (New York: Random House, 1990)

Gordon, John, *Fighting for MacArthur: The Navy and Marine Corps' Desperate Defense of the Philippines* (Annapolis: United States Naval Institute Press, 2011)

Green, William, "Brewster's Benighted Buffalo," *Air Enthusiast Quarterly*, No. 1 (1975), pp. 22–33

Hanyok, Robert J., "How The Japanese Did It," *United States Naval Institute Proceedings*, Vol. 23, No. 6 (December 2009)

Iyenaga, Saburo, *The Pacific War* (New York: Pantheon, 1978)

Lacroix, Eric and Wells, Linton, *Japanese Cruisers of the Pacific War* (Annapolis, Maryland: Naval Institute Press, 1997)

Manchester, William, *American Caesar: Douglas MacArthur 1880–1964* (Boston: Little, Brown, 1978)

Noah, Joe and Samuel L. Sox Jr., *George Preddy* (Greensboro: Preddy Memorial Foundation, 1991)

Foss, Joe and Brennan, Matthew, *Top Guns: America's Fighter Aces Tell Their Stories* (New York: Simon and Schuster Pocketbooks, 1991)

Gill, G. Hermon, *Royal Australian Navy 1939–1942* (Canberra: Australian War Memorial, 1957)

Lord, Walter, *Lonely Vigil: Coast Watchers of the Solomons* (New York: Viking Press, 1971)

Molesworth, Carl, *P-40 Warhawk Aces of the Pacific* (Oxford: Osprey Publishing, 2003)

Morison, Samuel Eliot, *History of United States Naval Operations in World War II*, Volume III: *The Rising Sun in the Pacific 1931–April 1942* (Boston: Little, Brown and Company, 1988)

Peattie, Mark R., "Akiyayama Saneyuki and the Emergence of Modern Japanese Naval Doctrine," *United States Naval Institute Proceedings*, Vol. 103 (January 1977), pp. 62–65.

Pelz, Stephen E., *Race to Pearl Harbor: The Failure of the Second London Naval Conference and the Onset of World War II* (Cambridge: Harvard University Press, 1974)

Persyn, Lionel, Stenman, Kari and Thomas, Andrew, *P-36 Hawk Aces of World War 2* (Oxford: Osprey Publishing, 2009)

Prange, Gordon W., *At Dawn We Slept: The Unknown Story of Pearl Harbor* (New York: McGraw-Hill, 1981)

Ruane, Michael E., "Unsealed 75 Years after the Battle of Midway: New Details of an Alarming WWII Press Leak," *The Washington Post* (June 5, 2017)

Sakai, Saburo, with Caidin, Martin and Saito, Fred, *Samurai!* (New York: Bantam Books, 1978)

Sakaida, Henry, *Japanese Army Air Force Aces 1937–45* (Oxford: Osprey Publishing, 1997)

Salecker, Gene Eric, *Fortress Against the Sun: The B-17 Flying Fortress in the Pacific* (New York: Da Capo Press, 2001)

Scott, James M., *Target Tokyo: Jimmy Doolittle and the Raid That Avenged Pearl Harbor* (New York: W.W. Norton Co., 2015)

Sherrod, Robert, *History of Marine Corps Aviation in World War II* (Novato: Presidio Press, 1980)

Shores, Christopher, Cull, Brian with Izawa, Yasuho, *Bloody Shambles*, Volume One, *The Drift to War to the Fall of Singapore* (London: Grub Street, 1992)

Shores, Christopher, Cull, Brian with Izawa, Yasuho, *Bloody Shambles*, Volume Two, *The Defence of Sumatra to the Fall of Burma* (London: Grub Street, 1993)

Spector, Ronald H., *Eagle Against The Sun: The American War With Japan* (New York: The Free Press, 1985)

Stenman, Kari and Davey, Chris, *Brewster F2A Buffalo Aces of World War II* (Oxford: Osprey Publishing, 2010)

Stout, Jay A., *Unsung Eagles* (Philadelphia: Casemate, 2013)

Thach, John S., "Flying Into A Beehive: Fighting Three At Midway," *United States Naval Institute Proceedings*, Vol. 21, No. 7 (June 2007)

Tillman, Barrett, *Enterprise: America's Fightingest Ship and the Men Who Helped Win World War II* (New York: Simon and Schuster, 2013)

Tillman, Barrett, *The Dauntless Dive Bomber in World War II* (Annapolis: Naval Institute Press, 1976)

Tillman, Barrett, *Corsair: The F4U in World War II and Korea* (Annapolis, Naval Institute Press, 1979)

Tillman, Barrett, *Wildcat: The F4F in World War II* (Annapolis: Naval Institute Press, 1983)

Toland, John, *Infamy: Pearl Harbor and its Aftermath* (New York: Doubleday & Co., 1982)

Toland, John, *But Not in Shame: The Six Months After Pearl Harbor* (New York: Random House, 1961)

Toland, John, *The Rising Sun: The Decline and Fall of the Japanese Empire, 1936–1945,*

vols. I and II (New York: Random House, 1970)

US Navy, *The Java Sea Campaign: Combat Narratives* (Washington, DC: Office of Naval Intelligence, 1943)

US Navy, "A Brief History of US Navy Aircraft Carriers: Part IIa – The War Years (1941–42)," NAVAIR 00-80P-1, *Dictionary of American Navy Fighting Ships* (Washington, DC: Office of the Chief of Naval Operations, 1959–81)

Vlahos, Michael, *The Blue Sword: The Naval War College and the American Mission 1919–1941* (Washington, DC: GPO, 1980)

Watson, R.L., "Loss of the Netherlands East Indies," in Craven, W. F. and Cate, J. L. (eds.), *Army Air Forces in World War II*, Vol. 1 (Washington, DC: Office of Air Force History, 1983), pp. 366–402

Winslow, Walter G., *The Fleet the Gods Forgot: The US Asiatic Fleet in World War II* (Annapolis: Naval Institute Press, 1994)

Yenne, Bill, *Aces High* (New York: Penguin, 2009)

INDEX